Transnationalisation and Legal Actors

Transnational tendencies have led to a pluralistic legal environment in which emerging and established legal actors, regulatory levels and types of legal norms co-exist, compete and interact in complex ways. This challenges and changes not only how legal norms are created, applied and enforced but also when these actors, norms and processes are considered legitimate. The book investigates how states and non-state actors interact in transnational settings and pays attention to the understudied question of what effect transnational tendencies have on the legitimacy of legal actors, norms and processes. It seeks to confront three fundamental questions: Has legitimacy significantly changed? Who creates norms and with which consequences for legal procedures and norms? The book considers the question of legitimacy from a broad range of legal perspectives, including environmental law, human rights law and commercial law. It maps out the contours of legitimacy today with an emphasis on the reactions of central actors like states and courts to transnational tendencies. The book thereby provides a conceptually powerful structure within which to further debate the complexity of transnational tendencies in law and proposes innovative approaches to problem solving while designing pathways for further reflection on the development of law in a transnational context.

Bettina Lemann Kristiansen is Professor of Sociology of Law at the Department of Law, BSS, Aarhus University. Her research interests focus on sociology of law, access to justice, legal aid, legal adjudication by non-lawyers and general tendencies in law (especially welfare regulation), such as globalisation, digitalisation and pluralism.

Kateřina Mitkidis is Associate Professor at the Department of Law, BSS, Aarhus University. Her research interests cover sustainability and law, international law of contracts, international environmental law and pharmaceutical law. She is interested in the use of private law tools to advance public interests.

Louise Munkholm is Postdoctoral Fellow at the Department of Law, BSS, Aarhus University. Her research interests include sociology of law and legal cultures with focus on the local enforcement of international and national labour law.

Lauren Neumann is PhD candidate at the Department of Law, BSS, Aarhus University. Her research interests include the law of armed conflict, international human rights law and the law relating to displacement.

Cécile Pelaudeix is Research Associate at PACTE Sciences Po. Her research interests include international law and international politics with emphasis on the international governance of the EU and the Arctic region.

Globalisation: Law and Policy

Globalisation: Law and Policy builds an integrated body of scholarship that critically addresses key issues and theoretical debates in comparative and transnational law and the principles, governance and policy on which they are developed. Volumes in the series focus on the consequential effects of globalisation, including emerging frameworks and processes for the internationalisation, legal harmonisation, juridification and democratisation of law among increasingly connected political, economic, religious, cultural, ethnic and other functionally differentiated governance communities. Legal systems, their harmonisation and incorporation in other governance orders, and their relationship to globalisation, are taking on new importance within a coordinated network of domestic legal orders, the legal orders of groups of states and the governance frameworks of non-state actors. These legal orders engage a number of important actors, sources, principles and tribunals – including multinational corporations as governance entities, contract and surveillance as forms of governance that substitute for traditional law, sovereign wealth funds and other new forms of state activity, hybrid supranational entities like the World Bank and the International Monetary Fund, and international tribunals with autonomous jurisdiction, including the International Criminal Court, the World Trade Organization and regional human rights courts. The effects have been profound, especially with respect to the role of states, and especially of developed states as their long-time position in global affairs undergoes significant transformation. Comparative and transnational law serve as natural nexus points for vigorous and sometimes interdisciplinary approaches to the study of state and non-state law systems, along with their linkages and interactions. The series is intended as a resource for scholars, students, policy makers, and civil society actors, and includes a balance of theoretical and policy studies in single-authored volumes and collections of original essays.

Larry Catá Backer is the W. Richard and Mary Eshelman Faculty Scholar, Professor of Law and International Affairs at the Pennsylvania State University. Previously he served as Executive Director of the Comparative and International Law Center at the University of Tulsa. He has published widely on comparative and transnational law.

Also in the series:

Power, Procedure, Participation and Legitimacy in Global Sustainability Norms
A Theory of Collaborative Regulation
Karin Buhmann

Chinese Constitutionalism in a Global Context
Peng Chengyi

Hostile Business and the Sovereign State
Privatized Governance, State Security and International Law
Michael J. Strauss

Legal and Rhetorical Foundations of Economic Globalization
An Atlas of Ritual Sacrifice in Late-Capitalism
Keren Wang

For more information about this series, please visit:
www.routledge.com/Globalization-Law-and-Policy/book-series/GLOBLP

Transnationalisation and Legal Actors

Legitimacy in Question

Edited by
Bettina Lemann Kristiansen, Kateřina Mitkidis, Louise Munkholm, Lauren Neumann and Cécile Pelaudeix

Routledge
Taylor & Francis Group
LONDON AND NEW YORK

First published 2019
by Routledge
2 Park Square, Milton Park, Abingdon, Oxon OX14 4RN

and by Routledge
605 Third Avenue, New York, NY 10017

First issued in paperback 2020

Routledge is an imprint of the Taylor & Francis Group, an informa business

British Library Cataloguing-in-Publication Data
A catalogue record for this book is available from the British Library

Library of Congress Cataloging-in-Publication Data
Names: Kristiansen, Bettina Lemann, editor.
Title: Transnationalisation and legal actors: legitimacy in question/ Bettina Lemann Kristiansen, Kateřina Mitkidis, Louise Munkholm, Lauren Neumann and Cécile Pelaudeix.
Description: Abingdon, Oxon; New York, NY: Routledge, 2020. | Series: Globalization law and policy.
Identifiers: LCCN 2019001665 | ISBN 9781138346970 (hardback) | ISBN 9780429437151 (ebook)
Subjects: LCSH: Law. | International and municipal law. | Sociological jurisprudence. | Law and globalization.
Classification: LCC K561 .T732 2020 | DDC 340.9–dc23
LC record available at https://lccn.loc.gov/2019001665

ISBN 13: 978-0-367-72796-3 (pbk)
ISBN 13: 978-1-138-34697-0 (hbk)

Typeset in Galliard
by Deanta Global Publishing Services, Chennai, India

Contents

Notes on contributors viii
Preface xi

Introduction
Transnational tendencies, law and legitimacy xii
LAUREN NEUMANN AND KATEŘINA MITKIDIS

PART I
Transnational tendencies in law 1

1 Five theses on the dialectic of unity and plurality in postnational law 3
KAARLO TUORI

2 The politics of transnational law 17
THOMAS GAMMELTOFT-HANSEN AND TANJA AALBERTS

3 Transnationalism in the Arctic Ocean: Legitimacy strategies of the Inuit Circumpolar Council, the European Union and China 33
CÉCILE PELAUDEIX

4 Transnational ecosystem-based norms covering the Danish/Greenlandic Arctic marine area 49
ELLEN MARGRETHE BASSE

5 Brexit: A note on the EU's interlegality 62
REZA BANAKAR

6 Beyond nations and continents?: Harmony and solidarity as common endeavours in a digital era of populism, propaganda and fiction? 82
HANNE PETERSEN

PART II
Developing regulatory legitimacy under transnationalisation **95**

7 Development of transnational contract law? 97
KATEŘINA MITKIDIS

8 Towards the participation of a global public in transnational law-making? Everyday ICT platforms as legitimacy opportunities for bottom-up governance 112
KARIN BUHMANN AND SAMEER AZIZI

9 Pushing back international human rights law – Counter reaction to transnational law? 127
JENS VEDSTED-HANSEN

10 Balancing legal obligations in Europe's cooperation with Libya in the fight against migrant smuggling 141
FENELLA M.W. BILLING AND NIKOLAS FEITH TAN

PART III
Application, enforcement and the challenges of legitimacy **157**

11 Enforcing transnational labour law in local contexts 159
LOUISE MUNKHOLM

12 The principle of equality as a transnational principle 173
NATALIE VIDEBÆK MUNKHOLM AND CHRISTIAN HØJER SCHJØLER

13 How domestic courts may shape international commercial law norms 187
THOMAS NEUMANN

14 Transnational religious law – Exemplified by the United Methodist Church 201
LISBET CHRISTOFFERSEN

15 Is formality legitimacy? Defining the obligations of non-state armed groups 216
LAUREN NEUMANN

Conclusion
Transnationalisation and legal actors: Legitimacy in question 230
LOUISE MUNKHOLM, CÉCILE PELAUDEIX AND BETTINA LEMANN KRISTIANSEN

Index 247

Notes on contributors

Tanja Aalberts is Professor of Law and Politics at the Department of Transnational Legal Studies, VU University, Amsterdam, and Director of the Centre for the Politics of Transnational Law. Her research focuses on the interplay between international law and international politics in practices of governance.

Sameer Azizi is Assistant Professor of Business Studies at the Department of Social Sciences and Business, Roskilde University, Denmark. His research interests include corporate social responsibility and information and communication technologies in developing countries.

Reza Banakar is Professor and Director of Research at the Department of Sociology of Law, Lund University, Sweden. His research interests are in the areas of law and social theory, legal cultures, legal profession and comparative law as well as socio-legal methodology.

Ellen Margrethe Basse is Professor of Environmental Law at the Department of Law, BSS, Aarhus University, Denmark. Her research focuses on the consequences of the design of environment, climate and energy law.

Fenella M.W. Billing is Postdoctoral Fellow at the Department of Law, BSS, Aarhus University, Denmark. Her research interests focus on transnational law enforcement and human rights, including migrant smuggling and the Law of the Sea as well as the principle of mutual trust in EU law.

Karin Buhmann is Professor, with special responsibilities, of Business and Human Rights at the Department of Management, Society and Communication, Copenhagen Business School, Denmark. Her research interests include business responsibilities for human rights and sustainable development from the perspective of public-private governance and regulation.

Lisbet Christoffersen is Professor of Law and Religion at the Department of Social Sciences and Business, Roskilde University, Denmark. Her research interests include religion law, ecclesiastical law, constitutional law, administrative law and EU law with focus on legal pluralism and socio-legal analysis.

Thomas Gammeltoft-Hansen is Professor of Legal Science with special responsibilities in regard to migration and refugee law at the Law Faculty, University of Copenhagen, Professor II at the University of Oslo and Honorary Professor at Aarhus University, Denmark. His research interests include international refugee law, human rights and the relationship between international law and politics.

Christian Højer Schjøler is Assistant Professor at the Department of Law, University of Southern Denmark. His research interests include national implementation of EU labour law with focus on collective bargaining and non-discrimination.

Bettina Lemann Kristiansen is Professor of Sociology of Law at the Department of Law, BSS, Aarhus University, Denmark. Her research interests focus on sociology of law, access to justice, legal aid, legal adjudication by non-lawyers and general tendencies in law (especially welfare regulation), such as globalisation, digitalisation and pluralism.

Kateřina Mitkidis is Associate Professor at the Department of Law, BSS, Aarhus University, Denmark. Her research interests cover sustainability and law, international law of contracts, international environmental law and pharmaceutical law. She is interested in the use of private law tools to advance public interests.

Louise Munkholm is Postdoctoral Fellow at the Department of Law, BSS, Aarhus University, Denmark. Her research interests include sociology of law and legal cultures with focus on the local enforcement of international and national labour law.

Natalie Videbæk Munkholm is Associate Professor at the Department of Law, BSS, Aarhus University, Denmark. Her research interests are in national, EU and international labour law, in particular the interplay between national and supranational systems, collective bargaining and fundamental rights at work.

Lauren Neumann is PhD candidate at the Department of Law, BSS, Aarhus University, Denmark. Her research interests include the law of armed conflict, international human rights law and the law relating to displacement.

Thomas Neumann is Associate Professor at the Department of Law, Aalborg University, Denmark. His research interests focus on commercial law. In this context, Neumann is the editor of the CISG Nordic Database and of the Albert H. Kritzer Database at Pace University, New York.

Cécile Pelaudeix is Research Associate at PACTE Sciences Po, France. Her research interests include international law and international politics with emphasis on the international governance of the EU and the Arctic region.

Hanne Petersen is Professor of Legal Cultures and Head of the Center for European and Comparative Legal Studies, Copenhagen University, Denmark. Her research interests include legal culture and legal pluralism, legal theory, gender and law and sociology of law.

Nikolas Feith Tan is PhD candidate at the Department of Law, BSS, Aarhus University, and the Danish Institute for Human Rights, Denmark. His research interests include international refugee law, human rights law, access to asylum and deterrence policies.

Kaarlo Tuori is Professor Emeritus of Jurisprudence at the University of Helsinki, Finland. His research interests include legal theory, European law and constitutionalism as well as transnational law and legal hybrids.

Jens Vedsted-Hansen is Professor at the Department of Law, BSS, Aarhus University, Denmark. His research focuses on human rights with emphasis on the right to protection under international law, including the development of common EU standards on asylum.

Preface

The core idea for this volume emerged at a workshop for researchers from the INTRAlaw Research Centre at Aarhus University in June 2015. INTRAlaw is a cross-disciplinary research centre with a focus on research in a broad range of transnational, primarily legal fields. From the presentations and discussions at a series of workshops in the period 2015–2017, it became clear that some topical, crosscutting issues were emerging, namely the changing roles of actors in transnational law development and law enforcement and the question of legitimacy in transnational law.

The contributors to this volume include a significant number of the INTRAlaw Research Centre's internal affiliates as well as invited scholars, who have participated in various INTRAlaw events over the past three years. We would like to thank the contributors for their significant efforts to ensure theoretical consistency in this volume and also for their patience with the length of the process of adequately defining the topics and the theme of this book.

In addition to the contributors, we are indebted to Jytte Mønster and Helle Hjorth Christiansen for preparing the final manuscript and to Michael McBarron for language revision and proofreading. We also want to thank Alison Kirk, Larry Catá Backer and Emily Summers at Routledge for impeccable editorial support.

Funding for this project has generously been provided by the INTRAlaw Research Centre and the Department of Law at Aarhus University.

The editors are listed alphabetically. This is due to the fact that this volume is the result of a close collaboration where all editors contributed equally, yet in different functions and in different phases of the work.

This volume reflects the law as it stood, to the best of the authors' knowledge, in November 2018. These areas of law are, however, by their nature still developing. Readers are advised to stay abreast of more recent legislation and case law.

Aarhus University, December 2018.
Bettina Lemann Kristiansen, Kateřina Mitkidis,
Louise Munkholm, Lauren Neumann and
Cécile Pelaudeix

Introduction

Transnational tendencies, law and legitimacy

Lauren Neumann and Kateřina Mitkidis

Legitimacy is an adaptive and transformative foundation of the law. It is not universal in its form or depth, yet its contours shape the definition and understanding of what law is. The concept of legitimacy – what it entails, its importance and how it is obtained, ensured or contested – has long occupied the minds of scholars and practitioners from fields such as law, political science and sociology.[1] Despite this, or perhaps because of it, a universal definition of legitimacy has remained elusive. It can be described as the justification of authority, of rules, actors and actions; but what is necessary for that justification, including the characteristics by which one can measure legitimacy, is somewhat fluid. Nonetheless, institutions exist at the national and international level that pronounce legally binding norms, and these are generally accepted as legitimate.[2] Based on an implicit understanding of what makes a norm binding, the legal system operates even when absent of a clear definition of legitimacy.

What then happens when that 'legal system' changes? What happens when legal actors change and become more numerous, and the system purporting to regulate behaviour no longer fits within the confines of what was previously perceived as legitimate? Transnational tendencies in law have created precisely such a situation, and this book examines what it means for the adaptable – but foundational – concept of legitimacy.

Transnational tendencies and their effect on law

Law is not static; it is constantly evolving and changing according to a variety of internal and external factors. Increasing global interconnectedness[3] – frequently

1 Some major works in this area include: Max Weber, 'The Three Types of Legitimate Rule' (1958) 4 *Berkeley Publications in Society and Institutions* 1, translated by Hans Gerth; Jürgen Habermas, *Legitimation Crisis*, (Beacon Press 1973); John Rawls, *The Law of Peoples* (Harvard University Press 1999); Harold Hongju Koh, 'Why Do Nations Obey International Law?' (1997) Yale Law School, Faculty Scholarship Series. Paper 2101. https://digitalcommons.law.yale.edu/fss_papers/2101 accessed 14 December 2018.

2 Not necessarily uncritically accepted, but broadly accepted, nonetheless.

3 In fields such as economics, finance and investment, technology, communications, society and culture.

a synonym for the loaded term 'globalisation' – is one such influencing factor. It has led to a decrease in the significance of the state's physical and jurisdictional boundaries through a process often referred to as transnationalisation.

Transnationalisation in a legal context brings to mind two opposing tendencies: on the one hand, the unification of legal regulation, and on the other, its fragmentation. Unification can occur not only through common international laws and norms adopted by states, but also through efforts by other actors with potentially transnational influence, such as the public at large and business communities. The emancipation of non-state actors, including individuals, private entities, international organisations and multi- or supranational bodies,[4] as regulatory actors has also contributed to the fragmentation of the legal environment and, thus, to legal pluralism. Legal pluralism describes the situation in which a social situation or phenomenon is regulated by multiple legal orders and is by now a well-established field of study.[5] The academic discourse has developed the notions of global and transnational legal pluralism[6] and included in the discussion not only different layers of law (national and international or state-made and religious law), but also hybrid and new forms of regulation, such as codes of conduct or guidelines developed by international organisations. The fragmentation of the legal environment is also fuelled by counter-reactions to transnationalisation, namely efforts by states to reclaim and/or restate their sovereign regulatory powers, leading to nationalistic tendencies not only in the political sphere, but also in the legal one.

With the changes in the variety of forms of legal regulation and in the legal actors participating at different stages of regulatory processes as a result of

4 While not necessarily new actors in the legal sphere, they are taking on new legal and quasi-legal roles and in so doing, testing the international, regional and domestic legal systems built around the supremacy and sovereignty of the nation state. See e.g. Gideon Boas, *Public International Law: Contemporary Principles and Perspectives* (Edward Elgar Publishing 2012) 9.

5 From the vast amount of literature, see e.g. Jacques Vanderlinden, 'Le pluralisme juridique: essai de synthèsé in John Gillissen (ed.), *Le pluralisme juridique* (Université libre de Bruxelles 1971); Jacques Vanderlinden, 'Return to Legal Pluralism: Twenty Years Later' (1989) 28 *Journal of Legal Pluralism* 149; John Griffiths, 'What is legal pluralism?' (1986) 24 *Journal of Legal Pluralism* 1; Sally E. Merry, 'Legal pluralism' (1988) 22 *Law and Society Review* 869; Jørgen Dalberg-Larsen, *The Unity of Law, an Illusion?: On the Legal Pluralism in Theory and Practice* (Galda & Wich Verlag 2000); Franz von Benda-Beckmann, 'Who's Afraid of Legal Pluralism?' (2002) 47 *Journal of Legal Pluralism and Unofficial Law* 37.

6 Paul Shiff Berman, 'From Legal Pluralism to Global Legal Pluralism' in Richard Nobles and David Schiff (eds.), *Law, Society and Community: Socio-Legal Essays in Honour of Roger Cotterrell* (Routledge 2014) Chapter 15; Peer Zumbansen, 'Transnational Legal Pluralism' (2010) 1 *Transnational Legal Theory* 141; Peer Zumbansen, 'Defining the Space of Transnational Law: Legal Theory, Global Governance, and Legal Pluralism' (2013) 21 *Transnational Law & Contemporary Problems* 305; Ralf Michaels, 'Global Legal Pluralism' (2009) 5 *Annual Review of Law & Social Science* 1; Keebet von Benda-Beckmann, 'Transnational Dimensions of Legal Pluralism' in Wolfgang Fikentscher (ed.), *Begegnung und Konflikt – Eine kulturanthropologische Bestandsaufnahme* (Verlag der Bayerischen Akademie der Wissenschaften 2001) 33.

transnationalisation, the fundamental questions of who can legitimately create, apply and enforce law, and when and how law becomes legitimate, re-emerge.

The focus of the book: Legitimacy in the transnational context

Issues of legitimacy in transnational contexts provide a common theme for this volume, which developed from reflections on the first three years of the INTRAlaw research centre at Aarhus University, Denmark.[7] The centre, focusing on INternational and TRAnsnational tendencies in law, was established by scholars working in widely disparate areas of law but encountering similar issues with respect to the (inter)relations between various systems and forms of law. The issues emerged along three theoretical and separate, yet interrelated, axes of regulatory change: state/non-state actors, soft/hard legal norms and public/private law.

After the inaugural three years and with numerous conferences, workshops and collaborative projects undertaken, the legitimacy of law in light of transnational tendencies emerged as an omnipresent theme worthy of greater examination. This was particularly obvious after the INTRAlaw conference, 'Law in transition – Interacting legal orders and changing actors', held in September 2017, where INTRAlaw members and invited speakers addressed the impact of transnational tendencies on (i) legal regulatory mechanisms, (ii) the role of the traditional legal actors and (iii) the subsequent challenges for legal research.

This volume adds to the existing scholarship on law and transnationalisation with an inductive approach to analysis. The individual chapters examine specific theoretical or practical problems, situations or initiatives and the effects these have for legitimacy. While the chapters employ various methods and frameworks to consider legitimacy in the transnational context, the inductive approach allows for identifying commonalities bridging the various legal branches and research methods.

The present book gathers a number of scholars with various backgrounds and expertise, who nevertheless encounter similar issues when working within the transnational context, in the endeavour of drawing common conclusions across legal areas on the relationship between transnationalisation, legal actors and legitimacy. The individual contributions study empirically or theoretically topical issues, such as human smuggling in the Mediterranean and developments in the Arctic, to address the changing legitimacy in transnational legal orders. In other words, the volume takes a snapshot of the state of law and legitimacy in a broad range of legal fields at different stages in the push-and-pull relationships between legal actors, states and their organs, individuals, public and private organisations, other non-state actors and the local, national, supranational and international legal systems in which they operate. This reveals interesting

7 http://law.au.dk/intralaw/ accessed 14 December 2017.

commonalities between the seemingly disparate areas, the non-linear directions in which the state and non-state actors move in relation to each other and the challenges – both normative and structural – that transnationalisation poses to law. This highlights innovative initiatives responding to practical and legal theoretical problems presented by new and changing actors and examines whether – and how – legitimacy in law is in fact changing. The three main research questions addressed in the book are:

1 Who are the legal actors on the transnational scene today and how do they generate or shape existing norms?
2 What are the emerging transnational tendencies in law?
3 What does this mean for how the legitimacy of norms is understood, defined, constructed and contested?

The book seeks, in line with the first research question, to identify and understand the conditions under which an actor is or becomes a 'legal actor' and how legal actors generate or reshape norms. The second research question identifies the tendencies in law that reflect current transnational issues and trends. This leads to the third and main research question asking how the identified transnational tendencies in law and analysis of the legal actors inform the concept of legitimacy. It is acknowledged that it is challenging, if not impossible,[8] to define the contours of legitimacy valid for all fields of law. The book aims, therefore, to focus on evolving nuances of legitimacy in the transnational context. Recognising that a comprehensive assessment is out of reach in the context of this volume, the chapters focus on specific actors to offer a possibility for generalisation.

Legitimacy in the transnational context

Despite its centrality to the work of legal scholars, legitimacy is not often explicitly conceptualised, especially in the transnational context. This could be due to the difficulty in doing so or perhaps as the result of an underlying assumption that legitimacy is so fundamental that one intuitively knows what the concept entails.

Most efforts to conceptualise legitimacy in the transnational context have been done in relation to one type of legal actor, one type of regulation[9] or a specific

8 Julia Black, 'Constructing and Contesting Legitimacy and Accountability in Polycentric Regulatory Regimes' (2008) 2 *Regulation & Governance* 137.

9 Such as transnational private regulation, see e.g. Fabrizio Cafaggi, *A Comparative Analysis of Transnational Private Regulation: Legitimacy, Quality, Effectiveness and Enforcement*, EUI Department of Law Research Paper No. 2014/145, https://papers.ssrn.com/sol3/papers.cfm?abstract_id=2530516 accessed 14 December 2018, or corporate codes of conduct, see e.g. Larry Catá Backer, 'A Lex Mercatoria for Corporate Social Responsibility Codes without the State?: On the Regulatory Character of Private Corporate Codes' (2016) 24 *Indiana Journal of Global Legal Studies* 115.

area.[10] Particular attention has been devoted to the legitimacy issues in connection to the activities and norms developed by non-state actors.[11] Legitimacy can and has indeed been widely discussed in relation to state-made law, especially in the international sphere.[12] The rising influence of non-state actors has brought new challenges to the intellectual discourse, with the activities and norms developed by international organisations being one largely discussed topic[13] and regulatory actions of private actors being another.[14] Yet another line of scholarship focuses on delivering theoretical, rather than empirical, accounts of changing legitimacy in the global sphere.[15] Finally, the legitimacy discourse in the transnational context has moved away from democracy towards less-demanding standards of legitimacy, such as accountability, deliberation and administrative procedure.[16] An explanation for this is that it is difficult, or more precisely illusory, to rely on a democratic process when adopting law or legal decisions at the transnational level. This trend could also be described as a move from normative to sociological (descriptive) legitimacy and a move from procedural to substantive legitimacy.[17] This book contributes to this debate and considers this transformation process within the various fields of focus in individual chapters.

Describing legitimacy

Traditionally, the legitimacy of law has been understood as the justification of the authority of legal rules stemming from the persuasion of the governed subjects that the law creator has the right and the authority to adopt prescriptions for their behaviour, and that (s)he will exercise its power appropriately and fairly,

10 Such as sustainability, see e.g. Karin Buhmann, *Power, Procedure, Participation and Legitimacy in Global Sustainability Norms. A Theory of Collaborative Regulation* (Routledge 2018).

11 Zumbansen (n. 6); Fabrizio Cafaggi, 'New Foundations of Transnational Private Regulation' (2011) 38 *Journal of Law and Society* 20; Andreas Maurer, 'The Creation of Transnational Law – Participatory Legitimacy of Privately Created Norms' (2012) ZenTra Working Paper in Transnational Studies No. 03/2012; Eric W. Orts, 'The Legitimacy of Multinational Corporations' in Lawrence E. Mitchell (ed.), *Progressive Corporate Law* (Westview Press 1995) 247; Larry Catá Backer, 'On the Tension between Public and Private Governance in the Emerging Transnational Legal Order: State Ideology and Corporation in Polycentric Asymmetric Global Orders' (16 April 2012). SSRN: http://ssrn.com/abstract=2038103.

12 Koh (n. 1).

13 Daniel Bodansky, 'Legitimacy in International Law and International Relations' in Mark A. Pollack and Jeffrey L. Dunoff (eds), *Interdisciplinary Perspectives on International Law and International Relations: The State of the Art* (Cambridge University Press 2013) 321.

14 Supra n. 9. See also Deirdre Curtin and Linda Senden, 'Public Accountability of Transnational Private Regulation: Chimera or Reality?' (2011) 38 *Journal of Law and Society* 163; Cafaggi (n. 11).

15 Most often these contributions are connected to the theory of transnational legal pluralism, see e.g. Phillip Paiement, 'Paradox and Legitimacy in Transnational Legal Pluralism' (2013) 4 *Transnational Legal Theory* 197.

16 Bodansky (n. 13).

17 See in the section immediately below.

this persuasion being expected to lead to compliance with the rules.[18] Most commonly, the legitimacy of national and international law stems from the mandate given to the national governments by the states' citizens.[19] On the transnational level, the issue of defining and ensuring legitimacy is less obvious. The absence of 'global government' not only questions who can create law in a transnational setting, but also, importantly, from where such law derives its legitimacy.[20]

Two conceptions of legitimacy are particularly useful in this volume. The first is that of normative and descriptive legitimacy.[21] Normative legitimacy depends on whether an institution objectively has a right to rule, this being assessed by the qualities of the ruler that morally justify its authority, including democracy, transparency and expertise. Descriptive legitimacy depends on empirical and explanatory arguments about what people believe and why; it focuses on the attitudes of the ruled. In the transnational context, the development of new actors ('rulers') raises questions as to the relationship between the ruler and the ruled, and whether normative or descriptive legitimacy (or a hybrid thereof) offers the strongest foundation for legitimate rule.

A second conception of legitimacy of relevance is that of procedural, substantive and effectiveness-based dimensions of legitimacy.[22] Procedural legitimacy is based on the process by which a norm or body is created; if the process follows accepted principles and procedures, it can be considered legitimate. Expert-based legitimacy is founded on the knowledge or specialisation of the actor or institution involved.[23] In contrast, substantive legitimacy 'stems from the congruence between the content of a rule or policy and the broader values that are privileged in a community at a given moment'.[24] Effectiveness-based legitimacy then focuses on the output of the norm or actor, with legitimacy resulting from 'effective solutions to shared problems'.[25] These types of legitimacy provide another interesting framework from which to consider legitimacy in light of transnational tendencies.

18 This understanding has origins in the work of John Locke (1632–1704), see Richard Ashcraft (ed.), *John Locke: Critical Assessments* (Routledge 1991) 524: 'The argument of the [Second] Treatise is that the government is not legitimate unless it is carried on with the consent of the governed'. For an in-depth analysis of the legitimacy concept from a political science perspective, see David Beetham, *The Legitimation of Power* (2nd edn, Palgrave 2013).

19 Though, there has been a long-lasting debate between scholars on what constitutes legitimacy of international law. For a comprehensive overview of this debate, see Koh (n. 1). See also Rüdiger Wolfrum and Volker Röben (eds), *Legitimacy in International Law* (Springer 2008).

20 Zumbansen (n. 6) 144.

21 See Bodansky (n. 13) 331 and Ian Hurd, 'Legitimacy and Authority in International Politics' (1999) 53 *International Organization* 379, 381.

22 See Magdalena Bexell, 'Global Governance, Legitimacy and (De)Legitimation' (2014) 11 *Globalizations* 289, 291.

23 Hurrell considers expert-based legitimacy (and reason-based legitimacy) to be separate dimensions of legitimacy; Andrew Hurrell, 'Legitimacy and the Use of Force: Can the Circle be Squared?' (2005) 31 *Review of International Studies* 15.

24 Bexell (n. 22) 292.

25 Hurrell (n. 23) 22.

The process (procedural legitimacy), content (substantive legitimacy) and outcome (effectiveness-based legitimacy) of law in transnational contexts can vary from their national or international counterparts, and how this affects legitimacy should be explored.

Conceptual clarification

There is little by way of authoritative or universally accepted definitions of a number of key terms and concepts in transnational legal literature. As such, it is necessary to devote a few words to clarify the position taken in this book to two key terms: transnationalisation and transnational law.

When speaking about changes in law resulting from transnationalisation, other terms are often used to describe the same or similar processes, such as the 'globalisation' or 'internationalisation' of law.[26] However, each of these concepts have particular nuances. Globalisation of law evokes the idea of a move towards unified legal norms applicable globally,[27] while internationalisation of law takes national law as a starting point and investigates the influences of other legal systems on it (including other national and international legal systems) and the transformation of it under these influences in such a way that the borders between different legal systems become obscured.[28] Transnationalisation of law takes a broader perspective and tries to capture various processes of mutual influence between, creation of new (also private-made) and change within various legal orders. It can be described as an umbrella over both internationalisation and globalisation, taking neither a national nor an international legal order as a firm starting point.

A major consequence of increased transnationalisation for legal theory and practice[29] has been the development of the concept of 'transnational law'. The term 'transnational law' as coined by Jessup over 60 years ago[30] has been used and redefined many times and in many ways; three main types of scholarship on transnational law can be identified. Firstly, there is a considerable amount of legal scholarship on transnational topics, such as transnational crime, transnational

26 From a vast amount of scholarship, see e.g. Martin Shapiro, 'The Globalization of Law' (1993) 1 *Indiana Journal of Global Legal Studies* 37; Amnon Lev, 'Internationalisation of Law: Historical and Cultural Aspects' (2011) 80 *Nordic Journal of International Law* 241.

27 Shapiro (n. 26) 38: ('By globalization of law, we might refer to the degree to which the whole world lives under a single set of legal rules'.); see also William Twining, *Globalisation and Legal Theory* (Cambridge University Press 2000) 50–51.

28 Lev (n. 26) ('It designates a displacement of legal discourse and legal thought towards a dimension, in which the differences which constitute legal orders as specific – and hence separate – entities have been superseded'.).

29 H. Patrick Glenn, 'Comparative Law and Legal Practice: On Removing the Borders' (2001) 75 *Tulane Law Review* 977, 980–981 (citing Laurel S. Terry, 'A Case Study of the Hybrid Model for Facilitating Cross-Border Legal Practice: The Agreement Between the American Bar Association and the Brussels Bars' (1998) 21 *Fordham International Law Journal* 1382, 1384).

30 Philip Jessup, *Transnational Law* (Yale University Press 1956) 1.

transactions or transnational reach of the internet. Secondly, there is a growing volume of studies on transnational law, studying transnational law as an object and developing theories of transnational law. Finally, transnational law is increasingly used as a perspective or even a method, when a theory or an analytical framework of transnational law is applied on a specific topic.[31]

The book builds on the analytical framework of Zumbansen, who describes transnational law as 'a methodological lens' through which we can 'study the particular transformation of legal institutions in the context of an evolving complex society'.[32] Actors, norms and processes are seen as the central building blocks in the analysis. The focus of this volume is on both established and emerging legal actors and their new or changing status and role in respect to norm creation, application and enforcement. In particular, it examines the effect of these developments on the legitimacy of the law within the fields of expertise of the individual contributors.

Structure and content of the volume

The volume is structured in three parts. Part I provides critical perspectives on transnational tendencies in law, Part II examines the genesis of law in transnational contexts and Part III considers the challenges of transnationalisation of law to the application and enforcement of law.

Part I takes a critical look at transnational tendencies in law with emphasis on how these tendencies challenge multilevel orders, norms and structures, and how legitimacy is framed at the transnational level. The volume opens with Chapter 1 by Kaarlo Tuori entitled 'Five theses on the dialectic of unity and plurality in postnational law'. The author is concerned with the unity and plurality of current legal orders and argues for the need for an ideal typical conceptual starting point from which to: identify instances of law; draw a boundary, however fuzzy and porous, between law and non-law; and separate, however tentatively, state law and non-state law. The chapter concludes by discussing whether internal and inter-instance unity of law can be constructed from the plurality of instances of law. The five theses have an impact on how legitimacy can be seen or described. The author purports that if our future lawscape is dominated by interlegality traversing the boundaries of national legal regimes, legitimacy must be increasingly based on cross-boundary discourses and deep legal cultural overlaps.

Chapter 2, 'The politics of transnational law' by Thomas Gammeltoft-Hansen and Tanja Aalberts, takes the perspective of international law. The chapter discusses the design choices in international institutions that mirror the discontent among states with liberal institutionalist governance. The authors argue that the expansion and increased institutionalisation of international law have created

31 Peer Zumbansen, 'Defining the Space of Transnational Law: Legal Theory, Global Governance, and Legal Pluralism' (2013) 21 *Transnational Law Contemporary Problems* 305, 307.
32 Zumbansen (n. 6) 307.

the structural premise for a 'darker' side of transnational law. This 'darker' side is characterised by increased legalisation used by states as a tool to manoeuvre within and against international law in ways that clearly challenge, if not outright undermine, the liberal assumptions underpinning most transnational legal theory.

These opening chapters discuss the possibility of achieving legal unity despite undeniable plurality. They are followed by two contributions that analyse and discuss how different actors, such as the EU, states and non-government organisations create, shape and challenge transnational norms when engaging in various strategies to impact policy development and institutional settings. The background for these two contributions is the Arctic region, which in some sense can be seen as a 'playground' for transnational law scholars since the area is characterised by a high number and wide variety of legal actors, norms and interests. Cécile Pelaudeix, in Chapter 3, 'Transnationalisation in the Arctic Ocean: Legitimacy strategies of the Inuit Circumpolar Council, the European Union and China', analyses the legitimisation strategies and arguments employed by the three actors using the framework of procedural, substantive and output legitimacy. Her presentation of the Arctic area as 'far from being a legal vacuum' should be considered in relation to the often-claimed view that transnational law develops as an answer to a lack of legal regulation. The author argues that there is a relationship between procedural and substantive legitimacy, and the former cannot substitute the latter. She points towards a need to include aspects of economics and power into analyses of legitimacy in transnational fora such as the Arctic Ocean.

Ellen Margrethe Basse then continues this discussion in Chapter 4, 'Transnational ecosystem-based norms covering the Danish/Greenlandic Arctic marine area'. In her chapter, the author discusses the role of diverse legal actors, including states, international and supranational organisations and non-governmental bodies in the protection of the Arctic marine area. The author specifically discusses the use of the ecosystem-based approach within the OSPAR regime[33] and EU law as a means of promoting the EU as a global normative power beyond its geographical borders. She further examines the division of responsibility between Denmark (an EU Member State) and Greenland (not part of the EU) for the marine area and the input and output legitimacy of the ecosystem-based transnational norms.

Reza Banakar provides another highly topical contribution in Chapter 5, 'Brexit: A note on the EU's interlegality'. This study argues that Brexit is as much an internal UK crisis of law, identity politics and democracy as it is an EU crisis of integration. Using the notion of 'interlegality' and the cartographic mechanisms of 'scale', 'projection' and 'symbolisation', the chapter draws attention to how EU laws and policies become inevitably distorted as they pass between legal spaces which are shaped by different scales of regulation. However, Brexit shows that these distortions do not, solely, sufficiently explain either the failure of the

33 Convention on the Protection of the Marine Environment of the North-East Atlantic (OSPAR Convention).

EU integration policies in respect to the United Kingdom or the success of the Leave Campaign in the 2016 referendum. To understand the double crisis which Brexit represents, the author argues that we need to explore how the EU's interlegality is shaped by the imbalance of power and authority which permeates the hierarchical structure of the EU. The chapter ends by arguing that to minimise the excessive distortions and to maximise the integrative potential of the EU law, we need to envisage the EU's interlegality outside its existing hierarchy of sources of power which create a primarily top-down flow of legal authority.

Part I of the volume closes with Chapter 6 by Hanne Petersen, 'Beyond nations and continents? Harmony and solidarity as common endeavours in a digital era of populism, propaganda and fiction?'. The author continues the critical discourse towards transnationalisation of law and reactions thereto. The author argues that transnationalism, as witnessed today, is shaped in practice through a highly asymmetrical relation between many small and few large countries and other legal actors. The chapter analyses the norms of solidarity and harmony as common endeavours on the transnational regulatory level, while discussing the strategies of populism, propaganda and fiction adopted by central actors in spreading (and undermining) these norms across borders. Following the discussion of these norms and strategies that overlap, interact and conflict with each other, the author calls for adopting a more pragmatic approach to understanding 'law', diverging from conceptual classification typical of the European setting.

Following Part I, which provides a conceptual springboard for the volume, Part II moves more specifically to the issue of genesis of regulation under transnationalisation. It analyses the role of different types of legal actors – primarily non-state legal actors – at the international, supranational, national and local levels. It considers their roles in developing regulation in transnational situations and addresses the conditions under which the actors and their activities are considered legitimate. Kateřina Mitkidis opens Part II in Chapter 7 by discussing businesses as legal actors. In her chapter entitled 'Development of transnational contract law?', the author examines the creation of contract law through business practice and asks the question whether we should speak in this context about legal transplant, (natural) legal convergence or transnationalisation of law. The chapter questions the legitimacy of businesses as norm creators and stresses the difference between transnationalisation of legal norms and of legal practice.

Also focusing on actual practice, Karin Buhmann and Sameer Azizi in Chapter 8, 'Towards the participation of a global public in transnational law-making? Everyday ICT platforms as legitimacy opportunities for bottom-up governance', explore opportunities for enhancing the legitimacy of transnational law-making by utilising information and communication technologies (ICT) to increase the role and contributions of a global public in the global sustainability governance. The chapter uses examples from the African mobile-phone revolution to provide insights into ICT as potentially instrumental for economic and political governance. The chapter concludes that ICT offers important potential for transnational governance that includes the views of a global citizenry. It argues that combining this with analytical technology can help solve the challenge of including vast numbers of individuals or representative organisations in such processes, thereby helping address problems regarding the feasibility of including a global public in transnational law-making.

Chapter 9, 'Pushing back international human rights law – Counter reaction to transnational law?' by Jens Vedsted-Hansen, is grounded in the current and ongoing discussions of the legitimacy of, and normative challenges to, the international human rights system. The author reviews a number of these challenges, including the seeming retaliation by domestic actors against the European Court of Human Rights. The chapter raises the question whether current struggles in international human rights law can be seen through the lens of transnationalism or whether this is yet another manifestation of a 'demarcation' exercise between state sovereignty and international law. The author draws an important distinction between general interpretation and the concrete application of international human rights law, suggesting that conscious awareness of this distinction may help both academics and practitioners tackle the complexities of transnationalisation of law phenomena.

The final chapter in Part II, Chapter 10, 'Balancing legal obligations in Europe's cooperation with Libya in the fight against migrant smuggling' by Fenella M.W. Billing and Nikolas Feith Tan, takes the discussion to the context of migrant smuggling. The chapter shows contradictions in EU and international law and asks under which conditions it is possible for the EU to balance its obligations as both an international and supranational legal actor. On that basis, the authors assess the role of trust and legitimacy for efficient and just cooperation. The authors argue that Europe's trust in the legitimacy of Libyan authorities may be determined – at least in part – according to the latter's respect for human rights standards, in law and in practice. However, the analysis shows that Libya lacks legitimacy in this regard.

The contributions in Part II share as a common theme the relationship between transnational norms and transnational practice. This theme is also central to Part III of the volume, which considers the practical challenges of applying and enforcing law in transnational contexts. It explores the processes of law application and enforcement in various legal areas with a focus on the extent to which different actors through the application of law contribute to the development of a transnational legal environment and what this means for how the legitimacy of transnational norms is understood.

Part III opens with Chapter 11 by Louise Munkholm entitled 'Enforcing transnational labour law in local contexts'. This contribution takes us to the town of Prato in Northern Italy that hosts approximately 5,800 Chinese firms, a significant number of which do not live up to the basic legal requirements regarding the employment, safety and health of their Chinese employees. The author explores the practice of labour inspectors on the ground, experimenting with innovative ways of legal enforcement and the use of pioneering tools for the enforcement of transnational norms. In particular, video campaigning, distribution of guidelines and the offer of consultancy are in focus. The chapter contributes to the debates about current attempts of legal actors to increase the legitimacy of existing transnational norms and ensure their compliance in local settings. The chapter thus addresses the application of law 'on the ground' by professionals who through their practice mould transnational law and build its legitimacy.

Chapter 12, 'The principle of equality as a transnational principle' by Natalie Videbæk Munkholm and Christian Højer Schjøler, stays within the area of labour law, however, it moves from ground level use of the law to higher levels of legal regulation. It investigates the application of the principle of equality as a transnational phenomenon by the Court of Justice of the European Union and examines national courts as legal actors in this context. The authors illustrate the difficulties of infusing national law with supra- or transnational law (in particular in the nationally sensitive areas of labour law and social law) by building on Kaarlo Tuori's theory of Critical Legal Positivism.

The role of courts in responding to transnational tendencies in law is also the focus in Chapter 13, entitled 'How domestic courts may shape international commercial law norms', by Thomas Neumann. The author discusses the divide between the textual unification of international sales law and its application and enforcement by national courts. The chapter addresses the process of judicial dialogue, that is, the use of foreign case law as a practical way for domestic courts to allow unification to slowly crystallise in practice. The chapter examines the use and non-use of judicial dialogue by Danish courts. It further calls for empirical studies to elucidate how national courts assess the legitimacy of foreign court decisions, and thus sources of transnational contract law.

Lisbet Christoffersen in Chapter 14, 'Transnational religious law – Exemplified by the United Methodist Church', moves the discussion from contract law to religious law. The author discusses religious law as transnational legal orders, analysing three aspects of a legal order – legal norms, actors and procedures. She concludes that the United Methodist Church fulfils all of them. The chapter then brings to the forefront potential conflicts between religious and societal law, namely in the context of discrimination on the basis of sexuality, and connected potential conflicts within internal legitimacy of the church.

The final chapter of Part III, Chapter 15 by Lauren Neumann, is entitled 'Is formality legitimacy? Defining the obligations of non-state armed groups'. The chapter introduces yet another type of non-state actor – non-state armed groups – and considers the applicability of international law to those actors. The author notes that non-state armed groups fall outside the scope of much of international law, at least according to traditional public international law theory. The chapter then describes and evaluates some of the formal and informal legal attempts made by various bodies to secure respect for international humanitarian and human rights norms by these non-state armed groups. Finally, the chapter considers the effect of such norm creation and enforcement for the general efficacy of, and therewith understanding of legitimacy in, international law.

The final chapter of the volume, Chapter 16, 'Transnationalism and legal actors', synthesises the findings of the individual chapters by identifying central legal actors on the transnational scene that generate or shape norms, mapping central transnational tendencies in law as well as counter reactions to those tendencies, discussing ways in which the research findings contribute to the advancement of theoretical understandings of legitimacy. The chapter also points to the future challenges and problem-solving mechanisms while designing pathways for further reflection on legal actors and legitimacy in a transnational context.

Part I

Transnational tendencies in law

1 Five theses on the dialectic of unity and plurality in postnational law

Kaarlo Tuori

The theses

Global law can no longer – if it ever could – be conceived of in terms of the black box model consisting of self-contained boxes of national (state) legal orders, complemented with the box of international law.[1] State law may still be the dominant type, but it does not hold a monopoly over law, nor can the relations among the instances of law which make up the postnational plurality any longer be thought in accordance with the black box model. In order to make sense of the lawscape of our postnational age, we have to rethink both unity and plurality, as well as their mutual relationship. In this chapter, I shall present and defend five theses about the dialectic of unity and plurality in postnational law:

1 The order in which we conceive of unity and plurality should be reversed: Instead of examining how plurality emerges from unity we should explore how unity arises from plurality.
2 Despite growing scepticism towards a general concept of law, I argue that we still need some basic general conceptual tools which facilitate identifying instances of law; drawing a boundary, however fuzzy and porous, between law and nonlaw; and separating, however tentatively and acknowledging fuzziness and porosity even here, state law and nonstate law.
3 Interrelations between the instances making up the postnational plurality of law are not only boundary-asserting but also boundary-crossing; not only conflictual but also consensual and dialogical, manifesting interlegality rather than simple diversity or radical pluralism.
4 Postnational plurality has fundamentally affected the internal unity of instances of law, including state law regimes. While formal unity of the national legal order is increasingly difficult to maintain, the emphasis has shifted from formal to substantive (legal cultural) and discursive unity.

1 'Black box model' is a term coined by William Twining in his *Globalisation and Legal Theory* (Northwestern University Press 2000).

5 Under the conditions of postnational plurality, a second-level unity of law can only be of a discursive and substantive nature, building on deep cultural affinities.

The theses I shall defend do not directly bear on the issue of legitimacy. Yet, indirectly they do. If the legal positivist notion of the law as hierarchically structured and self-contained state law is increasingly irrelevant, the reach of the legitimacy produced by state law's legislative practices and formal unity also diminishes. If our future – and to a great extent even present – lawscape is dominated by interlegality traversing the boundaries of national legal regimes, as well as by shifting legal cultural and discursive unities, legitimacy must also be increasingly based on corresponding substantive principles and discursive processes.

1 thesis: reversal of the hierarchy of unity and plurality

Legal positivism approaches law from the perspective of a singular national legal order. The default assumption is that law is state law, and that state law is positive law, posited by legislative and judicial bodies. The state enjoys exclusive and universal legislative and judicial sovereignty in its territory, defining its legal space. Positivist legal centralism goes together with state sovereigntism.

Positivism tends to treat national legal orders as mutually closed normative entities, isolated in their respective compartments. They are supposed to exist in plurality, but plurality is understood as *simple diversity*, as the mere co-existence of self-contained national legal orders, without any hint at their interconnections, be they of conflictual or cooperative and dialogical character. In the relationship between unity and plurality, plurality is subordinated to unity. Such a solipsist view is built on two problematic demarcations: first, the nonrecognition of nonstate law, such as indigenous and religious law, and secondly, the identification of the contents of the national legal order with their surface-level expressions. What success the largely mythical Westphalian state had in the policy of legal centralisation and state sovereigntism was limited to explicit law making and enforcement. What it did not achieve was national compartmentalisation of the legal cultural underpinnings of the surface-level legal order, i.e. annulment of the legal cultural transnationalism which was a legacy of the late medieval reception of Roman law. No *Grundnorm* or rule of recognition can identify and delineate the principles, concepts, theories and methodological devices which provide surface level law with the necessary legal cultural support. Here the black box model with its solipsist implications has never been able to convey an accurate picture of the plurality of law.

Little more than half a century has elapsed since the publication of the two major syntheses of positivist legal theory: the second edition of Kelsen's *Reine Rechtslehre* (1960) and Hart's *The Concept of Law* (1961).[2] In a relatively short

2 Hans Kelsen, *Reine Rechtslehre* (2. Auflage, Mohr Siebeck 1960); H.L.A. Hart, *The Concept of Law* (Clarendon Press 1961).

time, the state centralist positivist approach has lost its credibility even in the portrayal of the unity and plurality of surface-level law. State law can no longer claim monopoly and deny the existence of nonstate law, neither below nor above the state. Supported by international law, indigenous and religious legal regimes have waged at least partly victorious campaigns of recognition, and in some states also left their imprint on surface-level expressions of the state legal order. In tact with and as an epitome of general social denationalisation and globalisation, the significance of transnational normativity has expanded tremendously, with EU law as its most conspicuous epitome.

Not only has the rise of nonstate law enriched legal plurality with new instances of law. It has also proved the inadequacy of the black-boxist assumption of self-contained legal orders, subordinated to their respective Master Rules. Postnational plurality cannot be conceived of in terms of simple diversity, as a mere coexistence of distinct legal orders. Diversity has increasingly taken the guise of *legal pluralism*. In a situation of legal pluralism, diverse legal orders – or, to speak in broader terms – legal regimes, raise overlapping and rival claims of authority. And due to the reciprocal opening of state law regimes, too, simple diversity, implicit in the black-boxism of legal positivism, conveys a distorted image of their plurality as well.

Unity and plurality are interconnected. The way we conceive of the unity of law affects the way we conceive of its plurality, and vice versa. If the unity of law is depicted, in accordance with the centralist and state-sovereigntist tenets of legal positivism, primarily as formal unity, plurality is seen primarily as simple diversity. In the era of postnational law, characterised by the rise of nonstate law both below and above the state, the defects of the solipsist view are more evident than ever. The self-containment of legal orders has been punctured even at the surface level. Interlegality should substitute for state-sovereigntist solipsism as the main organising principle of legal plurality, and plurality, seen primarily as interlegality, should assume the dominant position in the dialectic between unity and plurality.

In a legal theory of and for the postnational era, the unity and autonomy of a particular instance of law must be recapitulated against the background of the plurality in which it partakes. Postnational plurality, which often enough amounts to a pluralism of overlapping and 'rival' legal regimes and which should be conceived of in terms of interlegality rather than exclusive solipsism, constitutes the context in which the internal unity of instances of law should be examined. This holds even for national legal orders, which legal positivism has recognised – together with international law – as the only instances of law.

2 thesis: the need for a conceptual framework

Acknowledging postnational plurality entails depriving state law of its monopolistic position: all law is not state law. Still, although states no longer hold a monopoly over law (if they ever did), state law is still the dominant type of law, and much of the functioning of nonstate law presupposes support from state law.

Consequently, even if its monopolistic pretensions are to be rejected, state law still deserves special attention.

Postnational variety of law, together with the findings of legal historians and anthropologists of pluralist phenomena accompanying even the rise of the nation-state and legal centralisation, have aroused scepticism as to the possibility of arriving at a general concept of law or led to defining law simply as what the community concerned calls law.[3] It may well be that a general concept of law is a chimera, not worth pursuing. Still, we need an ideal typical conceptual starting-point which serves us in clearing our way in the jungle of postnational legality – conceptual ladders which after use we might be able to throw away (to insert the obligatory Wittgenstein reference). In constructing such an ideal typical, tentative concept, the state tradition in legal theory may still have a legitimate task to perform.

State law is not only the dominant and most widespread but also the most developed instance of law. Such a characterisation may arouse familiar suspicions of ethnocentrism and bias for Western legal tradition. So let me briefly explain my point. As historically or sociologically oriented scholars from, say, Savigny, through Weber to Luhmann have emphasised, modern state law regimes have resulted from interrelated processes of differentiation. These include detachment of legal norms from socio-legal practices; specialised second-level legal practices, such as adjudication, law-making and legal scholarship, from everyday first-level socio-legal practices; and secondary, meta-level, rules from primary rules. Modern state law also facilitates insights into the multi-layered nature of law; i.e. into the inclusion in the normative legal order not only surface-level norms but also 'subsurface', legal cultural layers. Due to its high degree of differentiation, state law can serve as a basis for elaborating an ideal typical concept of law which encompasses as many aspects as possible of the kaleidoscopic character of law, attending to both norms and practices; first- and second-level socio-legal practices; primary and secondary rules; and surface-level law and legal culture. In sum, appraised by the yardstick of differentiation state law such as we know it in established Western democracies is undoubtedly the most advanced instance of law. This provides a justification for employing it as a model against which the law-like features of nonstate normativity can be assessed; a justification which can ward off at least some of the usual accusations of ethnocentrism and cultural imperialism.

The legal *Vorverständnis* of those of us who have received our education and made our careers under the auspices of Western state law is still impregnated by the state tradition, which still, especially in public law, colours our basic legal concepts. We can, to a certain degree, gain consciousness of the deep culture which we have internalised in our legal *Vorverständnis*. However, we can probably never wholly liberate ourselves from the concepts, principles, theories or methodologies of this *Vorverständnis* or change or modify these at will. So why not profit

3 See, e.g., Brian Z. Tamanaha, *A General Jurisprudence of Law and Society* (Oxford University Press 2001).

from this seeming misfortune and have recourse to the state tradition in forming the ideal typical concept of law which can assist us in orienting ourselves in the postnational lawscape and facilitate the necessary, though often merely provisional distinctions between law and nonlaw, state law and nonstate law, as well as among instances of nonstate law?

Legal positivism is a theory of modern state law, and Kelsen and Hart are its Masters. However, in proposing elaboration of an ideal typical general concept of law from the characteristic features of modern state law I do not recommend purchasing the whole package of positivist legal theory, in its either Kelsenian or Hartian version. On the contrary, the ideal typical conceptual framework I have in mind should cancel the positivist reductions with regard to both the sociality of law and the cultural layers of legal normativity. *Pace* legal positivism, law does not consist merely of the normative legal order, such as it appears at its surface. Our ideal typical conceptual framework should include the differentiation of and interaction among three modes of existence of law: namely, law as a normative legal order; law as it is embedded in first-level socio-legal practices; and law as it appears in second-level, specialised legal practices. And as concerns law as a normative legal order, the framework should be premised on the insight that legal cultural layers underlying surface-level normative manifestations should be treated as integral elements of the law.

In sum, the ideal typical general concept, based on the differentiations and interconnections characteristic of modern state law, would present a full blown legal regime where the surface level legal order is supported by legal cultural layers and where this legal order is primarily realised in first-level socio-legal practices and produced and reproduced in specialised secondary legal practices. It would constitute the general conceptual background for the examination of particular state law regimes: the law in Finland, the Netherlands and so forth. It would also constitute – so I propose – the conceptual starting-point for exploring instances of nonstate law and for drawing distinctions between law and nonlaw; between state law and nonstate law; as well as among instances of nonstate law. It is obvious that not all instances of what has been identified as nonstate law meet all the characteristics of a full blown legal regime, gathered together in the ideal typical concept of law. Thus, differing from typical state law regimes, most instances of nonstate law probably lack legal scholarship as a differentiated and specialised second-level legal practice. It may also be that an instance of nonstate law below the state – indigenous or religious law – wants specialised law-making practices. Furthermore, it is possible that in securing implementation and realisation of codified norms, instances of transnational law – say, standardisation regimes – are parasitic on state law. Where, exactly, we draw the borderline between law and nonlaw – i.e. what characteristics of a full blown legal regime we require an instance of nonstate normativity display to deserve to be called law – is not only controversial; it is also, at least to a certain extent, dependent on our specific research purposes. Consequently, watertight distinctions and clear-cut taxonomies, valid for all purposes, are not possible and should not even be aimed at.

However, I would argue that a minimum degree of differentiation – such as at least a rudimentary differentiation of norms from practices, and specialised second-level legal practices from first-level socio-legal practices – is necessary for transcending the threshold of law. What is often decisive is the existence of specialised dispute settling and/or sanction imposing mechanisms, guaranteeing the realisation of the normativity at issue. Yet, even here gradations exist, and, as I have already noted, instances of transnational normativity may rely on the specialised law-making and judicial practices of state law to meet the need for implementation and enforcement. This is an example of blurred boundaries, so characteristic of postnational law. Other examples abound in the normative dimension: the concept of soft law, in frequent use in studies on transnational law, already signals the shaking of the wall separating legal from nonlegal normativity; a wall that legal positivists tried to construct so solid and impenetrable.

3 thesis: primacy of interlegality over simple diversity and radical pluralism

In our postnational age, the plurality of law has taken decisive steps from simple diversity to legal pluralism. Not only has the rise of nonstate law enriched legal plurality with new instances of law. It has also provided additional proof of the inadequacy of the black-boxist assumption of self-contained legal orders, subordinated to their respective Master Rules. Post-national plurality cannot be depicted in terms of simple diversity, as a mere coexistence of distinct legal orders, even if we restrict our gaze to the surface level and shut our eyes to cultural interlegality. Legal diversity has increasingly taken the guise of legal pluralism. When Kelsen and Hart let off their owl of Minerva at the turn of the 1960s, legal plurality could still, at least in the parts of the legal world the Masters of positivism examined, be relatively credibly portrayed in terms of simple diversity; provided, of course, that one accepted the reduction of the legal order to its surface level and the bracketing of legal cultural transnationalism. This moment has passed: post-national legal plurality is essentially pluralist by nature. Diverse legal orders – or, to speak in broader terms – legal regimes raise overlapping and rival claims of jurisdiction. In assessing overlaps and rivalries of jurisdictional claims, all the four spheres of validity distinguished by Kelsen in his pure theory are relevant: not only spatial but also personal, material or substantive and temporal. Instances of law draw their boundaries in all spheres, but the emphasis they put on various spheres may differ. Accordingly, we can distinguish between territorial, substantive and personal principles of authority.

Even adherents of the black box model have reckoned with the possibility that legal issues have connections to more than one national legal regime and that, consequently, disputes over jurisdiction might arise. Yet, such disputes were supposed to be exceptional and manageable with private international law (conflict of laws). What makes such disputes relatively easy to solve is the fact that state law regimes obey the same territorial principle of authority; the crucial sphere for their reciprocal border drawing is the spatial one. Pluralist situations where instances of law raise overlapping and rival jurisdictional claims are more complex. They often involve instances falling under different types of law and obeying different principles of authority; i.e. emphasising different validity spheres in the (auto-) definition of their jurisdiction. A telling example is provided by the pluralist relations between EU law and Member State law: EU law defines its jurisdiction mainly in substantive (functional) terms, while Member State law adheres to the territorial principle of authority, specified, in state sovereigntist terms, by a claim to universal and exclusive jurisdiction within its territory. In turn, a central backdrop to the clashes between, on the one hand, indigenous or religious law and, on the other hand, national or transnational law, consists in the fact that the former follow primarily a personal principle of authority, distinct from the territorial or substantive principles of the latter. A pluralist constellation may also prevail between two instances of transnational law which both adhere to a substantive principle of authority but which specify this principle differently: between, say, EU law and European human rights law or EU law and WTO law. At issue in pluralist conflicts is no longer merely the exact course of the borderline but also, and even primarily, the mutual priority of different principles of authority. And, what is more, the pluralist clashes may also turn into what I would name *fundamental conflicts of authority*. In such conflicts, one of the parties tends to rebuff the other party's claim to either autonomy or identity; at least this is the reading of the latter party which thereby defines the situation as a *battle for recognition*.

The constitutional duelling between the European Court of Justice and Member State constitutional courts – primarily, the German Constitutional Court as the *primus inter pares* – provides us with salient examples of fundamental conflicts of authority. The celebrated *Kompetenz – Kompetenz* question – whether the ultimate basis of the competence of EU institutions lies in EU or national law – is a case in point: for the ECJ, constitutional courts' claim that EU institutions derive their competences from national constitutional law amounts to rejecting the autonomy of EU law. On the other hand, in exercising what it terms identity review of EU legal acts, the German constitutional court claims, not only that EU institutions recognise and respect German constitutional identity, but also that they recognise and respect it such as it is defined by the German side of the conflict.[4]

Two principal approaches exist to post-national pluralism. Some discussants stress the inevitability of fundamental conflicts of authority and the lack of an overriding reconciling principle or a third-party, neutral arbiter. Other theorists, while conceding the ever-looming possibility of conflict, lay more stress on the resources for dialogue, cooperation and normatively compatible intra-regime

4 The OMT case is the latest but will not be the last episode instance in the pluralist bickering between the German Constitutional Court and the ECJ. The contributions of the German Constitutional Court are **Beschluss vom 06. Juli 2014** – 2 BvR 2728/13 and Urteil vom 21. Juni 2016 – 2 BvR 2728/13, and the ECJ interventions Opinion of Advocate General Cruz Villalón delivered on 14 January 2015, Case C-62/14 *Gauweiler and Others v. Deutscher Bundestag*.

solutions. *Radical pluralists* of the former strand are reborn black-boxists. They admit that legal plurality has turned into pluralism, entailing new kinds of jurisdictional conflict. However, for these theorists, legal orders remain shut in their boxes so that their spokesmen approach the contested issue – say, the *Kompetenz – Kompetenz* question – from diverse perspectives, without any common legal ground facilitating compatible assessments. Alongside Koskenniemian and other legal strategists, invoking irreconcilable strategic interests and institutional biases, latter-day Kelsenians have been well represented among radical pluralists. On the Kelsenian account, each of the contending authorities – say, the ECJ and a national constitutional court – adopts the point of view of the legal order under which it has been established and whose *Grundnorm* it presupposes as a precondition for legal cognition; say, the ECJ the perspective of EU law and the German Constitutional Court the perspective of the national German legal order. The contestants guard jealously the autonomy of their legal orders against each other's imperialist pretensions, not because of strategic interests or institutional biases but because of the transcendental separation of their *Grundnorms*. Reborn black-boxists only release legal orders from their self-enclosures to let them collide in a way which ultimately leaves their normative isolation and solipsism intact.

The other party to the debate on post-national legal pluralism, *dialogical pluralists*, points to doctrinal, institutional and procedural devices which have been developed to prevent and to defuse inter-regime conflicts of authority, especially in Europe. Let me only allude to the general principles addressing the relationship between transnational EU law and national Member State law, such as direct effect and primacy, developed by the ECJ but subsequently accepted – although not without reservations – by national constitutional courts, too; to the fact that Member State courts act simultaneously as courts of both national and EU law; and to the preliminary ruling procedure by which Member State courts may obtain from the ECJ an authoritative interpretation of EU law. By and large, EU law has succeeded in overcoming the repercussions of, not only such legal diversity among national legal orders which is deemed harmful to European integration, but also legal pluralism, threatening to lead to constitutional deadlocks with Member State law. The above-mentioned devices are conspicuous manifestations of interlegality. They establish both permanent and issue-specific contacts between EU and Member State law and rupture the self-containment of national legal regimes. Furthermore, as the principle of mutual recognition demonstrates, the reciprocal closure of national Member State legal regimes has been broken as well.

What is significant for the purposes of my argument is that the devices construed to neutralise inter-regime conflicts draw on and are supported by legal cultural resources: overlapping and commonalities at the cultural levels of law where the black box model has never really worked. The doctrinal, institutional and procedural facilities expressly provided by EU law could never create inter-regime dialogue without the support of a unifying *legal deep culture*; i.e. without basic legal concepts, basic normative principles, legal theories and legal methodologies, shared by both Member State legal regimes and EU law. Interlegality is first and foremost a legal cultural phenomenon.

EU law is arguably the most advanced instance of nonstate law above the state – 'advanced' understood again in terms of differentiation – and in the ECJ, it possesses a powerful institutional spokesman. Not all the insights gained in exploring the interrelations of transnational EU law and national Member State law can be transferred to an analysis of other pluralist constellations. Yet, some of them evidently can. Fundamental conflicts of authority are not a specificity of EU law's relation to Member State legal systems, but can always – and are almost bound to – arise where the substantively or personally limited claims of nonstate law confront the territorially defined universal and exclusive pretensions of national law. Furthermore, clashes can occur not only between nonstate law and state law, but also between nonstate law and international law, as well as between two instances of nonstate law. Thus, as *Kadi* and *Bosphorus* testify, EU law has been engaged in fundamental conflicts of authority also with international law, as well as European human rights law as another instance of nonstate law.[5] Yet, as is the case with conflicts between transnational EU law and national Member State law, most often the conflicts receive a peaceful, consensual solution compatible with both overlapping legal orders. And, again, this testifies to legal cultural interlegality, facilitating dialogue and cooperation among the legal regimes finding themselves in a pluralist constellation. To a large extent, transnational law is *Juristenrecht*, 'jurists' law', using a common legal language and drawing from a transnational legal cultural fount.

Consensual and cooperative solutions may be more difficult to reach when the dispute involves an instance of indigenous or religious law, the other party being state law or transnational law. Nonstate law above the state, i.e. transnational law, is mostly instrumentally oriented, although here transnational human rights law constitutes a major exception. By contrast, indigenous and religious law are culturally deeply embedded and enmeshed with the daily life-world of the community, and address fields of comportment central to communal identity. Therefore, clashes with national or transnational law often touch on the very cultural identity of the community. The boundaries which national or transnational law question may turn out to be fault lines the adjustment of which exceeds the practical possibilities of the community, to employ Hans K. Lindahl's terms.[6] Then, a legal solution to the dispute could only be possible through a concession of the other party, for whom the dispute does not probably possess equal significance. Yet, prospects for consensual and dialogical outcomes may not be as bleak as they appear at first glance. Human rights discourses involving indigenous cultures, too, and adoption of indigenous legal concepts in the state law of some Latin American countries intimate that cultural resources for cross-border dialogue may exist here as well.

The possibility of a conflict transcending a mere border skirmish always looms over a pluralist constellation, and the perspectival approaches of the contending

5 Joined Cases C-402/05 P and C-415/05 P *Kadi and Al Barakaat* [2008] ECR I-6351; *Bosphorus Hava Yollari Turizm v. Ireland* App. No. 45036/98 (ECHR, 30 June 2005).

6 Hans K. Lindahl, *Fault Lines of Globalization* (Oxford University Press 2013).

authorities always imply the possibility that the conflict turns out to be legally intractable. In emphasising the conflictual aspect, radical pluralists do have a point. Yet, they do not turn the coin and look to the flipside. In their exclusive perspectivism, they downplay the significance of both the expressly regulated means for inter-regime dialogue and the cultural interlegality which facilitates the successful functioning of these means. Contrary to what radical pluralists tend to claim, inter-regime relations are not only about boundary-asserting; they are also about boundary-crossing. Radical pluralists commit a mistake similar to the reductionism of the legal positivism of Kelsenian or Hartian strand: with an eye only for surface-level boundary-maintaining, they tend to ignore the cultural interlegality which disregards the boundaries of the Kelsenian validity spheres of surface level law.

4 thesis: the need to rethink internal unity

The internal unity of instances of law should from the very beginning be analysed in the context of the plurality in which they partake. Yet, the discussion of postnational plurality must by necessity take off from a tentative reconstruction of internal unity; we cannot structure postnational plurality without a rough conception of the identity of its constituent entities. Yet, being consciously tentative, such a reconstruction must leave space for subsequent complements and corrections, necessitated by insights into postnational plurality and its characteristic interlegality. Here I shall restrict my observations of the effects of plurality on the internal unity of national legal orders.

The formal unity of these legal orders, cherished by legal positivists and, in their view, ultimately guaranteed by a criterial Master Rule (such as Kelsen's *Grundnorm* or Hart's rule of recognition), is increasingly difficult to maintain, even if the legal order is reduced to its surface-level and the supporting legal cultural layers are ignored. In Kelsen's pure theory of law, the formal unity is guaranteed by the subordination of the hierarchically structured legal order to a common basic norm. In Kelsen's hierarchical *Stufenbau*, the supremacy of higher-order norms is not reduced to primacy or *Anwendungsvorrang*, which presupposes setting aside contradictory lower-order norms in concrete cases, but also covers *Geltungsvorrang*, which implies invalidation of these norms as well. In addition, higher-order norms not only invalidate but validate, too: they establish the competence to issue lower-order norms. The supremacy of directly effective EU law with regard to national law only signifies *Anwendungsvorrang*. The EU law principle of supremacy dissects the three effects –*Anwendungsvorrang*, *Geltungsvorrang* and validation – which in Kelsen's *Stufenbau* go together. A further messing up of Kelsenian hierarchy ensues from the transposition of EU directives. Directives are EU law devices which, as a rule, require explicit transposition into state law by a national instrument; directives are only binding as to their purpose and effect. EU law endows the national legal instrument effectuating the transposition – say, a parliamentary statute – with legal consequences which set it apart from 'purely' national instruments of the same hierarchical rank. The national instrument – whatever its hierarchical level in municipal law – participates in the supremacy of EU law. Thus, validation and *Geltungsvorrang* follow the hierarchy of state law, while *Anwendungsvorrang* is determined by criteria of EU law. By the same token, standards which in state law govern the relations between norms of one and the same hierarchical level – such as *lex posteriori* and *lex specialis* – are set out of effect. The principles with which EU law positions itself in respect of national law, principles grown out of policy considerations, pose a threat to both the formal unambiguity and the principle-based substantive coherence of the latter.

In the legal positivist understanding, formal unity was also supposed to guarantee the autonomy of distinct national legal orders. As the example of EU law's impact on Member State law shows, the contours of national legal orders seem increasingly fuzzy, even if we – in the vein of legal positivists – restrict our gaze to its surface level. Kelsen's and Hart's Master Rules are increasingly incapable of covering all the normative material which national courts rely on and drawing exact borderlines between law and nonlaw, as well as state and nonstate law. Formal unity even in its very thinnest sense, as subordination to the same *Grundnorm* or rule of recognition, is wavering. Because of the problematisation of formal unity, it would seem natural to look to substantive criteria in the reestablishment of the lost unity.

Kelsen was right in his observation that his predecessors' efforts to create unity through systematisation by means of law's divisions – classification, as it was called in the US – involve substantive criteria, which for him were an anathema. Where Kelsen erred in his criticism was his claim that building unity on substantive principles, concepts and theories, which were an essential part of the classification project, would necessarily entail embracing natural law premises. *Pace* Kelsen, postnational plurality has not quelled interest in the divisions of law, and grouping surface level legal material into distinct fields and elaborating field-specific general doctrines is discussed as eagerly as ever. Indeed, we are witnessing a revival of classification debates. However, their focus has shifted, so that 19th-century discussants – or even those of, say, the first post-World War II decades – would have a hard time in orienting themselves in present debates on putative legal departments, such as social law, medical and bio-law, sports law, information law or communications law. But systematisation through the law's divisions has changed its character and can no longer create a comprehensive unity, which could, by the same token, be unambiguously demarcated from other legal orders. Now law's divisions tend to be boundary-crossing rather than boundary-asserting. New putative fields of law comprise normative material from not only diverse sources – manifesting new kinds of polycentricity – but even diverse legal orders. The coherence they aim at is of local and, at the same time, boundary-crossing rather than comprehensive but boundary-maintaining character. Distinct branches of law are not expected to add up to constitute a single and unified, self-contained legal order. Divisions of law are not static but in constant movement. Nor are they excluding but overlapping, so that a set of norms can be examined as belonging to more than one branch of law: for instance, provisions on patient insurance fall under both tort law and medical law. Divisions of law and the legal fields they imply are openly perspectival: they admit that other classifications, for other purposes and adopting another perspective, are both conceivable and justifiable.

In sum, systematisation through the law's divisions is still a pertinent objective, not only for pedagogical purposes, but also for elaborating general doctrines and thus rationalising legal argument. Still, in contrast to the objectives pursued by systems preceding contemporary legal plurality, the unity that postnational systematisation can bring about is not of a comprehensive but a local character; not boundary-asserting but boundary-crossing; not stable but shifting and not valid for all purposes but openly perspectival. Current systematising efforts demonstrate that under the conditions of postnational law, the unity there can be in the law's normative dimension can only be of a substantive character, deriving from unifying principles, as well as common legal concepts, theories and methodologies, also possessing normative implications. The supports of unity lie in the cultural, sub-surface layers of law which positivist theorists in their reductive normativism tend to overlook. And the cultural layers have always been – even in the heyday of state sovereigntism and legal centralism – the privileged site for interlegality where the black-boxist self-containment embraced by positivist theorists breaks down.

5 thesis: from universal law to the plurality of discursive-cultural unities

Unity of law is a two-level issue. It can – and should – be examined both at the level of instances of law – the constituent entities of postnational plurality – and at the level of the plurality of these instances; i.e. as internal and inter-instance unity. These two levels obviously interact, so that insights gained on the impact of the postnational condition on the internal unity of state law regimes are relevant also for a discussion of inter-instance unity. Thus, the fracturing of the formal unity supposedly guaranteed by a Kelsenian or Hartian Master Rule also affects the way the unity of the law's plurality can be conceived of.

In his obsession with formal unity, Kelsen was not content with reconstructing the internal unity of national legal orders and international law. His ambitious objective was to demonstrate the unity of all law; universal law, consisting of all national legal orders and international law. He argued that, ultimately, international law defines the validity of national law and that, consequently, all law constitutes a unity. In our postnational era, Kelsen's recapitulation of universal law can hardly convince as a portrayal of the unity of global law, although it may still provide in particular international lawyers with valuable insights and inspiration. Kelsen's universal law does not recognise nonstate law at all, and, as we have seen, national legal orders can no longer – if they ever could – be depicted in terms of a hierarchical normative *Stufenbau*.

Instead of Kelsenian formal unity, inter-regime unity of postnational law must be conceived of in discursive and cultural terms, keeping in mind that in addition to its normative aspect law also consists of socio-legal practices, including legal discourses, and that the normative aspect involves 'sub-surface', cultural layers, too. What unity there is, is primarily produced through cross-boundary discourses which, in turn, would not be possible without legal cultural overlaps, commonalities and boundary-transcending influences. I have found it fruitful to make assumptions of a common deep culture which is shared by diverse legal orders and which facilitates inter-regime discourses.[7] Thus, for instance, the sufficiently uniform application of EU law or European integration as legal integration in general would hardly have been possible without such a deep culture, common to the national legal orders of the Member States, as well as EU law.

Klaus Günther talks about a ***universal legal code*** which allows for discursive links between legal regimes. This code is not reduced to the Luhmannian distinction between law and nonlaw or legal and illegal (*Recht/Unrecht*) – a strict binary distinction which postnational developments in fact have questioned – but constitutes a richer legal cultural package with normative, conceptual and methodological elements.[8] It is neither possible nor necessary to engage here in a detailed examination of the ingredients Günther suggests be included in the universal code of legality. What is important to me to note are the similarities between Günther's code and my notion of legal deep culture. We could contend that at its core, globalisation of law amounts to globalisation of a common legal deep culture or – to put it in Günther's terms – the formation and spread of a universal legal code. This code would facilitate inter-regime discourse and be the major cause for what unity the plurality of law can display at the global level. Yet, such a contention must be accompanied by at least three vital qualifications.

First, we should be careful with universalist terms and pretensions, and not equate globalisation with universalisation.[9] How widespread the deep culture is, is an empirical question. The answer evidently depends on how thick terms we use in defining the contents of this deep culture. The more we enrich the normative contents the more controversial universalist claims become. This also means that it is possible to speak of legal deep cultures with wider and narrower reaches. Even when abandoning universalist pretensions, it may still make sense to talk of European legal deep culture. And, to narrow the scope, the Nordic legal deep culture, common to the national legal orders of the Nordic states, may be given a thicker definition than the European one. This entails – and this is my second qualification – that we can talk of a plurality of unities, constructed at different levels and with different extensions.

7 Kaarlo Tuori, *Critical Legal Positivism* (Ashgate 2002); Kaarlo Tuori, *Ratio and Voluntas* (Ashgate 2011).

8 Klaus Günther, 'Rechtspluralismus und universaler Code der Legalität: Globalisierung als rechtstheoretischer Problem' in Luc Wingert and Klaus Günther (eds), *Die Öffentlichkeit der Vernunft und die Vernunft der Öffentlichkeit* (Suhrkamp 2001) 539–567.

9 Because of the universalist connotations, 'denationalisation' is often a more recommendable term than 'globalisation'.

My third qualification is related to the lesson of perspectivism which can learn from Kelsen's discussion of universal law. For a legal theorist, no bird's-eye-view from above and outside all differentiated legal cultures exists: legal theorists always engage in reconstructing both the unity and the plurality of law carrying with them the legal cultural package they have internalised in their legal *Vorverständnis.* For those of us who are pupils of Western legal culture(s) there is no escape from a certain imposed legal cultural Eurocentricism. Yet, among us, too, culturally determined perspectives vary, producing variety in our legal theoretical reconstructions.

So, plurality of unities there is, and in the dialectic of unity and plurality it is plurality which finally gains the upper hand.

Sorry to say, dear Kelsen.

2 The politics of transnational law

Thomas Gammeltoft-Hansen and Tanja Aalberts

Introduction[1]

When Philip Jessup first proposed the term 'transnational law' to describe 'all law which regulates actions or events that transcend national frontiers', he hardly knew what he would spark. Emerging out of his 1956 Storrs lectures at Yale Law School, Jessup was primarily concerned with breaking down traditional distinctions in the legal discipline, between public and private, and between international and domestic. The world, he argued, far from always fits these neat categorisations, and if students 'are nourished on the pap of old dogmas and fictions, it is not to be expected that they will later approach the solution of transnational problems with open-minded intelligence instead of open-mouthed surprise'.[2] Still, for Jessup, transnational law was to be considered a residual category or, as the Danish physicist Niels Bohr would describe it, a 'border theorem',[3] capable of bringing a wider tool box of law to bear on actions and events clearly transcending these categories. As one review of Jessup's book noted, 'Transnational law is not likely to become a term of art [...] nor does Jessup so intend it'.[4]

Sixty years later, 'transnational law' has become a term of art employed in a wide variety of contexts within legal scholarship. The term has – as the editors to this volume outline – effectively become a placeholder for multiple different theories and understandings of the mutually reinforcing developments in international law and the world it claims to govern. From the 1990s onwards, transnational legal theory, or simply transnationalism, came to be one of the main approaches to international law and many of its sub-branches across several leading law schools in both the United States and Europe. Part of this literature further involves more

1 The present chapter draws in part on material from Thomas Gammeltoft-Hansen and Tanja Aalberts, 'Politics in an Age of International Law' in Tanja Aalberts and Thomas Gammeltoft-Hansen (eds), *The Changing Practices of International Law* (Cambridge University Press 2018).

2 Philip Caryl Jessup, *Transnational Law* (Yale University Press 1956) 108–109.

3 Niels Bohr, *Atomfysik og Menneskelig Erkendelse* (Schultz 1957).

4 James N. Hyde, 'Review of Phillip C. Jessup, "Transnational Law"' (1957) 66 *Yale Law Journal* 813.

interdisciplinary research agendas, in particular, re-linking international law with its estranged offspring discipline, international relations (IR).

The onset of transnationalism in the 1990s was initially met by scepticism among many international lawyers. The shift of governance towards transnational and more loosely-structured networks of professionals (governmental, judicial or non-state actors) as well as the development of more informal and non-binding normative structures were argued to spell the death of the liberal institutionalist paradigm dominating international politics in the post-World War II period and its emphasis on treaty law and centralised legal institutions. For international relations scholars such as Robert Keohane and Joseph Nye, transgovernmentalism was seen as a change from the repeated political deadlocks and slow response time of formal international decision-making.[5] However, the informality of such networks, Sol Picciotto pointed out, creates 'a chronic lack of legitimacy'.[6] Moreover, transnationalism, or 'the myopia of handmaidens', as Philip Alston called it in 1997, 'actually relies rather heavily on the marginalization of traditional multilateral organizations. It also seems to leave increasingly little significant or relevant space for international law'.[7]

Subsequent international legal scholars have, however, often embraced transnationalism not as a paradigm shift but rather as an inescapable and perhaps even beneficial evolution of international law. For these scholars, transnationalism provides a much-needed support system to aid the efficiency of international law. Transnational networks support, rather than displace, the continued development of treaty law.[8] Transnationalism provides for global advocacy alliances of non-governmental organizations (NGOs), academics and activists serving as 'norm entrepreneurs' to push certain issues and help the gradual development of new international law, while, as part of an alleged global civil society, creating a broader basis for its legitimacy.[9] Furthermore, transnational networks of government officials, Kal Raustiala argues, further 'smooth the negotiation of new treaties by fostering convergence in ideas, policies and institutions' and further help create different modes of cooperation, e.g. 'soft law', which fill an important gap in politically sensitive areas, where binding international agreements are difficult

5 Joseph S. Nye and Robert O. Keohane, 'Transnational Relations and World Politics: An Introduction' (1971) 25 *International Organization* 329.

6 Sol Piccioto, 'Networks in International Economic Integration: Fragmented States and the Dilemmas of Neo-Liberalism' (1996–1997) 17 *Northwestern Journal of International Law and Business* 1014; Kal Raustiala, 'The Architecture of International Cooperation: Transgovernmental Networks and the Future of International Law' (2002) 43 *Virginia Journal of International Law* 2, 25.

7 Philip Alston, 'The Myopia of Handmaidens: International Lawyers and Globalization' (1997) 8 *European Journal of International Law* 435, 446.

8 José E. Alvarez, 'Do Liberal States Behave Better? A Critique of Slaughter's Liberal Theory' (2001) 12 *European Journal of International Law* 183.

9 Kathryn Sikkink, 'Transnational Politics, International Relations Theory, and Human Rights' (1998) 31 *Political Science & Politics* 517. Margaret E. Keck and Kathryn Sikkink, *Activists Beyond Borders Advocacy Networks in International Politics* (Cornell University Press 1998).

to obtain.[10] Last, but not least, according to scholars such as Harold Koh, transnational legal processes provide an important interface between international law and domestic law through which 'interpretive communities' are constituted and provide for 'norm internalisation'.[11]

All these claims, however, assume a certain normative underpinning. A liberal trajectory is often assumed to either precede or ensue from this encounter between transnationalism and international law, ensuring that transnational networks and processes work to promote rather than undermine the liberal premise of the international legal project. With the immense benefit of hindsight, the present chapter argues that this assumption, if ever valid, is particularly challenged in today's political environment, in which many states feel unduly constrained by international legal commitments and liberal internationalism no longer holds the currency in foreign policy discussions it used to.

This chapter proceeds in two parts. The first part highlights five traits of institutional design that characterise the current discontent among states with liberal institutionalist governance. This section then correlates these traits with current states' critiques of transnationalism. The second part analyses how states respond to such frustration by developing policies and practices designed to reclaim sovereign manoeuvrability by circumventing or creatively navigating these same international legal structures. This development draws on the very same transnational structures and modus operandi as foreseen by transnational law scholars. Indeed, the expansion and increased institutionalisation of international law itself seem to have created the structural premise for this type of politics of international law. The chapter thus argues that, in contrast to the predictions of previous transnational legal scholarship, this form of transnationalism is increasingly used as a managerial tool to limit the impact or development of more traditional and liberal forms of international law.

Design choices in international law

The second part of the 20th century has seen an exponential multiplication of multilateral treaties, specialised legal regimes and international institutions. Together they weave an increasingly dense net for the international rule of law as an apparently prevalent factor in international relations. As described in the introduction to this volume, this development covers several distinct but related phenomena at the empirical level – from the multiplication of actors, or subjects, of international law to the ensuing growth in treaty law in conjunction with new types of law; and from the proliferation of international organisations,

10 Ibid., fn. 1, p. 92; See also Anne Marie Slaughter, *A New World Order* (Princeton University Press 2005); Thomas Gammeltoft-Hansen, John Cerone and Stephanie Lagoutte, 'Introduction: Tracing the Roles of Soft Law in Human Rights' in Stephanie Lagoutte, Thomas Gammeltoft-Hansen and John Cerone (eds), *Tracing the Roles of Soft Law in Human Rights* (Oxford University Press 2016) 1.

11 Harold Hongju Koh, 'Transnational Legal Process' (1996) 75 *Nebraska Law Review* 181.

transnational corporate entities and other non-state actors challenging the notion of sovereign states as the exclusive subjects and arbiters of international law, to the recognition of non-state entities as holding obligations and bolstering of international judicial institutions.

More fundamentally, international law can be seen to have developed to reflect a number of more or less deliberate design choices in the turn to law as the predominant form of international diplomacy.

The dissolution of the national–international divide

Alongside the quantitative expansion of treaty law, international law has seen an equally important qualitative transformation in terms of the content of the treaties. A substantial part of the treaties concluded during the past half century governs qualitatively different issues, often deeply impacting domestic politics and challenging traditional conceptions of state sovereignty based on a separation of internal and external affairs. Wolfgang Friedmann famously coined this development as the difference between the international law of co-existence and the international law of co-operation.[12] As he foresaw as early as 1964, international law has gradually developed beyond the traditional law of sovereign states, ensuring peaceful co-existence and regulating conflict among states, and has been supplanted by a drive towards deeper cooperation, concerned with topics hitherto considered 'domestic affairs', such as economic development, welfare and good governance.[13] From trade law, to human rights, to environmental law, the growing international law of co-operation presupposes a fundamentally different commitment of participating states to correspondingly adjust domestic affairs. This is epitomised in the development of 'community interests' that overrule individual interests states may have as well as the principle of consent, as the International Court argued in the Reservations to the Genocide Convention opinion.[14] Similarly, with the expansion of the commons of mankind, sovereignty increasingly seems to function as a fiduciary logic, a responsibility rather than a right, with states as trustees of the global commons.[15] Last but not least, inter-operation between different legal institutions also works to break down the national–international divide.[16] A crucial development is the increasingly important role that national institutions play in the enforcement of international law,

12 Wolfgang Friedmann, *The Changing Structure of International Law* (Stevens & Sons 1964).

13 Ibid.

14 *Reservations to the Convention on the Prevention and Punishment of the Crime of Genocide*, Advisory Opinion, [1951] ICJ Reports 15. Bruno Simma, 'From Bilateralism to Community Interest in International Law' (1994) 250 *Recueil des Cours* 217.

15 Tanja E. Aalberts and Wouter G. Werner, 'Mastering the Globe: Law, Sovereignty and the Commons of Mankind' in Rens van Munster and Casper Sylvest (eds), *The Politics of Globality since 1945: Assembling the Planet* (Routledge 2016) 89.

16 André Nollkaemper, 'Inside or Out: Two Types of International Legal Pluralism' in Jan Klabbers and Touko Piiparinen (eds), *Normative Pluralism and International Law: Exploring Global Governance* (Cambridge University Press 2014) 94.

stimulated by, inter alia, the development of universal jurisdiction in international criminal cases and domestic incorporation of, e.g. human rights instruments.[17]

The proliferation of international legal institutions

Furthermore and related, international law has been backed by a much broader and stronger panoply of international legal institutions (some 125 to date) in the hope of solving the age-old problem of enforcement in international law.[18] Not only do we have more courts, they are also overloaded with work. A clear illustration of this development is the reach and caseload of regional courts; for instance, the European Court of Human Rights alone receives around 60,000 applications and issues some 1,500 substantive judgments annually.[19] Moreover, several new adjudicatory mechanisms have emerged since the 1990s. The fragmentation of international law in numerous specialised legal regimes has brought with it a whole landscape of specialised adjudicatory and dispute resolution mechanisms. Importantly, many of them include powerful states that have traditionally avoided submitting to international jurisdiction.[20] Maybe even more significantly, in the last decades, the International Court of Justice has been granted jurisdiction in a number of controversial and security-related cases. This shows that here too, we witness not only a quantitative but also a qualitative expansion of the international rule of law. Another key development in this regard is that new protocols have expanded the right to individual petition under a number of human rights treaties, as well as the role of human rights committees and national institutions to monitor domestic implementation (e.g. the Optional Protocol to the Convention Against Torture). These developments further illustrate the transformation of the divide between national and international matters. The two ad hoc International Criminal Tribunals for Rwanda and the former Yugoslavia were succeeded by the establishment of the International Criminal Court, allowing for the international prosecution of government officials for, e.g. war crimes and crimes against humanity. Last but not least, the expansion in treaty law, such as bilateral investment treaties, has also led to an increase of inter-state arbitrations before the Permanent Court of Arbitration (PCA). Moreover, as a telling illustration of the transnationalisation of

17 Benedict Kingsbury, 'International Courts: Uneven Judicialisation in Global Order' in James Crawford and Martti Koskenniemi (eds), *The Cambridge Companion to International Law* (Cambridge University Press 2012) 203, 222; B.S. Chimni, 'Legitimating the International Rule of Law' in James Crawford and Martti Koskenniemi (eds), *The Cambridge Companion to International Law* (Cambridge University Press 2012) 290, 296.

18 Calculation from the Project on International Courts and Tribunals www.pict-pcti.org accessed 23 January 2017.

19 Kingsbury (n. 17) 208.

20 J.H.H. Weiler et al., 'Special Issue: Changing Paradigms in International Law' (2009) 20 *European Journal of International Law* 21; Georges Abi-Saab, Laurence Boisson de Chazournes and Vera Gowlland-Debbas, *The International Legal System in Quest of Equity and Universality = L'ordre Juridique International, Un Système En Quête D'équité et Universalité : Liber Amicorum Georges Abi-Saab* (Martinus Nijhoff Publishers 2001).

international law, today the PCA also provides dispute resolution services in cases involving claims concerning non-state actors such as transnational corporations.

Shifting dynamics of law formation

Third, the expansion and qualitative reorientation of treaty law has implied a shift of law-making powers towards international organisations as well as non-state actors. While states undoubtedly remain the principal authors of international law, the model of legal decision-making pursued in most areas of international law has facilitated a more heterogeneous and inclusive multilateralism. As the number of states negotiating expands and the topics under consideration become more complex, international organisations are increasingly charged with preparing draft text and facilitating the negotiation process. As part of this development, international organisations have similarly drawn in other non-state actors in the consultation and/or drafting process. Nowadays, it is thus far from unusual to see NGOs,[21] academics,[22] technical experts[23] and private corporations[24] take on important roles in the development of international law.

New modalities of international law

Fourth, the relative dominance of law and legal expertise means that legal forms and legal language are being employed far beyond what we traditionally recognise as formal international law. An increasing part of the normative standards in the last decades has taken the form of non-binding agreements and other instruments short of positive international law. The trend towards the increasing use of soft law is particularly pronounced in the area of human rights. While relatively few human rights treaties have been adopted at the UN level in the last two

21 Christine Chinkin, 'Human Rights and the Politics of Representation: Is There a Role for International Law?' in Michael Byers (ed.), *The Role of Law in International Politics* (Oxford University Press 2000) 131. Richard Price, 'Reversing the Gun Sights: Transnational Civil Society Targets Land Mines' (1998) 52 *International Organization* 613. See also n. 9.

22 Lianne J.M. Boer, 'Chapter 5: Call me again if you're ever ready to begin answering the questions' in *International Law as We Know It: Cyberwar Discourse and the Construction of Knowledge in International Legal Scholarship*, Dissertation Vrije Universiteit Amsterdam (2017). Of course, the involvement of academics has already been the practice since long in the International Law Commission (1947), whose membership is composed of 'persons of recognized competence in international law' (Article 2.1 ILC Statute). Members are drawn from the various segments of the international legal community, including academia, the diplomatic corps, government ministries and international organisations (http://legal.un.org/ilc, accessed 27 March 2019).

23 Anna Leander and Tanja Aalberts, 'The Co-Constitution of Legal Expertise and International Security' (2013) 26 *Leiden Journal of International Law* 783; Jaye Ellis, 'Legalization in International Environment Law' in Tanja Aalberts and Thomas Gammeltoft-Hansen (eds), *The Changing Practices of International Law* (Cambridge University Press 2018).

24 Jonathan Charney, 'Transnational Corporations and Developing Public International Law' (1983) 4 *Duke Law Journal* 748.

decades, the number of declarations, resolutions, conclusions and principles has grown almost exponentially.[25] This new realm of soft law can be seen to shape and impact upon the content of international law in multiple ways: from being a first step in a norm-making process to providing detailed rules and more technical standards required for the interpretation and the implementation of existing rules of positive law.

Growing regime interdependence

Fifth and finally, the different components of international law today display a high degree of both legal and political interdependence. More than 6,000 multilateral treaties have been signed since the beginning of the 20th century.[26] Many of them, for example the United Nations Convention on the Law of the Sea (UNCLOS), are general in nature and package a wide and diverse range of commitments that states are presented with as a single package. At the regional level, the EU is probably the most paradigmatic example of an integrated legal regime, the membership of which bundles a vast number of directives, regulations as well as intergovernmental legal commitments together, which are difficult (though not impossible) to selectively opt out of.[27] A clear illustration is that one can only join the EU if also ratifying the European Convention on Human Rights and becoming a member of the Council of Europe. Moreover, despite the development (or fragmentation) of international law in a variety of specialised regimes, these are far from isolated bodies of law. Interestingly, both legal instruments themselves and international legal institutions increasingly make cross-references to other treaties and institutions.[28] It is thus common practice for bilateral agreements to cross-reference multilateral obligations. For instance, foreign investment treaties often require signatory parties to also commit to a variety of other international standards in order to establish a secure investment climate. At the level of the judiciary, the European Court of Justice and the European Court on Human Rights seek to avoid potential adjudicative conflicts through informal coordination.

Together, these developments give the impression of an ever widening and more dense net of legal rules and network of institutions across a wide range of issue areas. Moreover, reference to international law and institutions has become more commonplace. It confirms that international law no longer is

25 Gammeltoft-Hansen, Cerone and Lagoutte (n. 10).

26 A development that seems to have slowed down somewhat the last two decades.

27 Rebecca Adler-Nissen, *Opting out of the European Union: Diplomacy, Sovereignty and European Integration* (Cambridge University Press 2014).

28 Imelda Higgins, 'Human Rights in the International Court of Justice' (2007) 20 *Leiden Journal of International Law* 745; Philip Liste, 'The Politics of (Legal) Intertextuality' (2010) 4 *International Political Sociology* 318; Antje Wiener and Philip Liste, 'Lost Without Translation? Cross-Referencing and a New Global Community of Courts' (2014) 21 *Indiana Journal of Global Legal Studies* 263.

the Buchrecht of esoteric academics, but has become the everyday language in diplomacy and public discourse.[29] We seem to live in an unprecedented era of 'legalisation',[30] with 'law at every turn'.[31] The question is, however, if this means that the room for politics is concomitantly narrowing, as a part of this scholarship seems to suggest.

The backlash against international law

If the empirical developments underpinning the success story of international law in the 20th century are undeniable, recent events arguably show that the international legal project facing substantial political challenges.

Since a few years, we are witnessing a political backlash to the increased role of international law within global governance. Different states have voiced concern that international law is imposing unrealistic burdens and that international legal institutions are undermining democratic decision-making and national sovereignty.[32] In Europe, several states have criticised its two regional courts, the Court of Justice of the European Union (CJEU) and the European Court of Human Rights (ECtHR), for 'judicial activism' and overly dynamic interpretation, not least in regard to sensitive political issues such as welfare distribution, immigration and minority rights.[33] In 2016, the Danish Supreme Court, in clear defiance of the interpretation of the CJEU, reasserted the pre-eminence of Danish domestic law in a case concerning employment rights.[34] Resistance to the jurisdiction of the CJEU similarly played a prominent role in the United Kingdom campaign to

29 James Crawford and Martti Koskenniemi, 'Introduction' in James Crawford and Martti Koskenniemi (eds), *The Cambridge Companion to International Law* (Cambridge University Press 2012) 1, 1; Ian Johnstone, *The Power of Deliberation: International Law, Politics and Organizations* (Oxford University Press 2011).

30 While this concept has been incorporated as part of a theoretical framework to scrutinise the phenomenon of international law (see Judith Goldstein, Miles Kahler, Robert O. Keohane and Anne-Marie Slaughter, 'Introduction: Legalization and World Politics' (2000) 54 *International Organization* 385), we use it here as a descriptive term to identify the expansion of law in the international realm.

31 As David Kennedy observes, 'Although it is easy to think of international affairs as a rolling sea of politics over which we have managed to throw but a thin net of legal rules, in truth the situation today is more the reverse. There is law at every turn – and only the most marginal opportunities for engaged political contestation.' David Kennedy, 'Challenging Expert Rule: The Politics of Global Governance' (2005) 27 *Sydney Law Review* 5, 5.

32 Ivan Anthony Shearer, 'In Fear of International Law' (2005) 12 *Indiana Journal of Global Legal Studies* 345.

33 Mark Dawson, B. De Witte and Elise Muir (eds), *Judicial Activism at the European Court of Justice* (Edward Elgar 2013); Mikael Rask Madsen, 'The Challenging Authority of the European Court of Human Rights' (2016) 79 *Law and Contemporary Problems* 141.

34 Mikael Rask Madsen, Henrik Palmer Olsen and Urska Sadl, 'Competing Supremacies and Clashing Institutional Rationalities: The Danish Supreme Court's Decision in the *Ajos* Case and the National Limits of Judicial Cooperation' (2017) 23 *European Law Journal* 140.

leave the European Union, just as it has in the ensuring negotiations of the Brexit process.[35] In the United States, the Trump administration announced withdrawals from both the Trans-Pacific Partnership Agreement (TPPA) on trade and the Paris Agreement on climate change, in addition to introducing a moratorium on new multilateral treaties.[36]

Looking at some of these incidents, and the political discourse surrounding them, the different criticisms by states often correlate with the core traits set out above. That is to say, these criticisms seldom amount to the full-scale rejection of international law as such; rather, it is often voiced as objections directed at the particular way international law-making and legal institutions have been designed and developed.

The flipside to the growing web of international legal commitments is the revival of traditional sovereignty discussions. Across different parts of the world, national-conservative forces have capitalised on this dynamic to mobilise domestic political support with various promises of re-establishing stronger boundaries between domestic and international regulation. The issues at stake differ from country to country – immigration in Australia, sexual minorities in Uganda, EU opposition in Hungary and labour production in the United States – but the core political arguments in terms of rebalancing sovereignty and self-determination vis-à-vis international obligations and pressures remain the same. Similarly, the proliferation of broadly scoped multilateral treaties and increased legal and political regime inter-dependency is seen by many states as creating a lock-in effect, making it different to isolate, opt-out or renegotiate particular international legal agreements without wide-ranging and in many cases unforeseeable legal, political let alone economic consequences.

Closely related, the strengthening of international legal institutions has prompted accusations of judicial activism and international courts being portrayed as fundamentally undemocratic.[37] Such sentiments were repeatedly cited by the Danish government as the reason to critically examine existing human

35 As noted by Theresa May in her speech at Lancaster House on 17 January 2017, 'We will take back control of our laws and bring an end to the jurisdiction of the European Court of Justice in Britain. Leaving the European Union will mean that our laws will be made in Westminster, Edinburgh, Cardiff and Belfast. And those laws will be interpreted by judges not in Luxembourg but in courts across this country.' www.gov.uk/government/speeches/the-governments-negotiating-objectives-for-exiting-the-eu-pm-speech accessed 7 November 2018.

36 Jack L. Goldsmith, 'The Trump Onslaught on International Law and Institutions' (*Lawfare Blog*, 17 March 2017) www.lawfareblog.com/trump-onslaught-international-law-and-institutions accessed 7 November 2018; Monica Hakimi, 'International Law in the Age of Trump' (*EJIL:Talk!*, 28 February 2017) www.ejiltalk.org/international-law-in-the-age-of-trump accessed 7 November 2018.

37 Mikael Rask Madsen, Pola Cebulak and Micha Wiebusch, 'Backlash Against International Courts: Explaining the Forms and Patterns of Resistance to International Courts' (2018) 14 *International Journal of Law in Context* 197; Armin von Bogdandy and Ingo Venzke, 'In Whose Name? An Investigation of International Courts' Public Authority and Its Democratic Justification' (2012) 23 *European Journal of International Law* 7.

rights commitments and using its 2017–2018 Council of Europe presidency to initiate a reform process with regard to the European Court of Human Rights intended to further cement the principle of subsidiarity and limit the influence of the Court on politically sensitive issues such as asylum and immigration.[38]

In addition, the inclusive and facilitated decision-making processes led by international organisations are seen by some states as imposing a substantive bias not shared by a majority of states and, in some cases, furthering organisational rather than state interests. Hence, the arguments by both governments and commentators that it is time to 'bring back international law on state hands'.[39] Concretely, this has led to both calls for institutional reform, including threats to withhold or cut funding as well as attempts by states to negotiate political and legal agreements around alternative, state-led and more selective coalitions. As such, soft law processes have similarly become the battleground for interpretive struggles. In some cases, state-led soft law processes are clearly used as a strategy for parties actively seeking to backtrack or hedge against dynamic developments in the interpretation of international human rights law.[40]

In sum, international law has developed to a point where some states feel threatened by their own creation. We agree with David Kennedy in his observation that never before has international law been so important; yet, based on the above examples, his conclusion that this has limited the possibilities for political contestation seems to be premature.[41] The paradoxical result of the increased legalisation of world politics is not only the development of an increasingly dense net of rules, but also the parallel emergence of a catalogue of loopholes in its wake, thus enhancing the room for politics within international law.

The dark side of transnationalism: State strategies to cope with transnationalism

So, we have a situation where, on the one hand, international law is seen as sine qua non for doing international politics, and, on the other hand, the increasing constraints of international law create a certain fervour amongst states to try and recoup sovereign power by making the rules work for them in areas of particular political importance.

38 Danish Presidency of the Council of Europe, 'Draft Copenhagen Declaration', 5 February 2018, paras 22–30. https://menneskeret.dk/sites/menneskeret.dk/files/media/dokumenter/nyheder/draft_copenhagen_declaration_05.02.18.pdf, accessed 27 March 2019. The final version of the Copenhagen Declaration adopted by the Council, however, somewhat toned down demands for subsidiarity and does not include mention of specific approaches to certain issues such as asylum and immigration.

39 Interview with former Under-Secretary of Legal Affairs at the Danish Ministry of Foreign Affairs, Ambassador Thomas Winkler, September 2012. See more generally Eric A. Posner, 'Liberal Internationalism and the Populist Backlash' (2017) 49 *Arizona State Law Journal* 795.

40 Gammeltoft-Hansen, Cerone and Lagoutte (n. 10).

41 See quote in n. 31.

Such a scenario may of course lead some states to resign from existing multilateral agreements. There are serious worries that Brexit and the US withdrawal from, e.g. TPPA and the Human Rights Council, might have far reaching implications for development and rule of international law, also beyond these specific regimes. Yet, this does not necessarily spell a diminished role for international law as such. In their wake, different forms of international law may well emerge, replacing broader multilateral with webs of bilateral intergovernmental agreements. Thus, we may be seeing a further qualitative transformation of international law towards different and more 'disaggregated' forms of international cooperation[42] as well as of legal instruments themselves.

In this situation, transnationalism takes on a completely different role. As states are increasingly required to translate and justify their actions in legal terms, governments have become much more adept at navigating and manoeuvring legal structures. As such, governments begin to rely on their legal advisors not just to check for compliance with international law but also to actively engage in creative thinking around the design of new policies vis-à-vis international law.[43] Notably, this is facilitated by the very developments in international law that we claim to be part of its success story; the multiplication of legal regimes, overlapping jurisdictions and shifting centres of authority seem to have opened up an increased playing field for political contestation within international law.

Transnationalism, both in the sense of transnational networks and transnational legal structures, plays a particular role here. It allows governments to apply different forms of governance in order to design policies and actions to work at the fringes or in-between the formal structures of international law. And it enables transnational networks of policy-makers to come together in order to explore legally complicated policy areas or counter more expansive interpretations of sensitive areas of international law by international judiciaries and other actors engaged in the ongoing negotiation of international law.[44]

42 Itamar Mann, 'The Disaggregated Law of Mass Surveillance' in Tanja Aalberts and Thomas Gammeltoft-Hansen (eds), *The Changing Practices of International Law* (Cambridge University Press 2018).

43 Kennedy (n. 31) 5; see also Matthew Windsor, 'Consigliere or Conscience? The Role of the Government Legal Advisor' in Jean d'Aspremont et al. (eds), *International Law as a Profession* (Cambridge University Press 2017) 355; Fernando G. Nuñez-Mietz, 'Lawyering Compliance with International Law: Legal Advisers in the "War on Terror"', (2016) 1 *European Journal of International Security* 215. Yet, these analyses might imply too much in terms of the increasing role and power of legal advisors within government. See Tanja Aalberts and Lianne J.M. Boer, 'Entering the Invisible College: Defeating Lawyers on Their Own Turf' (2018) 87 *British Yearbook*. Their analysis of the Chilcot inquiry supports our contention that indeed international law is a crucial language to justify foreign policy, but that this does not automatically mean that the legal advisors themselves have gained more power (as the literature quoted here suggests).

44 Gammeltoft-Hansen, Cerone and Lagoutte (n. 10).

The range of these practices is broad. We see it in very diverse subject areas, from migration control to surveillance to trading of emission and to fishing quotas.[45] The kind of strategies employed are surprisingly similar across different regions and policy areas, suggesting learning or mimicry aspects through which policies are transferred from one issue area or one country to another.[46]

Perhaps the oldest form of such policies to shift or avoid legal liability under either domestic or international law involves the use of extraterritorial venues. A clear and topical example of such 'jurisdiction shopping' is the increasing state practice to interdict migrants on the high seas (as the United States has done with Haitian refugees since the 1980s, is the basis of Australia's 'Pacific Solution' and has become a normalised practice for EU states and Frontex in the Mediterranean Sea since the turn of the millennium). The argument is that this nullifies any right to claim asylum as a matter of international refugee or human rights law, as the right to seek asylum allegedly is only activated when a migrant enters a state territory.[47] It can also involve deals to make use of another state's territory, as Australia's deal with Nauru on detention centres for asylum seekers illustrates.

Jurisdiction shopping is equally evident in regard to commercial interests. States may thus be seen to negotiate agreements to allow industrial manufacturing in third countries with fewer or lower environmental and labour rights restrictions. The effort to establish national fishing quotas as a matter of international law has thus equally seen a number of southern European states negotiate agreements with their African neighbours to allow European trawlers to fish within their territorial waters and exclusive economic zones.[48] Things become even more complex the more fragmented processes are. Global value chains not only are commercially attractive, but also make it difficult to govern these processes through the international rule of law.

International cooperation is another way through which states may try and circumvent or shift particular legal obligations. The active, or even nominal, involvement of another state's authorities is regularly used to make claims on behalf of sponsoring states to avoid legal liability in regard to, e.g. law enforcement. Some states have thus been known to send terrorist suspects to partner states in order to effect interrogations with techniques that would not be allowed in the sponsoring state under either domestic or international law. This may involve the concomitant commercialisation of sovereignty by the territorial state, as in the

45 For case studies, see the contributions in Tanja Aalberts and Thomas Gammeltoft-Hansen (eds), *The Changing Practices of International Law* (Cambridge University Press 2018).

46 A dynamic specifically tracked by Daniel Ghezelbash in regard to immigration policy. Daniel Ghezelbash, *Refuge Lost* (Cambridge University Press 2018).

47 A practice subsequently accepted to entail jurisdiction as a matter of international human rights. Thomas Gammeltoft-Hansen, 'Sale's Legacy – "Creative Legal Thinking" and Dynamic Interpretation of Refugee Law' (*Opinio Juris*, 15 March 2014). www.opiniojuris.org, accessed 27 March 2019.

48 Francisco Orrego Vicuna, *The Changing International Law of High Seas Fisheries* (Cambridge University Press 1999).

case of Guantanamo Bay. Or it may involve more complex arrangements between multiple states, as in the case of the Central Intelligence Agency (CIA) rendition programme. Similar arrangements are common in efforts to fight different forms of transnational organised crime, where international law otherwise poses a range of constraints in regard to intercepting foreign vessels on the high seas suspected of smuggling or carrying out raids inside the territory of another state. The use of ship-riders – authorities of a territorial or neighbouring state – has thus become an increasingly popular part of maritime law enforcement.[49] Last, but not least, this kind of pro forma involvement of the authorities of another state has been employed in the context of international military operations by countries hoping to avoid triggering extraterritorial human rights jurisdiction when taking persons into custody.[50]

Moreover, in both Iraq and Afghanistan, the United States has also made increasing use of private military and security companies like Blackwater and Carlyle. Similar use of private contractors can be seen in regard to, e.g. anti-piracy operations[51] and migration control.[52] This is another example of how transnationalism is enacted, namely through the blurring boundary between public and private as a matter of international law and practice. The involvement of private military and security companies raises a number of different issues in terms of state responsibility and accountability under both domestic and international law – often at least de facto insulating states from any associated responsibility for, e.g. violations of international humanitarian or human rights law.[53] Often these arrangements involve several layers of subcontracting or take place as part of extraterritorial operations, thereby further complicating questions of accountability and the possibility to 'pass the buck' for any subsequent wrongdoing.[54]

49 Ibid., 72ff.

50 Denmark, for instance, has routinely involved British soldiers when undertaking military patrols in Iraq. Anders Henriksen, 'Fanger, folkeret og "brite-finter". (Detainees, International Law and "the British Trick")' (2014) 87 *Økonomi & Politik* 6.

51 John J. Pitney Jr and John-Clark Levin, *Private Anti-Piracy Navies: Warships for Hire Are Changing Maritime Security* (Lexington Books 2013); Jill Harrelson, 'Blackbeard Meets Blackwater: An Analysis of International Conventions that Address Piracy and the Use of Private Security Companies to Protect the Shipping Industry' (2010) 25 *American University International Law Review* 283.

52 Thomas Gammeltoft-Hansen, 'Private Security and the Migration Control Industry' in Rita Abrahamsen and Anna Leander (eds), *Routledge Handbook on Private Security* (Routledge 2015).

53 Anna Leander, 'The Paradoxical Impunity of Private Military Companies: Authority and the Limits to Legal Accountability' (2010) 41 *Security Dialogue* 467; A. Claire Cutler, 'The Legitimacy of Private Transnational Governance: Experts and the Transnational Market for Force' (2010) 8 *Socio-Economic Review* 157; Carsten Hoppe, 'Passing the Buck: State Responsibility for Private Military Companies' (2008) 19 *European Journal of International Law* 989.

54 Hoppe (n. 53).

The co-existence of complex, partly overlapping and non-hierarchical treaty regimes[55] may furthermore afford states opportunities to deal with issues through different legal regimes with different responsibilities towards different parties. For instance, the issue of intellectual property rights is regulated via the World Trade Organization's (WTO's) trade regime through the Agreement on Trade-Related Aspects of Intellectual Property Rights (TRIPS) but is also addressed by the World Health Organisation (for instance in the case of patented pharmaceuticals in the fight against HIV/Aids in developing countries) and the Convention on Biological Diversity. The latter enables the subordination of intellectual property rights to environmental protection and development goals, which goes against the TRIPS arrangements.[56] The dynamics of regime complexity are further enhanced by the expansion of 'soft law' instruments, such as declarations, guidelines, standard-setting and recommendations.[57]

As a result, states are likely to try and resolve legal disputes through whatever litigation mechanism or body of international law that is likely to afford them the most favourable view or work most to their benefit. For example, North American trade disputes can be brought both to the WTO and to North American Free Trade Agreement (NAFTA), each of which have different approaches and legal effects in regard to the parties. This kind of judicial forum shopping is not only a matter of strategic choice in regard to specific cases but can also involve the simultaneous or successive litigation of claims,[58] or to discriminate among overlapping memberships[59] in light of a legal 'shadow of the future logic'.

What is significant here is the way each of these practices are enabled by wider developments in international law itself. Most of the examples set out above are framed by bilateral or multilateral international agreements. The international law of cooperation, in other words, is the very vessel through which they are implemented. As such, it is difficult to see how more international rules or stronger international institutions alone can provide a solution to this issue. In sum, much

55 Karen J. Alter and Sophie Meunier, 'The Politics of International Regime Complexity' (2009) 7 *Perspectives on Politics* 13; cf. Kal Raustiala and David Victor, 'The Regime Complex for Plant Genetic Resources' (2004) 85 *International Organization* 277.

56 Raustiala and Victor (n. 55); Laurence R. Helfer, 'Regime Shifting: The Trips Agreement and the New Dynamics of International Intellectual Property Making' (2004) 29 *Yale Journal of International Law* 1. Raustiala and Victor push the argument even further and identify this as a practice of 'strategic inconsistency', which is the creation of contradictory rules in parallel regimes in order to undermine existing rules in other agreements.

57 Cf. mapping of the regime complex for climate change in Robert O. Keohane and David G. Victor, 'The Regime Complex for Climate Change' (2011) 9 *Perspectives on Politics* 7.

58 Laurence R. Helfer, 'Forum Shopping for Human Rights' (1999) 148 *University of Pennsylvania Law Review* 285. He sees this not as a threat to the unity of the legal system, but emphasises the aforementioned practice of inter-decision making which makes international human rights litigation a 'shared and ongoing enterprise' producing 'harmonious, though not necessarily uniform, set of human rights standards' (*Helfer*, 'Forum Shopping for Human Rights' 400).

59 Mark L. Busch, 'Overlapping Institutions, Forum Shopping, and Dispute Settlement in International Trade' (2007) 61 *International Organization* 735.

against the liberal expectations of its original proponents, transnationalism seems to have pushed a range of political-legal strategies designed not to further promote international law, but in response to and as a reaction to international law's increasing influence.

Conclusions

Governments have become more strategic in their relationship to international law. The result is a distinctive form of transnationalism, at once shaped and constrained by the wider landscape of international law. Existing scholarship often considers the policies listed above as exceptions or aberrations to the ordinary modus operandi of international law. Such perspectives, however, fail to acknowledge the extent to which, across a wide array of issue areas and jurisdictions, these practices have come to represent a systemic feature of the international legal landscape today.

This is not to say that the kind of practices examined in the present chapter are representative of states' commitment to all aspects of international law. These practices rather represent a particular kind of political response in areas where states feel unduly constrained by international law in light of important political priorities, and where the two obvious alternatives – openly disregarding legal obligations or seeking to renegotiate or step down from international legal instruments – are considered unfeasible or too costly.

Two additional points should be made in this connection. Firstly, the emergence of these practices far from always entails a rejection of international law as such. Rather, strategies to avoid or circumvent legal obligations presume, inter alia, that these norms do actually matter and, under ordinary circumstances, affect state action. If governments felt they could simply disrespect international law 'at home', then there would be little need to engage in cumbersome and often costly schemes of this nature. These transnational governance strategies allow states to simultaneously apply a more managerial approach to international law, but still formally present themselves as countries abiding by their international law commitments.

Secondly, at a time when the legitimacy and continued political viability of the international legal order is intensely debated, attention to this kind of transnationalism necessarily raises difficult ethical and normative questions. Depending on one's vantage point, many of the examples set out above might be described as intentional circumvention of international law, violating if not the letter of the law, then core principles such as implementing treaties in good faith. International law is by design poorly equipped to deal with that kind of political speculation and may suffer more generally as a result. Others may conversely point to the domestic political support many states enjoy when engaging in the kind of strategies described in this chapter. More pragmatic scholars may thus argue that this kind of politics ultimately serves as a political pressure valve and avoids more direct confrontations against international law. Vice versa, scholars attentive to global social justice might argue that at least some states have legitimate interest in regaining political control of international law. Regardless of how one judges the legality of the kind of creative legal thinking described in this chapter, such practices are one of the few options available to many states in the Global South hoping to re-establish public control vis-à-vis international investors.[60]

60 See Malcolm Langford, Daniel Behn and Ole Kristian Fauchald, 'Backlash and State Strategies in International Investment Law' in Tanja Aalberts and Thomas Gammeltoft-Hansen (eds), *The Changing Practices of International Law* (Cambridge University Press 2018).

3 Transnationalism in the Arctic Ocean

Legitimacy strategies of the Inuit Circumpolar Council, the European Union and China

Cécile Pelaudeix

Introduction

The dramatic changes affecting the Arctic region and pertaining to climate change and globalisation, and the resulting increase in economic activities have sparked many discussions and initiatives about the governance of the region and the legal framework. Far from being a legal vacuum, the region, which is governed by eight Arctic states, shows a high level of complexity stemming from political and cultural diversity whereby law and norms arise from territorial entities (for instance, regional governments or administrations), states, regional organisations (such as Ospar, the Arctic Council), the EU and international institutions (for instance, the International Maritime Organisation and the UN). As global governance develops, new regimes are also expected to affect the region (the Paris Agreement and the under-discussion Convention on Biodiversity Beyond National Jurisdiction, to name a few examples). This governance complexity, in which the state is not the sole provider of norms and which characterises a situation of transnationalism, increases with the involvement of actors such as Indigenous Peoples (IP) organisations or powerful non-Arctic states like China entering the Arctic scene and claiming to be involved in norm-setting.

This chapter analyses the relation between transnationalism and legitimacy in the Arctic Ocean (AO) by focusing on three actors: the Inuit Circumpolar Council (ICC), the EU and China. These actors – a non-governmental indigenous organisation, a supranational organisation and a non-Arctic state – are challenging the normative status quo: their claims to be associated in norm shaping relate to legitimacy as a right to rule.[1] Transnationalism is here conceived in a wider perspective than Jessup's mainly geographic acceptance whereby transnational law refers to law that 'transcends national frontiers'.[2] The approach

1 Daniel Bodansky, 'Legitimacy in International Law and International Relations' in Jeffrey L. Dunoff and Mark A. Pollack (eds), *International Perspectives on International Law and International Relations* (Cambridge University Press 2013) 321.

2 Philip Jessup, *Transnational Law* (Yale University Press 1956).

in this chapter embraces Zumbansen's definition of transnational law as 'a methodological lens' through which we can 'study the particular transformation of legal institutions in the context of an evolving complex society'.[3] With the inclusion of China as a case study, this chapter also points to legal challenges posed by the rise of a non-Western country. Indeed, the three types of actors in this chapter reflect major legal shifts in the contemporary world: the increasing recognition of IP's rights, the development of a supranational organisation in an international system still dominated by a Westphalian model and the rise of a country, in a Western dominated world, claiming an equal right to norm making (see Figure 3.1).

Questions thus arise as to how legitimacy in the governance of the AO is being shaped. Currently, the five Arctic coastal states (Canada, Denmark, Norway, the Russian Federation and the United States) assert their legitimacy of actors in 'a unique position' to govern the AO through the Ilulissat Declaration, and they establish the United Nations Convention on the Law of the Sea (UNCLOS) as the basic legal framework. The present chapter analyses in three distinct sections the arguments that the ICC, the EU and China associate with their legitimacy claims. The fourth section discusses the results and compares the strategies of the three actors in the analytical terms of procedural (input), substantive and output legitimacy.[4] Procedural (input-based, democratic) legitimacy claims propose that a policy or institution is legitimate to the extent that it has come into being in accordance with generally accepted principles of right process. Substantive legitimacy is premised on the need for policies or rules to be justifiable on the basis of shared broader norms and values. Substantive legitimacy thus stems from the congruence between the content of a rule or policy and the broader values that are privileged in a community at a given moment. Finally, output (efficiency-based) legitimacy is obtained by providing effective solutions to collective problems.[5]

The ICC

A number of issues transcend national borders and have led the Inuit people to require to be involved in decision-making that might affect their lives. This consideration was one of the main arguments for the creation of an international Inuit body in the 1970s. The exploitation of oil resources in the Beaufort Sea, which covers both Canadian and American territorial seas, and the Exclusive Economic Zone (EEZ) had convinced Eben Hopson of the necessity of creating a circumpolar Inupiat Assembly to work with the multinational oil industry:

3 Peer Zumbansen, 'Defining the Space of Transnational Law: Legal Theory, Global Governance, and Legal Pluralism' (2012) 21 *Transnational Law and Contemporary Problems* 305, 307.

4 Magdalena Bexell, 'Global Governance, Legitimacy and (De)Legitimation' (2014) 11 *Globalizations* 289, 291.

5 Andrew Hurrell, 'Legitimacy and the Use of Force: Can the Circle Be Squared?' (2005) 31 *Review of International Studies* 15.

Figure 3.1 Map of the Arctic Ocean and the circumpolar Arctic.

Source: © Arctic Portal. Map provided by www.arcticportal.org

> There is only one Beaufort Sea. It is a single Arctic ecological system shared by the North Slope Borough, and the Northwest Territories. We Inupiat are [...] living under two national flags. We must contend with two different political systems, and two sets of rules governing oil and gas development, to protect our environmental values within our larger Beaufort coastal community.[6]

6 Mayor Eben Hopson's testimony before the 'Berger Inquiry on the Experience of the Arctic Slope Inupiat with Oil and Gas Development in the Arctic', 1976 www.ebenhopson.com/papers/1976/BergerSpeech.html accessed 30 August 2018.

The creation of the ICC one year later emphasised in its resolution the need to protect the interests of the Inuit at the international level.[7]

Normative claims

The ICC represents the interests of the 160,000 Inuit living in Alaska, Canada, Denmark/Greenland and Russia. Indeed, the arrangements and agreements involving Inuit and Arctic jurisdictions show great differences throughout the Arctic. While the Inuit people have been granted various administrative and management rights in Alaska and in Canada, no agreement has been signed with Inuit in Siberia. Inuit rights over the offshore are even more limited,[8] although some authors are of the opinion that the central principle of free, prior and informed consent, which is not (yet) a hard law requirement in every case, can be applied both by developers and by the states governing such procedural rights.[9] Amongst Inuit regions, Greenland definitely stands apart, with a striking evolution towards self-government within the Danish Kingdom and competences over offshore mineral resources. The ICC claims focus on two main concerns: protecting the environment, which is the basis for cultural practice and subsistence, and enjoying economic benefits from activities deployed in the Arctic. The ICC's main objective is that all circumpolar Inuit get the right to self-determination.

The ICC claims insist on normative aspects of participation and implementation of policies. This includes, inter alia, asking states for direct participation in bi- and multilateral meetings, to be involved in UNCLOS submissions, in UNCLOS processes to promote and protect Inuit sovereignty and Inuit rights to the offshore, asking states to advocate for rights and interests, to advocate for regulatory policies and to ratify and implement international instruments.

Legitimacy strategies

For many years the ICC has promoted the concept of good stewardship based on 'traditional knowledge' as an argument to be associated to scientific research projects and to decision-making processes.[10] As the ICC is strong in the global arena, and actually stronger than in the regional arena, one major legitimisation avenue is to refer to international law to put pressure on the domestic level.

7 'There is a need for an international organization of Inuit to study, discuss, represent, lobby and protect our interests on the international level'. Resolution ICC 77-01.

8 Øyvind Ravna and Kristoffer Svendsen, 'Securing the Coastal Sami Culture and Livelihood' in Cécile Pelaudeix and Ellen Margrethe Basse (eds), *Governance of Arctic Offshore Oil and Gas Activities* (Routledge 2017) 186; Thierry Rodon, 'Offshore Development and Inuit Rights in Inuit Nunangat' in Cécile Pelaudeix and Ellen Margrethe Basse (eds), *Governance of Arctic Offshore Oil and Gas Activities* (Routledge 2017) 169.

9 Rachael Johnstone, 'Indigenous Rights in the Marine Arctic' in Céline Pelaudeix and Ellen Margrethe Basse (eds), *Governance of Arctic Offshore Oil and Gas Activities* (Routledge 2017) 72.

10 A Circumpolar Inuit Declaration on Sovereignty in the Arctic, Art. 3.2.

In 2009, the ICC took a significant step in its legitimacy strategy by putting forward a political argument. Just a year before, on 27–29 May 2008, the AO Conference in Ilulissat had brought together the Arctic coastal states. Whereas cooperation in the Arctic usually relies on the Arctic Council and its Permanent Participants (IP organisations), the Ilulissat meeting excluded representatives of the Arctic indigenous peoples, along with Arctic Council members Iceland, Finland and Sweden. Since this meeting, which was followed by other so-called Arctic 5 meetings, the ICC has put forward on its political agenda the notion of Inuit sovereignty and released a Declaration of Sovereignty in 2009.

The Sovereignty Declaration refers to a geographical space called Inuit Nunaat and defined as 'Inuit homeland', which stretches over Alaska, Canada, Greenland and Russia. The Inuit reaffirm their rights, as a people, to self-determination. They require to be partners of states, industry and other actors and that their land claims and self-government agreements be respected. The objective is clearly to challenge the Westphalian model of sovereignty for relying on state borders. However, the ICC does not fully reject the notion of sovereignty, and it actually sticks to its foundations: the association of the notion of a territory to a claimed legitimate authority, both notions which usually characterise sovereignty as the attribute of independent states. The ICC cannot fully challenge the concept of sovereignty, as it is the basis of international law on which, as a people and as an IP, the Inuit rely in order to support their claims and impact domestic policies: Articles 1.3 and 1.4 of the Declaration of Sovereignty quote the UN Charter, the International Covenant on Economic, Social and Cultural Rights, the International Covenant on Civil and Political Rights and the United Nations Declaration on the Rights of Indigenous Peoples (UNDRIP). The ICC contends itself with claiming for an 'evolving concept of sovereignty in the Arctic' (Section 2). Whereas the A5 grounds its legitimacy in the governance of the AO on UNCLOS, which contains no provisions for IP[11] and could appear in contradiction with UNDRIP when it comes to IP's rights to resources on the ocean, the ICC challenges the notion of sovereignty and at the same time sticks to the Westphalian inspired model of UNDRIP.

One year later, the ICC launched another Declaration more specifically focusing on resources: the Circumpolar Inuit Declaration on Resource Development Principles in Inuit Nunaat. This Declaration is also based on UNDRIP core rights and draws on the principles asserted in the 2009 Sovereignty Declaration.

At the same time as it is trying to improve international law (cf. the role of ICC in the negotiations and drafting of UNDRIP and its role in the United Nations Economic and Social Council) and putting pressure on states to comply with international norms through a general declaration of sovereignty and a more specific declaration on resources, the ICC is acting from a bottom-up perspective. The ICC has recently launched an innovative initiative: an Inuit led management

11 However, Art. 140 on Benefit of Mankind in the Area provides for 'consideration to the interests of peoples who have not attained full independence'.

regime, for an Arctic polynya situated between Canada (Baffin Island) and North West Greenland. The management would incorporate traditional knowledge and be based on the concept of Indigenous Protected Area (IPA).[12] An authority led by Inuit representatives from the communities is to establish a framework for regulating activities (including transportation, shipping and off-shore industrial development).[13] The Pikialasorsuaq region would include a protected area, comprised of the polynya itself, and a larger management. It would be a free travel zone for Inuit.

The concept of IPA is a class of protected area used in Australia formed by agreement with Indigenous Australians, declared by Indigenous Australians and formally recognised by the Australian Government as being part of its National Reserve System. The concept embodies Indigenous Values, and it is also consistent with principles of international instruments like UNDRIP: in that sense, the use of the IPA concept stands as a substantive legitimacy argument. The legal status of the Inuit-led management plan has not been established yet.[14] Interestingly, the Commission is asking states to make a request to the International Union on the Conservation of Nature (IUCN) to formally recognise IPAs as a valid conservation designation under the 'other acceptable conservation measure' category.[15]

Thus, in terms of procedural legitimacy, the ICC pushes forward the principles of UNDRIP and, in particular, the Free Prior and Informed Consent principle, but also the principle of self-determination to support a sovereignty claim over Inuit Nunaat. In terms of procedure, the ICC also innovates with a bottom-up approach of management that intends to demonstrate its capacity to manage transnational issues. In terms of substantive legitimacy, the ICC further innovates in recommending the creation of an IPA to bring definition to the idea of a 'conservation paradigm shift in the Arctic'.[16]

The European Union

Although the EU policies in the High North date back to the integration of Finland, Sweden and Denmark in the Union and the participation of the Commission in the subsequent establishment of regional bodies (Barents Euro-Arctic Council in 1993), the EU's Arctic policy per se, e.g. with a circumpolar scope, was initiated in 2008 in the context of a growing awareness of the global impacts of climate change on international security. Acknowledging the 'evolving geo-strategy of the Arctic region', the EU emphasised the need to secure its

12 'People of the Ice Bridge: The Future of the Pikialasorsuaq'. Report of the Pikialasorsuaq Commission. November 2017.

13 Ibid.

14 Ibid.

15 Mary Simon, 'A New Shared Arctic Leadership Model'. Report to the Ministry of Indian Affairs and Northern Development, Canada, December 2017.

16 Ibid.

trade and resource interests.[17] Since then, the EU has been developing its Arctic policy, which relies on three pillars: support knowledge (on the environment and climate change), act with responsibility with regard to sustainable development and intensify the EU's engagement in terms of international cooperation.[18]

Normative claims

In coherence with its objectives and values enshrined in Articles 2 and 3 of the Lisbon Treaty, EU normative claims in the AO mainly relate to environmental protection, sustainable development (fisheries, energy, shipping) and to international cooperation. The EU deems 'the need for a solid framework for sound stewardship is particularly high in the Arctic'.[19]

The EU's contribution to sustainable development in the governance of the AO in terms of normative impacts can be characterised as five-fold. First, the normative impact of the EU on the AO originates from the EU legislation that applies to the EEZ and the continental shelf of European Economic Area/ European Free Trade Association (EEA/EFTA) countries (Norway and Iceland). Second, it originates from the EU environment legislation that applies to waters under EU Member States' jurisdiction (vertical harmonisation); this, according to Basse, could be the case of Greenland.[20] Environmental protection in the EEZ of Greenland marine areas, which is Denmark's responsibility, could fall under EU jurisdiction. Third, EU normative impact originates from external competences (e.g. EU companies like Shell operating in Alaskan waters). Fourth, the EU as a member of IOs or regional organisations (like Ospar) and as a party to international agreements (as UNCLOS) can push for more ambition in resolutions on oceans that promote global membership of maritime governance (horizontal harmonisation). This is also the case for the International Maritime Organization (IMO), to which the EU is not a party (it only accepts states): indeed, parties to Ospar or Marpol (e.g. the EU) can raise the need for new initiatives at the IMO.[21]

17 Javier Solana and Benita Ferrero-Waldner, 'Climate Change and International Security'. Paper from the High Representative and the European Commission to the European Council, S113/08, 14 March 2008.

18 European Commission and High Representative. Joint communication to the European Parliament and the Council. JOIN(2016) 21 final p. 2. 'A safe, stable, sustainable and prosperous Arctic is important not just for the region itself but for the European Union and for the world. The EU has a strategic interest in playing a key role in the Arctic region'.

19 Ibid., 4.

20 The case of Greenland, which opted out of the EU treaties in 1985 and has an overseas countries and territories (OCT) status, is a complex one, accounted for in Ellen Margrethe Basse, 'The EU's Role as a Facilitator in the Development of Maritime Environmental Law in the Arctic, with Focus on Offshore Hydrocarbon Activities' in Cécile Pelaudeix and Ellen Margrethe Basse (eds), *Governance of Arctic Offshore Oil and Gas Activities* (Routledge 2017) 47.

21 Ibid.

Finally, EU norms originate from case law emanating from the Court of Justice of the European Union (CJEU).

Concretely thus, normative activity of the EU of relevance for the Arctic, in addition to its input in major instruments (Polar Code, etc.), mainly includes the following Directives which are all relevant for EEA states: the Offshore Safety Directive, the Habitats Directive, the Wild Birds Directive, the EIA Directive, the SEA Directive, the Framework Directive for Marine Spatial Planning, etc. Furthermore, the EU is promoting principles such as the ecosystem based standards, and wishes to extend the Marine Protected Areas in the Arctic.[22] The EU insisted on being included in the negotiations on the regulation of fisheries in the high seas of the central AO: the EU was *not* associated in the first round, which resulted in a Declaration of the Arctic 5.[23] The fishery resources are still unknown in the high seas,[24] but in periods overfishing has been reported in the high seas of the Bering and Barents Seas.[25] At the moment, most of the Arctic high seas are not covered by international conservation regimes but are covered by some management rules. UNCLOS (Articles 63, 64, 116, 117 and 118) provides a very general provision to define the duties of States for the conservation of the living resources of the high seas. The 1995 UN Fish Stocks Agreement, in force in 2001, establishes that international cooperation is to be organised in Regional Fisheries Management Organizations or Arrangements.

The EU considers it should work with Arctic states to develop an instrument under UNCLOS for the conservation and sustainable use of Biodiversity Beyond National Jurisdiction. Finally, the EU is asking for the respect of the freedom of navigation in the Arctic; some sections of the Arctic sea routes are considered international straits by the United States and the EU whereas Canada and Russia consider them internal waters.

Legitimacy strategies

In terms of procedural legitimacy, the EU reminds that three EU Member States are Arctic states (Denmark, Sweden, Finland), and two others are EEA members (Norway, Iceland); the latter are of more relevance when it comes to the governance in the AO, although the case of Greenland could be of more focus in terms of legitimate normative claims by the EU in the context of environmental aspects

22 European Commission and High Representative (n. 18) 7.

23 The Arctic coastal states took the initiative to design and sign a Declaration Concerning the Prevention of Unregulated High Seas Fishing in the CAO of 16 July 2015 without including other parties.

24 FISCAO. January 2017. Final Report of the Fourth Meeting of Scientific Experts on Fish Stocks in the Central Arctic Ocean. www.afsc.noaa.gov/Arctic_fish_stocks_fourth_meeting/pdfs/FourthFiSCAOreportfinalJan26_2017.pdf accessed 30 August 2018.

25 Edward Struzik, 'The Future of Fishing in the Central Arctic' (*World Policy Blog*, 2015) www.worldpolicy.org/blog/2015/03/11/future-fishing-central-arctic accessed 30 August 2018.

of marine areas. Regarding the involvement of the EU in the negotiations on fisheries in the high seas of the central AO, the EU recalls that fisheries is a field that falls under the EU's exclusive external competences. These legal arguments are supported by an argument of responsibility (the EU is a contributor to Arctic pollution) and by a commercial argument.[26]

As far as substantive legitimacy is concerned, as shown earlier, the EU provides an impressive range of norms and directives that represent an outstanding force of normative proposal in coherence with international values of environment protection and sustainable development.

In terms of output legitimacy, the EU advances a pragmatic argument for its association to Arctic governance that because of the transnational nature and scope of Arctic challenges (e.g. pollution, climate change), these challenges can be more effectively addressed through regional or multilateral cooperation.[27] Another argument in terms of output legitimacy relates to means deployed by the EU: its outstanding investment in Arctic research (€200 million in the past decade) and its commitment to fighting climate change.[28] It is used as a pragmatic argument to support its legitimacy in the governance of the region which had been contested after the EP 2008 Resolution on Governance and its article on an Arctic Treaty.[29] The funding instruments it intends to develop in the context of the establishment of the Arctic stakeholder forum[30] is also an argument of means relevant in the output legitimacy strategy.

China

As it is opening on the global stage and wants to contribute to the world order, China aims at weighing on international law and at designing the law itself. 'China must lead the way in reforming global governance', recently stated President Xi Jinping.[31] Rising as a sea power, China also applies this normative ambition to the governance of the oceans. The Arctic is no exception. Although China cannot be

26 The EU 'believes that such a framework can only be established in an open and inclusive manner, and welcomes the broadening of the negotiations to involve major fishing nations'. *European Commission and High Representative* (n. 18) 16.
27 European Commission and High Representative (n. 18) 2. Council of the European Union, Council conclusions on the Arctic Foreign Affairs Council, 20 June 2016.
28 European Commission and High Representative (n. 18).
29 The ban on the trade in seal products has impacted the EU policies' reception in the Arctic but is not an Arctic policy per se. See Cécile Pelaudeix and Thierry Rodon, 'The EU Arctic Policy and National Interests of France and Germany: Internal and External Policy Coherence at Stake' (2014) 37 *Northern Review* 57. See also Nikolas Selheim, 'The Goals of the EU Seal Products Trade Regulation: From Effectiveness to Consequence' (2015) 51 *Polar Record* 51, 274.
30 European Commission and High Representative (n. 18).
31 Xi Jinping cited by the Foreign Ministry www.reuters.com/article/us-china-diplomacy/xi-says-china-must-lead-way-in-reform-of-global-governance-idUSKBN1JJ0GT accessed 30 August 2018.

considered a new actor in the Arctic – it became a party to the Svalbard Treaty in 1925 – the Chinese Arctic Policy (CAP), released in 2018, confirmed Chinese ambitions to be a significant player in the region; the project of establishing a 'Polar Silk Road' encompasses access to energy resources and minerals, infrastructure building, shipping and fisheries.

Legitimacy strategies

In an effort to strengthen its position in this region where it has no sovereignty or sovereign rights, China puts forward several procedural arguments. It first uses a rather unexpected geographical argument to call itself a 'near-Arctic State'; it does so on the grounds that, as stated by Vice Foreign Minister Zhang Ming, 'the changing natural environment and exploration of resources in the Arctic have a direct impact on China's climate, environment, agriculture, shipping, trade and social and economic development'. The argument is repetitively used in official texts, official speeches and by Chinese scholars. Another procedural argument, dealing with the principle of equity, refers to China as a developing country or as a country supporting the rights of developing countries that has to work hard to bring all countries, particularly the developing countries, into the rule-making process as equals.[32] China uses the equity argument to support claims in the Area of the AO.[33] China's official position on the Area of the AO was first articulated in June 2009:

> When determining the delimitation of outer continental shelves, the Arctic States need to not only properly handle relationships among themselves, but must also consider the relationship between the outer continental shelf and the international submarine area that is the common human heritage, to ensure a balance of coastal countries' interests and the common interests of the international community.[34]

In the AO, the largest claims for extended continental shelves come from Denmark, Russia and potentially Canada. The specific seafloor features of the Arctic seabed, which includes four ridge-like structures, allow for coastal states to claim vast areas of extended continental shelf; if all claims were accepted,

32 Yi Wan, 'China, a Staunch Defender and Builder of International Rule of Law', 24 October 2014. http://en.people.cn/n/2014/1024/c90883-8799769-2.html accessed 30 August 2018.

33 The Area is made of the seabed beyond national jurisdiction, which has the status of common heritage of mankind. See, OHCHR, OHRLLS, UNDESA, UNEP, UNFPA, 'Global governance and governance of the global commons in the global partnership for development beyond 2015', UN System Task Team on the Post-2015 Development Agenda, January 2013.

34 Hu Zhengyue, Chinese assistant minister of foreign affairs, quoted by Shijie Zhishi, 中国对北极事务的看法 [China's Perspective on Arctic Matters], 55, 15, 2009 (author's translation).

only very small areas would be left for the common heritage of humankind. The International Sea-Bed Authority, which administers the deep seabed, has estimated the potential value of non-living resources in the outer continental shelf areas of the world to amount to a total of 10,328 trillion US dollars, mainly held in iron-manganese nodules and crusts, conventional oil and gas and gas hydrates.[35] The rationale behind the creation of the Area was to grant land-locked states and developing countries the same rights as coastal states (Article 136 of UNCLOS). The safeguarding of the common heritage of mankind was a key point of the Chinese position during the negotiations of UNCLOS[36] to the drafting of which it contributed significantly.[37] The delimitation of the continental shelves is the responsibility of the Commission on the Limits of the Continental Shelf, which issues recommendations, and the decisions made by coastal states on the basis of the recommended limits are final and binding (Articles 76.8 of UNCLOS). China advances the argument of a balance of rights to the Area with rights of developing countries in order to limit Arctic coastal states claims to the seabed. It grounds its claims in the Area on UNCLOS.[38] Doing so, it refers to Article 136 ('The Area and its resources are the common heritage of mankind') but seems to also make an implicit reference to Article 150;[39] yet, the notion of balance in this article relates to the sharing of resources of the Area – i.e. once the Area has already been delineated. It is actually possible for a distant state, whose coasts are neither opposite nor adjacent, to initiate a dispute that would concern the Commission on the Limits of the Continental Shelf (CLCS);[40] yet, it remains to be seen on a pure procedural perspective what weight the balance argument would be given by the CLCS (or the International Tribunal for the Law of the Sea, the International Court of Justice, the Legal Counsel of the UN Office of Legal Affairs or other authorities).

Substantive arguments advanced by China refer to 'conservation in a scientific manner' and to a 'rational use' of resources.[41] Both concepts lack clarity. The first concept is actually a re-interpretation and weakening of the precautionary

35 International Sea-Bed Authority 2000, 7.

36 Third United Nations Conference on the Law of the Sea 1982, 102.

37 Mincai Yu, 'China Being a Maritime Power under the UNCLOS: Issues and Ways Ahead' (2014) 7 *Journal of East Asia and International Law* 1.

38 China's Arctic Policy, The State Council Information Office of the People's Republic of China, January 2018. www.scio.gov.cn/zfbps/32832/Document/1618243/1618243.htm accessed 30 August 2018.

39 Art. 150 'Activities in the Area shall [...] be carried out in such a manner as to foster healthy development of the world economy and balanced growth of international trade, and to promote international cooperation for the over-all development of all countries, especially developing States'.

40 Rudiger Wolfrum, 'The Role of International Dispute Settlement Institutions in the Delimitation of the Outer Continental Shelf' in Rainer Lagoni and Daniel Vignes (eds), *Maritime Delimitation* (Martinus Nijhoff Publishers 2006) 19; Michael Sheng-ti Gau, 'The Commission on the Limits of the Continental Shelf as a Mechanism to Prevent Encroachment upon the Area' (2011) 10 *Chinese Journal of International Law* 3.

41 China's Arctic Policy (n. 38).

principle. The use of the second term has already raised much concern when discussing fisheries in the Antarctic where its meaning is all but clear;[42] the Chinese delegation's statement indicated in 2013 a clear interpretation of 'rational use' as meaning an unrestricted right to fish.[43] In a legal sense, there is actually no definition of what 'rational use' means, but its use clearly intends to blur the distinction between environmental protection and economic use of resources, thus to re-interpret the concept of 'sustainability'. Furthermore, China adopted a law dedicated to the international seabed area to conform with UNCLOS and secure effective compliance from all parties. Despite its merits, the law puts emphasis on the 'benefit for mankind' rather than 'heritage of mankind', which, according to legal scholars, signals a preference for an economic perspective rather than a conservation one.[44]

In the AO, under UNCLOS, China also enjoys shipping rights. The Northern Sea Route, a Russian term for the shipping lanes running along the Russian Arctic coast and connecting the Pacific to the Atlantic, is the Arctic sea route of most interest to China. Some of its sections are regarded by Russia as internal waters, meaning that no ship can navigate without Russia's consent.[45] Like the EU, China claims freedom of navigation and remains clear and firm on this position; however, China has not put much emphasis on this claim so far. It is to be noted that, anyway, as long as the sea is packed with ice, Russia maintains the right to administer navigation through its EEZ with reference to UNCLOS Article 234 – the 'ice clause'.

Comparing legitimisations

All three actors put forward procedural legitimacy claims, but these claims are grounded in different types of arguments. The ICC relies on human rights (the post-colonial norms of self-determination) defined in the UN Charter and on the rights of indigenous peoples as established in UNDRIP, in particular the Free, Prior and Informed Consent (FPIC). Dissatisfied with being excluded from international discussions over the AO, the ICC innovates with a declaration of sovereignty over Inuit Nunaat. It also initiates at the local level a transnational bottom-up approach of management, which challenges the traditional governance both vertically (in terms of hierarchy) and horizontally (across borders).

The EU refers to international law on statehood and on EU law reminding that three EU Member States are Arctic states, and two (Norway and Iceland) are EEA states. The EU also insists on its responsibility as a co-producer of pollution

42 Jennifer Jacquet et al., '"Rational Use" in Antarctic Waters' (2016) 63 *Marine Policy* 28.

43 Ibid.

44 Zhang Guobin and Zheng Pai, 'A New Step Forward: Review of China's 2016 Legislation on International Seabed Area Exploration and Exploitation' (2016) 73 *Marine Policy* 244.

45 Frédéric Lasserre, 'Vers une autoroute maritime? Passages arctiques et trafic maritime international' in Frédéric Lasserre (ed.), *Géopolitique d'une région en mutation* (Presses de l'Université du Québec 2010) 449.

and on its commercial dependency on some products like fisheries. China, in terms of procedure, consistently uses a geographic argument of 'near-Arctic state'. For a specific zone of the sea, the Area, China pushes forward an equity argument which it bases on UNCLOS.

In terms of substantive legitimacy, the ICC has long claimed Inuit values embedded in the concept of 'traditional knowledge' and is now innovating with the concept of IPAs. The EU provides an important set of substantive arguments to support its legitimacy: concepts and norms created at the international level (e.g. Marine Protected Areas) or at the EU level (environmental liability) and promotes them in the Arctic through various mechanisms (e.g. external competence, extraterritoriality and membership of the EEA). By contrast, China has not promoted many arguments of substantive legitimacy and puts forward the contested concept of 'rational use' of resources.

Finally, the conclusion regarding output legitimacy is less clear, both in terms of means and results. Usually, less attention is being paid to that legitimacy aspect, both by academics and by policymakers. The ICC has participated in many reports to the Arctic Council – such as the Arctic Marine Shipping Assessment – to encourage policies that respect Inuit rights and safeguard the environment. Yet, the impact of the specific contribution of the ICC has not been highlighted, and might be complex to isolate from the contributions of other stakeholders. Thus, the relevance (legitimately speaking) of the ICC local experiment in the Polynya area. The EU, which in terms of means, has contributed €200 million to scientific research, has released an inventory of its Arctic activities[46] and has recently launched a policy assessment framework to assess the impact of its policies in the Arctic and enable recommendations on how to develop the EU's Arctic policy 2025–2030. China has not provided any assessment of its – recent – policies in the Arctic (see Table 3.1).

Conclusion

The increasing accessibility of the AO is giving rise to diverse and sometimes conflicting approaches to its use. Consequently, depending on the actor, normative approaches of governance differ and are legitimised through distinct arguments and strategies. This chapter has analysed the legitimacy strategies of the ICC, the EU and China through the analytical framework of procedure (participation), substance and output (impact) legitimacies. From a descriptive legitimacy perspective (legitimacy as a subjective quality, here considered by the ruler), there is a great variance amongst the three actors. The ICC, which is a very small organisation compared to the EU and to China, takes advantage of the support of international law it benefits from (human rights and indigenous peoples' rights) to circumvent

46 European Commission and High Representative, Joint Staff Working Document. The inventory of activities in the framework of developing a European Arctic Policy. JOINT (2012) 19 final.

Table 3.1 Legitimacy arguments of the ICC, the EU and China

Legitimacy arguments	*ICC*	*EU*	*China*
Procedural (participation)	Int. law (self-determination) IP rights (UNDRIP with FPIC) Bottom-up management	Int. law EU law Responsibility argument Commercial argument	Geographic argument Commercial argument UNCLOS
Substantive	Traditional knowledge (values of *Inuit* Qaujimajatuqangit) Indigenous Protected Areas	Art. 2 and 3 Lisbon Treaty Ecosystem-based approach Marine Protected Areas Offshore Safety Directive (including the environment liability principle) Habitats Directive Wild Birds Directive EIA Directive SEA Directive Framework Directive for Marine Spatial Planning	'Conservation in a scientific manner' 'Rational use'
Output (impact)		Policy assessment in process	

the state restrictive approach of these rights and advance legitimacy claims. The ICC also relies on its proximity to the local communities, which peoples it represents, to produce a very innovative approach, both in procedure (bottom-up approach) and in substance (the IPAs norm) that has the potential to result in effective output. Consistent with its values and aims enshrined in the Lisbon Treaty, the EU promotes a wide range of norms and standards to protect the environment and facilitate sustainable development and engages in an assessment of the output of its policies. China enjoys less procedural legitimacy than the ICC or the EU, a disadvantage that is not compensated by a substantive legitimacy; the initial support of China for IP in official discourses when China was a candidate for observer status at the Arctic Council has not been incorporated in Chinese Arctic Policy. The normative proposition of China on the use of the AO remains discreet (e.g. the concept of 'rational use') and could furthermore have a negative impact in lowering the international standards of protection of the environment and sustainable development. The legitimacy strategy of China so far relies more on rhetoric, but this might shift to a more legal argumentation; China can increase its legal capacity – as it did to handle World Trade Organization (WTO) litigation[47] – and it is paying more attention to institutions like the CLCS.[48]

This study of the issue of legitimacy in a transnational context in the AO informs the relations between transnationalism and legitimacy in three ways. First, it illustrates, regarding procedural legitimacy, how democracy and political legitimacy can be articulated in a transnational context. The ICC approach could contribute to the reflection on the solving and implementation of a deliberative democracy in such context although the geographical scale of the Polynya area is not commensurate with a global scale. The way the territorial governments of Nunavut and of Greenland will support or not support the transnational initiative will be very informative in that regard.

Second, this chapter shows the interdependence between procedural and substantive legitimacy. Although actors can strategically emphasise one type of legitimacy or the other, the various types of legitimacy appear to be hardly independent of each other. This consideration shifts the reflection towards a more normative lens (normative legitimacy assessed on objective standards). Indeed, procedural legitimacy cannot substitute substantive legitimacy; shared broader norms and values are at the core of any transnational order. Another argument is a contextual one; as highlighted by Ellen M. Basse in her chapter,

> As the geographical particularity, the ecological characteristics as well as the sensitivity of the Arctic marine area are very clear, it is a precondition in this chapter that these issues of global interest will have some effect on the legitimacy of any norms that are designed to protect the marine ecosystems.[49]

When states and other actors can try to manoeuvre with various dimensions of legitimacy, and when state self-interest can actually be the rationale to challenge the legitimacy of international law,[50] the relation of dependence between procedural legitimacy and substantive legitimacy needs to be underlined.

Third, legitimacy aspects would gain from not only being analysed from a regulatory governance approach but also in terms of power relations, including economic aspects and how the market can act as a regulator at the global level. As a state, China enjoys a number of rights on the use of the ocean, yet it does not have as strong geographical arguments as the ICC or the EU, not does it

47 Pasha L. Hsieh, 'China's Development of International Economic Law and WTO Legal Capacity Building' (2010) 13 *Journal of International Economic Law* 997. Research Collection School of Law.

48 Xia Liping, 'The Impact of Change in the Arctic Environment on Global Security and China's National Security'. Paper presented at the 4th China-Nordic Arctic Cooperation Symposium, Rovaniemi, 8 June 2016.

49 Ellen Margrethe Basse, 'Transnational Ecosystem-based Norms covering the Danish/Greenlandic Arctic Marine Area', Chapter 5 in this volume.

50 Rüdiger Wolfrum, 'Legitimacy in International Law from a Legal Perspective: Some Introductory Considerations' in Rüdiger Wolfrum and Volker Röben (eds), *Legitimacy in International Law* (Springer 2008) 1, 11.

provide fully convincing substantive arguments, yet it has a huge economic leverage through foreign direct investment that provides China weight in regards to norm shaping.[51] In that respect, the ICC innovative approach looks even more thought-provoking, considering the contrast in scale and power relationships with the EU and China. Finally, the role of courts will also deserve attention in future research in the transnational governance of the Arctic Ocean.

51 Cécile Pelaudeix, 'Along the road, China in the Arctic'. Institute for Security Studies, Connectivity and Security Brief, 13, 2018. https://www.iss.europa.eu/content/along-road-%E2%80%93-china-arctic accessed 21 April 2019.

4 Transnational ecosystem-based norms covering the Danish/ Greenlandic Arctic marine area

Ellen Margrethe Basse

Introduction

The Arctic marine area is characterised by many authorities, international and regional organisations as well as intergovernmental fora/partnerships with different jurisdictions and mandates to regulate. Greenland is located in the Arctic.[1] It is part of the Danish Realm, and it is covered by the Danish ratification of the United Nations Convention on the Law of the Sea (UNCLOS), the United Nations Convention on Biodiversity (Biodiversity Convention) and the Convention on the Protection of the Marine Environment of the North-East Atlantic (OSPAR Convention). Greenland is not included in Denmark's EU membership, but it is one of the overseas countries and territories (OCTs) associated with the EU with a special legal status.[2] The EU's direct or indirect impact on the legislation of the Kingdom of Denmark as one of its Member States is of special interest in the context of Arctic marine governance, as Denmark is one of the five Arctic coastal states. The question to be answered is whether – based on the legitimacy of the transnational norms that are developed by the European Union (EU) and the OSPAR Commission[3] as part of the fulfilment of the Biodiversity Convention – there is a Danish obligation to respect and to implement these norms with their ecosystem-based approach in the marine law covering the Danish/Greenlandic Arctic area.

The ecosystem-based approach – that was introduced under the Biodiversity Convention[4] – has triggered a change of structure and development of new legal

1 Greenland is located in the Arctic as the largest island in the world. It lies 700 km from the North Pole and goes to 2,600 km further south.

2 This legal position is based on the Greenland Treaty of 30 March 1984 with the Protocol on special arrangements for Greenland.

3 The marine protection of the Nares Strait, Baffin Bay and Davis Strait – the western part of the Danish/Greenlandic marine area – are outside the OSPAR area and consequently also outside the EU-based Arctic regional seas cooperation. The OSPAR Convention is, however, respected in all the Greenlandic marine areas, see David Boermann (ed.) *Miljø og råstoffer i Grønland* (in English: *Environment and Raw Materials in Greenland*) (Miljøbiblioteket, Aarhus Universitetsforlag 2018) 46.

4 The ecosystem approach was introduced at the Second Meeting of the Conference of the Parties (COP) held in Jakarta, Indonesia (CDB COP 2), decision 8, UNEP/CBD/COP/2/19,

instruments as well as institutional development and cooperation. It is a regulatory approach integrating a specific focus on ecological preconditions and environmental governance features, aiming to consider the multi-level dynamics of polycentric regulatory institutions and the many actors taking part in the governance, as well as satisfying human needs in a way that does not compromise the integrity, or health, of ecosystems.[5]

The transnational dimension of law is, in the following, defined with a focus on the regulatory actors, their common regulatory approach, their decision-making and cooperation processes as well as the functions of their transnational norms.[6] The processes of normative settlement on the use of an ecosystem-based approach in the management of marine environment, and the alignment – involving the EU and the OSPAR Commission in cooperation with monitoring the environmental status, on reporting and on enforcement – are important parts of this understanding of the concept of 'transnational law'.[7]

As a geographical particularity, the ecological characteristics as well as the sensitivity of the Arctic marine area are very clear, and it is a precondition in this chapter that these issues of global interest will have some effect on the legitimacy of any norms that are designed to protect the marine ecosystems. The question of legitimacy of the transnational norms – with their ecosystem-based approach – as governing law in the management of the Danish/Greenlandic Arctic marine areas is consequently expected to be important in this chapter. There are different legal and political approaches to the understanding of the term 'legitimacy'.[8] The concepts used in the following are: the *input legitimacy* – understood as Denmark's delegation of regulatory power to each of the two cooperating and coordinating regional actors (the European Union and the OSPAR Commission) and the cooperation process and common monitoring/reporting systems established between them – and the *output legitimacy* – understood as the adequate performance of power that responds best to the expectations and the needs of the public in respect to a sustainable future for both the existing and future generations, and the outcomes compliance with international law (including the

p. 12, concerning this COP 2, see Britta Bohman, *Transnational Law for Social-Ecological Resilience?: A Study on Eutrophication in the Baltic Sea Area* (Stockholm University 2017) 83 and 196ff.

5 Bohman (n. 4) 22 and 48.

6 This understanding of translational law as a methodological shift in legal theory is described in Peer Zumbansen, 'Defining the Space of Transnational Law: Legal Theory, Global Governance, and Legal Pluralism' (2012) 21(2) *Transnational Law & Contemporary Problems* 305–336; and in Peer Zumbansen, 'Governance: An Interdisciplinary Perspective' in David Lévi-Faure (ed.), *Oxford Handbook of Governance* (Oxford University Press 2012).

7 The approach to transnational law is consequently also inspired by the theory of Terence Halliday and Gregory Shaffer (eds), *Transnational Legal Orders* (Cambridge University Press 2015) 27–28.

8 Linda Senden, 'Soft Post-Legislative Rulemaking: A Time for More Stringent Control' (2013) 19 *European Law Journal* 57, 58; and Brad R. Roth, *Governmental Illegitimacy in International Law* (Clarendon Press 2000).

obligations under the Biodiversity Convention), as well as its capability to solve problems affecting the marine ecosystems.[9]

The relevance of the use of the transnational ecosystem-based approach in the cooperation between the EU and the OSPAR Commission in their transnational governance, as well as the relevance of the Marine Strategy Plan of the Arctic Council (as a legitimating support to this transnational governance approach), are described in section 2.

The EU's legal order and the consequences of this in the national implementation of international obligations and transnational norms are described in section 3. One of the aims of the EU is to promote its values globally so as to support its role as a normative global power[10] – e.g. by the involvement in the cooperation on the design of ecosystem-based transnational norms.[11] The EU's external environmental competence of importance for the legitimacy and binding effects of the norms that it develops and controls together with the OSPAR regime (that the EU is a party to) is partly a consequence of the Lisbon Treaty, partly a consequence of the case law of the European Court of Justice (CJEU), which has an important role to play with its doctrine of parallelism between internal and external competences.[12]

Section 4 aims to explain the relationship between Denmark and Greenland as well as the separation and limitation of their respective responsibilities in the marine area. It gives the answers to two important questions: *who* has – as the 'state' – jurisdiction to decide on the use of the marine hydrocarbon in the exclusive economic zone (EEZ) around Greenland and *who* is – in the internal relation as well as the external relations – responsible as the 'state' for the marine protection against the negative environmental consequences caused by such offshore activities.

The answer to the last-mentioned question is found neither in the subnational Inatsisartut Mineral Resources Act[13] nor in the Danish Act on the Protection of the Marine Area in the Exclusive Economic Zone (EEZ) around Greenland.[14] The missing marine protection in the national and subnational acts – as well as the missing ecosystem-based approach in the mentioned acts – are issues that are covered by section 5.

On the basis of the legal position of Denmark as described in section 3 – and the fact that Greenland has (as described in section 4) not taken over the

9 Bohman (n. 4) 260; and Linda Senden, 'Soft Law and Its Implications for Institutional Balance in the EC' (2005) 1(2) *Utrecht Law Review* 79.

10 Art. 3(5) Treaty of the European Union (hereinafter TEU).

11 Concerning the use of this approach in the regulation of water, see Henrik Josefsson, *Good Ecological Status. Advancing the Ecology of Law*, LL.D. diss. (Uppsala University 2015).

12 Tom Delreux, 'EU Actorness, Cohesiveness and Effectiveness in Environmental Affairs' (2014) 21 *Journal of European Public Policy* 1027.

13 Inatsisartut Act No. 7 of 7 December 2009 on Mineral Resources.

14 Act No. 1534 of 19 December 2017 on the Protection of the Marine Area in the Exclusive Economic Zone (EEZ) around Greenland.

responsibility for the marine environment in the EEZ – it is still the Danish authorities that have the competence and responsibility. It is concluded in section 6 that the norms have to be respected by Denmark in its management of the Danish/Greenlandic Arctic marine area inside the EEZ. The legitimacy of the transnational ecosystem-based marine governance of the activities in the Danish/Greenlandic marine area inside the EEZ is also assessed in this section.[15]

Transnational cooperation on ecosystem-based marine protection norms

The Biodiversity Convention and the Law of the Sea Convention (UNCLOS) both impose duties on the parties to cooperate directly or indirectly regarding the implementation of their obligations through competent international and regional organisations. The EU is a party to these conventions, and its institutions are – based on the Lisbon Treaty – in their relations with the wider world, obligated to do all that lies in their power to enhance the international legal order and to do this under the guidance of the principles that inspired the creation of the Union and its subsequent development.[16] They are also required to define and pursue common policies and actions and to work for a high degree of cooperation in all fields of international relations.[17] As part of this, the EU's institutions are strengthening their efforts in the international maritime and marine areas by pushing for more ambition in resolutions on the environmental protection of the marine areas.[18] The seventh Environment Action Programme, entitled *Living well, within the limits of our planet*, for the period 2013–2020, objective 9 highlights that 'particular emphasis should be given to the [...] Arctic regions, where there is a need for intensified cooperation and increased Union involvement'.[19]

The OSPAR Commission (covering the North-East Atlantic) and the HELCOM[20] made already at their first joint Ministerial Meeting in June 2003 a common statement on their ecosystem-based approach to the management of human activities. Their application of the ecosystem-based approach was explained to be part of – and a support to – the future development of the EU's marine strategy and its marine directives as well as measures adopted by other

15 Concerning output legitimacy, see Colin Scott, 'Regulatory Governance and the Challenge of Constitutionalism,' *EUI Working Paper RSCAS 2010/07*, 13–14; and Jean D'Aspremont, 'Legitimacy of Governments in the Age of Democracy' (2010) 38 *International Law and Politics* 877–917.

16 Art. 21 TEU.

17 Art. 21(2) litra f) TEU.

18 Commission COM(2012) 491 final, p. 10; see European Commission 2012.

19 European Parliament and Council 2013b.

20 The HELCOM is covering the Baltic Marine area (its name is also the Baltic Marine Environmental Protection Commission and the Helsinki Commission). Britta Bohman has made a very interesting analysis of the cooperation and coordination between the EU and HELCOM that this chapter of the book is using as part of its argumentation, see Britta Bohman's thesis mentioned above in n. 4.

international organisations.[21] This statement is relevant as an important basis for the designing of transnational ecosystem-based norms, as the EU has now passed its Integrated Maritime Policy (IMP) that set the objective and guidelines for a coherent policy approach to the marine areas, with the aim of protecting the ecosystem, based in harmony with the Biodiversity Convention, and also taking the economic, environmental and social issues into account.[22] This ecosystem-based perspective is part of the EU's Marine Strategic Framework Directive (MSFD),[23] the Framework Directive for Maritime Spatial Planning (FMSP)[24] and the Offshore Safety Directive.[25]

The MSFD is of special relevance in the assessment of the legitimacy of the transnational governance of the Arctic marine area, as the OSPAR Commission is taking part in the fulfilment of the aims laid down in the Directive. It is stated in recital 44 of the MSFD: 'Programmes of measures and subsequent action by Member States should be based on an ecosystem-based approach to the management of human activities'.

The Directive aims at achieving 'good environmental status' by the year 2020 through the implementation of two overreaching principles: the ecosystem-based approach to the management of human activities and an integrated and coordinated approach at regional and sub-regional levels. It refines how cooperation between EU's Member States and other parties to the regional regimes inside the territory of the EU – including cooperation with the OSPAR Commission – should take place.[26] Where practical and appropriate, the OSPAR regime should be used to ensure coordination among Member States and with third countries in the development of marine strategies. At the same time, the Directive should contribute to the fulfilment of the obligations and important commitments of the EU and/or its Member States under OSPAR. This cooperation on transnational governance is also ensured by several OSPAR rules and guidelines, see, for example, the OSPAR Regional Implementation Framework for the EU Marine Strategy Framework Directive. OSPAR has adopted some common indicators

21 Statement at the First Joint Ministerial Meeting of the Helsinki and OSPAR Commissions of 25–26 June 2003 on the Ecosystem Approach to the Management of Human Activities, 'Towards an Ecosystem Approach to the Management of Human Activities', p. 3.

22 Concerning the relevance of EU IMP in the Arctic, see Erik J. Molenaar, 'Status and Reform of International Arctic Shipping Law' in Elizabeth Tedsen, Sandra Cavalieri and R. Andreas Kraemer (eds), *Arctic Marine Governance: Opportunities for Transatlantic Cooperation* (Springer 2014) 127, 11ff. and 14ff.

23 European Parliament and the Council Directive 2008/56/EC of 17 June 2008 establishing a framework for community action in the field of marine environmental policy, *OJ L* 164 of 25 June 2008, pp. 19ff.

24 European Parliament and the Council Directive 2014/89/EU of 23 July 2014 establishing a framework for maritime spatial planning, *OJ L* 257 of 28 August 2014, pp. 135–145.

25 European Parliament and the Council Directive 2013/30/EU of 12 June 2013 on safety of offshore oil and gas operations and amending Directive 2004/35/EC Text with EEA relevance. *OJ L* 178 of 28 June 2013, pp. 66–106.

26 Art. 6 of MSFD.

for application under the MSFD. The OSPAR Strategy for the Protection of the Marine Environment of the North-East Atlantic 2010–2020 (OSPAR Agreement 2010-3) is one of the most important examples of the harmonisation of OSPAR and EU standards. The cooperation between the OSPAR Commission and the EU under the mentioned strategy is important, as it often prepares the presentation of new approaches and principles that afterwards support the EU directives once they 'take over' and make the soft law 'harder'.[27] Such regional programmes of measures intend to make a large contribution to the coherent, efficient and effective implementation of both the EU's marine environmental law and the Biodiversity Convention.

It is not only the cooperation between the EU and the OSPAR Commission that is important for the impact of the transnational norms in the Arctic marine area. The ecosystem-based approach is supported by the Arctic Council that is established as a high-level intergovernmental forum with the mandate to promote cooperation, coordination and interaction between Denmark and the other seven Arctic states.[28] Its non-binding Arctic Marine Strategic Plan (AMSP) – covering the period 2015–2025[29] – is based on the same environmental governing tools as the tools used in the just mentioned transnational cooperation and coordination of marine governance. The AMSP recognises the multitude of environmental and human aspects of Arctic change that emphasise the need for place-specific implementation of an integrated and participatory ecosystem-based approach to managing the Arctic marine environment.[30]

Transnational norms as an integral part of the EU's legal order

In environmental matters, the EU ratifies regional and international agreements as 'mixed agreements', together with its Member States. The Lisbon Treaty emphasises the shared nature of the competences, as the EU and its Member States

27 However, it is stated in an assessment of the OSPAR monitoring procedures and assessment that there is a need for a better aligning of these activities with the requirements of MSFD, see Ingmar van Homeyer, Leonie Reins and Claire Dupont, *Analysis of Regional Sea Convention needs ensuring better coherence of approaches under the Marine Strategy Framework Directive* (Milieu Ltd. 2013) 74–75, published at https://webgate.ec.europa.eu/maritimeforum/sites/maritimeforum/files/Final%20Report_RSC%20needs.pdf, accessed 27 March 2019.

28 The member states of the Arctic Council are Norway, Sweden, Iceland, Finland, Denmark/Greenland, Russia, Canada and USA (Alaska). Greenland has the right to take part in the meetings of the Council, but it is not a member of the Council. The six organisations representing the different indigenous people living in the Arctic are permanent participants of the Council. Several observers and some ad hoc observers (including the EU) are involved in the Council's discussions and initiatives.

29 Arctic Council, 'Arctic Marine Strategic Plan 2015–2025. Protecting Marine and Coastal Ecosystems in a Changing Arctic' (AMSP) (2015). The Arctic strategy was adopted at the ministerial meeting in Iqaluit, Canada the 24–25 April 2015.

30 Ibid., 9.

each intervene 'within their respective spheres of competences'.[31] However, when the Treaty confers a shared competence, the EU – which has legal personality – has exclusive competence in all areas as to the conclusion of an international or regional agreement when its conclusion is provided for in its own law (treaties as well as secondary legislation).[32] The EU also has the exclusive competence to ratify international and regional agreements when such a competence is necessary to enable the EU to exercise its internal competence – including to ensure that the conclusion of such international or regional agreements may not affect the EU's own rules or alter their scope. The ratification by the EU Council – for example, of UNCLOS,[33] OSPAR and the Biodiversity Convention – has the consequences that the decisions made by the parties to these conventions automatically start to form 'an integral part' of EU law and have primacy over secondary EU and national legislation.[34]

The agreements that the EU is making with the OSPAR Commission on the transnational ecosystem-based norms on the protection of the marine area inside the jurisdiction of the EU are consequently an integral part of the EU legal order and are binding on it. The CJEU has jurisdiction to interpret such norms. Conflicts concerning the correct understanding and use of the international and regional agreements, ratified by the EU, are handled *only* by the CJEU. This is important as the practice of the Court ensures vertical harmonisation[35] through a legal hierarchy putting the international and regional conventions above the EU's own secondary legislation to show third parties that the EU is a reliable international partner which respects the Vienna Convention on the Law of Treaties. It is also important in the argumentation for the binding effect of the transnational cooperation and coordination described in section 2 that the Member States are obliged to respect the fact that EU treaties and secondary legislation take precedence over national law.[36]

This hierarchy of the legal sources – including customary international law – is a consequence both of the Vienna Convention, which is binding on the EU institutions and part of the EU legal order,[37] and the principle of sincere

31 It is stated in Art. 191(4) TFEU.

32 The exclusive competence is stated in Art. 3 TEU.

33 See e.g. Case C-459/03 *Commission v. Ireland (The MOX Plant Case)* concerning the provisions of the UNCLOS that have become part of the EU's legal order.

34 Arts 216 (6) and 288 TFEU.

35 See the vertical harmonisation ensured in the judgments C-6/04 *Commission v. United Kingdom and Northern Ireland*, C-181/73 *Haegeman v. Belgium*, C-12/86 *Demirel v. Stadt Schwäbisch Gmünd* and C-240/09 *Lesoochranarske zoskupenie v. Ministerstvo životného prostredia Slovenskej republiky*.

36 It has been established by the CJEU in a number of cases where the first principle judgment is C-6/64 *Costa v. E.N.E.L.* Priority also applies to older national legislation and practice, cf. C-106/77 *Italian Finance Administration v. Simmenthal*.

37 Case C-266/16 *Western Sahara Compaing UK v Commissioners for Her Majesty's Revenue and Customs and Secretary of State for Environment, Food and Rural Affairs*, para. 58; and Case C-15/17 *Bosphorus Queen Shipping Ltd. Corp v. Rajavartiolaitos*, para. 67.

cooperation, established by the Lisbon Treaty.[38] What is also important in the argumentation for the obligation to respect the result of the EU's cooperation and coordination with the OSPAR Commission is the fact that the Court has used functional criteria and has hereby held that the geographical scope of the application of EU law follows that of Member States' jurisdiction, an approach that makes EU legislation relevant to all the marine area under Danish jurisdiction.

The Danish responsibility for the marine area around Greenland

Jurisdiction – which plays an important role when assessing the legal regulatory competence, the legitimacy and the responsibility of different public authorities – has a geographical component, including when the focus is on the marine environment. In this analysis of the marine protection of the Danish/Greenlandic marine area, it is therefore of importance that Greenland is part of the Danish Realm. The consequence of this is that the marine areas around Greenland is part of the jurisdiction of Denmark – and included in Denmark's international obligations under the UNCLOS, the Biodiversity Convention and the OSPAR Convention ratified without reservations for Greenland.

The 2009 Agreement between the Government of Denmark and the Government of Greenland (Naalakkersuisut) on the Act on Greenlandic Self-Government (Kalaallit Nunaanni)[39] gives the Greenlandic people the right to take over most of the legal, administrative and judicial competences. The Greenlandic population also has the right under this Act to withdraw from the Danish Realm (Kunngeqarfik Danmark) if it so desires, when expressed in a referendum in Greenland and subject to approval by the Greenland Parliament (Inatsisartut) and the Danish Parliament.[40] The right to withdraw from the Danish Realm has not been used until now.

The Greenlandic population is – as many other populations in the Arctic – an indigenous people. Eighty-five percent of the people living in Greenland are Inuit (Kalaalit). Their minimum rights to protection of their way of life and culture that are based on their own aspirations and priorities are ensured by the Danish ratification of the International Labour Organisation's Convention 169 (ILO 169). However, it is the general understanding both in Denmark and in Greenland that the Inatsisartut and the Naalakkersuisut represent the interests of all the people living in Greenland. There is *neither* any specific regulations or

38 Art. 4(3) TEU.

39 Danish Act No. 473 of 12 June 2009 on Greenlandic Self-Government. The Act covers the overall structure for the authorities that consist of a directly elected Greenland Parliament (Inatsisartut) and the Government (Naalakkersuisut).

40 There is a political agenda in Greenland of acceding to independence of subsidies from Denmark and being a sovereign state with its own constitution.

provisions for the Inuit's rights of ownership and possession over the lands, *nor* any special procedural rights for the Inuit in the legislation.

The Self-Governmental Act does not apply to international agreements which also apply to Denmark, or agreements to be negotiated within an international organisation of which the Kingdom of Denmark is a member. The Act gives only powers to the Naalakkersuisut to negotiate and to conclude under international law where such agreements relate solely to Greenland. This limitation of the Greenlandic self-government is a consequence of the Danish Constitution.[41]

The UNCLOS gives coastal states the exclusive right to regulate and to give licences for extraction in their EEZ[42] and on the continental shelf.[43] The legal competence to regulate and administrate offshore extraction has been taken over by Greenland. The competence was used to pass the Inatsisartut Mineral Resources Act in 2009. The public regulatory power and responsibility for the protection of the marine area in the EEZ has not been taken over by Greenland. Therefore, in the internal relations between Greenland and the Kingdom of Denmark, it is the authorities of the Kingdom that are primarily responsible for the protection of the marine area beyond three nautical miles.[44] The 'responsibility' for the environmental quality of the marine water is under the UNCLOS attributed to the national norms of the 'Arctic five'[45] national states. It is only Denmark that currently has a status as a state, as Greenland is not a state.

The missing legal protection as well as the missing ecosystem-based approach

The Marine Strategic Framework Directive (MSFD) – described in section 2 as an important part of the transnational ecosystem-based norms – requires Denmark to develop a marine strategy to ensure that good environmental status is achieved or maintained for its marine waters no later than December 2020. This Danish environmental marine strategy should include an initial assessment of the environmental status, the determination of what good environmental status means for the different Danish marine waters and the setting of environmental targets to reach good environmental status. The Danish obligations under the directive also include a monitoring programme to check and test the state of the marine environment on a continuing basis, the updating of the environmental targets and the use of a coherent programme of measures, setting up the necessary actions to achieve good

41 Act No. 169 of 5 June 1953.

42 The EZZ is defined in Art. 57 of the UNCLOS as an area beyond and adjacent to the territorial sea, extending a maximum of 200 nautical miles from the baseline.

43 Art. 193 of the UNCLOS.

44 It is the Danish military authorities that act in situations of oil spills in this Arctic area to fulfil the international obligations of the Kingdom of Denmark.

45 Norway, Denmark/Greenland, Russia, Canada and USA (Alaska).

environmental status by 2020.[46] However, Denmark does not accept that these obligations are relevant in the Danish/Greenlandic marine area. Consequently, the Danish Act on the Protection of the Marine Area in the Exclusive Economic Zone (EEZ) around Greenland is based on the old traditional 'pollution reducing approach', and it is only the pollution from ships that is covered by this Act. The limitation of the scope of the Act in relation to environmental consequences of offshore hydrocarbon extraction is explicitly stated in section 2(3).

The Inatsisartut Mineral Resources Act establishes the overall competence of Naalakkersuisut over the mineral resources – onshore as well as offshore. It includes the rules that both Naalakkersuisut and other Greenlandic authorities have to respect in their decision-making. Among these rules are some framework rules on the reduction of climate effects, protection of the environment and conservation of nature. It is the only environmental obligations that have to be respected by the Greenlandic authorities responsible for the administration of offshore hydrocarbon extraction activities, and the scope of these environmental rules only cover decision-making on extraction projects onshore and inside the territorial waters (the three nautical miles). It is stated explicitly in section 9, subsection 3, of the Act that the responsibility for the marine environmental protection outside three nautical miles is outside the scope of these environmental rules.[47] The rationale behind this subsection is explained in the preparatory works with very few words:

> The area of marine environment has not been transferred to Greenland's self-government, so the proposal's environmental provisions do not apply to the continental shelf area outside of Greenland's territorial sea and in the exclusive economic zone to the extent that otherwise follows from the marine environment legislation.

The intention is very clear. The Greenlandic authorities are of the opinion that the protection of the environmental quality of the marine environment in the exclusive economic zone – including the protection against the consequences of the offshore extraction activities – is the responsibility of the Danish authorities. The rationale behind this position is the fact that the competence on this marine area has not been taken over by Greenland. The Danish authorities – as it is indicated by section 2(3) of the Danish Act on the Protection of the Marine Area mentioned above – are of another opinion. Denmark deems that the competence to regulate the hydrocarbon extraction, with any environmental consequences, has been taken over by Greenland.

None of the environmental rules of the Greenlandic Parliament cover the environmental consequences of hydrocarbon extraction on the EEZ of Greenland *insofar as* the marine environmental acts provide otherwise. The ecosystem-based

46 Arts. 8–13 of MSFD.
47 Section 9(3) of the Act.

approach is part of a new Inatsisartut Act on Marine Environmental Protection[48] covering the territorial water (the three nautical miles) around Greenland. However, it is explicitly stated in section 6 of this act that it does *not* cover offshore hydrocarbon activities. It is the Inatsisatut Mineral Resources Act mentioned above that is the relevant Act.

The consequences of the just mentioned acts are that there are no rules in the above-mentioned Danish nor in the Greenlandic acts of relevance for the protection of the Danish/Greenlandic marine environment inside the exclusive economic zone against pollution from offshore hydrocarbon extraction. Neither are there any rules in these acts on the protection of the marine ecosystem. The ecosystem-based management approach established under the Biodiversity Convention and in the transnational cooperation between the EU and OSPAR is totally missing.

Legitimacy of the transnational actors and their norms

It is the conclusion – based on the description in sections 3–4 – that the interpretation of the EU's marine directives in the Danish legislation covering the Danish/Greenlandic EEZ marine area has to be in harmony with the transnational norms described earlier in section 2. The objectives underlying the transnational norms with their ecosystem-based approach must be respected in the Danish legislation.[49] The Danish Act on the Protection of the Marine Area in the Exclusive Zone (EEZ) around Greenland, however – as described in section 5 – does not protect this marine area against pollutions caused by offshore hydrocarbon extractions, and it is not legislation based on the ecosystem approach. The general pollution-based approach is still very strong in Danish environmental law. The gap in the geographical protection of the Danish/Greenlandic EEZ marine area is a consequence of the historical discussions between Denmark and Greenland about rights and obligations in respect of the Greenlandic resources – as well as a consequence of the current conflicting interests between Greenland and Denmark on sovereignty issues.

The legitimacy of the transnational norms as a protection of the Arctic marine area is, on this basis, of special importance.

The *input legitimacy* of the transnational norms described in section 2 is ensured by Denmark's membership of the EU as well as the ratification by Denmark and the EU of the OSPAR Convention, the UNCLOS and the Biodiversity Convention – ratifications made by Denmark without reservations

48 Inatsisartut Act No. 15 of 8 June 2017 on Marine Environmental Protection section 6.

49 J.P.M. van Tatenhove, 'Marine Governance: Institutional Capacity-building in a Multi-level Governing Setting' in Michael Gilek and Kristine Kern (eds), *Governing Europe's Marine Environment: Europeanisation of Regional Seas or Regionalisation of EU Policies* (Ashgate 2015) 47.

for Greenland.[50] The consequences of this are important in the assessment of the transnational norms, as it is stated in Article 31 of the Vienna Convention that the ratified conventions shall be interpreted in good faith and in the light of their objects and purpose. The parties shall consider, together with the context of the Convention, any relevant rules of international law – including transnational norms – applicable in the relations between the parties.

The input legitimacy of the transnational ecosystem-based norms is also a consequence of the wording of the MSFD, in combination with the CJEU's case law, and the other legal mechanisms mentioned above in sections 2 and 3. It is important to remember that Denmark has a narrow discretionary power when the EU uses its external competence to cooperate under the international and national regimes covered by the EU's secondary legislation. Denmark has the power to use its legal competences and responsibilities on the protection of the Greenlandic Arctic marine area *only* in so far as its regulatory activities do not harm EU interests.[51] There is no strong Greenlandic interest that could constitute a reason for Denmark not to respect the principle of sincere cooperation to the EU and its international obligations under the Biodiversity Convention and the OSPAR Convention in respect of the protection of the ecosystems of the Arctic marine area.

The *output legitimacy* implies both that the exercise of public power must be limited and subject to some higher form of control by reference to the law – including international law. It is relevant to mention that the transnational norms, developed by the EU and OSPAR – as their fulfilment of obligations under the Biodiversity Convention, and supported by the Arctic Council – are based on a sustainable development perspective.

One aspect of importance for the output legitimacy is that the transnational cooperation between the EU and OSPAR on the use of a holistic, ecosystem-based approach, as an important part of a functionally oriented policy of sustainable development,[52] is controlled by integrated monitoring, assessment, data collecting and reporting activities. The output legitimacy is also ensured by the possibility for other EU Member States and for the EU Commission to bring legal cases on the outcome of the transnational governance under the control of the CJEU.[53] The just mentioned 'control possibilities' can be relevant, as

50 Several international and regional environmental conventions and declarations have been ratified by Denmark – some with reservation, others without reservations for Greenland. The conventions mentioned above in sections 1–2 are all ratified by Denmark without reservation for Greenland.

51 This right for Denmark to act in the interest of its OTCs was ensured by Declaration No. 25 of the Treaty on European Union attached to the earlier Maastricht Treaty from 1992. The declaration is not appended to the Treaty of Lisbon.

52 Josefsson (n. 11) 26 and 78.

53 However, the risk of enforcement by the EUCJ has also negative impact on the level of environmental ambition of OSPAR targets, see van Homeyer, Reins and Dupont (n. 27) 24 and 28.

Denmark was criticised, in 2017, by the European Commission for its monitoring programme covering the environmental status of its marine area.[54]

The concern in the EU's environmental directives and in the transnational norms for procedural rights is another indicator of the output legitimacy of decision-making on the rule of law.[55] One example on the EU's coordination with OSPAR on such procedural rights of private actors economically involved in the hydrocarbon activities is the Offshore Safety Directive that includes references to the OSPAR decision 98/3 on the disposal of disused offshore installations.[56] The just mentioned decision is based on the common approach that marine governance of offshore hydrocarbon extraction must involve all stakeholders.[57] The EU's marine environmental directives involve public participation obligations in accordance with the Aarhus Convention[58] and the Rio Declaration. Denmark has ratified this Convention, but the ratification is with reservation for Greenland. As mentioned in section 4, Denmark is also a party to the ILO Convention 169 on the rights of indigenous peoples that specifies rights to consultation and participation. However, the Danish and Greenlandic acts described earlier in sections 4–5 do not ensure such clear relations to international obligations and procedural rights. Ensuring that Greenlanders are meaningfully involved in processes to impact decision-making in mineral resources projects remains a challenge.[59]

The Arctic Council – by its marine strategy as well as its own structure – supports both the input legitimacy and the output legitimacy of the transnational ecosystem-based norms described in section 2. The ecosystem-based approach laid down in its Arctic Marine Strategic Plan is in harmony with the just mentioned transnational norms,[60] and as a bridging organisation[61] – accepted by the actors having interests in the Arctic marine area – the Council has the potential to ensure the transnational governance of the Arctic marine area social legitimacy.[62]

54 European Commission, COM(2017) 3 final, pp. 15–20.

55 Jonas Ebbesson, 'The rule of law in governance of complex socio-ecological changes' (2010) 20 *Global Environmental Change* 414.

56 Seline Trevisanut, 'The Role of Private Actors in Offshore Energy: Shifting Models of Participation' (2014) 29 *International Journal of Marine and Coastal Law* 647–48f.

57 Ibid., 648.

58 The UNECE Convention on Access to Information, Public Participation in Decision-Making and Access to Justice in Environmental Matters (the Aarhus Convention).

59 Cécile Pelaudeix, Ellen Margrethe Basse and Natalia Loukacheva, 'Openness, Transparency and Public Participation in the Governance of Uranium Mining in Greenland: A Legal and Political Track Record' (2017) 53 *Polar Record* 603; and Mark Nuttall, *Climate, Society and Subsurface Politics in Greenland: Under the Great Ice* (Routledge 2017) 40ff. and 50ff.

60 Concerning social legitimacy, see Trevisanut (n. 56) 648; and Bohman (n. 4), 252ff.

61 Concerning bridging organisations, see Bohman (n. 4) 47 and 55.

62 Concerning social legitimacy, see Linda Senden, *Soft Law in European Community Law* (Hart Publishing 2004) 65–66; and Bohman (n. 4), 259–271.

5 Brexit

A note on the EU's interlegality

Reza Banakar

Introduction

The United Kingdom (UK) has been one of the influential members of the European Union (EU) for more than four decades, during which time it has contributed to shaping EU rules, policies and institutions, while being shaped by them. Yet, the people of the UK voted in a referendum on 23 June 2016 to leave the EU by a margin of 51.9% to 48.1%, thereby ending their participation in what has been described as the most successful transnational project to date.[1] The outcome of the referendum was determined by a complex set of socio-political factors and historical forces, some of which are specific to the UK while others can be also found in other EU Member States. These include the British conception of sovereignty, a UK-wide crisis of identity politics, a largely EU-hostile UK press and a long-standing Eurosceptic attitude among many British politicians belonging to the right and the left of the political spectrum. Notwithstanding the distinctively British character of Brexit, the result of the referendum is the evidence of the EU's failed integration policy and its inability to generate a collective European identity that could appeal to the majority of Britons and cultivate a sense of solidarity between them and other Europeans.

In the following, we shall regard EU law as a transnational regime which is interlocked with the legal systems of its Member States, thus comprising a hierarchically ordered, multiple legal space. The notion of 'interlegality' coined by Boaventura de Sousa Santos helps us to explore how these spaces are 'superimposed, interpenetrated and mixed' within the EU's hierarchy of authority.[2] It also allows us to consider the 'porous legality' and 'legal porosity'[3] that enable the law to move through these spaces, interpenetrating layers of legality, from the governance of the EU at the transnational level to the national legal systems of the Member States and to the everyday life of its citizens at the local community level.

1 Ralf Michaels, 'Does Brexit Spell the Death of Transnational Law?' (2016) 17 *German Law Journal* 51, 52.

2 Boaventura de Sousa Santos, 'Law: A Map of Misreading: Toward a Post Conception of Law' (1987) 14 *Journal of Law and Society* 279, 297–298.

3 Ibid., 298.

Bearing these preliminaries in mind, this chapter will explore Brexit as an expression of the interlegality of EU laws and policies gone astray. Why did EU law and policies, which were designed to enhance the economic and political integration of the Member States, fail so miserably when it came to integrating Britain into the EU community? Does Brexit bring us a new insight into how the legal order of the EU and its Member States is interrelated at the transnational level? Does it throw new light on the EU law's ability to produce a sense of collective European identity and solidarity?

This chapter starts by explaining how Santos' 'Law: A Map of Misreading' and ideas borrowed from cartography can be applied to the study of EU law. This is followed by a brief account of some of the factors which influenced the outcome of the 2016 referendum in favour of leaving the EU. Next, the chapter examines how EU law has been used to devise a set of core values and a collective European identity aimed at conferring legitimacy on EU institutions and integrating the Member States into a political union. Why the EU's efforts to build a collective identity has not had the desired effect on British society is examined next by exploring the British crisis of national identity, which has evolved largely independently of the EU. The chapter ends by arguing that the EU's failure to generate a collective European identity needs to be examined in view of how its hierarchy of political power and legal authority constrains its interlegality.

Maps, scales and the notion of interlegality

In his seminal work entitled 'Law: A Map of Misreading', Santos uses cartography to describe how law operates sociologically by using the idea of different scales. To be practical, maps use certain apparently neutral 'mechanisms' to compress, reduce and generalise the features of the landscape they portray. This procedure transforms three-dimensional spaces into two-dimensional surfaces, but it does so at the price of distorting the objects that maps portray. 'There is thus', writes Santos, 'a permanent tension in maps between representation and orientation' in the sense that 'too much representation may hinder orientation', and inversely, 'accurate orientation may require omitting details in the environment which is being described'.[4] Santos' main point is that law misreads and, subsequently, distorts social reality in a way resembling how maps generalise, compress and distort geographical spaces. Therefore, he goes on to suggest that the 'dialectic of representation and orientation applies to law as much as it applies to maps'.[5] Crucially, this type of misreading is neither arbitrary nor chaotic or divorced from the truth, but is a form of practice that 'occurs through determinate and determinable mechanisms'.[6] These mechanisms or techniques include

4 Ibid., 283.
5 Ibid.
6 Ibid., 282.

scale, *projection* and *symbolisation*, each requiring a particular procedure. Starting with *scale*, Santos writes:

> The legal developments reveal the existence of three different legal spaces and their corresponding forms of law: local, national and world legality. It is rather unsatisfactory to distinguish these legal orders by their respective objects of regulation because they often regulate or seem to regulate the same kind of social action. Local law is a *large-scale legality*. Nation state law is a *medium-scale legality*. World law is *small-scale* legality. This concept has broad implications. First, it means that since scale creates the phenomenon, the different forms of law create different legal objects upon eventually the same social objects. They use different criteria to determine the meaningful details and relevant features of activity to be regulated. They establish different networks of facts. In sum, they create different legal realities.[7]

Following Santos' cartographic metaphor, the legal order of the EU becomes small-scale law designed to regulate the exclusive areas which fall within its competence. The volume of EU legislation has increased dramatically over the last three decades and yet remains considerably smaller than the corpus of laws of the Member States. More importantly, EU laws are projected in *general* terms that allow maximum orientation or effective steering across the legal systems of the Member States. They may be, for example, projected at a high level of generality to avoid micro-regulatory interference in the domestic affairs of the Member States, or because the EU wishes to leave 'certain aspects of the regulatory regime to be dealt with at the national level'.[8] The domestic legal order of the Member States represents medium-scale legality. At this level, the principles of subsidiarity and proportionality, as set out in Articles 5(3) and 5(4) of the Treaty on European Union (TEU), apply to guarantee a degree of independence for the national and regional authorities and to avoid detailed and nationally intrusive EU legislation.[9] The legally relevant experiences of EU citizens (involving rights claims, disputes, contracts, customary practices, etc.) and their attitudes towards, and expectations of, national EU law represent large-scale local legality. This level is highly fluid and changes rapidly as the seemingly disconnected fragments of legal experiences and streams of legal consciousness form new, but transitory, kaleidoscopic patterns of normativity. The public sphere, where the EU is discussed by politicians and citizens alike and reported on by the media, marks one of the intersections between the national and local levels of legality.

In cartography, *projection* is a neutral technique used to transform spherical objects into two-dimensional flat surfaces, thus reducing the complexity of

7 Ibid., 287.

8 For a discussion subsidiarity, see Paul Craig, 'Subsidiarity: A Political and Legal Analysis' (2012) 50 *Journal of Common Market Studies* 72.

9 Ibid., 73.

the real-life spaces. Varying types of projection organise the space differently by creating dissimilar representations of the same object. Moreover, they place certain objects at the centre of the map, thus privileging their representation, while relegating other objects to the margins of the map where they are excessively distorted. Turning to the study at hand, issues which are privileged at the EU law's small-scale level and thus placed at the centre, such as the EU's 'four freedoms' set out in the Treaty of Rome, are created and projected as different objects at the national and local levels and even relegated to the margins of the local law. Inversely, starting at the local level, as we shall see, central issues, such as the right to have one's local culture and job market protected, are translated into, and projected as, very different legal objects at the national and EU levels. This particular effect of projections distorts social reality more at the peripheries than at the centres although Santos hastens to add that it is on the peripheries that 'interpenetration between different legal orders is most frequent'.[10] The public political debates on the role of EU law and policies, involving both national actors (e.g. Parliament, government officials and political interest groups) and ordinary citizens and grassroot movements, mediated largely through the media, exemplify how the national and local levels overlap and interact on the margins of legal spaces. Finally, each cartographic scale uses a special *symbolisation* that concerns how particular sign systems are used to form a representational style for depicting physical features of various objects. As we shall argue later, how EU law and policies are projected at the national and local levels of governance is largely influenced by symbolisation mechanisms that reflect each level's specific identity, cultural makeup, history and purpose.

Since referring to law and legality does not capture the complexity arising out of the interaction between, and intersection among, these spaces of legality, Santos uses instead the notions of *interlaw* and *interlegality*. Interlegality is 'legal porosity'; it is about how different legal orders intersect, overlap and interact; it is the 'multiple networks of legal orders forcing us to constant transitions and trespassing'. As such, interlegality is not produced by any particular scale, but is reconditioned by the scope and logic which govern different scales. Different scales establish different 'sequences of action' that are structurally governed by their boundaries; large-scale legality conditions 'tactical and edifying' actions while 'small-scale invites instrumental action packages'.[11] Santos recognises that the distortions and concealments of reality create a basis for exercising power, but he does not problematise the power dimension of the interactions between legal spaces which generate interlegality. It is as if interlegality is realised in a power vacuum.

In the context of EU governance, interlegality works top-down or bottom-up. Legislation, directives, regulations, decisions and judgments as well as political priorities and agendas emanating from specific EU institutions and bodies work

10 Santos (n. 2) 292.
11 Santos (n. 2) 290.

top-down and carry considerably more political and legal weight than bottom-up processes of legality which start with civil society organisations or social movements. EU regulations, directives and decisions, which are binding on Member States, trickle down into the lower layers of domestic and local legality where they are translated into new legal objects and projected by Member States' legal systems as legal rules and regulations of their own. The bottom-up process of interlegality, on the other hand, involves the large-scale concerns of the local law and the legal experiences of citizens making their way upwards into the national and transnational levels and being projected as new legal events. It should be stressed here that these two processes can be formed with two different types of rationality and power relations. As a rule, interlegality, which is initiated top-down, has political force behind it and is conditioned by what Santos calls 'instrumental action package'. It is strategic, has a long-term perspective on regulation and is, therefore, universalistic in its scope. By contrast, the bottom-up movement of interlegality is propelled socio-culturally. It is 'tactical and edifying', but also particularistic in a way that benefits transitory local interests or mirrors localised conflicts.

Brexit

The EU referendum showed that the population of the UK was divided along lines which defy the traditional left-right political divisions. Those who voted to leave the EU came from both the left and the right of the political spectrum to demand to have their sovereignty, their laws and control of their borders back from the EU.[12] These demands are the defining features of the nation-state and express the wishes of the majority of the electorate to turn back the clock and reverse the process of globalisation, which has 'blurred and splintered the boundaries between the domestic and external spheres of nation-states and of regional integration organisations' such as the EU.[13] Assuming that Brexit runs its course and the UK succeeds in securing a divorce from the EU in March 2019, it will damage both the UK and the EU. It will deprive the UK of its political influence on the affairs of the EU, restrict its access to the EU internal market and force it to recast its future in an increasingly uncertain world. It will also deprive the EU of 16% of its gross domestic product (GDP) and free access to the UK market. However, focusing on economic gains and losses for the UK after Brexit misses the point that at the heart of this process is a conflict of values which does not lend itself to rational economic calculation. 'The referendum result was defined',

12 Using a left-right political scale, 53% of voters on the right and 50% of those on the left opted to leave the EU. See Heather Stewart, 'UK Politics Mired in "Culture Wars", Study Suggests' *The Guardian* (London, 7 December 2016).

13 Francis Snyder, 'Governing Economic Globalization: Global Legal Pluralism and European Union' (1999) 5 *European Law Journal* 334, 335–336.

writes Tim Oliver, 'also by views on what type of country Britain should be in terms of values, identities and outlook'.[14]

As these lines are written in October 2018, a fiercely divisive, angry and at the same time confused public debate is raging in Britain between 'remainers' and 'Brexiteers' over the UK's terms of withdrawal from the EU. One government faction seeks 'soft' Brexit, which would allow access to the single market, whereas another group advocates 'hard' Brexit, which would take Britain out of the single market and the customs union, falling back instead on the World Trade Organisation (WTO) rules for trade with the EU and the rest of the world. As the national debate on hard and soft Brexit is raised to the level of the EU and is projected through the small-scale legality of EU law and governance, it is transformed into technical talks on a range of issues such as 'hard' or 'soft' borders between the UK and the EU (e.g. how to ensure that the border in Northern Ireland remains open to trade, services and people), the rights of Britons living in Europe and the rights of EU citizens living in the UK after the UK's departure from the Union, or the 'financial settlement' (i.e. the amount that the UK must pay until 2020 to cover its commitment to the EU budget).

At the large-scale local level, the symbolisation mechanism of Brexit finds its expression in protectionism (protecting the local job markets), but also in nationalism and anti-migration sentiments, projecting itself as identity politics, more specifically as cultural threats to Englishness and Britishness. These are captured in the rising hate crime statistics and the growing number of violent offences against ethnic minorities and EU migrants in the UK after the referendum.[15] At the national level, the same identity politics manifests itself in the UK government's attempts to curb migration. At the EU level, these translate into challenges to the principle of free movement of EU citizens.

The European political elite, who planned the EU's integration policy, knew that without a collective European identity that enabled the citizens of the Member States to recognise their shared values and interests, the EU could neither legitimise its authority nor foster a collective sense of belonging, allegiance and solidarity among its Member States.[16] They also knew that there would always be tension between national or regional identities and a collective European identity, in the same way as there would be tension between national and transnational systems of law and governance. Hence the idea of multiple identities and belongings, which in theory allows attachment to both a collective

14 Tim Oliver, 'Fifty Shades of Brexit: EU Referendum and its Implications for Europe and Britain' (2017) 52 *The International Spector* 1, 3.

15 Figures for England and Wales show that violent offences against migrants soared after the referendum. See *The Guardian* (London, 16 October 2018), 'Hate crime surge linked to Brexit and 2017 terrorist attacks' www.theguardian.com/society/2018/oct/16/hate-crime-brexit-terrorist-attacks-england-wales accessed 21 October 2018.

16 Roberta Capello, 'Cohesion Policies and the Creation of a European Identity: The Role of Territorial Identity' (2018) 56 *Journal of Common Market Studies* 489.

European identity and to a national identity.[17] Such hybridised identities were to be created through EU law and policy processes, much of which were introduced and implemented in a top-down process of governance, driven by the conviction that an EU machinery can direct and control a uniform development across the Member States.

A European identity

The EU is a political project with a legal architecture designed with the objective to integrate its Member States into a transnational community which then governs itself. The EU treaties, legislation, regulations, directives and decisions together form a legal framework at the transnational level, empowering and restricting the authority of EU bodies and institutions. By transferring the political sovereignty of the Member States to the EU Council and Commission, it generates a shift of power from the democratically elected national parliaments to the EU Parliament, which suffers from low democratic legitimacy.[18] This creates a three-layered hierarchical legal space permeated by power disparity with the EU institutions at the top, the Member States in the middle and the EU citizens at the bottom. At the national level, this can translate into policies which undermine the sovereignty of national parliaments, while directly or indirectly regulating certain social and economic activities and developments. At the local level, it protects EU citizens' right to free movement, settlement and employment across the EU and to participate in elections in the country of their residence.[19] This framework gains legal force at the domestic level when the legal systems of the EU Members States recognise EU law as one of their primary sources of law. In this way, to borrow from Matthias Albert,[20] the EU legal system becomes part of the 'self-deceptions' of the Member State's national legal systems and, subsequently, part of their collective identity. This is also a description of how the EU's interlegality works, i.e. how the legal systems of the EU and its Member States intersect and overlap to create one territory without borders for the movements of goods, services, capital and people. This borderless entity is dependent on Member States,

17 Thomas Risse, 'The Euro between National and European Identity' (2003) 10 *Journal of European Public Policy* 487, 488.

18 The average turnouts at the elections to the European Parliament are far lower than the average turnouts at most national elections. In 2014, 35.60% of the UK electorate took part in the EU Parliament election, while the turnout at the 2017 General Election in the UK was 68.8%. This reflects among other things Britons' lack of trust in the EU. See *European Parliament* (2014) 'Results of the 2014 European Elections' www.europarl.europa.eu/elections2014-results/en/turnout.html accessed 20 August 2018.

19 For a comprehensive overview of the rights of the EU citizens, see the Charter of Fundamental Rights of the European Union, which is part of the EU's primary law and, thus, binding on the European institutions and Member States when they implemented EU law. It is noteworthy that the UK attempted to secure a partial opt-out from the Charter.

20 Matthias Albert, 'Governance and Democracy in European Systems: On Systems Theory and European Integration' (2002) 28 *Review of International Studies* 293, 302.

which paradoxically continue to define themselves, among other things, in terms of their national borders. Similarly, the EU's constitutive force – its so-called 'competence-competence' or ability to enact legally binding decisions addressing the Member States – is a function of the Member States' ratification of EU treaties and treaty amendments which give the EU competence over new areas of regulation.[21] EU law also integrates (or ought to integrate) EU citizens into one socio-political community by shaping their individual rights and duties. In this way, EU law becomes a medium for creating a collective, transnational, European identity, which transcends its internal borders and national identities, and thus, to borrow from Mayer and Palmowski, expresses 'what Europe is and what it aspires to be'.[22]

There is a large body of scholarly work which demonstrates that the potential of the law in integrating the EU is rather limited. This is not to deny the jurisprudential achievements of the Court of Justice of the European Union (CJEU) and the role of doctrines such as direct effect and supremacy for the formation of the European Community. Nor is it to deny that EU law has brought about a degree of Europeanisation of the legal systems of its Member States. Instead, the scholarly debates draw our attention to EU law's double-edged property, i.e. its interlegality integrates as well as disintegrates relationships at national and local levels. It engenders trust in EU institutions at a transnational level, but spawns distrust of them at national and local levels. Landmark judgments such as *Viking Line*[23] and *Laval*[24] exemplify how EU law integrates the economic relations at the macro level of the Member States, while engendering political conflicts at the local levels of interaction, organisation and collaboration between EU citizens.[25]

21 As Craig explains, 'the scope of EU competence is also affected by the interpretation accorded to treaty provisions by the EU courts'. Craig (n. 8) 74.

22 Franz Mayer and Jan Palmowski, 'European Identities and the EU – The Ties that Bind the Peoples of Europe' (2004) 42 *Journal of Common Market Studies* 573, 587.

23 C-438/05 International Transport Workers' Federation and Finnish Seamen's Union v. Viking Line ABP and OÜ Viking Line Eesti [2007] ECR I-10779.

24 C-341/05 Laval un Partneri Ltd v. Svenska Byggnadsarbetareförbundet, Svenska Byggnadsarbetareförbundets avdelning 1, Byggettan and Svenska Elektrikerförbundet [2007] ECR I-11767.

25 In judgments such as *Viking Line* and *Laval*, the CJEU illustrated the EU's determination to uphold the principles of a free market economy at the transnational level even if it amounted to eroding the workers' rights at the national and local levels. Both cases were concerned with the right to strike in Community law and with 'social dumping', i.e. attempts by employers to replace workers in one Member State with lower-paid workers from another Member State. In both cases, the CJEU held that it was a matter for national courts to decide if the right to strike was justified and proportionate. Nevertheless, it provided that the right to take industrial action was established in Community law and, thus, could only be exercised in a manner compatible with that law. This meant that the right to strike at national level was restricted by the right to freedom of movement and freedom of establishment which are supranational rights. For a discussion, see Ann-Christine Hertzén, *The European Social Dialogue in Perspective: Its Future Potential as an Autopoietic System and Lessons from the Global Maritime System of Industrial Relations* (PhD monograph, Lund University 2017) 242ff.

Its integrative properties operate at the macro level of EU governance, while the disintegrative forces materialise when EU laws and policies intersect with the socio-cultural conditions which define national and local laws.

Aware of the limits of EU law's integrative/disintegrative force and the inevitability of its legal rules being reconstructed differently within the different scales of national and local laws, the EU tries to establish a symbolisation mechanism capable of bringing some type of uniformity to how laws are projected across the legal systems of its Member States, thus reducing distortions produced by the mechanisms of projection. To this end, the EU has attempted to produce a collective European identity using a top-down and a bottom-up method, both of which are intimately tied up to solidarity and forms of legitimacy-building. These two approaches assume that democratic institutions at the national level will provide the public political spaces for developing a collective identity, while democratic processes enable the active participation of citizens in those spaces, thus fostering their ownership of the EU and trust in its institutions, which in turn strengthen their collective European identity. According to Prutsch,[26] these two approaches should jointly give rise to 'a democratic political culture which is grounded in institutionally guaranteed civil rights and political participation and which is per se open to everyone', i.e. operates at the large-scale local levels of the Member States, but is at the same time 'conceived in opposition to "closed" national(ist) cultures that represent and are (pre-)defined by specific ethno-cultural values'.

Top-down identity building

The 'top-down' method of constructing a collective identity uses European law and governance to establish democratic structures and institutions that are supported by a set of shared norms and core values. To create and maintain a common identity top-down, the EU resorts to using collective symbols such as the European flag, the EU anthem, a European day, and community rituals, but also producing a set of shared values and principles such as the need to secure a lasting peace, unity among the Member States, equality, freedom, security and solidarity. Once in place, these should, in theory, bring uniformity to how EU laws and policies are projected at national and local levels. The most fundamental value of the EU, as articulated by the Council of the European Union,[27] is the 'shared determination to promote peace and stability and to build a world founded on respect and human rights, democracy and the rule of law'. EU citizens should be

26 Markus J. Prutsch, *Research for CULT Committee – European Identity, European Parliament, Policy Department for Structural and Cohesion Policies* (European Parliament 2017) 17. Posted at www.europarl.europa.eu/RegData/etudes/STUD/2017/585921/IPOL_STU(2017)585921_EN.pdf accessed 1 September 2018.

27 *Council of the European Union*, 'EU Strategic Framework and Action Plan on Human Rights and Democracy' (European Council 2012) www.consilium.europa.eu/uedocs/cms_data/docs/pressdata/EN/foraff/131181.pdf, accessed 1 June 2018.

united not by national cultures, religious allegiances and ethnic belonging, but by a set of democratic values and rights based on respect for difference and plurality. Thus, as Hirsch notes, international human rights norms become a 'constitutive norm' used to define the membership of the community:

> The EU bodies have repeatedly stated that human rights protection constitutes a constitutive norm. [...] The EU's institutions are legally committed to comply with fundamental human rights and may suspend certain membership rights of members which seriously and persistently breach these norms.[28]

This method of identity building relies, to borrow from Habermas,[29] on 'a consensus on the procedures for the legitimate enactment of laws and the legitimate exercise of power', rather than on national cultures and ethnic belonging.[30] Therefore, it functions as a source of 'normative legitimacy', i.e. guiding how authorities or state institutions constrain arbitrary exercise of power by satisfying certain objective operational criteria, such as accountability, consistency, autonomy, transparency and the rule of law generally. These are, incidentally, the key properties of any constitutional democracy which impose what Thornhill calls 'external norms (usually expressed as rights) on political power' and ensure that 'the exercise of power is controlled and limited by relatively formalized normative principles'.[31] This creates 'normative legitimacy', which in contrast to 'descriptive legitimacy' is independent of the public's attitude to legal and political institutions.[32]

The EU's constitutional framework for human rights protection provides a basis for creating a liberal democratic identity which is produced both internally within the EU's small-scale legal order and projected externally onto outsiders, i.e. to criticise countries outside the EU which violate human rights. Thus, EU law and treaties, including the Charter of Fundamental Rights of the European Union, which places human rights at the centre of the legal order of the EU, are the underpinnings of the top-down project of creating a European identity; an identity which is to trickle down the layers of law through the medium of interlegality and permeate both national and local spaces. This identity is reconstructed under the auspices of the CJEU and other EU institutions by urging Member States to comply with EU norms and standards at the national level,

28 Moshe Hirsch, *Invitation to the Sociology of International Law* (Oxford University Press 2015) 109–110.

29 Jürgen Habermas, 'Struggles for Recognition in the Democratic Constitutional State' in Charles Taylor and Amy Gutmann (eds), *Multiculturalism: Examining the Politics of Recognition* (Princeton University Press 1994) 107, 135.

30 Prutsch (n. 26) 17.

31 Chris Thornhill, 'Niklas Luhmann and the Sociology of Constitution' (2010) 10 *Journal of Classical Sociology* 315, 316.

32 For a discussion on the distinction between normative and descriptive legitimacy, see Joseph H.H. Weiler, 'In the Face of Crisis: Output Legitimacy and the Political Messianism of European Integration' (2012) 34 *Journal of European Integration* 825.

generally, but with the EU's 'constitutive norms' in particular, thus enhancing socio-political integration across the Union. The problem is, as Hirsch notes, that once 'the existing constitutional framework (with the exception of anti-discrimination law)' is reconstructed and projected at national levels of Members States, it 'assigns a more circumscribed role to human rights within the context of internally focused EU policies'.[33] Instead, it appears to be more interested in projecting human rights externally, i.e. 'to promote human rights actively in its international policies'.[34] By using human rights norms to take non-EU Member States to task, the EU constructs a transnational 'other' for its community, but it also draws attention away from the political accountability of the EU itself which, as Weiler puts it, is 'remarkably weak'.[35] 'It is difficult', Weiler writes, 'to point out to one single instance of accountability for political failure as distinct from personal accountability for misconduct in the annals of the European integration'.[36] This structural failure of European governance is not conducive to the construction of a collective European identity that helps social actors at national and international levels to envision the EU's human rights values in their minds and reproduce it in their actions.

Bottom-up identity building

The bottom-up identity formation requires the type of experience-near understanding of other Europeans which can be produced socio-culturally at the large-scale level of local communities. One has to start with how ordinary citizens make sense of themselves where relationships with other European people are of primary concern. This type of identity is experience-based, generated through first-hand interaction and association with other Europeans and, thus, not uniform. In theory, it works when social actors realise that values and experiences that they have in common as Europeans outweigh the national, ethnic, religious or cultural differences which distinguish them from each other. In that sense, it also involves trust and a feeling of solidarity towards the other. This self-understanding as a European has a symbiotic relationship with collective action at national levels (e.g. in labour movements, environmental movements and various civil society organisations which operate across national borders) among Europeans because one needs a degree of identification with other people before one can associate and collaborate with them. At the same time, such cross-national collaboration strengthens a collective identity because 'it necessarily involves taking the perspective of others who are co-jointly involved in the project or movement and

33 Hirsch (n. 28) 112.

34 'Since 1992, the EU's trade agreements with third parties have included a "human rights clause" requiring the parties to respect human rights and democratic principles'. Hirsch (n. 28) 113–114.

35 Weiler (n. 32) 829.

36 Weiler (n. 32) 829.

dwelling on features shared with them'.[37] For the civic engagement to work and allow collaboration, the EU needs to uphold individual rights and duties of the citizens towards each other and guarantee their autonomy vis-à-vis the national authorities and EU institutions. The collective identity creates closer relations of interdependency and trust between the various groups belonging to different Member States. This, in turn, confers legitimacy in its descriptive sense – i.e. reflecting the citizens' attitude to, and perception of, the law and authority – on the EU institutions which facilitate a closer cross-border collaboration among EU citizens.

Two points attract attention when we compare the top-down and bottom-up processes of identity building. First, the top-down efforts are carried out through the binding force of the EU's interlegality and are impregnated with instrumental rationality of macro administrative systems. As such, they strengthen the normative legitimation of the EU's transnational governance, without necessarily having a direct impact on the local levels of legality, i.e. how EU citizens perceive EU's institutions. By contrast, the collaborative cross-border identity-building, which is to work its way up the EU's hierarchy of legal spaces, has neither the binding force of EU's authority behind it nor enjoys its own locally based source of authority. It is instead reliant on mutual understanding and collaboration which, given time, will enhance intercultural intersubjectivity and solidarity among EU citizens. Even the citizenship rights enshrined in the Charter of Fundamental Rights of the European Union were not devised to provide an independent source of authority for EU citizens. As Article 51(1) clarifies, the Charter is addressed at the EU institutions, bodies and the Member States, which implement EU law. Second, there is an intrinsic tension between an EU identity, which is projected as cross-border collaboration and solidarity to other EU members, and local national identities which are projected through the cultural and ethnic markers of various European populations. The former emphasises in the first place similarities, whereas the latter is based on the construction of differences between social groups. In the context of Brexit, for example, the other Europeans were conceptualised, viewed and experienced as out-groups and a threat to British culture and the job market. This is yet another example of the integrative/disintegrative properties of the interlegality of EU laws and policies. To unfold this point, we should take a closer look at how British identity evolved over time and how it came to define itself, at least in part, against the EU.

British identity

The data on EU citizens' self-identification, which was collected prior to the 2016 referendum, showed that UK citizens had the weakest sense of belonging

37 European Commission, *The Development of European Identity/Identities: Unfinished Business: A Policy Review* (2012) 13. www.mela-project.polimi.it/publications/920.htm accessed 25 August 2018.

or attachment to the EU. According to the *Eurobarometer survey* conducted in 2015, nearly two thirds of the people of the UK did not identify themselves as Europeans, compared with 40% of French and Italians and 30% of Germans and Spanish.[38] Who did Britons identify themselves with and why? According to the right-wing politician Enoch Powell,[39] British identity consisted of four essential, but interrelated, unique elements: (1) parliamentary sovereignty, (2) individualism and individual rights, (3) the ethnic unity of the British people, which excluded the Asian and black migrants and (4) detachment from the European continent. Since, according to Powell, 'British national identity was singular, it would be suicidal to join Europe. [Britain] was not a European nation, and its geographical proximity to Europe was a contingent matter of little political and cultural significance'.[40] Margaret Thatcher[41] largely shared Powell's conception of British identity although she did value the UK's membership of the EU, which she thought was economically beneficial, and believed that the black and Asian migrants should be assimilated rather than deported back to their countries of origin, as Powell advocated. New Labour[42] adopted a different approach to Britishness and national identity, which arguably reduced it to what Parekh calls a 'corporate brand', a largely London-based cool image that harboured its own 'seeds of exclusion and intolerance'.[43] It pursued a British identity based on a business model committed to market economy, but also sought a communitarian alternative to the neoliberal individualism and the economic egoism that had become the hallmark of the Thatcher era. However, it was not New Labour's notion of Britishness, but versions of Powell's definition which were revived by populist groups in the wake of the 2008 financial crisis in Britain to strengthen the anti-EU, anti-migration and anti-establishment sentiments in the country.

As Henderson et al. stress, there has never been a homogeneous or fixed British identity, and Britishness has neither existed uniformly across England, Wales, Scotland and Northern Ireland nor has meant the same thing to different communities in different parts of the UK.[44] Moreover, as a result of 'globalization

38 European Commission, *European Citizenship* (Standard Eurobarometer 83 Spring 2015) 22.

39 Enoch Powell (1912–1998) was a Conservative Member of Parliament between 1950 and 1974, a member of the Ulster Unionist Party from 1974 to 1987. Although he did not regard himself a racist, he left a 'lasting and malign effect (…) on the way in which race and migration are discussed, or not discussed'. See *The Economist*, '*"Rivers of Blood": The Lasting Legacy of a Poisonous Speech*' (London, 21 April 2018) www.economist.com/britain/2018/04/19/rivers-of-blood-the-lasting-legacy-of-a-poisonous-speech accessed 20 August 2018.

40 Bhiku Parekh, 'Defining British National Identity' (2000) 71 *The Political Quarterly* 4, 9.

41 Margaret Thatcher served as UK Prime Minister from 1979 to 1990.

42 'New Labour' refers to the Labour Party under Tony Blair and Gordon Brown's leadership. They were in Government from 1997 to 2010.

43 Parekh (n. 40) 12–13.

44 Ailsa Henderson, Charlie Jeffery, Dan Wincott and Richard Wyn Jones, 'How Brexit was made in England' (2017) 19 *The British Journal of Politics and International Relations* 631, 635.

and international interdependence, most strikingly through the developing institutions of the European Union', Heath and Roberts argue, 'British identity is now in decline'.[45] However, it was the parliamentary devolution of power to Scotland, Wales and Northern Ireland in 1998 which partly aroused a new interest in Englishness (in contrast to Britishness) and in England's place in the world. Various terrorist incidents following the Iraq war, such as the terrorist attacks of 7 July 2005 which were perpetrated by young Muslim converts who were born and bred in England, also helped to awaken the public's interests in identity politics. The 'London bombings' were seen as a failure to create a unifying and inclusive civic British identity and a justification for using 'ethnic and religious signifiers' to divide the nation into insiders and outsiders.[46]

Although national identities become fluid and fragmented in a late modern setting, they nevertheless maintain their ties with the past. This is true in the case of English national identity, which continues to be reconstructed partly in the shadow of the British Empire and Britain's diminished role in the world.[47] The social anthropologist Andrew Garner describes the circumstances which drove many English and Welsh people to choose to leave the EU as the unfolding of a long historical process which culminated in 'the collapse of the British Empire, and transformation of British identity, in the post-Second World War era'.[48] Similarly, Chris Rojek points to the swift decline of the British Empire, 'the enormous loss of British power and prestige', as a traumatic experience which 'still casts a long shadow over British culture and identity'.[49] The British identity remains, therefore, in flux. Although fragmented by its multinational constitution (consisting of England, Wales, Scotland and Northern Ireland) and fractured by multiculturalism, part of which (the post-war Black and Asian migration) is a legacy of its imperial past, it nevertheless continues a nostalgic quest for continuity in a transient world, where social interactions, norms, relationships and structures are increasingly liquified. These types of national revival and nationalistic search for 'the good old days' are hardly specific to Britain and can be found across and beyond the EU. In the case of Britain, the reinvention of the past is played out in the historical context of the British Empire with its own symbols and myths, which were used to construct Powell's notions of Britain as a separate entity from Europe, with its own unique brand of sovereignty, individual rights and the ethnic unity.

45 Anthony Heath and Jane Roberts, 'British Identity: Its Sources and Possible Implications for Civic Attitudes and Behaviour.' Research Report for Lord Goldsmith's Citizenship Review (HMSO 2008) 4.

46 Eva-Maria Asari, Daphne Halikiopoulou and Steven Mock, 'British National Identity and the Dilemmas of Multiculturalism' (2008) 14 *Nationalism and Ethnic Politics* 1, 1.

47 Ibid., 9–10.

48 Andrew Garner, 'Brexit, Boundaries and Imperial Identities: A Comparative View' (2017) 17 *Journal of Social Archeology* 3, 19.

49 Chris Rojek, *Brit-myth: Who Do the British Think They Are?* (Reaction Books 2007) 180.

In some ways, this is the antithesis of 'cool Britain' of the New Labour era which, with its open corporate borders, celebrated the idea of the European Union and globalisation. Despite its communitarian aspirations, its critique of neoliberal individualism and its efforts to educate the populace to 'accept personal responsibilities and the right of others in the community',[50] New Labour did not succeed in strengthening the sense of community and solidarity in Britain. Once EU law and policies, which were designed to create a European identity and integrate the Member States, managed to interpenetrate the national legal space in the UK, they raised alarm among sections of the political establishment which had not adapted to the decline of the British Empire. Britain's national identity crisis impacted on the way these laws and policies were projected and recreated at the national level as bureaucratic and often contradictory constraints forced on Britain against its sovereign will. Once they reached the local level, they were projected through a British national identity, which besides being individualistic and seeing itself largely separate from continental Europe was largely formed in confrontation with the type of solidarity-based identity which the EU had been fostering.

The Human Rights Act 1998

In view of the constitutive role that human rights play in the EU's collective identity-building, we should take a brief look at how the Human Rights Act 1998 (HRA) has fared in the UK. The HRA was introduced by the 'New Labour' government and passed by the UK Parliament independently of the EU to incorporate the fundamental rights and liberties enshrined in the Convention on Human Rights adopted by the Council of Europe after World War II. Once the HRA was enacted, 'anyone living within the jurisdiction of the UK, regardless of citizenship or nationality, [could] claim the protection of the convention'.[51] Those whose rights had been violated under the Convention no longer needed to take their case to the European Court of Human Rights in Strasbourg. They could instead seek remedy in British courts. In that sense, we might expect that the enactment of the HRA places human rights at the centre of the UK's national map of law and creates a culture of respect for human rights that increases the affinity between UK law and the EU's constitutive norms. At the level of local law, where the interface between the law and ordinary citizens' conception of legality takes place, one would expect the HRA to help citizens to envision the human rights norms and values similar to those at the core of the EU's collective identity project. At the national level, one would expect the HRA to help UK courts and other public authorities to incorporate more effectively the idea of human rights protection as part of their institutional identity. Indeed, by transferring

50 Jack Straw, 'Jack Straw Sets Out New Vision of Society' Press Release (Lord Chancellor's Department 18 May 1999).

51 Anthony M. Clohesy, 'Human Rights Act: Politics, Power and the Law' in David Howarth and Jacob Torfing (eds), *Discourse Theory in European Politics* (Palgrave 2005) 170, 170.

political power from the executive and legislature to the judiciary, this act gave courts a more active role in protecting individual rights. It empowered judges to review legislation and administrative decisions for compliance with the European Convention on Human Rights (ECHR), subsequently enhancing the power of the judiciary. However, this created tension between Parliament (or parliamentary sovereignty) and the judiciary, giving rise to a public political debate on the constitutional impact of the HRA.

In the wake of the 9/11 and the 2005 terrorist attacks in London, judges' interpretation and application of the HRA were criticised heavily for being against the will of Parliament and in defiance of the legislature. Judges were said to protect 'only the undeserving, such as criminals and terrorists, at the expense of the law abiding citizens'.[52] In its 2009 report, the UK Equality and Human Rights Commission explained that although the 'Ministry of Justice [had] actively promoted the HRA and disseminated guidance and best practice through its Human Rights Programme', the evidence showed that 'a culture of respect for human rights [had] largely failed to take root among public authorities in England, Scotland and Wales in the way that [had been] anticipated a decade ago' when the HRA had come into force.[53] Moreover, 'surveys of general public opinion, like those of public service staff and service users, [revealed] a degree of hostility to the way in which the HRA [was] perceived to operate as a charter for people wanting to cheat the system'.[54] The reports also found a tendency among UK Government ministers and various politicians to misrepresent the HRA. To exemplify, Daniel Hannan, a Conservative member of the European Parliament, complained in 2006 that the UK Parliament was no longer sovereign because courts had to consider the European Convention on Human Rights, the UN Declaration on Refugees and the Treaty of Rome and so on when deciding cases. Underpinning all these evils was the HRA:

> The Human Rights Act is becoming the first refuge of the scoundrel. It is snatched at by illegal immigrants wishing to avoid repatriation, and by prisoners who want to receive pornography in their cells (on grounds of "freedom of expression"). It is invoked against stop-and-search powers, school uniform policies and "wanted" posters. It has frustrated the attempts of four successive home secretaries to deport the Stansted Afghan hijackers.[55]

52 *Joint Committee on Human Rights Act: The DCA and Home Office Review, Thirty-second Report of Session 2005–06* www.publications.parliament.uk/pa/jt200506/jtselect/jtrights/278/ 278.pdf accessed 25 September 2018.

53 Alice Donald, Jenny Watson, Niamh McClean, Philip Leach and Jörn Eschment, *Human Rights in Britain since the Human Rights Act 1998: A Critical Review* (Equality and Human Rights Commission 2009) 2.

54 Ibid., xviii.

55 Daniel Hannan, 'Good for Crooks, Bad for Human Rights' *The Telegraph* (16 November 2006) www.telegraph.co.uk/comment/personal-view/3634310/Good-for-crooks-bad-for-human-rights.html accessed 20 August 2018.

The UK Parliament's *Joint Committee on Human Rights* had a year earlier claimed, in a similar vein, that the HRA prevented the democratically elected government of the UK 'from responding effectively to serious challenges that threaten the country', thus, calling for the repeal of the act and recommending to the UK government to withdraw from the ECHR.[56] In their 2015 party manifesto, the Conservatives pledged to curtail the influence of the ECHR on UK courts by repealing the HRA and replacing it with the 'British Bill of Rights', which had a much weaker link with the ECHR (this has, however, not happened yet).

Considering the numerous obstacles which stood in the way of the HRA, we find several issues of relevance to our discussions regarding the EU. *First*, by enabling national courts in the UK to decide cases which were previously brought before the European Court of Human Rights in Strasbourg, the HRA widened – albeit inadvertently – the distance between the British public and continental Europe. *Second*, unlike the EU's human rights engagement, which is 'messianic' and directed in the first place at promoting human rights internationally, the HRA turned on the UK legal system. Its supporters saw it as an attempt to cultivate moral communitarianism, i.e. to introduce new shared community values and social justice in opposition to the extreme individualism of the Thatcher era, while its many critics described it as a cynical attempt by New Labour to 'bolster government power'.[57] How it was ultimately reconstructed and projected was a function of symbolisation mechanisms which were triggered by anti-terrorism fears and the identity crisis described in the previous section. *Third*, there is tension between the type of outward-looking HRA, based on the small-scale 'world law' of the ECHR, which is aimed at protecting rights and freedoms of everyone equally, and the sort of inward-looking charter of citizens' rights, which was sought by national political groups who claimed to protect the British public at the local level more effectively against the threat of terrorism. This tension reappears in different guises in our discussions regarding how identity and solidarity are reproduced at different national and transnational levels. *Fourth*, Hannan's misrepresentations (quoted above) exemplify attempts by political interests to project the HRA negatively at the local level of legality. These misreadings of the HRA illustrate how the act was projected at the intersection of local and national politics. They also indicate the role of political interest groups in influencing how laws are projected, reminding us that interlegality does not take place in a political vacuum and is shaped by power relationships between the EU, its Member States and citizens. It is, therefore, not surprising if the HRA was also invoked by Eurosceptics to blame EU law for protecting terrorists and criminals.[58] *Fifth*, New Labour ministers, such as Jack Straw, knew all too well that the British public

56 *Joint Committee on Human Rights* (n. 52).

57 Clohesy (n. 51) 175.

58 See Anoosh Chakelian, 'How Much of our Law is Made in Brussels?' *New Statesman* (16 June 2016) www.newstatesman.com/politics/uk/2016/06/how-much-our-law-made-brussels accessed 20 August 2018.

needed to learn that the rights enshrined in the HRA had to be balanced with individual obligations and responsibilities towards others.[59] Being confronted with numerous administrative obstacles and misrepresented in the public political discourse, the values enshrined in the HRA could not flow down the hierarchies of social organisation to be projected and recreated by the grassroots at the local level. The failure to morally project the HRA at the large-scale local level of legality meant that in public opinion, individual rights promoted by the HRA were not balanced with corresponding responsibilities towards others. Thus, Britain remained a largely rights-claiming, individualistic culture with the second (only after the Netherlands) lowest level of solidarity towards others.[60]

Concluding remarks

Brexit shows that Britain's crisis of identity politics influenced the way EU laws and policies were projected, recreated, but also excessively distorted, at the national and local levels. It shows that the top-down introduction of human rights values, intrinsic to the EU's identity and solidarity building project, were not matched with a bottom-up recognition of rights and responsibilities. These points need to be considered further in the context of our discussions on the flow of interlegality within the hierarchy of the EU spaces. The EU's interlegality flows top-down and bottom-up interconnecting the EU institutions at the transnational level, the Member States at the national level and the EU citizenry at the local levels, although this is not a free flow of interlegality of the type Santos appeared to be suggesting. As we saw, laws and policies which integrate Member States at the transnational level of the internal market can disintegrate relations at the national level by depriving, for example, labour movements of their right to strike in certain instances, which violates the principles of the EU law. The disintegrative effects of EU law are caused by the power disparity which hierarchically forms the relationship between the EU, its Member States and citizens and, as such, should not be confused with the distortions generated by the cartographic mechanisms described by Santos.

When flowing top-down, the EU's interlegality has the authority of the EU behind it and is mediated through the legal systems of the Member States. By contrast, when the flow takes place bottom-up, it lacks an authority or a source of legality of its own large-scale legal order. As we explained above, even EU citizenship rights did not emerge at the local level and were not designed specifically to empower the individual citizens; instead, they emanated from the EU and were addressed to the Member States. The upward flow of EU interlegality

59 Jack Straw, 'Human Rights in the 21st Century', *Mackenzie-Stuart Lecture* (University of Cambridge, Faculty of Law, 25 October 2007) http://sms.cam.ac.uk/media/1172324 accessed 2 September 2018.

60 See *Special Eurobarometer 461, Designing Europe's Future* (European Commission 2017) 63. http://ec.europa.eu/commfrontoffice/publicopinion/index.cfm/ResultDoc/download/DocumentKy/79157 accessed 25 August 2018.

can start at the lowest level of legality with the citizens' experience of EU laws, policies and regulations. Lacking in legal authority, it cannot manifest itself as rules and policies, but as disputes between individuals and national governments, rights claims, search for social change and reform, or defiantly as an expression of political resistance to the disintegrative effects of EU laws. Brexit exemplifies how power disparities embedded in social structures and upheld with law create a condition for resistance to the exercise of top-down authority of the EU. Part of the resistance manifests itself in *excessive* distortions – i.e. distortions which go beyond misrepresentations caused by cartographic mechanisms – of legal rules and policies which move from higher to lower subordinate spaces of legality. As we saw, the HRA 1998, aimed at strengthening the human rights protection of all those who lived within the national borders of the UK, was projected as the charter of criminals and terrorists who sought to evade justice, once it moved from the national to the local community level of legality. Instead of bringing the UK and EU closer, the HRA widened the distance between them. Even though the HRA had been enacted independently of the EU, it nevertheless became the most hated piece of legislation among Brexiteers because it incorporated the *European* Convention on Human Rights.[61]

To neutralise the imbalance of power which disproportionately distorts the flow of interlegality, the EU needs to reconstruct itself as a community, or a network of communities, which is simultaneously active at the transnational, national and local levels. Such a network needs to be structurally fluid to allow legal porosity and trespassing between spaces and levels of legality and yet maintain enough continuity in its constitutive relationships to operate as a social and legal order. This type of community network cannot stem from the small-scale reality of transnational level and cannot emanate from the authority of the EU and its Member States alone. Its legal authority can no longer emanate from one single unifying source or from several sources which are organised hierarchically with respect to each other. Its legitimacy must become as much dependent on ethical properties embodied in the organisation of the EU institutions and the modus operandi of EU authorities as it is on the EU citizens' willingness to identify themselves with them. Instead, to borrow liberally from Roger Cotterrell, this network of communities has to create its norms, relationships and authority 'in a "bottom-up" process of negotiation and consensus formation'.[62]

The constant renegotiations cannot be limited to the small-scale legality of the EU Parliament and Commission or the CJEU, but must take place also at the local level where many EU citizens are struggling with a crisis of identity and many Member States with the rise of extremist populist political movements. This can be carried through while the Member States are grappling with their own national identity crisis and may, indeed, serve to turn the tide of regionally based nationalism that is currently fuelling the anti-EU sentiments across Europe.

61 Chakelian (n. 58).

62 Roger Cotterrell, *Sociological Jurisprudence* (Routledge 2018) 110.

Admittedly, it will not be easy to initiate such a transformation which compels EU institutions, EU's policymakers and its jurists, not to mention the Member States, to envisage the EU's legal architecture in a fundamentally new way, i.e. not as a force of normativity which acts top-down through a hierarchy of authority, but as a form of interlegality which permeates and shapes the local, national and transnational spaces in equal measures. This will be a 'high risk/high gain' project, but the alternative, i.e. failure to see EU law's regulatory mechanisms and potential in a radically different light, will gradually, but inevitably, erode the political and legal foundations of the EU.

6 Beyond nations and continents?[1]

Harmony and solidarity as common endeavours in a digital era of populism, propaganda and fiction?

Hanne Petersen

Introduction

The end of World War II led amongst many other things to the establishment of the United Nations (UN), process(es) of decolonisation, the establishment of The People's Republic of China and the European Economic Community, later to become the European Union (EU), which required the transfer of national legal sovereignty. Some have described this as the end of the Westphalian order.[2] The world has moved towards more states but also towards smaller and not always well-functioning states. Issues of scale and economy thus achieve importance besides and beyond (state) status. Transnational law is here understood as transcending or crossing borders but not necessarily being formally enacted by states. Thus, the growing influence of non-state actors in the regulatory arena results in an increased questioning about legitimacy. This chapter deals with the role of China and the EU in shaping transnational norms in the 21st century (mainly based upon Danish and Nordic examples), drawing on my experience with these parts of the world and my longstanding interest in and work with changing legal cultures. Anti-globalism in the form of (sometimes) populist, political developments has been strengthened[3] in this period, as has a professed return to the 'nation first' in a digital era, where market and political propaganda has a reach maybe never witnessed before. Lately, market legitimacy is increasingly questioned also due to increased economic inequalities. Perhaps, therefore, transnational norms of solidarity and harmony have (re)appeared in especially European and Chinese contexts.

1 In the Online Etymology Dictionary, 'trans-' is defined as a 'word-forming element meaning 'across, beyond, through, on the other side of, to go beyond,' from Latin trans (prep.) 'across, over, beyond', perhaps originally present participle of a verb *trare-, meaning 'to cross', from PIE (proto-Indo European) *tra-, variant of root *tere- (2) 'cross over, pass through, overcome''. www.etymonline.com/word/trans- accessed 4 July 2018.

2 See Hanne Petersen, 'Lange krigsballetter: før og nu' in H.M. Motzfeldt, S. Schaumburg-Müller, R. Gottrup and K. Østergaard (eds), *Mod og mening: Hyldestskrift til Frederik Harhoff* (Djøf Forlag 2016) 423–34.

3 Anna Libak, *Forstå populismen!* (Gyldendal 2018).

The first part of this chapter discusses the concept of transnationalism with an emphasis on the current transformation of the global legal landscape and world order. The second part presents norms of solidarity and harmony focusing on their role in Chinese and European history in this transformation process. The third part analyses populism, propaganda and fiction, highlighting the role of central actors in spreading the norms of solidarity and harmony across borders. There is a cross-over and interaction going on in many fields, however, without any clear pattern or image emerging at this moment.

Transnationalism in a world of asymmetry and disparity[4]

In 2017, the UN had 193 Member States. In the dominant (Western) legal theories and in the UN treaty, these states are considered sovereign and equal.[5] However, a closer look at the figures shows that about 40 of these states have populations below 1.5 million – a minor Chinese city – and 106 of the states have populations below 10 million, fewer than many megacities of the world, and added together they make up less than each of the two biggest states in the world, China and India.[6] Only 11 out of the UN Member States have populations of more than 100 million (China, India, United States of America, Indonesia, Brazil, Nigeria, Bangladesh, Russian Federation, Japan, Mexico and Philippines).[7] The world club of major countries is quite small in numbers, but not in populations. Size and scale matter in a globalised world. The 11 biggest countries in the world cover all continents apart from Europe. These big countries, some of which have experienced substantial economic growth over the last few decades, will have a considerable future impact on normative globalisation. Being small is, however, not necessarily negative. The ten richest countries in the world are small – and very diverse in political models and strategic positions. Several of them are in practice city-states. They are in certain respects occasionally highly competitive. When one compares and links China and Europe, the geographical status is not clear. '*Eurasia*' is a contested term sometimes defined as *one continent* combining the landmasses of Europe and Asia. At other times they are considered *two* continents. 'Eurasia' comprises about 70% of the world's population.[8] Of the

4 See also Hanne Petersen, 'Chinese Contributions to Global Normative Pluralism?' [2016–2017] *Naveiñ Reet, Nordic Journal of Law & Social Research. Special Issue on Law and Transitional Society: Chinese and Global Perspectives* 53 www.jsl.tors.ku.dk.

5 See Charter of the United Nations Art. 2, The Organization is based on the principle of the sovereign equality of all its Members.

6 See United Nations (DESA / Population division), 'World Population Prospects 2017' http://esa.un.org/unpd/wpp/Download/Standard/Population/ accessed 14 March 2018.

7 Ibid.

8 See Wikipedia, 'Eurasia' https://en.wikipedia.org/wiki/Eurasia accessed 14 March 2018; see also Alfred W. McCoy, 'The Geopolitics of American Global Decline: Washington Versus China in the Twenty-First Century' (Tomdispatch.com, 7 June 2015) www.tomdispatch.com/post/176007/tomgram%3A_alfred_mccoy%2C_washington%27s_great_game_and_why_it%27s_failing_/#more accessed 2 July 2018.

world's about 7 billion people, more than 50% live in the Eastern and Southern parts of Asia.[9]

The present global legal landscape is undergoing reconstitution. The EU and China are two central actors when it comes to the development of transnational norms. Over the years from 1957 to 2004, the EU expanded from originally 6 countries to 27, encompassing a population of about half a billion people. Of the present 28 countries (still including the UK), 16 have populations of less than 10 million people.[10] The European Union and several of its Member States are challenged strongly, economically, politically and in terms of internal cohesion. Nonetheless, it seems that many of these rather small states still consider it beneficial to be part of a both transnational and in some respects supranational union.

China is one of the world's biggest countries and one of the world's oldest civilisations. It is a country with a recent record of high economic growth and a so-called 'socialist market economy'. In a world of asymmetry and disparity in terms of populations, economic growth and history, a country like China will have a significant impact on the development of transnational norms. Global geopolitical – and thus arguably normative power is shifting, as exemplified in the Chinese decision to remain in the Paris Accord, which the United States has left under President Trump.[11] The 2018 changes to the Chinese constitution cancelled the earlier time limits on the office of the president.[12] This will allow the present president, Xi Jinping (who is also leader of the Communist Party and of the military – positions without time limitations), to continue in power after 2023. This is a development in line with autocratic developments and practices in the major states of the world such as Russia, the Philippines, Turkey and Brazil. Similarly, the US president, Donald Trump, is a case of an elected erratic leader under whom the US legal landscape is likely also to change. Thus, a large part of the bigger countries of the world at present seem to favour 'strong man' regimes, being either semi-democratic or autocratic. China's relationships to international law is reluctant.[13] The impact of that remains to be seen.

The Chinese author Yu Hua writes in his essay 'Disparity' about a Chinese saying, which goes, 'The weak fear the strong … the strong fear the violent, and the violent fear the reckless'.[14] Big countries may lead or influence normative processes

9 See United Nations (n. 6).

10 See Eurostat, 'Demographic Balance, 2016' https://ec.europa.eu/eurostat/statistics-explained/index.php?title=File:Demographic_balance,_2016_(thousands).png accessed 19 September 2018. Countries below 10 million by year of accession and as of 1 January 2017: Luxembourg, Denmark, Ireland, Austria, Finland, Sweden, Cyprus, Estonia, Hungary, Latvia, Lithuania, Malta, Slovakia, Slovenia, Bulgaria, Croatia.

11 See McCoy (n. 8), see also Uffe Østergaard, 'Kina vinder' *Weekendavisen* (Copenhagen, 10 March 2017).

12 See www.bbc.com/news/world-asia-china-43361276/ accessed 10 August 2018.

13 See The South China Sea Ruling: China's International Law Dilemma, https://thediplomat.com/2016/07/the-south-china-sea-ruling-chinas-international-law-dilemma/ last accessed 10 September 2018.

14 Yu Hua, *China in Ten Words* (Anchor Books 2012).

globally by way of size and power – be it military, political, economic or cultural in a very broad sense. Small – or very small – countries and communities may probably lead by (good or bad?) example, by being rich and/or providing different attractive models. These may be models which benefit bigger parts of the small populations in terms of politics and economy, sustainable living conditions, welfare, educational and health models, high trust and low corruption, modernised intergenerational and gender relations, which make these models workable. The small Nordic states have managed to deliver such examples for the last half century. Other very rich small countries like Singapore, Qatar and Macao benefit from resources, strategic positions and specific economic structures. Whether this will continue remains to be seen. Other models offering 'protection of wealth', tax havens and possibilities of luxury consumption of different kinds may be more attractive to the wealthy elites of the world.[15] Recently, the world has witnessed the relationship between North Korea and the United States, which in my view may be a case of the strong fearing (but perhaps also using) the violent and the reckless.

Harmony and solidarity as common endeavours?

In a world of blatant asymmetry in terms of size between (state) actors, it is perhaps not surprising to witness a development of a discourse on transnationalism and transnational law, which involves big actors beyond and besides states. The political, economic and legal landscape during the last generation has not only been characterised by asymmetry *between nations*. It has also witnessed increased economic inequality *between citizens* within and beyond nations across the world. This has happened during a process where legal regimes have supported market reforms and market (de)regulation *de facto* undermining equality as political value and economic practice. In 1980, the richest 1% of the population in the United States and Western Europe owned 10% of the wealth in their countries. Today they own 12% in Western Europe and 20% in the United States, writes Anna Libak, referring to the *World Inequality Report 2018*.[16] *The World Inequality Report 2018* shows

> that income inequality has increased in nearly all world regions in recent decades, but at different speeds. The fact that inequality levels are so different among countries, even when countries share similar levels of development, highlights the important roles that national policies and institutions play in shaping inequality.[17]

15 See Rebecca Adler-Nissen & Ulrik Pram Gad (eds), *European Integration and Postcolonial Sovereignty Games. The EU Overseas Countries and Territories* (Routledge 2013) and my review Hanne Petersen, 'Nye politiske relationer i Europa og verdenssamfundet' [New political relations in Europe and World Society] (2013) 16(4) *Politik* 62.

16 Libak (n. 3) 94.

17 Facundo Alvaredo, Lucas Chancel, Thomas Piketty, Emmanuel Saez and Gabriel Zucman (eds), 'World Inequality Report' (2018) https://wir2018.wid.world/ accessed 4 July 2018.

The period of combined globalisation and neoliberalism has led to an increased economic inequality inside mega-nations such as China, as well as in transnational communities such as the European Union, even if those less well-off have also experienced growth. The combined developments of increased market dependency of (sm/all) nations and increased inequality amongst citizens (often) in large nations and communities are probably some of the reasons for the introduction of trans/intercontinental discourses on harmony and solidarity in China and Europe.

Economic growth has been used to secure legitimacy both in the one-party state of China and in the multi-state community of the EU. However, since the Asian economic crisis in 1997–1998 and the Western economic crisis in 2007–2009, this strategy is no longer sufficiently convincing. Both these parts of the world have thus returned to ideas and perhaps even ideologies of cohesion which belong to earlier times. China has been going back to historical morality older than Christianity. In the case of Europe, we also see increased focus on religion in the *fin de siècle* period – particularly on Islam, but in the case of former Eastern European countries also on almost fundamentalist forms of Christianity (Catholicism in Poland and the Orthodox Church in Russia), which all are in favour of conservative developments, including 'conservative jurisprudence'[18] and gender conservatism.[19]

In the beginning of the 21st century, former Chinese President Hu Jintao (2002–2012) reintroduced the concept of harmony as part of a Neo-Confucian value orientation aiming at securing stability in a country which had experienced unprecedented growth alongside growing social inequality and confusion. Solidarity was a historical concept reintroduced by sociologist Durkheim (1858–1917) in his book on the division of labour from 1893 to describe forces of societal cohesion (and anomie) in times of major changes.[20] In the beginning of the 21st century, several EU documents (the EU Charter on Fundamental Rights from 2000 – slightly revised in 2012 – and the Lisbon Treaty from 2009) again made use of the concept of solidarity during a period of considerable expansion of the number of EU Member States. Individuals and members of the European Union clearly foresaw that social, political and economic disparities were going to widen.[21]

18 Professor Elena Zdravomyskova (St. Petersburg) used the term 'conservative jurisprudence' in her keynote address to the Swedish Sociology Conference held in Lund 7–9 March 2018. The title of her address was 'The Conservative Turn and Politicization of Gender in the Russian Context Today'.

19 See Eszter Kováts & Maari Põim (eds), *Gender as Symbolic Glue. The Position and Role of Conservative and Far Right Parties in the Anti-Gender Mobilizations in Europe* (FEPS – Foundation for European Progressive Studies 2015). The countries treated in the report are France, Germany, Hungary, Poland and Slovakia.

20 Emile Durkheim, *Om den sociale arbejdsdeling* (First published 1893, Hans Reitzels Forlag 2000).

21 See especially the articles in Krzysztof Michalski (ed.), *What Holds Europe Together?* (Central European University Press 2006).

It is unclear whether this introduction of top-down normative arguments of *harmony* and *solidarity* will transform into bottom-up national or transnational expressions and practices. Harmony is historically a very strong value in Chinese society both within the family as 'filial piety' and towards the head of state or emperor. However, the economic developments, the one child policy and the considerable migration from the countryside to an ever-more urbanised China to a certain extent have undermined the conditions of harmony. This has meant, for example, an introduction of a number of laws in China, which have underlined the moral, practical and economic obligations of (grown up) children towards their elderly parents.[22] The American essayist Evan Osnos has described several of these examples of 'moral collapse' in his book *Age of Ambition: Chasing Fortune, Truth, and Faith in the New China*.[23]

Practices of solidarity were particularly influential in Europe during the industrial era, as were legal expressions of solidarity – increasingly conveyed through welfare policies and legislation. Ironically, in 1980 the Polish workers' movement took the name *Solidarnosc*. In the former Eastern Bloc, 'solidarity' was considered a top-down activity mainly used in international relations and hardly considered legitimate in a local context. 'Under communism, solidarity was a subject of black humour rather than of scholarship. An altruistic interpretation of transnational solidarity could not be accepted under the conditions of "forced solidarity", to use a euphemism for dictatorship and military occupation.'[24] Solidarity was hardly valued amongst the population in Western Europe in the neo-liberal late 20th century either. The somewhat similar 21st century conditions of growth (and decline), instability and insecurity have in China led to the propagation of harmony and in the EU to the propagation and inclusion of claims of solidarity in several major legal documents, such as the Lisbon Treaty (2009) and the European Charter (2000/2012). In this respect, it is interesting to note the resurgence of a discourse on solidarity in transnational relations by religious actors, not least in relation to the destiny of refugees and migrants entering first Italy or Greece and later other EU countries after the so-called 'refugee crisis'.[25]

On March 24, 2017, Pope Francis spoke of *peace and harmony* but especially *solidarity* in his speech to 'the European Union leaders' in Rome on the occasion of the 60th anniversary of the signing of the 'Rome Treaty' establishing the European Economic Community and the European Atomic Energy Community.

22 Simona Novaretti, sinologist and law professor at the University of Torino, highlighted this development in a joint presentation *In Between – Gender, Solidarity and Legality?* we gave on 4 May 2017 in Torino, at an event on 'Genere, diritto e solidarietà' organised by Centro Interdisciplinare di Richerche e Studi delle Donne e di Genere.

23 Evan Osnos, *Age of Ambition: Chasing Fortune, Truth, and Faith in the New China* (Farrar, Straus and Giroux 2014).

24 See Janos Matyas, 'Between Resentment and Indifference. Narratives of Solidarity in the Enlarging Union' in Krzysztof Michalski (ed.), *What Holds Europe Together?* (Central European University Press 2006) 54.

25 See Steinar Stjernø, *Solidarity in Europe. The History of an Idea* (Cambridge University Press 2005).

He mentioned that the Treaty could have remained dead letter, and that they needed to take on spirit and life. The first element of this vitality 'must be solidarity', a spirit, which according to the Pope remains 'as necessary as ever today, in the face of centrifugal impulses and the temptation to reduce the founding ideals of the Union to productive, economic and financial needs. Solidarity gives rise to openness to others.'[26]

Later he continued:

> Europe finds new hope in solidarity, which is also the most effective antidote to modern forms of populism. Solidarity entails the awareness of being part of a single body, while at the same time involving a capacity on the part of each member to "sympathize" with others and with the whole. When one suffers, all suffer … For solidarity is no mere ideal; it is expressed in concrete actions and steps that draw us closer to our neighbours, in whatever situation they find themselves. Forms of populism are instead the fruit of an egotism that hems people in and prevents them from overcoming and 'looking beyond' their own narrow vision.

Pope Francis further said:

> [T]oday's prosperity seems to have clipped the continent's wings and lowered its gaze. Europe has a patrimony of ideals and spiritual values unique in the world, one that deserves to be proposed once more with passion and renewed vigour, for it is the best antidote against the vacuum of values of our time, which provides a fertile terrain for every form of extremism. These are the ideals that shaped Europe, that "Peninsula of Asia" which stretches from the Urals to the Atlantic.[27]

Solidarity is not considered a particularly Christian value – rather it has its origin in Roman law, as already mentioned by Emile Durkheim.[28] It is also not necessarily a Western value. It has been propagated more or less convincingly by socialist and communist regimes around the world. In this context, it is noteworthy that the head of the Vatican state and the transnational Catholic Church underlines its importance in view of populism in the world. A populism, which seems to be a way to handle fear – of globalism amongst others – by withdrawing back into the confines of 'the nation'. Harmony is also not only a Chinese value or a national value. As solidarity, it has the potential to move beyond the nation – but need not do so.

26 Pope Francis, 'Pope Francis' Full Speech to the European Union leaders' (24 March 2017) www.romereports.com/en/2017/03/24/pope-francis-full-speech-to-the-european-union-leaders/accessed 28 March 2019

27 Ibid.

28 Durkheim (n. 21).

Populism

The insecurity caused by globalisation has called harmony, solidarity *and* populism to the fore at mostly national levels. However, populism also has transnational expressions – populist parties are found in almost all European and EU countries. In Europe, populism has become an important normative force, which makes an understanding and implementation of (other forms of) solidarity across differences and nations difficult. The legitimacy of populist policies is growing as seen in the present developments in Sweden and Germany, where populist parties are gaining more influence.

According to Jan Werner Müller, populism has as its main characteristic anti-pluralism.[29] The Danish specialist in ancient Greek history and society, Mogens Herman Hansen, claims that modern populism is not an ideology. It exists both in autocracies such as Putin's Russia and Erdogan's Turkey, where it has become a popular movement, which legitimises the rulers.[30] According to Herman Hansen, populism and populists seek to create bigger economic and social equality, to uphold the nation state and national sovereignty as well as to fight corruption. He does not mention China, where nationalism, anti-corruption and anti-poverty campaigns clearly legitimise the politics of Xi Jinping. Herman Hansen mentions that populism is found in both the right and the left part of the political landscape. It is more widespread among men than among women, more among older than younger parts of the populations, more amongst the less educated and more in the private sector than in the public sector, as well as more in the middle class, working class and underclass than amongst the upper class and upper middle class. More supporters of populism live in the countryside and in provincial towns.[31] In his discussion about President Trump as an expression of populism, Herman Hansen draws attention to a development, where *suffrage* has become democratised, while *eligibility* has not.[32]

Anna Libak, a Danish journalist specialised in Russia and foreign affairs, understands the rise of populism and its concomitant wish for change as a result of an emerging new world order, where the Western world has lost its dominant position. The dominant question is no longer how the West can create peace and freedom in the rest of the world, but how it can avoid that the rest of the world creates chaos and unrest in a broad sense in 'our' part of the world.[33] According to her, this contributes to anti-globalisation, which she considers the characteristic of populism. Populism is a method for political self-performance, which does not indicate anything about whether the person using this method is a democrat or not. She suggests that one should distinguish between democrats, semi-autocrats

29 Jan-Werner Müller, *Hvad er populisme? Et essay* (Informations Forlag 2016).
30 Mogens Herman Hansen, *Hvordan forvrænger populismen demokratiet?* (Informations Forlag 2017).
31 Ibid 21.
32 Ibid 50.
33 Libak (n. 3) 8 and 9.

and autocrats using populism.[34] *Victimhood* is for her the core of populism. Right and left wing politics, mostly called identity politics in left wing politics and populism in right wing politics, share a culture of victimhood.[35] Libak suggests an 'open and unprejudiced discussion about how globalization can be controlled', in order that 'our countries' can continue to exist 'as solid democracies based on the rule of law [retsstat] and created for the benefit of citizens and not for the market'.[36] She considers it a necessity to revise international conventions, which nation states no longer respect or follow. Conventions, which inculcate false hopes (of asylum), must be reformed.[37] The consequence of this approach seems to be that international law should be reformed (and protection of asylum seekers reduced) in order to secure the idea that Western states are governed by the 'rule of law'. Her suggestion seems to indicate that saving the 'rule of law' is more important than saving people. This is a suggestion that hardly looks beyond the 'narrow vision' mentioned by Pope Francis.

Immigration from poorer regions *within* China and from poorer third countries – mainly in the Middle East and Africa – to the European Union (and the United States) is perceived as challenging both harmony, stability and solidarity. Insular economic policies, import restrictions and market policies, anti-corruption policies and law, local or transnational, do not seem to be instruments sufficiently suitable to meet today's global challenges, inequalities and insecurities. Levelling down protections of 'the other' perhaps produces and secures a form of insular 'solidarity' and 'harmony', but does not necessarily include transnational hopes and visions.

Propaganda

In the modern history of the West, law has been understood as a major, legitimate normative tool. That was not always the case. Propaganda – from Latin 'propagare' – literally means, 'that which ought to be spread'. In 1622 (at the beginning of the Thirty Years' War), Pope Gregory XV established the *Congregatio de Propaganda Fide*, an institution and clerical order to spread Catholicism as well as analyse the spread in non-Catholic areas. As already mentioned, the Catholic Church is a transnational institution besides being a state and a member of the UN. This is not the case for any other of the world religions, perhaps because they are not organised along the same centralised and hierarchical lines. The Catholic Church was a creator of transnational law in Europe in the form of Canon law until the split of the Christian churches after the Reformation in 1517. Spreading Christian – and legal – ideas to the world had gone along with colonisation, the printing press and later the Reformation. Spain lost the Thirty Years' War – and

34 Ibid 19.
35 Ibid 30ff.
36 Ibid 145.
37 Ibid 155.

the Catholic Church, which had supported this empire, was weakened. However, the Catholic Church continues to be a normative and influential institution in Europe and in the world.

The instrument of propaganda – as a means to spreading ideas – has clearly lived on. Absolutist kings and emperors used newspapers and pamphlets for centuries after the Gutenberg Revolution. Nazism and fascism made wide use of propaganda in the technological forms dominant in the first part of the 20th century – film and radio were used extensively. Propaganda has been widely used by authoritarian regimes in Europe, the Soviet Union and in a Chinese political context. Soviet and Chinese propaganda used large-scale posters and images, which is still the case in China. Today, propaganda is often understood as a means of one-way, top-down communication of limited legitimacy. Present 'political propaganda' is making use of contemporary social media, and in the case of the US president, especially Twitter, where the short messages may bear resemblances to the slogans of Soviet and Chinese earlier propaganda.

'Commercial propaganda' or advertisements have had a similar goal of spreading ideas – however, mostly about the benefits of certain goods in a market-dominated society. Steven Heller writes that

> The design and marketing methods used to inculcate doctrine and guarantee consumption are fundamentally similar. And branding is not just smoke and mirrors; the results are often quantifiable because public awareness and brand loyalty can be measured by sales – or votes.[38]

The election of Trump as president of the United States has given rise to a flood of discussions about 'fake news' with their intention to influence public discourse normatively. Hendricks and Vestergaard claim that technological progress is not necessarily progress for humanity, but is not automatically a drawback either. In the information age, attention is a scarce resource and hard to access. Harvesting attention may give rise to both misinformation, political bubbles, populism and post-factual democracy.[39] In the information age, it is possible without censorship or transgression of rights of free speech to achieve an effect similar to propaganda by flooding citizens, voters and the press with misinformation. 'The economy and the market for media products, which follows the internet, give political and ideological interests favourable propaganda conditions. Strong economic incentives to produce and spread twisted stories, loose rumours and fake news are part of the whole package'.[40]

Trump's one-way, top-down Twitter policy is clearly both a transnational source of (mis)information about American domestic and foreign policy and

38 Alexander Rich Henningsen, 'Kompromisets æstetik' (Atlas Magasin 9 May 2018) http://atlasmag.dk/samfund/kompromisets-%C3%A6stetik accessed 2 July 2015.

39 Vincent F. Hendricks and Mads Vestergaard, *Fake News. Når virkeligheden taber* (Gyldendal 2017) 8 and 9.

40 Ibid 18–19.

intentions and a (propaganda) tool for attention harvesting. International legal conventions and obligations are cancelled on Twitter, speeding up the spread of messages and ideas across the globe through brief communications. International law, as we thought we knew it, is transformed. The digital era clearly makes it easier to spread ideas, but perhaps more difficult to make them broadly trustworthy. What will be the consequences of this for Western legal culture? There are many countries in the world where popular trust in law and legal systems and culture is very limited. Will people in the West also stop trusting and respecting existing legal norms more broadly?

The United States has been propagating the American Dream in the 20th century, and the Chinese are now trying to propagate a Chinese Dream. The EU and its Member States seem to fear their own attraction to third country nationals and refugees and find it difficult to demonstrate solidarity in practice.

Fiction in a digital era

Films have long been co-produced transnationally due to the high production costs.[41] According to commentators, films shown at the Cannes Film Festival in 2017 focused on dysfunctional families, such as Michael Haneke's *Happy End* – with the European migration challenge as its dystopian backdrop and a transnational UK-French relationship and marriage as part of the centre. To what extent is 'law as we knew it' becoming dysfunctional in a transnational and digital era?

The Gothenburg Film Festival in 2018 had a special section 'Electric Shadows of China' showing Chinese documentaries and feature films. The ones I saw demonstrated love; broken love and broken societies (Spring in a Small Town); left-behind children in villages, where parents have left as workers for the city; claustrophobic lives of hypocritical middle class couples; highly competitive life styles of contemporary Chinese actors making them imitate practices of ostracism from the Cultural Revolution; interviews with and about Shanghai residents – and perhaps even dissidents – in a film made for the Shanghai Expo in 2010.

Before the fall of the Berlin Wall, literature was known to play an important role for life and living in Eastern Europe and the Soviet Union. The decline of the West may have led to a growing interest in fiction as tools to describe our societies and make us understand what is happening around us. Elizabeth Long 'finds reading for club members to be an active and social pursuit, a crucial way for women to reflect creatively on the meaning of their lives and their place in the social order'.[42] For the Danish author of fiction, Inge Eriksen, rereading the classics and writing her own three-volume novel about the momentous changes

41 Hanne Petersen, 'The Lion King and the Lady and the Unicorn: Jurisprudential Considerations on Visual Normativity' in Alberto Febbrajo, David Nelken & Vittorio Olgiati (eds), *Social Processes and Patterns of Legal Control. European Yearbook in the Sociology of Law* (Giuffrè Publisher 2001).

42 Elisabeth Long, *Women and the Uses of Reading in Everyday Life* (University of Chicago Press 2003).

in Europe and the world after 1989 was a way of dealing with transitions and transformations of values and norms.[43]

A number of major novels all deal with individual and/or societal collapse or dramatic changes in the 19th–21st centuries. Marcel Proust (1871–1922) describes the fall of the aristocracy in his seven volumes *In Search of Lost Time*. Thomas Mann (1875–1955) describes the fall of an upper class bourgeois family in *Buddenbrooks*. Robert Musil (1880–1942) wrote about the collapse of the Austro-Hungarian Double Monarchy in his monstrous monumental novel *The Man without Qualities*. James Joyce (1882–1941) wrote his avant-garde challenging paraphrase of Greek mythology, *Ulysses*.

In the 21st century, Karl Ove Knausgård (1968–) published his mammoth six-volume 'novel' or 'autofiction' that he describes as 'reality literature' with the provocative title *My Struggle*, paraphrasing Hitler's 'Mein Kampf'.

Grasping and understanding a breakdown of political institutions, social structures and legal cultures can be painful, as we have witnessed during the period after 1989.[44] Making sense of major transitions and understanding the concomitant individual transitions are a challenge. The difficulties in describing the 'genre' of Knausgård's hyper detailed 'auto-narrative' may perhaps resemble the difficulties in making sense of the 'crossing over' or 'passing through' from national to trans-national legal culture or a genre beyond that. It is not easy to pin down what 'transnational law' is or might be.

A great example of the role of fiction in shaping transnational norms can be found in the novels of criminal law professor, He Jiahong. Jiahong (1953–) has written crime fiction besides writing 'ordinary' law books. He says in an interview that everyone knows that this type of academic literature becomes obsolete after a few years. 'Conversely, my novels enjoy a long shelf life'.[45]

Jiahong's novel demonstrates a difference in the trust in law in different legal cultures, which also needs to be taken into consideration when discussing transnational law.

In his novel *Hanging Devils*, the protagonist describes law in the following way:

> "The law?" Xiao Xiong cut in, and let loose a roar of incredulous laughter. "The law, it sounds so great, doesn't it?" he shouted. "It was the cloak of justice, but it's always double-dealing. To the ordinary people it behaves like

43 Inge Eriksen, *Sommerfuglens vinge. Vol. 1, Tørvegraverne* (Gyldendal 1997) [The Wing of the Butterfly. Vol. 1, The Peat Diggers]; Inge Eriksen, *Sommerfuglens vinge. Vol. 2, De rumænske bøfler* (Gyldendal 1999) [The Wing of the Butterfly. Vol. 2, The Romanian Buffalos]; Inge Eriksen, *Sommerfuglens vinge. Vol. 3, Vinterhaven* (Gyldendal 2001) [The Wing of the Butterfly. Vol. 3, The Winter Garden].

44 See also Kishore Mahbubane, *Has the West Lost It? A Provocation* (Penguin 2018).

45 Elisa Nesossi, He Jiahong 何家弘, 'Working Between Law and Literature' www.thechinastory.org/2012/09/he-jiahong-%E4%BD%95%E5%AE%B6%E5%BC%98-working-between-law-and-literature/ last accessed 10 September 2018).

> a stern grandfather, but when it comes to dealing with the ones who make the rules, the Party officials, it turns into a cowardly son of a bitch. And the more important the official, the more insignificant the law becomes. In this world, if you have power, then you are the law…" … "You can take your law and feed it to the dogs. But I tell you", he added, wagging his finger, "even the dogs wouldn't want to eat it".[46]

Literature – be it auto-fiction, science-fiction or other (hybrid) types of fiction – has not (yet?) become obsolete in our digital era, but some of its stories are being transplanted into other types of media. Visuality is becoming ever more important – also for law and transnational law. Film has been the visual expression par excellence of the 20th century, which positivist law dominated. In the digital era, both of these Western dominated, normative expressions are probably challenged, perhaps leading to more competition between normative actors and expressions.[47]

Conclusion

There is a process of interaction and 'cross-over' going on in many fields – in literature, between literature and science, beyond national and continental understandings of values, moralities and 'law'. We need to understand other normative expressions beyond the written – be they visual, oral, factual or customary – both in local and personal relations and beyond.

Maybe we should be more pragmatic – as the Chinese seem to be – and less concerned with strict conceptual approaches – as Europeans tend sometimes to be. How should we understand transitions in diverse and fluid fields – including what some call 'law'? Religious norms have lost – and regained – power, (moving and commercialised) images appeal beyond linguistic borders, as do (some) fashions.

Do we need less narrow visions of cooperation across borders, countries and cultures? Doesn't the digital age with all its flaws offer us challenges and opportunities we have not experienced before?

46 He Jiahong, *Hanging Devils. Hong Jun Investigates* (Viking 2010) 242–243.
47 Petersen (n. 42) 173.

Part II

Developing regulatory legitimacy under transnationalisation

7 Development of transnational contract law?

Kateřina Mitkidis

Introduction

National borders have been constructed for centuries with great difficulty and resulting in high costs in resources and lives.[1] Now, while still in place, national borders are to a great extent losing their significance both in the physical and jurisdictional sense. This does not necessarily mean that the world is getting more interconnected or unified. In fact, we experience two opposing tendencies of unification and fragmentation.[2] These tendencies appear in various areas, including culture, politics, economics and law. This chapter concerns itself with the unification tendencies in law, namely in the area of contract law.

Predictable legal framework is a precondition for efficient international commerce.[3] That is why the international community has been striving to determine such a framework. Arguably, the most successful effort so far has been the adoption of the United Nations Convention on Contracts for the International Sale of Goods of 1980 (CISG). The CISG, however, suffers from the lack of an international dispute resolution body and therefore also the lack of unified application and interpretation. Such fragmented and national-based adjudication of the international convention questions its actual contribution to the establishment of a truly international regime for commercial contracting and, thus, to legal

1 H. Patrick Glenn, 'Comparative Law and Legal Practice: On Removing the Borders' (2001) 75 *Tulane Law Review* 977, 978 (referring to Michael Biggs, 'Putting the State on the Map: Cartography, Territory, and European State Formation' (1999) 41 *Comparative Studies in Society and History* 374, 377).

2 See also Gralf-Peter Calliess, 'Making of Transnational Contract Law' (2007) 14 *Indiana Journal of Global Legal Studies* 469, 473–476 (noting the tension between unification and fragmentation in respect to the development of commercial law in the 19th century: 'domestic legal unity came paradoxically at the price of external legal divergence').

3 Ralph Amissah, 'The Autonomous Contract – Reflecting the Borderless Electronic-commercial Environment in Contracting', Lex Mercatoria, https://www.jus.uio.no/lm/the.autonomous.contract.07.10.1997.amissah/doc.html accessed 6 November 2018.

certainty for commercial actors.[4] Similar criticism has also been expressed in relation to soft law efforts in the international commercial area, all leading to a disillusion over the efforts for unification of private law at the international level.[5]

This chapter deals with an understudied way of unification of contract law on the global level: the practice of reusing standard (boilerplate) contractual provisions regardless of the governing law. A US-originated boilerplate provision of an 'Entire Agreement' clause (EA clause) used in contracts governed by Danish law will be taken as an example to demonstrate this practice.[6] The aim is not to conduct a comparative analysis between the effects of EA clauses in the two jurisdictions,[7] but to engage into a more theoretical discussion on the topic from a comparative law perspective, using theories of legal transplants, legal convergence and transnational law. The focus is then on private actors (companies) as 'legislators' creating a legal framework that is considered binding by the business community and to which the business community adapts its behaviour, and on the legitimacy of this framework. Such a legal framework – transnational contract law – develops beyond nation states, largely independently both from national and international contract law.[8]

The questions asked in this chapter are: How and to what extent does the practice of reusing common law contractual standards and provisions impact on the development of national law? Does the practice create a legitimate source of law applicable beyond bilateral contractual relations, allowing us to predict the results of any future disputes? And more generally, what is the relationship between national and transnational contract law and practice?

The chapter proceeds as follows. It first introduces the phenomenon of boilerplate contractual provisions, specifically the EA clause, and the practice of using such provisions in contracts governed by Danish law. Then the chapter employs two comparative law theories in an effort to describe and explain the phenomenon of using common law-originated contractual clauses in Danish contracts; specifically, it discusses (i) whether we can consider EA clauses to be legal transplants in the Danish setting, meaning that they become a part of the Danish legal system and have a role to play there, and (ii) considering the theory of legal convergence, whether we experience US and Danish contract law getting closer to each other and becoming more similar. This section closes with a discussion of contracts and contract law under transnationalisation, preparing ground for the next section

4 Yet, an argument could be put forward that CISG with its reliance on the application and interpretation by national courts creates a transnational regime when national courts are expected to consult foreign court decisions when adjudicating a CISG dispute. See also contribution of Thomas Neumann in this volume.

5 Calliess (n. 2) 474.

6 The term 'entire agreement clause' is used primarily in the European context while in the American context the terms 'merger clause' and 'integration clause' are more widely used.

7 Such comparative analysis can be found in Kateřina Peterkova Mitkidis and Thomas Neumann, 'Entire Agreement Clauses: Convergence Between US and Danish Contract Law?' (2017) *Nordic Journal of Commercial Law* 182.

8 Calliess (n. 2) 472.

focused on the issue of legitimacy of contract law rules evolving from transnational practice. Finally, the chapter concludes with some general observations.

Introduction to EA clauses

A typical Entire Agreement (EA) clause may read as follows: 'This Agreement constitutes the entire Agreement between the parties pertaining to the subject matter contained herein and supersedes all prior agreements, representations and understandings of the parties'.[9] An EA clause is a typical boilerplate provision that has origins in common law jurisdictions.[10] Boilerplate provisions are contractual provisions often subsumed under the headline 'Final provisions' or similar, towards the end of (commercial) contracts. They are rarely negotiated and often used unchanged in different types of contracts and regardless of jurisdiction. Boilerplate provisions are not generally perceived as 'deal breakers' and are in fact often considered to be the best practice regarding the allocation of risks in respect of contract interpretation and application.[11]

Danish business, and contract drafting, are influenced by the globalised economy. English has become the common language not only of international commercial contracts, but many times also of domestic ones.[12] The language is then connected with the use of common law contract models, originating in the UK and the United States.[13] When common law contract models are used in civil law jurisdictions, it might cause some misunderstandings and even disputes. Common law contracts are traditionally much longer as they aim to become self-sufficient[14] in order to secure predictability in the transaction,[15] particularly in

9 Example taken from *Corbin on Contracts* (n. 17) para. 25.8.

10 For origins of EA clauses in the USA, see Richard A. Lord, *Williston on Contracts* (4th edn, Thomson Reuters 1990) § 33.23.

11 Marcel Fontaine and Filip De Ly, *Drafting International Contracts: An Analysis of Contract Clauses* (2nd edn, Martinus Nijhoff 2009) 105.

12 In interviews on the use of EA clauses by Danish companies conducted by the author, several interviewees stated that they prefer to have all contracts drafted in English, also those concluded with Danish partners, as the same templates can be used. Most of the interviewees stated that they keep only few local and 'smaller' contracts in Danish. The interviews are reported in Kateřina Mitkidis, 'The Use of Entire Agreement Clauses in Contracts Governed by Danish Law' (2017) *Erhvervsjuridisk Tidsskrift* 198.

13 Giuditta Cordero-Moss, 'International Contracts Between Common Law and Civil Law: Is Non-State Law to Be Preferred? The Difficulty of Interpreting Legal Standards Such as Good Faith' (2007) 7 *Global Jurist* 1, 1.

14 Giuditta Cordero-Moss, 'Conclusion: The Self-sufficient Contract, Uniformly Interpreted on the Basis of its Own Terms: An Illusion, but Not Fully Useless' in Giuditta Cordero-Moss (ed.), *Boilerplate Clauses, International Commercial Contracts and the Applicable Law* (Cambridge University Press 2011) 344.

15 Tomas Lindholm in Mads Bryde Andersen and Jonas Christoffersen (eds), *Forhandlingene ved Det 38. Nordiske Juristmøde i København, 21–23. August 2008*, vol. 2 (2008), 616, http://nordiskjurist.org/meetings/fremmede-retsbegreber-i-nordisk-kontraktsret/ accessed 28 March 2019.

relation to the outcome of any eventual dispute. In contrast to civil law countries where predictability is secured by codification of law accompanied with reliance on parties' mutual trust and protection of their legitimate expectations (typical for a civil law subfamily of Scandinavian jurisdictions), in common law countries – based rather on the system of precedents than codification – predictability has been secured by the *parol evidence* rule.[16] The *parol evidence* rule prevents a party to a written contract from presenting extrinsic evidence in a dispute that contradicts or alters the written contract, if that appears to be fully integrated, meaning that it incorporates all prior or contemporaneous agreements on the subject matter between the parties.[17] The *parol evidence* rule is then supplemented by the formalistic style of contract interpretation.[18]

It is thus typical for parties from common law jurisdictions to cover as many details as possible in their contracts in order to limit the possibility of going beyond the four corners of the contract when determining its content (though extrinsic evidence can still be used to clarify any ambiguities). An EA clause serves to express the intention to conclude a completely integrated contract and to reinforce the *parol evidence* rule.

The *parol evidence* rule and EA clauses are considered questions of substantive law in common law jurisdictions.[19] But to Danish lawyers, they may seem to be rather procedural law issues as they deal with the limitation of what can be furnished as proof in a proceeding. Belonging to the Nordic legal subfamily of civil law, the Danish legal system uses the subjective contract interpretation style, looking first for the intention of the parties at the time of the contract's execution.[20] Logically, the intention is proven predominantly by the text of the contract.[21] However, based on the principle of free admissibility of evidence, any kind of communication exchanged between the parties prior to the contract execution (including letters of intent, negotiation documents, statements and agreements) may be supplied by the parties to document that the actual agreement between the parties differs from the contractual text.[22] Inclusion of an EA clause

16 It is important to note here that although we experience the shift from precedent-based law-making to written codification in common law jurisdictions, the *parol evidence* rule remains an important rule in the major common law orders.

17 *Williston on Contracts* (n. 10) para. 33.1; Arthur Linton Corbin, Joseph M. Perillo and John E. Murray, *Corbin on Contracts* (Lexis Nexis, Matthew Bender 2015; Release No. 15S2), chapter 5; UCC § 2-202 (amended 2002); Restatement (Second) of Contracts § 213 (1981).

18 Mark L. Movsesian, 'Formalism in American Contract Law: Classical and Contemporary' (2012) 12 *Ius Gentium* 115; cf. Larry A. DiMatteo, 'False Dichotomies in Commercial Contract Interpretation' (2012) 11 *Journal of International Trade Law and Policy* 27.

19 *Williston on Contracts* (n. 10) para. 33.1

20 Peter Møgelvang-Hansen, 'Contracts and Sales in Denmark' in Børge Dahl et al., *Danish Law in a European Perspective* (2nd edn, Karnov 2002) 254.

21 Nis Jul Clausen et al., *Dansk Privatret* (19th ed., Jurist- og Økonomforbundets Forlag 2016) 140.

22 Lovbekendtgørelse af 13.10.2016 nr. 1257 Retsplejeloven § 344.

into a contract challenges the free admissibility of extrinsic evidence and directs the judges towards objective and formalistic contract interpretation. As such, EA clauses are foreign to the Danish legal system.

Despite the contradictory approaches to contract interpretation, Danish firms increasingly often use a common law contract drafting style and engage in execution of lengthy contracts including EA clauses in contradiction to their legal tradition and thinking. They do so under the pressure of transnationalisation. If they want to conclude contracts with international partners, they need to adjust to the current contracting practice, whose development is led by large multinational companies, often based in common law, in English speaking countries.[23] In an interview-based study conducted with representatives of Danish industry, judiciary and legal profession, it has been found that EA clauses are used in the majority of contracts concluded by Danish companies, regardless of the governing law of the contract.[24] In line with the research questions raised in this chapter, we may ask: whether and to what extent does the practice influence the development of national contract law; whether the practice amounts to the creation of a transnational norm; and how can we theoretically frame the process we experience in order to predict future development and outcomes of possible legal disputes.

Comparative law

When studying interactions between different legal orders, a scholar may turn to comparative law theories and methods to explain the similarities and differences between the legal orders as well as the core of the interaction. Comparative law has dominantly engaged with macro and micro comparison of state-made law, from the 19th century this being mainly positive law.[25] However, as law in general is responding to the transnationalisation processes, so is comparative law as a legal discipline. Michaels describes three major changes to law under transnationalisation influencing comparative legal endeavours: the rise of non-state actors ('beyond the state'), the change in the sources of law ('beyond positive law') and the necessity to consult other disciplines, such as sociology or anthropology, to understand and evaluate law ('beyond legal science').[26] Despite the changing object of study, comparative law theories provide a helpful conceptual

23 Dorthe Plechinger, 'Der skal være en udløbsdato på sådan en post' (based on an interview with Søren Jenstrup) (2015) *Advokaten* 21.

24 The empirical study is described and its results reported in Mitkidis (n. 12).

25 Ralf Michaels, 'Transnationalizing Comparative Law' (2012) 23 *Maastricht Journal of European and Comparative Law* 352, 354. See also William Twining, 'Globalisation and Comparative Law' in Esin Örücü and David Nelken, *Comparative Law: A Handbook* (Hart Publishing 2007) 77 ('during the 20th century and before, Western academic legal culture has tended to be state-oriented, secular, positivist, "top-down", North-centric, unempirical, and universalist in respect to morals').

26 Michaels (n. 25).

background and methodological 'toolkit' to study law under transnationalisation.[27] From the large array of comparative law methods and theories, the legal transplant and the legal convergence theories seem particularly apt to analyse the practice of reusing boilerplate provisions, including EA clauses, in commercial contracts and the effect of this practice on the national legal orders.

Legal transplants

The legal transplant theory is used to study how a legal order or parts of it are copied by or imposed on another jurisdiction in order to fill in regulatory gaps or replace existing norms.[28] Traditionally, the theory was concerned with transplanting laws in the form of statutes or full legal orders, but now it is recognised that the transplanting process may happen also in respect of a single rule or even a concept.[29]

The legal transplant theory has mostly been discussed and applied in the public law area, and its use within private law is rather limited. This might be surprising as it seems well suited to explaining some of the current phenomena. But it may not be surprising after all when thinking about who has the legislative competence. If we accept that new rules can enter a national legal system through commercial contracting, we assume that companies can, as a matter of fact, create generally binding law, which is a highly-disputed issue covered later in this chapter. What is accepted in contract law is that commercial parties can create binding 'law' for their relationship.[30] However, if a particular provision foreign to a national legal system is repeatedly included into contracts in that jurisdiction, the original purpose and legal effects of such provision may influence the behaviour of the parties, the decisions of disputes and ultimately also the legal system. Can EA clauses be seen as an example of this process?

The question whether EA clauses can be considered legal transplants leads to the question of *transferability*. As discussed above, only formal law has been and still is considered transferable by some.[31] If this position is correct, the discussion in this chapter should be about transplanting the *parol evidence* rule. However, this view of transferability limited to formal law has been rejected by the very father of the legal transplant theory, Alan Watson, who purports that 'what is borrowed and what can be borrowed are legal rules, principles, institutions and

27 Peer Zumbansen, 'Transnational Comparisons: Theory and Practice of Comparative Law as a Critique of Global Governance' (2012) *Comparative Research in Law & Political Economy.* Research Paper No. 1/2012, 1.

28 Alan Watson, *Legal Transplants: An Approach to Comparative Law* (2nd edn, University of Georgia Press 1993).

29 William Twining, 'Diffusion of Law: A Global Perspective' (2004) 49 *Journal of Legal Pluralism* 1, 17.

30 In the limits of mandatory provisions of contract law.

31 Pierre Legrand, 'The Impossibility of "Legal Transplants"' (1997) 4 *Maastricht Journal of European and Comparative Law* 111, 112.

even structures'.[32] Nowadays, legal transplants through commercial contracts are considered a recognised variant of legal transplants.[33] Moreover, regarded as not morally loaded but rather 'mechanical' rules (especially so when talking about boilerplate provisions), they are considered more easily transferable than 'organic' contractual provisions embedded in the values and culture of a particular society.[34]

If we conclude that EA clauses can be seen as legal transplants, we should investigate whether they kept their original purpose and legal effects in the new setting. Some authors consider this to be a sign of a 'success' of the transplanting process,[35] while others point out that a transplanted norm does not need to have the same or similar legal consequences for the process to be successful.[36]

Considering the original purpose of EA clauses, namely, to exclude extrinsic evidence for the purpose of determining the content of a contract, two problems arise. Firstly, even in common law jurisdictions, the original purpose assigned to the clauses is often not achieved. For example, in the United States, the treatment of EA clauses has developed from considering them to be the ultimate proof of the intention to conclude a fully integrated agreement (and thus reinforcing the *parol evidence* rule) to perceiving them as only one piece of rebuttable evidence in this respect.[37] Moreover, while the original purpose was limited to the substantive question of contractual content determination, some American courts also ascribed interpretative effect to EA clauses.[38] Secondly, EA clauses are not consistently interpreted in the Danish context either. Two available cases provide opposite solutions although they were both decided by the Copenhagen Maritime and Commercial Court. On one occasion, the Court upheld an EA clause and decided a dispute solely on the basis of the contractual text.[39] On another occasion, the Court ignored an EA clause and considered prior communications and documents when deciding the case.[40] While there were differences

32 Alan Watson, *Legal Transplants: An Approach to Comparative Law* (University Press of Virginia 1974) 107.

33 See e.g. Li-Wen Lin, 'Legal Transplants through Private Contracting: Codes of Vendor Conduct in Global Supply Chains as an Example' (2009) 57 *American Journal of Comparative Law* 711.

34 Otto Kahn-Freund, 'On Uses and Misuses of Comparative Law' (1974) 37 *Modern Law Review* 1, 12–13.

35 Legrand (n. 31) 124.

36 Michele Graziadei, 'Comparative Law as the Study of Transplants and Receptions' in Mathias Reimann and Reinhard Zimmermann (eds), *The Oxford Handbook of Comparative Law* (Oxford University Press 2006) 441.

37 Mitkidis and Neumann (n. 7) 191–195.

38 On the overlap of contractual content determination and contract interpretation under the US law, see Margaret N. Kniffin, 'Conflating and Confusing Contract Interpretation and the Parol Evidence Rule: Is the Emperor Wearing Someone Else's Clothes?' (2009) 62 *Rutgers Law Review* 75, 80–81.

39 *Rotate Aviation v. Air Kilroe*, SH2012.H-0011-11.

40 *Sandrew Metronome International v. Angel Scandinavia*, SH2005.H-0132-02. For further analysis of both cases, see Mitkidis and Neumann (n. 7).

in the facts and the Court's reasoning was obscure due to brevity,[41] it seems fair to say that there is no legal certainty about how a Danish adjudicator will handle an EA clause.

The differences in the results of American and Danish cases concerning EA clauses are thus not as big as it could be expected.[42] However, this does not prove that the transplanting process has been successful.[43] The actual handling of the legal questions regarding EA clauses and the underlying contract law concepts and principles differ significantly between the two jurisdictions. Yet, at least in the written form of contracts, we observe the transplanting process taking place.

Legal convergence

The legal transplant theory is relevant for analysing the way in which norms are borrowed and get new life in the receiving system. However, the analysis raises new questions, such as to what extent does the transfer lead to convergence of legal systems. Thus, perhaps a better explanation of the use of EA clauses in contracts governed by Danish law can be found considering the theory of legal convergence.[44]

In order to achieve efficiency of international transactions supported by simplicity and predictability of contractual parties' behaviour and legal framework, the participants of global business community instinctively align their conduct.[45] Unifying contractual content through its reuse by companies is one way to achieve such a convergence. The bottom-up (natural) convergence is considered by Merryman as 'the most effective mode of convergence of laws, superior to legal transplantation and to active unification in the depth and permanence of its consequences'.[46]

However, the question here may be posed whether we experience convergence between (the understanding of a legal concept in) two legal systems or rather convergence of contracting practice. There seems to be no doubt that the contracting practice across the globe is converging. This is, for example, apparent from the

41 See also contribution of Thomas Neumann in this volume.

42 Lars Gorton, 'Merger Clauses in Business Contracts' (2008) *Erhvervsjuridisk Tidsskrift* 344, 352.

43 Considering the framing of success by Pierre Legrand, see (n. 35).

44 Ugo Mattei and Luca G Pes, 'Civil Law and Common Law: Toward Convergence?' in Gregory A. Caldeira, R. Daniel Kelemen and Keith E. Whittington, *The Oxford Handbook of Law and Politics* (Oxford University Press 2008).

45 Luke Nottage, 'Comment on Civil Law and Common Law: Two Different Paths Leading to the Same Goal' (2001) 32 *Victoria University of Wellington Law Review* 843, http://www.nzlii.org/nz/journals/VUWLawRw/2001/43.html (citing Merryman) accessed 28 March 2019.

46 John Henry Merryman, 'On the Convergence (and Divergence) of the Civil Law and the Common Law' (1981) 17 *Stanford Journal of International Law* 357, 371 ('Often legal transplantation and unification of laws are merely ways of formalizing a legal consensus already reached by political-cultural rapprochement').

reuse of contract models. However, looking at the varied treatment of EA clauses by local courts in the US and Danish jurisdictions, there seems to be no evidence of convergence in the approach of legal systems to this concept as such.

Von Mehren suggests that a high level of convergence in private law matters can only be achieved if two conditions are fulfilled: first, there is a consensus on the transnational level about the rules, and second, those rules are administered by a transnational justice system where the adjudicators are trained in a shared legal tradition.[47] The CISG was an attempt to fulfil the first condition and partly succeeded in this, but we have not seen fulfilment of the second condition just yet.[48] The second condition could possibly be fulfilled if national courts' decisions among participating states also converge. However, in relation to EA clauses (and generally contract law), the available court decisions from the two studied jurisdictions do not show mutual appreciation between the two legal systems.

If we look for another area of law where such a convergence has been achieved, or is in the process, the area of human rights comes into mind, with international and regional courts establishing, interpreting and applying international rules. However, although human rights as a public law area might be further along the convergence process, it chokes on a third issue not mentioned by von Mehren: enforcement. Even if we achieve transnational consensus on rules in a specific area and establish a court or other body to decide disputes, the question then appears if those decisions are in reality (how and by whom) enforced.[49] Thus, in the human rights sphere, we might actually experience the exact opposite than in contract law – while positive laws are converging, the practice (the application of the law) lags behind.

Contract law and contracts under transnationalisation

From the above, it seems that while providing some helpful conceptual frameworks and methodological tools, comparative law theories struggle to describe the current relationship between national and international law of contracts and the realities of the globalised legal world. With respect to EA clauses, as with many other issues, this may be caused by the high intensity of the three changes in law described by Michaels ('beyond the state', 'beyond positive law' and 'beyond legal science').[50] Reusing contractual standards and provisions moves law creation fully beyond the state's control and from the realm of positive law to the realm

47 Arthur T. von Mehren, 'The Rise of Transnational Legal Practice and the Task of Comparative Law' (2001) 75 *Tulane Law Review* 1215, 1216–1217.

48 Such a convergence can possibly be achieved on a local level, e.g. the EU. Although the failure in adopting the Common European Sales Law (Proposal for a Regulation on a Common European Sales Law, COM/2011/0635 final) can be seen as a failure of the top-down convergence exercise.

49 See also contribution of Jens Vedsted-Hansen in this volume.

50 Michaels (n. 25).

of law in action.[51] Moreover, other than legal considerations, especially economic and social ones are the drivers for the inclusion of EA clauses even in contracts governed by civil law systems.

This is not new in the history of contract law. Throughout different stages of human history, commercial relations have been to a larger or lesser extent governed and developed independently from national laws and adapted to the needs of cross-border relations. The flourishing *lex mercatoria* during the medieval period is of course a prominent example here. Some authors claim that the commercial reality we live in today can be understood as *new lex mercatoria*,

> an autonomous legal system beyond the nation state, which is based on general legal principles, i.e. the common core of national legal systems as explored by functional legal comparison (e.g., the UNIDROIT principles), and on trade customs of international merchants as expressed in standardised contract terms (e.g., the Incoterms or model contract forms of the ICC).[52]

However, some also point to the fact that *lex mercatoria* has developed against the background of long experience of the nation state in the area of commercial practice and related substantive and procedural law,[53] thus saying that the system was not fully disconnected from the state. This seems also to fit well with respect to *new lex mercatoria*. Basically, while we witness transnationalisation tendencies in global commercial practice, evidenced, for example, by the reusing of the same boilerplate provisions, including EA clauses in various jurisdictions, these tendencies collapse at the same point as the internationalisation efforts led by the CISG – the lack of unified dispute settlement. In the words of Shapiro, 'there emerges a global commercial law independent of any global law giver or enforcer, although dependent on national legal and judicial institutions already long in place'.[54] So while companies use EA clauses on a regular basis and largely align their behaviour with those provisions if a problem appears, they resort to a dispute resolution body applying a national legal system or common sense rather than the prevailing understanding of the clause developed in global practice.

51 'Law in action' generally refers to the fact that a gap exists between the law in books and the law as it is applied in society. The idea of law in action has been developed in the United States and is primarily associated with the legal realism movement and empirical legal methods of research. E.g. the Wisconsin University Law School bases all its education on the concept of 'law in action'. See https://law.wisc.edu/law-in-action/index.html accessed 18 August 2018 ('Knowing the rules is like learning to play scales when you study a musical instrument. Playing scales is essential, but it isn't music. And knowing the rules is essential, but it isn't being a lawyer (…) Solving a problem requires looking beyond the rules and into the entire set of relationships surrounding the dispute.').

52 Calliess (n. 2) 476.

53 Peer Zumbansen, 'Piercing the Legal Veil: Commercial Arbitration and Transnational Law' (2002) 8 *European Law Journal* 400, 402.

54 Martin Shapiro, 'The Globalization of Law' (1993) 1 *Indiana Journal of Global Legal Studies* 37, 39.

In this regard, one may say that dispute resolution institutions and their unified interpretation of transnational contract law are not needed, as commercial parties solve the majority of their disputes among themselves. While this is a fact, the background possibility of bringing a case to an official dispute resolution body is arguably an important factor in these private dispute settlements. Basically, the threat of legal sanctions as well as economic, business and reputational repercussions of starting a legal proceeding motivate companies to deal with any dispute privately, out of court.

While relying on contractual standards and provisions, companies act in the context of globalisation. In 1993, Shapiro summarised that '(b)y globalization of law, we might refer to the degree to which the whole world lives under a single set of legal rules'.[55] While there has not been any global government yet, in some areas (and commercial law is an example), one jurisdiction can prevail over others, thus in fact exercising a regulatory power. In this respect, some authors have been speaking about the Americanisation of commercial law generally and contracting specifically. The political power of the United States, the economic power of American and British companies, common law lawyers and legal education and the English language combined have led to a situation where commercial actors across the globe actively use the American contract drafting style.[56] Shapiro even says that

> it is now possible to argue that American business law has become a kind of global *jus commune* incorporated explicitly or implicitly into transnational contracts and beginning to be incorporated into the case law and even the statutes of many other nations.[57]

However, such process of Americanisation is not obvious when considering the example of EA clauses in contracts governed by Danish law. While it is a fact that EA clauses are used in the majority of those contracts, there is (as already stated) no evidence that Danish contract law or court practice is aligning with American law and decision practice. However, the process may already have started without being immediately apparent.

Here we come back to the legal transplant theory. Teubner has presented a variation of the theory using the term 'legal irritants'.[58] He purports that it can be expected that the contract drafting practice will in turn influence national legal rules and the Courts' approach, though this process might be slow and subtle.

55 Ibid., 37.

56 Wolfgang Wiegand, 'Americanization of Law: Reception or Convergence?' in Lawrence M. Friedmann and Harry N. Scheiber (eds), *Legal Culture and the Legal Profession* (Westview Press 1996) 148; Wolfgang Wiegand, 'The Reception of American Law in Europe' (1991) 39 *American Journal of Comparative Law* 229.

57 Shapiro (n. 54) 39.

58 Gunther Teubner, 'Legal Irritants: Good Faith in British Law or How Unifying Law Ends Up in New Divergences' (1998) 61 *Modern Law Review* 11.

This effect can already be seen in Danish legal scholarship and its presumption that the judges will not entirely disregard EA clauses, but take a middle road in interpreting them.[59] However, the presumption that contracting practice influences the legal rules and judiciary approach would imply that there is a clear and unified purpose behind the inclusion of EA clauses into contracts by Danish companies, which the legislative and judiciary powers will aim to protect. The empirical evidence though shows that the reasons behind the inclusion of EA clauses into contracts governed by Danish law are largely varying, ranging from power issues to ignorance.[60]

Companies as legislators and legitimacy

The *new lex mercatoria* reality is built on the fact that private international law and convention-based international law do not keep pace with transnationalisation, thus allowing for 'privatization of law-making'.[61] National and international legal rules become substituted by private standards, including contract standards. The variants of private law-making and types of regulation cannot be aligned with the traditional sources of legitimacy in the constitutional state.[62] 'The democratic control of the sovereign by parliament is replaced by markets that select efficient private standards and eliminate "bad" ones'.[63] While this can be seen as a good development seconded by nation states, it can also be criticised, especially with respect to the legitimacy of the 'new' legal rules. Considering contracting practice and the content of contracts to be 'law' exposes us to the danger that economic transactions are assigned legitimacy only based on their efficiency, thus immunising them from 'all legal and political criticism'.[64] However, even state-made contract law's legitimacy may be disputed, as has been done by Calliess, who states that the democratic legitimacy of current state-made private law is largely overstated.[65] He speaks about the fact that common law is judge-made law without the involvement of parliament (in most cases) while civil law codifications were often prepared by experts from ministries or during various times of weaker democracies or even totalitarian regimes (such as many laws in the states behind

59 Peter Møgelvang-Hansen, 'The Nordic Tradition: Application of Boilerplate Clauses Under Danish Law' in Giuditta Cordero-Moss (ed.), *Boilerplate Clauses, International Commercial Contracts and the Applicable Law* (Cambridge University Press 2011) 236; Eigil Lego Andersen, 'Hvorledes indgår erhvervslivet aftaler?' (2008) *Erhvervsjuridisk Tidsskrift* 34, 37; Mads Bryde Andersen, *Grundlæggende aftaleret* (4th edn, Gjellerup 2013) 328; Bernhard Gomard et al., *Almindelig kontraktsret* (5th edn, Jurist- og Økonomforbundets Forlag 2015) para. 3.2.2.

60 Mitkidis (n. 12) 199–201.

61 Calliess (n. 2) 469.

62 Ibid., 470.

63 Gerald Spindler, 'Market Processes, Standardization, and Tort Law' (1998) 4 *European Law Journal* 314, 317.

64 Zumbansen (n. 53) 406.

65 Calliess (n. 2) 477.

the Iron Curtain). Moreover, he points towards the lack of democratic legitimacy in preparing and adopting EU private law as national legislators are not involved.[66]

In their very important contribution to the transnational law debate, Calliess and Zumbansen discuss and develop the concept of 'rough consensus and running code' as a process of law creation.[67] The idea here is that contract law is developed through an iterative action where first a group reaches a consensus about a new standard and then they test the standard on a small sample before it is released for global use. Afterwards, the global community can accept or reject the new standard, and if and when the standard achieves broad acceptance, such that non-compliance would jeopardise cooperation, it becomes binding. This law creation is very close to customary law; in fact, the authors have described it as 'timely interpretations of the production of customary law'.[68] This way of law creation has been observed by the authors, for example, in the area of internet governance.

The 'rough consensus and running code' law-creation process seems applicable also in the area of contract law. If we consider the EA clauses, we could claim that Article 2.1.17 of the UNIDROIT Principles of International Commercial Contracts (PICC) constitutes a global consensus on the effects of an EA clause in international contracts. The article, in general, follows the US legal understanding of EA clauses as excluding the possibility of furnishing extrinsic evidence when determining contractual content, while allowing extrinsic evidence when interpreting ambiguities. The PICC are soft law principles. Yet, they are often perceived as a legitimate source of law by the business community. UNIDROIT is an independent intergovernmental organisation, comprised of 63 members from 5 continents, representing various legal cultures, traditions and socio-political backgrounds.[69] The PICC thus base their legitimacy firstly on the expertise of the working group drafting the principles (procedural, expert-based legitimacy).[70] The working group has based their work on the practical need for certainty rather than theoretical foundations, using the format of law restatement known from the American Law Institute (USA).[71] Moreover, the legitimacy of PICC with respect to EA clauses could be seen as based on the consensus of the governed (descriptive legitimacy)[72] since companies largely use EA clauses

66 Ibid., 478.

67 Gralf-Peter Calliess and Peer Zumbansen, *Rough Consensus and Running Code: A Theory of Transnational Private Law* (Hart Publishing 2010).

68 Calliess (n. 2) 481.

69 www.unidroit.org/about-unidroit/overview accessed 18 August 2018.

70 Magdalena Bexell, 'Global Governance, Legitimacy and (De)Legitimation' (2014) 11 *Globalizations* 289, 292.

71 Klaus Peter Berger, 'International Commercial Contracts in International Contract Practice: The UNIDROIT Model Clauses' (2014) 19 *Uniform Law Review* 519, 519–520.

72 Ian Hurd, 'Legitimacy and Authority in International Politics' (1999) 53 *International Organizations* 379, 381; Daniel Bodansky, 'Legitimacy in International Law and International Relations' in Jeffrey L. Dunoff and Mark A. Pollack (eds), *International Perspectives on International Law and International Relations* (Cambridge University Press 2013) 331.

drafted in compliance with Article 2.1.17 of the PICC in their contracts (as discussed earlier). We could argue that both the global consensus and observance of Article 2.1.17 of PICC are in place in compliance with the theory of the 'rough consensus and running code', and thus this Article constitutes a piece of binding law. However, this might be questioned. For example, we may ask whether a consensus is indeed achieved when facing the situation where companies use EA clauses in line with PICC, but national courts do not recognise the effects of such clauses in the same way. In order to achieve a consensus, we may therefore need not only acceptance by the governed subjects but also by enforcers. Moreover, how does the fact that these clauses are not negotiated but often accepted without discussion due to power imbalance between contractual parties or the aim to focus on more important issues in negotiations impact on the legitimacy of the rule? The absence of protection of the weak compromises the legitimacy of the rule as weaker parties are not represented in establishing the consensus and their compliance is forced. This has been confirmed in an empirical investigation conducted by the author, where Danish companies repeatedly commented on the fact that they include EA clauses in their contracts because those come from their stronger contractual partners.[73] Furthermore, the focus of contractual parties on other parts of a contract, due to negotiation strategies and economic considerations, questions the existence of the consensus even among stronger companies as conscious ignorance of this contractual provision cannot be considered to constitute consensus on its legal effects.

In conclusion, the role of companies as legislators may be accepted with respect to individual transactions, but raises many doubts regarding the legitimacy of the rules created both among and beyond contractual parties. In other words, the convergence of contractual practice (contractual content) does not necessarily create legitimate rules.

Conclusion

This chapter has analysed the use of EA clauses in contracts governed by Danish law. Particularly, this phenomenon was analysed using the legal transplants and legal convergence theories. It has been concluded that the contractual practice indeed amounts to the transplanting of foreign contractual provisions into Danish contracts, and that we observe convergence, and therefore transnationalisation, in contract drafting practice. The same has, however, not been observed with respect to national contract law or its application by courts. Companies create a *new lex mercatoria*; yet, this law remains resting on the national dispute resolution institutions and thus lacks uniformity in application and enforcement. This is seen, for example, in the different treatment of EA clauses in various jurisdictions. Possibly, we should be more patient and simply wait for the national laws and jurisprudence to catch their breath and get on board with transnationalisation.

73 Mitkidis (n. 12) 199–200.

One way is to simply learn from each other's decision practice, eventually reaching consensus of both companies and enforcers on the legal effects of EA clauses. Such mutual learning is also stressed by Glenn:

> I do mean to say that when courts from around the world have written well-reasoned and provocative opinions in support of a position at odds with our familiar American views, we would do well to read carefully and take notes. Indeed, we can cross the divide separating us from other jurisdictions around the world. And if we do so with the modest intent to borrow ideas on classifying, discussing, and solving a particular problem, we should not be deterred by unfamiliarity with foreign legal systems. We may fail to understand a particular system of law or even misinterpret some foreign decisions. Nevertheless, we may also find unexpected answers or new challenges to domestic legal issues.[74]

For now, the question of where to seek legitimacy in the transnationalised contracting world remains unanswered. Some theories, such as the 'rough consensus and running code', exist. Such theories interpret contractual practice and demonstrate that the rules developed in practice fulfil individual evaluation aspects for law's legitimacy, such as the level of democratic procedure, expertise of lawgivers and consent by the governed subjects. They help us to understand the process of the bottom-up development of law and to assess its legitimacy. However, they also adopt various views on legitimacy. Bottom-up development will continue to be the predominant way of law creation in order to fulfil practical cross-border needs of the commercial community unless we achieve globalisation of law otherwise. Companies will continue to develop norms for themselves, such as standard contracts and, in that way, replace nation states as legislators. However, we should be aware of, and keep alive, the difference between practice (content of contracts) and law (background norms – found in statutes, customs or otherwise). It has been stated that transnational legal practice has 'vastly outpaced the theory of whether and how such practice should be regulated'.[75] It is the role of legal scholarship to build the theory up. In order to do that, we need to study in detail, and in a comparative perspective, the attitudes of national legal systems to norms that, on the surface, have transnational potential.

74 Glenn (n. 1) at 986 (citing the judge in *Abrahamson v. Fisher*).
75 Glenn (n. 1) at 980–981.

8 Towards the participation of a global public in transnational law-making? Everyday ICT platforms as legitimacy opportunities for bottom-up governance

Karin Buhmann and Sameer Azizi

Introduction[1]

Recent years have witnessed a series of initiatives by the United Nations (UN) to develop policy and law to advance social, environmental and economic sustainability holistically. While some breakthroughs have been achieved in terms of agreement on new international (soft) instruments, implementation still challenges the effective governance of global sustainability concerns. This applies to the Sustainable Development Goals ('SDG')[2] as well as the Paris Climate Change Accord.[3] The overall objectives of both, as well as their effective implementation, have significant implications for social and environmental sustainability at the level of individuals. The SDG introduced a global focus on sustainability and development that the 2001–2015 Millennium Development Goals did not have but remain somewhat top-down both in their approach to addressing sustainability concerns of relevance to citizens in all regions and in the process through which they were created. Transforming their visions into change on the ground requires knowledge of the needs and perceptions of local citizens. For this reason, it is reasonable to consider how individuals can be included in the onward shaping of the steps that will be taken to transform the SDG and Climate Accord into practice on the ground. Moreover, given the global surge in sustainability awareness and concerns, it is also reasonable to consider how individuals, forming part of a global public, can be actively included in future transnational sustainability-related law-making.

1 Acknowledgements: This chapter builds in part on empirical studies funded by the Danish Research Council for the Social Sciences for project ref. 09-060314. Audiences at the 'Leadership challenges that matter' conference 2017 (Johannesburg, South Africa) and the Participatory Design conference 2014 (Windhoek, Namibia) provided useful comments to papers that have been elaborated into this chapter.

2 UN (2015) Transforming our world: the 2030 Agenda for Sustainable Development, UN Doc. A/Res/70/1, 21 October 2015.

3 UN (2015) Framework Convention on Climate Change: Conference of the Parties, Adoption of the Paris Agreement, UN Doc. FCCC/CP/2015/L.9/Rev.1, 12 December 2015.

Another UN initiative, which despite also being ground-breaking has received less attention in terms of international policy and literature concerning global sustainability concerns, deserves to be considered for the insights it may offer in regard to the points set out above. This is the evolution of the United Nations' (UN) business and human rights (BHR) 'regime',[4] which came about through a multi-stakeholder process that helped the outcome gain legitimacy, supported by electronic communication platforms to share preliminary ideas and invite input from around the world. Supported by civil society and business organisations, the UN's Human Rights Council's agreement reached in 2008 on the UN Protect, Respect and Remedy Framework ('UN Framework')[5] was a breakthrough on several accounts: First, because it broke the stalemate that had caused previous efforts to flounder.[6] Second, because the UN Framework delivers specific normative guidance not only for states but also for business enterprises on their impact on society, thereby challenging the state-centric approach of much international law, even on sustainability issues. In 2011, this was followed by an agreement on the soft-law UN Guiding Principles on Business and Human Rights ('UNGP'),[7] which spell out the implications of the UN Framework into operational steps for states and businesses. The process towards this UN-brokered transnational regime relied on a participatory process that was unusually inclusive of non-state actors, even for a UN and human rights process.[8] Besides physical meetings, information and communication technologies (ICT) was deployed to engage stakeholders globally and facilitate their participation. Hence, from a process-oriented perspective on international law and law-making,[9] the case of the UN's BHR regime is interesting with regard to how a global public can participate in defining sustainability norms and implementing steps.

Participation is relevant from a sustainability perspective for a number of reasons. Participation in political decision-making at various levels of governance is inherent in the ideals of democracy and legitimacy.[10] Participation in public

4 Karin Buhmann, *Changing Sustainability Norms Through Communicative Processes: The Emergence of the Business & Human Rights Regime as Transnational Law* (Edward Elgar 2017).

5 UN Human Rights Council, *Protect, Respect and Remedy: A Framework for Business and Human Rights*, Report of the Special Representative of the Secretary-General on the issue of human rights and transnational corporations and other business enterprises, John Ruggie, (2008) UN Doc. A/HRC/8/5.

6 John Ruggie, *Just Business* (Norton 2013).

7 UN Human Rights Council, *Guiding Principles on Business and Human Rights: Implementing the United Nations 'Protect, Respect, Remedy' Framework* (2011) UN Doc. A/HRC/17/31.

8 Karin Buhmann, 'Development of the "UN Framework": A Pragmatic Process Towards a Pragmatic Output' in Radu Mares (ed.), *The UN Guiding Principles on Business and Human Rights: Foundations and Implementation* (Martinus Nijhoff Publishers 2012) 85.

9 Rosalyn Higgins, *Problems and Process: International Law and How We Use It* (Clarendon Press 1994).

10 Jürgen Habermas, 'A Political Constitution for the Pluralist World Society?' (2007) 34 *Journal of Chinese Philosophy* 331; Jürgen Habermas, *Between Facts and Norms: Contributions to a Discourse Theory of Law and Democracy*, translated by William Rehg (Polity Press/Blackwell 1996).

decision-making affecting one's life is also a human right, found in the Universal Declaration of Human Rights[11] and the Vienna Declaration and Programme of Action on human rights and sustainable development.[12] International development literature shows that participation in development-related processes caters for ownership and institutional sustainability.[13] The social-science literature within the field of 'participatory design' confirms the benefits of bottom-up involvement of actually or potentially affected citizens and groups for ownership and relevance of solutions and confirms the significance for the successful implementation.[14] Socio-legal reflexive or responsive regulatory strategies apply similar lines of thinking.[15] Much of this socio-legal literature was developed for the 'regulatory crisis' of the 1970s–1980s with regard to the economic, social, migratory and environmental challenges facing states at the national level. Many of these concerns have now shifted onto the global stage, calling for innovative solutions. In this context, bottom-up participation may feed into regulation at the super-national[16] level of global sustainability concerns.

The current global political, economic and legal order is marked by a blurring of conventional boundaries between nation states and global interactions. Economic activities, climate change and even public governance[17] carry effects beyond nation-state-based jurisdiction. Much of the impact of economic activity and climate change caused by actors in the Global North affects the

11 *Universal Declaration of Human Rights*, G.A. res. 217A (III), 10 December 1948, UN Doc A/810.

12 UN General Assembly, *Vienna Declaration and Programme of Action* (1993) UN Doc. A/CONF.157/23.

13 E.g. Elizabeth Kleemeier, 'The Impact of Participation on Sustainability: An Analysis of the Malawi Rural Piped Scheme Program' (2000) 28 *World Development* 929; S.J. Marks and J. Davis, 'Does User Participation Lead to a Sense of Ownership for Rural Water Systems? Evidence from Kenya' (2012) 40 *World Development* 1569.

14 Toni Robertson and Jesper Simonsen, 'Participatory Design: An Introduction' in Jesper Simonsen and Toni Robertson (eds), *Routledge International Handbook of Participatory Design* (Routledge 2013) 1.

15 E.g. Jørgen Dalberg-Larsen, *Ret, styring og selvforvaltning* (Juridisk Bogformidling, Aarhus 1991); Gunther Teubner, 'Substantive and Reflective Elements in Modern Law' (1983) 17 *Law and Society Review* 239; Sally Falk Moore, *Law as Process: An Anthropological Approach* (Routledge & Kegan Poul 1978); Philippe Nonet and Philip Selznick, *Law and Society in Transition: Toward Responsive Law* (Harper & Row 1978); John Griffiths, 'What Is Legal Pluralism?' (1986) 24 *Journal of Legal Pluralism and Unofficial Law* 1; Jay A. Sigler and Joseph E. Murphy, *Interactive Corporate Compliance: An Alternative to Regulatory Compulsion* (Quorum Books 1988).

16 'Super-national' in here refers to any regulatory level above the nation state (regional, international, transnational).

17 E.g. Karin Buhmann and Iben Nathan, 'Regulating Sustainability by Combining Legality Verification and Market Access: Critical Reflections on the EU's FLEGT Scheme as "smart-mix" Multi-level Regulation for the Timber Sector' in Tonia Novitz and Clair Gammage (eds), *Sustainable Trade, Investment and Finance* (forthcoming).

Global South.[18] This necessitates ensuring the views of affected stakeholders in developing regulatory responses. The process towards the SDG sought to take account of this through online questionnaires but did so in a manner that presumed a high level of technical and (English) language skills.[19] This underscores the importance of identifying solutions that are accessible and easily applied for the billions of people who live far from urban-based decision-making centres and whose voices are rarely heard in global governance. Indeed, the idea of using the Internet to gain input from a global citizenry is becoming increasingly viable through smartphone devices or computers connected to low-cost or even free Internet access.

In this chapter, we look at the role that ICT may play in involving people in remote areas in processes that feed into global law- and policy-making. We particularly focus on the potential of mobile phones. As an early example of innovative use of ICT, several African countries have seen mobile phones used as payment platforms (for much longer than in the Global North) as well as for other purposes that go beyond spoken communication between individuals.

We argue that the use of ICT offers unique opportunities to provide bottom-up input to transnational law-making. We do not harbour utopian visions of every citizen on this planet actively participating in transnational law-making. What we have in mind is to draw the attention of scholars and practitioners of transnational law and global law-making to the potential of ICT for including otherwise marginalised individuals and groups and to place this into existing theoretical debates on popular participation and legitimate law-making in a 'post-national constellation'.[20] Specific experiments, analyses and modalities for channelling (or funnelling) views upwards to formal decision-makers can, and should, follow later, as outlined in the conclusion.

The next section presents the methodology, introducing the applied pragmatic approach, the grander theoretical framework with an emphasis on transnational law; and the BHR regime as a case for studying broadly inclusive multi-stakeholder transnational law-making on issues of global concern. The subsequent sections address core elements of Habermasian theory on legitimate law-making in a transnational context, the deployment of ICT in the evolution of the BHR regime and the role that ICT already plays in the Global South for economic and political participation. Next, the chapter analyses the potential of

18 John H. Knox, 'Human Rights Principles and Climate Change' in Kevin R. Gray, Richard Tarasofsky and Cinnamon Carlane (eds), Oxford Handbook of International Climate Change Law (Oxford University Press 2016).

19 UN World Global Survey, *MY World* (communication platform) launched in 2013 by the UN as a global survey for citizens, aimed to 'capture people's voices, priorities and views' (2013) www.worldwewant2015.org/inequalities accessed 11 March 2013 (link no longer operative).

20 Habermas, 'A Political Constitution for the Pluralist World Society?' (n. 8); Jürgen Habermas, 'The Constitutionalization of International Law and the Legitimation Process of a Constitution for World Society' (2008) 15 *Constellations* 444, 444–445.

ICT in the context of legitimacy in transnational law-making on global concerns, drawing on the BHR case to identify challenges as well as opportunities. Based on this, it outlines research perspectives and finally concludes.

Methodology

This article adopts the approach of legal pragmatism to combine the human rights perspective of participation in law-making, a specific case of transnational law-making within the context of a conventional international organisation, and ICT, all set within the theoretical framework of transnational law and Habermasian theory on legitimate law-making for global concerns in the postnational constellation. Our legitimacy-focus is on input into a law-making process rather than on the output itself. This is based on arguments by various scholars who like Habermas (originally in a national law-making context)[21] and Franck (for an international law-making context)[22] argue that legitimacy of a normative output is contingent on the legitimacy of the process leading to that output and, therefore, of the input that is gathered through that process.[23] For an output that is relevant to the needs and concerns of individuals, transnational law and law-making addressing global (or regional or local) concerns should adequately target the relevant geographic area and its citizenry.

We understand transnational law to merge elements of conventional public international, regional and sometimes even national law and private law, as well as new forms of law and rule-making, including private self-regulation such as codes of conduct for companies with transnational operations.[24] Transnationalisation of law is partly a result of the fact that markets have internationalised while governments remain by definition bound by their borders. Transnational law may appear to be private, but is fundamentally public in character, represented by such fields as human rights, labour, environmental and public health law.[25]

Transnational law may pragmatically allow for novel forms of law and law-making to reach across the institutional limits of conventional legal systems. From this perspective, the UN's BHR regime may be considered a type of transnational law, which builds on conventional international law but goes beyond this in seeking to regulate business conduct across territorial borders through

21 Habermas, *Between Facts and Norms* (n. 8).

22 Thomas M. Franck, *The Power of Legitimacy Among Nations* (Oxford University Press 1990).

23 For a more detailed explanation of this, see Karin Buhmann, *Power, Procedure, Participation and Legitimacy in Global Sustainability Regulation: A Theory of Collaborative Regulation* (Routledge 2017).

24 Compare Peer Zumbansen, 'Transnational Law, Evolving' in Jan M. Smits (ed.), *Elgar Encyclopaedia of Comparative Law* (2nd edn, Edgar Elgar 2012) 898; Harold H. Koh, 'Why Do Nations Obey International Law? (Review essay)' (1997) 106 *The Yale Law Journal* 2599, 2626–2627.

25 Harold H. Koh, 'Opening Remarks: Transnational Legal Process Illuminated' in Michael Likosky (ed.), *Transnational Legal Processes: Globalisation and Power Disparities* (Butterworths 2002) 327, 331.

state regulation, business self-regulation and mixed forms of law.[26] The process towards the BHR regime was pragmatic in inviting for-profit, non-state actors into the process along with the non-profit organisations that are more commonly included in processes of international human rights law-making. It was innovative in broadly using electronic resources to gain views beyond the participants/stakeholders involved in physical meetings.[27]

We have also considered participatory design, a social-science approach to participation in processes to deliver solutions to everyday needs (hence, 'design') to advance relevance and ownership.[28] The participation in processes of 'designing' solutions brings a 'bottom-up' perspective that complements the opportunities offered by ICT.

A pragmatic approach focuses on solving problems of reality and is open to interdisciplinarity. A pragmatic legal approach allows for identifying opportunities within other scientific fields. In this chapter, we incorporate ICT as providing part of the solution to the challenge of how to involve a global citizenry in transnational law-making in line with Habermas' ideas. This challenge is further detailed later. We do not address the technical aspects of ICT but, rather, draw on the experience of ICT as a modality to extend participation (in the economy and in governance) to individuals who could otherwise be excluded from such roles.

Inclusive transnational law-making and legitimacy: Habermasian perspectives

Several scholars of legal philosophy,[29] political science,[30] socio-legal studies,[31] international and transnational law[32] discuss legitimacy of law-making with regard to the output as well as the process (compare also chapter by Pelaudeix) and agree that there is a need for theory-based insights on transforming the ideals of legitimate law-making into practice. Much of this has been spurred by Habermasian theory, which posits that law-making attains its legitimacy from

26 Buhmann (n. 2).
27 Buhmann (n. 21).
28 Robertson and Simonsen (n. 12).
29 Esp. Habermas, *Between Facts and Norms* (n. 8).
30 Thomas Risse and Mareike Kleine, 'Deliberation in Negotiations' (2010) 17 *Journal of European Public Policy* 708; Thomas Risse, '"Let's argue": Communicative Action in World Politics' (2000) 54 *International Organization* 1.
31 E.g. Teubner (n. 13); Gerlinde Berger-Walliser and Paul Shrivastava, 'Beyond Compliance: Sustainable Development, Business, and Pro-active Law' (2015) 46 *Georgia International Law Journal* 417.
32 E.g. Salomone Picciotto, 'Rights, Responsibilities and Regulation of International Business' (2003) 42 *Columbia Journal of Transnational Law* 131; Gráinne De Burca, 'Developing Democracy Beyond the State' (2008) 46 *Columbia Journal of Transnational Law* 221; Joshua Cohen and Charles F. Sabel, 'Global Democracy?' (2005) 37 *NYU Journal of International Law and Politics* 763.

a clear connection to the views and needs of citizens affected by the rules and their results. Yet a great deal of the prevalent theory remains top-down, despite formal emphasis on the importance of input.[33] Our focus is on how input may be generated from individuals whose voices are rarely heard but who – whether they be farmers, fishermen, women, youths, etc. – are at least as affected by global sustainability changes as those whose positions, education and geographical locations provide closer access to decision-making.

In his major work on legitimate law-making,[34] Habermas perceives the legitimacy and effectiveness of law as closely related. Both are connected to qualified participation in the law-making process by those who are subjected to the rules.[35] Public discourse mobilises reasoning drawing on citizens' interests and values. This feeds into law- and policy-making through deliberation or through bargaining where concessions are needed to reach a compromise.[36] The expression of differences in ideas, perception and outlook towards a commonly agreed solution provides legitimacy.[37]

The Habermasian approach to legitimate law-making relies on civil society, not only as bearers of rights and duties, but also as law-makers. The theory was originally developed for a national context but in recent years has been turned to global governance, particularly with regard to the UN and the need for addressing global sustainability concerns. Habermas notes that globalisation and the growth of trade place human and environmental sustainability and equitable distribution under pressure.[38] Addressing this requires global collaboration for adequate policy-making and regulation. As currently both the institutional framework and actors are lacking,[39] it is necessary to identify suitable forms for a democratic process beyond the nation state:[40] a constitutionalisation of international law that 'can secure a democratic legitimation for new forms of governance in transnational spaces'.[41] This needs not be a constitution as known from nation states. As Zumbansen observes, transnational constitutionalism challenges but does not negate the distinction between the national and the international legal order.[42] Habermas argues that individuals should enjoy a status as members of a politically constituted global society, with the UN and other international

33 See e.g. E.A. Zoomers and K. Otsuki, 'Addressing the Impacts of Large-scale Land Investments: Re-engaging with Livelihood Research' (2017) 83 *Geoforum*, 164.

34 Ibid.

35 Ibid.

36 Habermas, *Between Facts and Norms* (n. 8) 165–166.

37 Ibid., 165–166; Risse and Kleine (n. 28).

38 Habermas, 'The Constitutionalization of International law' (n. 18) 444–445.

39 Habermas, 'A Political Constitution for the Pluralist World Society?' (n. 8).

40 Habermas, 'The Constitutionalization of International Law' (n. 18) 444–445.

41 Ibid., 445; see also Jürgen Habermas, (2005) 'Den postnationale konstellation og demokratiets fremtid' in Heine Andersen (ed.), *Demokrati og retsstat: En tekstsamling* (Reitzel 2005) 220.

42 Peer Zumbansen, 'Comparative, Global and Transnational Constitutionalism: The Emergence of a Transnational Legal-pluralist Order' (2012) 1 *Global Constitutionalism* 16–52.

governance systems (such as the WTO trade system) becoming more inclusive of the views, needs and influence of the world's public.[43] Habermas' vision of a transnational decision-making system embodying a global civil society has been criticised, partly because of the technical difficulties of establishing deliberation at a transnational level.[44] Habermas does recognise that national forms of deliberative discourse as a legitimacy foundation cannot be directly transferred to the international level, but maintains that the views of the public can be channelled by national governments and regional organisations as well as by civil society.[45] But again, for these organisations to represent ordinary citizens, they too must be aware of the views, needs and concerns of those citizens. ICT offers an important bottom-up tool for such purposes.

The use of ICT in the evolution of the business and human rights regime

The use of ICT in processes for including views for policy- and law-making is not a novelty in itself. For example, the EU has been using electronic platforms for generating input to various policies, but the reach tends to remain limited to those who are already in the know or recognised stakeholders. The evolution of the BHR regime differed because the use of electronic communication was both more experimental and more explicitly aimed at reaching out not only to stakeholders already involved or included, but also to those that were not in such a position.

To respond to concerns regarding the societal impacts of transnational business and their local partners, various initiatives have been launched to provide normative guidance for business conduct; until the early 2000s, most of these were private in nature due to political disagreements between states, institutional limitations of the international law system and territorial limits of national legal systems. In 2011, however, the UN, whose overall objective is to promote solutions to international problems of an economic, social and cultural character, reached a turning point in relation to specific normative guidance for business impact on society. This came about through the agreement that was reached on the UN Framework and the UNGP. Both evolved through extensive multistakeholder consultation in contrast to the conventional state-based process of international law-making.[46] To enhance public involvement in the process, draft

43 Jürgen Habermas, 'Jenseits des Nationalstaates: Bemerkungen zu den Folgeproblemen der wirtschaftlichen Globalisierung' in Ulrick Beck (ed.), *Politik der Globalisierung* (Suhrkamp 1998).

44 See also William E. Scheuerman, 'Critical Theory Beyond Habermas' in John S. Dryzek, Bonnie Honig and Anne Phillips (eds), *The Oxford Handbook of Political Theory* (Oxford University Press 2006) 85.

45 Jürgen Habermas, 'Folkeretten i overgangen til den postnationale konstellation' (2004) 8 *Distinktion* 9.

46 Ruggie (n. 4); Buhmann (n. 21).

texts and other documents were made available through the Internet, and views were invited from stakeholders.

The UN Framework was, for politically pragmatic reasons, entitled a 'policy framework', but its content is highly normative. It does not develop new human rights or obligations but explains the implications of already existing human rights for states and companies. With regard to states, there is a particular focus on their duty to protect against human rights infringements occurring in the horizontal relationship between non-state actors (e.g. a company and an individual). With regard to companies, their responsibilities (regardless of the form, size, sector, etc. of the specific business enterprise) are explained with regard to their human rights impacts.

The development of the two instruments involved not only states, but also a range of private business organisations, individuals and civil society representatives. Doing so through meetings and online platforms exceeded what is common in the state-centric system of international law, not least international human rights law.[47] From the Habermasian perspective, this inclusion of civil society as a channel for communication of individuals' views can be argued to have strengthened the legitimacy of the process and its normative output (the UN Framework and the UNGP). For the purposes of the legitimacy of the output with companies, the inclusion of business in the process also mattered.

In order to share information on various reports and other documents, a website was set up by the Business & Human Rights Resource Centre, a voluntary organisation. This occurred soon after the launch of the process to develop what became the UN Framework. Later, the website became an Internet platform,[48] helping to share the preliminary results and receive comments from stakeholders across the globe.

ICT and bottom-up governance: Incremental developments at the local level

The growth and employment of ICT as channels of communication in remote or less developed areas offers opportunities to expand the inclusion of individuals through direct forms of participation.[49] Even if non-governmental organisations (NGOs) still act as intermediaries to collate and process information, such a process can offer enhanced participatory legitimacy through the active involvement of individuals. However, ICT can also enable individuals to communicate directly to the top levels of decision-making.

The diffusion of mobile phone technology in the African continent has been phenomenal, with particularly Sub-Saharan Africa having more than 420 million

47 See further Buhmann (n. 6).

48 www.business-humanrights.org/SpecialRepPortal accessed 13 June 2018.

49 Jørn Braa and Sahay Sundeep, 'Health Information Systems Programme: Participatory Design Within the HISP Network' in Jesper Simonsen and Toni Robertson (eds), ***Routledge International Handbook of Participatory Design*** (Routledge 2013) 235.

mobile phone subscribers in 2016, making this region the fastest growing globally in terms of unique subscribers.[50] This development has contributed significantly to small-scale commercial activity in rural areas, economic growth and employment. This has occurred at the same time as several African countries and African mobile phone firms have become global leaders in applying innovative M4D (mobile technology for development) systems that enable 'self-governance' beyond Internet-accessible areas and beyond Euro-centric governance models.[51]

The advanced evolution of mobile phones as instruments for facilitating mobile banking[52] and/or agribusiness[53] for poor individuals or small firms in Africa dates back to the late 1990s and is a convincing example of the potential for using even limited numbers of ICT devices for broader socio-economic purposes.[54] Innovative use of mobile technology to create change and to enable those otherwise excluded originated with the development of mobile money-transfer platforms, based on technical developments that were applied in East Africa already during the 1990s. This enabled farmers and other rural residents far from banks to transfer funds to economic partners and make bank deposits electronically,[55] meaning real changes for individuals who had been excluded from easy access to the modern economy based on simple money transfers. This led to new opportunities for rural residents to build their lives. While mainly of economic character, these transfers and opportunities testify to the transformative power of ICT to empower people far from conventional centres of transactions and activity.

Giving a voice and access to participation to those otherwise disadvantaged, mobile technology is increasingly a tool not only for private and professional communication or money transfers,[56] In the political sphere, however, studies have increasingly debated the role of mobile phones as the rapid expansion of

50 GSM Intelligence Research, *The Mobile Economy: Sub-Saharan Africa 2017* (2017) www.gsmaintelligence.com/research/?file=7bf3592e6d750144e58d9dcfac6adfab&download accessed 13 June 2018.

51 Sharath Srinivasan, 'FrontlineSMS, Mobile-for-Development, and the "Long Tail" of Governance' in *Bits and Atoms: Information and Communication Technology in Areas of Limited Statehood* (Oxford University Press 2014); Primož Kovačič and Jamie Lundine, 'Mapping Kibera. Empowering Slum Residents by ICT' in *Bits and Atoms: Information and Communication Technology in Areas of Limited Statehood* (Oxford University Press 2014).

52 Jonathan Donner and Marcela X. Escobari, 'A Review of Evidence on Mobile Use by Micro and Small Enterprises in Developing Countries' (2010) 22 *Journal of International Development* 641.

53 Jenny C. Aker, 'Information from Markets Near and Far: Mobile Phones and Agricultural Markets in Niger' (2010) 2 *American Economic Journal: Applied Economics* 46.

54 Jenny C. Aker and Isaac M. Mbiti, 'Mobile Phones and Economic Development in Africa' (2010) 24 *The Journal of Economic Perspectives* 207.

55 Ibid.

56 Leopoldina Fortunati, Franxis Lee and Angel Lin, 'Introduction to the Special Issue on Mobile Societies in Asia-Pacific' (2008) 24 *The Information Society: An International Journal* 135; Jan H. Pierskalla and Florian F. Hollenbach, 'Technology and Collective Action: The Effect of Cell Phone Coverage on Political Violence in Africa' (2013) 107 *American Political Science Review* 207.

low-cost phones and of connectivity has enabled marginalised groups to get involved in discussing local sustainability needs, norms and their implementation. We identify three ways in which mobile phones have affected the political engagement of the marginalised through bottom-up approaches.

First, the direct person-to-person communication enabled by mobile phones has been important in mobilising masses for political purposes. A study of the African continent shows that during economic downturns between 1998–2012, mobile phones have been instrumental in involving individuals and groups for collective actions and protests.[57] The role of mobile phones has been described as pivotal in the mobilisation of people during 'the Arab Spring' in both Northern Africa and the Middle East.[58] Although these mobilisations did not in all places lead to democratic outcomes, the fact that mobile phones served to give a voice to many individuals who were otherwise formally, or de facto, disenfranchised, testifies to the potential role of ICT for inclusive governance. Studies on African countries have also stressed the positive relationship between mobile phone coverage and incidents of political violence in the same geographic areas,[59] indicating that the mobilisation potential of mobile phones can lead to violent protests. In contrast, studies from Iraq show that increased mobile phone network expansion led to decreased presence of insurgent groups, as mobile phones enabled the public to report on insurgency activities.[60]

Second, studies highlight that innovative mobile phone applications have been developed based on SMS messaging technology in order to create communication channels for political campaigning and to increase political participation for marginalised voters. Findings from the 2009 election in Mozambique indicate that new applications were utilised not only to inform voters about the election process, but also to report on electoral misconduct at village and district levels.[61] In Uganda, similar applications were implemented to enable voter-politician communication, with the result that marginalised populations (such as the poorest groups and women) in particular benefitted from such low-cost and impersonal channels of communication to contact and express views to local politicians.[62]

57 Marco Manacorda and Andrea Tesei, *Liberation Technology: Mobile Phones and Political Mobilisation in Africa* (2016) Working paper, Centre for Economic Performance, LSE.

58 Sean Aday, Henry Farrell, Marc Lynch, John Sides and Freelon Deen, *Blogs and Bullets II: New Media and Conflict after the Arab Spring* (2012) Tech. rept. United States Institute of Peace; Anita Breuer, Todd Landman and Dorothea Farquhar, 'Social Media and Protest Mobilization: Evidence from the Tunisian Revolution' (2015) 22 *Democratization* 764; Habibul H. Khondker, 'Role of the New Media in the Arab Spring' (2011) 8 *Globalizations* 675.

59 Pierskalla and Hollenbach (n. 54).

60 Jacob N. Shapiro and Nils B. Weidmann, 'Is the Phone Mightier than the Sword? Cellphones and Insurgent Violence in Iraq' (2015) 69 *International Organization* 247.

61 Jenny C. Aker, Paul Collier and Pedro C. Vicente, 'Is Information Power? Using Mobile Phones and Free Newspapers During an Election in Mozambique' (2017) 99 *Review of Economics and Statistics* 185.

62 Guy Grossman, Macartan Humphreys and Gabriella Sacramone-Lutz, '"I wld like u WMP to extend electricity 2 our village": On Information Technology and Interest Articulation' (2014) 108 *American Political Science Review* 688.

Third, the utilisation of mobile-phone applications is not limited to election periods. Findings suggest, for example, that mobile phone applications enable marginalised groups to also voice their concerns to politicians and account for their public service deficiencies between elections.[63] In addition, the recent 'smart' generation of mobile phones has enabled 'citizen journalism'[64] for citizens of the Global South, as they can record and share both audio and video evidence of events to address and share misuses of power.[65]

These uses of mobile phones for bottom-up governance purposes have been incremental but speak for the potential of using the technology through organised processes for individuals or groups to share their views and express needs and concerns with regard to the lives they live and would like for their children to have.

Challenges and opportunities

The extensive use of the Internet during the construction of the UN's business and human rights regime, particularly the 2011 UNGP, was innovative, but the process has not been unanimously perceived as inclusive or sufficiently so. Part of the process functioned in a top-down manner, an approach that reflected the relative novelty of the use of ICT for these purposes by inviting criticism of its legitimacy.[66] This, at the same time, speaks to the need for development of bottom-up approaches. There was no overall strategy for ensuring that involved NGOs represented individuals broadly. Thus, while business representatives had gained a measure of direct participation, the large group of individuals whose enjoyment of human rights may be affected by business activities remained, at best, indirectly represented. Civil society organisations' presence around the globe is not evenly dispersed, and many pursue interests particular to their expertise and missions. This adds to the legitimacy challenge if such collaborative rule-making is to be employed in other international or transnational contexts and underscores the importance of utilising communication platforms that enable individuals to voice their own views.

63 Guy Grossman, Kristin Michelitch and Marta Santamaria, 'Texting Complaints to Politicians: Name Personalization and Politicians' Encouragement in Citizen Mobilization' (2017) 50 *Comparative Political Studies* 1325.

64 Manuel Castells, *Communication Power* (Oxford University Press 2009); Gerard Goggin and Jacqueline Clark, 'Mobile Phones and Community Development: A Contact Zone Between Media and Citizenship' (2009) 19 *Development in Practice* 585.

65 J.T. Wisdom, 'Mobile Telephony and Democracy in Ghana: Interrogating the Changing Ecology of Citizen Engagement and Political Communication' (2017) 41 *Telecommunications Policy* 685.

66 E.g. Surya Deva, 'Treating Human Rights Lightly: A Critique of the Consensus Rhetoric and the Language Employed by the Guiding Principles' in Surya Deva and David Bilchitz (eds), *Human Rights Obligations of Business: Beyond the Corporate Responsibility to Respect?* (Cambridge University Press 2013) 78.

Although, as a matter of principle, individuals were able to access the draft documents online and offer their views online or in writing, in practice the views of individuals (such as actual or potential victims of business-related human rights abuse) were mainly represented by civil society organisations, typically NGOs[67] rather than at a direct, personal level. As ICT develops, possibilities for individuals to give direct personal input can also grow.

When the UN begins to discuss the post-2030 agenda to consider what should follow the SDG, ICT potentially offers a channel for bottom-up governance in a manner that responds to Habermas' call for citizens' views to strengthen the legitimacy of transnational law-making. Questionnaires such as those that were used for generating input to the SDG can be shared electronically through mobile phones, and individuals can respond through mobile phone technology. Questionnaires should be written in every-day language spoken locally and should avoid specialised terminology. Translation can be assisted through electronic platforms too (and closer to 2030 will likely be more precise than currently). Digital analysis can help analyse replies, thereby offering an alternative to civil society acting as channels/funnels to decision-makers and addressing reservations on the feasibility of Habermasian global regulation ideals for legitimate law-making. ICT can also serve a role sooner, for example, to provide input to SDG implementation. This can help ensure that localised solutions to the goals are relevant to the needs and concerns of the people who will be affected.

Future inclusive stakeholder engagement for input to governance (whether law-making or its implementation) may deploy mobile phone networks that individuals already use for texting or money transfers. To facilitate such participation, mobile credits can be provided by the organiser of the consultation (e.g. the UN). That will help eliminate needs for individuals to prioritise use of their mobile online time that may be required for tasks related to daily communication and money transfers.

Studies on the nexus between politics and ICT and in particular mobile phone technology have provided various examples of anecdotal evidence and outlined immense possibilities for 'leadership from below'[68] through the participation enabled. Scholars recognise that future studies need to distinguish between the multiple ICT-led media as means for political engagements by different user segments,[69] for example, by addressing the impact and consequences of mobile phones versus laptops for the elite vis-à-vis marginalised groups.

67 Karin Buhmann, *Normative Discourses and Public-private Regulatory Strategies for Construction of CSR Normativity: Towards a Method for Above-national Public-private Regulation of Business Social Responsibilities* (Multivers Publishing 2014).

68 Jason A. Martin, 'Mobile Media and Political Participation: Defining and Developing an Emerging Field' (2014) 2 *Mobile Media and Communication* 173.

69 Scott W. Campbell and Nojin Kwak, 'Political Involvement in "Mobilized" Society: The Interactive Relationships Among Mobile Communication, Network Characteristics, and Political Participation' (2011) 61 *Journal of Communication* 1005.

The discussion earlier underscores that ICT holds a large potential for democratic participation. More knowledge is needed to release that potential in a systematic way with regard to transnational law-making and the implementation of adopted soft or hard law. Through theory and experiments, scholars can help contribute knowledge on how to design ICT-based participatory processes so that they are perceived to be legitimate by those involved in the processes, and by stakeholders who will apply the outputs of the process.

Conclusion

This chapter has discussed prospects for increasing the participation of a global public in transnational law-making through the use of everyday information and communication technology (ICT) platforms. Actively including ICT for public participation can enhance the legitimacy of law-making with regard to global (or local) sustainability concerns by increasing awareness of the views and needs of ordinary citizens. An increased usage of ICT, including low-cost communication and externally paid mobile credits, can serve to enhance the inclusion of views and concerns harboured by the many individuals who live far from the city centres where public policy- and law-making often occur. Use of ICT can help address the challenge highlighted by legitimacy-scholars of how to include a global public in transnational law-making. The use of mobile phone technology in Africa and some other places shows that technically, ICT offers a voice to otherwise marginalised individuals. Involving individuals in global governance no longer requires getting them to polling booths or having experts or civil servants travel to far-away places to collect views and information. Information can be shared through ICT, both top-down with regard to the idea and objectives entailed in a new prospective governance instrument, providing individuals with the facts and knowledge they need to make informed decisions and input; and in a bottom-up direction for such decisions and input to be communicated. Where Internet access is available, it may be expedient to provide the former type of information through Internet sites. Individual responses may be given through mobile phones as well as Internet sites. In this manner, citizens around the world may in principle help shape, for example, the implementation of the Paris Accord to fit local needs or help provide ideals for locally relevant SDG interventions.

The evolution of mobile phones as instruments of economic participation and incremental bottom-up governance in the Global South provide convincing examples of the potential for using even limited numbers of ICT devices for including otherwise marginalised individuals and groups. The technology provides a technical response to Habermas' call for enhancing the legitimacy of transnational law-making through the voices of a global citizenry. There is no reason in principle why the investigation of the needs, concerns and expectations of individuals should not actively and directly include those populations otherwise excluded.

The use of ICT for broadly inclusive public decision-making on policies and law is a quite novel field for both practice and theory. To fully benefit from the technology for social science purposes, there is a need for theoretical insight into how to design participatory processes of global rule-making by using available technical solutions. This is underscored by the criticism of web-based consultation for the business and human rights regime for not being fully inclusive and balanced, despite intentions to enable global input. Obviously, design of these platforms will call for care to preserve the privacy of individuals and information. Clever design should also go into technical solutions that will allow large numbers of individuals to share their input, and to categorise such input for use in the onward transnational law-making process or as input to its implementation. These and other issues call for collaboration between social scientists and technical experts.

Establishing a basis for expanding bottom-up participation in law-making research could start by systematically mapping the ICT practices of citizens during the Arab Spring and in various African countries in situations where ICT gave a voice to the otherwise marginalised. Along with this, an analysis of the ICT modalities employed by the UN in the process towards the UNGP could be undertaken. This should be followed by an investigation of critiques of the democratic and inclusive character of those processes, analysing this against existing theoretical insights on methods, tool and techniques for participatory design. The aim should be to allow the collating, processing and transmitting of individuals' views for the use of organised collaborative decision-making. Benefits, drawbacks and procedural challenges of available ICT modalities should be discussed in relation to communication networks available to population groups in different areas and regions. Combining this with theory on legitimacy and participation could feed into future deployment of ICT for representative bottom-up governance. This could add to the validity and representativeness of the views shared by ICT, enhancing the legitimacy of the output. Ultimately, this insight could be deployed in other instances of collaborative transnational rule-making on sustainability or other global, regional or local concerns, generating a basis for further analysis and refinement of theory.

9 Pushing back international human rights law – Counter reaction to transnational law?

Jens Vedsted-Hansen

Current challenges to human rights law

Against the background of recent debates criticising the international human rights system, the question arises whether, and to which extent, they reflect a legitimacy crisis for human rights as normative principles that gained political support and legal status at the international level in the aftermath of the Holocaust and World War II. Alternatively, the criticism may be seen as addressing structural or institutional problems that threaten the effective functioning of international human rights monitoring bodies. In either case, the crisis or criticism appears to reflect dissatisfaction, frustration or resistance towards key aspects of international cooperation and the ensuing transnational phenomena affecting national legal systems.

At the level of political discourse, the main challenge seems to be that of international human rights obligations reducing the scope of manoeuvre for sovereign states and their democratically elected bodies at the national level. This factor is frequently exacerbated by domestic policymakers' frustration over judicial control – at the national or international level, or both – of the legislative and executive branches of government. Such judicial control and the ensuing political discontent are inevitably linked to the application and enforcement of human rights norms in situations where their protective scope is most directly affected by political decisions. Although regularly concerned with human rights norms protecting ethnic, religious, sexual and other minorities, the challenges have been increasingly presented in politico-legal terms that appear to question the general legitimacy of human rights as a normative concept and an institutional structure.

Whatever the level and precise nature of the current crisis of the human rights system, a search for relevant causes is called for in order to understand and address the challenges to the principles and underlying values of human rights law. The following will attempt to present and analyse the most central issues and challenges in the light of recent debates. Some of these issues will be identified and examined by reference to the European level while others can be amply illustrated by debates and initiatives in Denmark that are of interest beyond the country as they were closely interwoven with policy processes within the Council of Europe.

First, the contested legitimacy of the human rights system will be discussed with a focus on the interconnectedness between the sources of law and the actors of the system who are interpreting, enforcing and to some extent developing the normative standards. Second, the main features of the criticism raised against the human rights system will be presented in order to identify the nature of the alleged popular discontent, test the accompanying political rhetoric and discuss the role of academics in this context. Third, attempted political interference with the monitoring system under the European Convention on Human Rights will be illustrated by reference to the Danish chairmanship of the Council of Europe and its resulting Copenhagen Declaration of April 2018. In conclusion, certain conceptual distinctions will be suggested with a view to clarifying the legal nature of the problems underlying the criticism of the human rights system and, at least potentially, of the transnational challenges to national legal systems in general.

International actors – Questioned legitimacy?

The international human rights system and its actors are often being identified with the sources of law that they interpret, apply and develop. As a significant example, the European Court of Human Rights has been increasingly exposed to criticism, often in a somewhat unclear combination of quantitative criticism against the Court's backlog of cases and qualitative criticism reflecting dissatisfaction with the Court's approach to the interpretation and application of the European Convention on Human Rights. As will be discussed later, this type of criticism can be seen as part of a broader tendency of domestic actors pushing back international human rights law and its actors, sometimes even questioning the legitimacy of the international sources of law as interpreted by the various international monitoring bodies.

While interconnectedness between the sources of law and the actors in charge of their interpretation and application is indeed a general phenomenon in legal systems, it can be considered a special and even paramount feature of the legal sources concerning international human rights. This follows from the nature and purpose of human rights treaties as the basis of protection for individuals and groups of persons vis-à-vis the contracting states, and from the general and rather vague or imprecise wording of most treaty provisions, the vast majority of which were adopted decades ago. Therefore, in accordance with the principle of effectiveness as recognised in public international law, international human rights bodies normally have a rather active role in the interpretation and application of the various treaties.[1] This *evolutive approach* to human rights norms is probably most clearly illustrated by the principle of *dynamic interpretation* that has become a well-established practice of the European Court of Human Rights aiming to ensure that the Convention rights and freedoms will be 'practical and effective, not theoretical and illusory'.[2]

1 See Martin Scheinin, 'Characteristics of Human Rights Norms' in Catarina Krause and Martin Scheinin (eds), *International Protection of Human Rights: A Textbook* (2nd edn, Åbo Akademi University 2012) 19.

2 See, as significant examples, *Christine Goodwin v. UK* (ECHR 2002-VI 1) para. 74; *Mamatkulov and Askarov v. Turkey* (ECHR 2005-I 293) para. 121; *Stoll v. Switzerland* (ECHR 2007-V 267) para. 128; *Magyar Helsinki Bizottság v. Hungary* (ECtHR 8 November 2016) paras 121 and 155.

Although not beyond dispute and controversy, this interpretive principle seems to be generally recognised as an important means towards the effective application in the light of 'present-day conditions' of the human rights norms laid down in international treaties. At the same time, the principle implies some potential for 'judicial activism' as it has been pointed out both in general theory on the European Convention on Human Rights and its monitoring system and in more specific contexts where the European Court of Human Rights has been subjected to criticism.[3] Notably, the latter kind of criticism has often been rather imbalanced, either focusing on specific aspects or areas of the Court's case law which may or may not be adequately reflecting its review of European Convention on Human Rights cases in general, or based on particular preunderstandings or selective approaches to the impact of the Court's monitoring on domestic decisions or policies.[4] Not infrequently, these two kinds of sceptical positions appear in combination.

The various international human rights bodies have certainly not been unaware of the issues and phenomena underlying such criticism. Perhaps most importantly, the European Court of Human Rights has made persistent and gradually enhanced efforts to pre-empt or accommodate accusations of 'judicial activism' by developing the *principle of subsidiarity* and the ensuing *margin of appreciation* as a general feature of its examination of the cases brought before it. As early as 1990, it was posited that, as far as the European Convention on Human Rights is concerned,

> the dilemma of activism versus restraint is more apparent than real, in that activism and restraint are complementary components of the methodology of judicial review inherent in the very nature of the Convention as an international treaty intended to secure effective protection of human rights and fundamental freedoms.[5]

In addition to this method of reviewing the decisions adopted by domestic authorities, the Court has also based significant rulings concerning the interpretation of the European Convention on Human Rights and other kinds of general development of Convention standards on the so-called *comparative method*. In doing so, the question of a European 'consensus' is normally considered decisive to the Court in settling issues of either dynamic interpretation, modification of

3 See William A. Schabas, *The European Convention on Human Rights. A Commentary* (Oxford University Press 2015) 47–50; Bernadette Rainey, Elizabeth Wicks and Clare Ovey, *Jacobs, White, and Ovey, The European Convention on Human Rights* (7th edn, Oxford University Press 2017) 72, 76–80.

4 See, for instance, Marc Bossuyt, *Strasbourg et les demandeurs d'asile: des juges sur un terrain glissant* (Bruylant 2010); additional examples from recent Danish debates will be given *infra*, notes 20, 21 and 23.

5 Paul Mahoney, 'Judicial Activism and Judicial Self-Restraint in the European Court of Human Rights: Two Sides of the Same Coin' (1990) 11 *Human Rights Law Journal* 57, 66–68.

the balancing of interests or other kinds of development of standards that might extend the protective scope of the Convention and could therefore be seen as an expression of judicial law-making.[6] As a result, dynamic developments of the interpretation or application of the Convention provisions do not come out of the blue or depend on judicial whim. Rather, such developments are to be seen as the outcome of supposedly rational reasoning that is normally based on the domestic standards prevailing in Europe as developed over time, sometimes in conjunction with relevant human rights standards that have been adopted by other international organisations at the European or universal level. Nonetheless, this review approach cannot and does not prevent criticism of the European Court or other international human rights bodies for that sake. Rather, it may actually expose them to additional acceptability challenges insofar as their intensity of review may vary to a degree that may be perceived as inconsistent or even as a separate cause for uncertainty regarding the human rights standards to which states will have to adhere. The following will attempt to illustrate this as one possible part of the reasons for criticism or scepticism.

Human rights scepticism: political rhetoric and popular frustration?

In order to depict the criticism levelled against the international human rights system, it seems reasonable to focus on three major strands of critical engagement with human rights: one concerned with the interaction between international and national authorities; one invoking the inherent democratic nature of national authorities; and one discarding human rights outright. These strands of criticism cannot be precisely distinguished from each other as they are partly overlapping, addressing the same issues from different perspectives and formulated in a variety of combinations. This is reinforced by the fact that they are not infrequently characterised by little conceptual clarity as to which aspects of human rights norms and institutions they are addressing. It should also be noted that while the examples below are taken from recent debates, criticism of the international human rights system and not least of the European Convention and Court of Human Rights has occurred quite frequently over the years.[7] It seems, however, to have increased and possibly evolved into more radical positions in recent years, in all

6 On the comparative method of interpretation applied by the European Court of Human Rights, see Ida E. Koch and Jens Vedsted-Hansen, 'International Human Rights and National Legislatures – Conflict or Balance?' (2006) 75 *Nordic Journal of International Law* 3, 11–13; Jonas Christoffersen, *Fair Balance: Proportionality, Subsidiarity and Primarity in the European Convention on Human Rights* (Martinus Nijhoff Publishers 2009) 57–66; Rainey, Wicks and Ovey (n. 3) 80–81.

7 For a wider exploration of criticism of the European Court of Human Rights, including counter-dynamics at the political and judicial level in 15 States Parties to the Convention and the EU, see Patricia Popelier, Sarah Lambrecht and Koen Lemmens (eds), *Criticism of the European Court of Human Rights. Shifting the Convention System: Counter-Dynamics at the National and EU Level* (Intersentia 2016).

likelihood closely connected to tendencies of resistance towards binding international cooperation mechanisms more in general, sometimes articulated with reference to ideas of 'taking back control' in policy areas characterised by dissatisfaction with the modalities or outcomes of international cooperation.[8]

International monitoring as a disputed exercise

First, the scope and intensity of review as conducted by international human rights bodies has been the subject of almost constant debate and criticism for many years, both among outside observers and within these bodies themselves. This kind of debate was already discussed earlier, pointing at the methodological devices by which human rights bodies are attempting to prevent or modify criticism in this regard. It is mentioned here again, however, as parts of such debates tend to evolve into more fundamentally questioning international monitoring of states' compliance with their human rights obligations.

In some instances, critics mostly from the legal profession have addressed the working modalities of international human rights monitoring bodies, pointing to the lack of consistency in their case law that may cause legal uncertainty, and their failure to respect the boundaries of international review of domestic authorities' decisions. Insofar as inconsistency is concerned, the various mechanisms employed to prevent real or perceived activism, as described earlier with regard to the European Court of Human Rights, are obviously not a linear exercise, and they may therefore result in incoherence in the Court's approach to its review functions. Such preventive mechanisms, often disguised as application of the *margin of appreciation* doctrine, may in themselves be a cause for legal uncertainty due to self-restraining factors that are not necessarily conducive to rational decision-making. Thus, it can be argued that attempts to avoid judicial activism can potentially result in precisely that. In any event, the European Court of Human Rights as well as other international monitoring bodies cannot avoid critical observation and monitoring of their review activities, and they can and should be considered as structurally exposed to constant review of the legitimacy of their activities.

Parts of the criticism against the human rights system, not least that levelled by certain members of national judiciaries, can be explained by the enhanced complexity of the sources of law that have to be taken into account by domestic decision-makers in order to adhere to international obligations. As far as EU Member States are concerned, this is further exacerbated by the existence of supranational norms of EU law which may in turn add to the complexity due to the sometimes uneasy relationship between EU fundamental rights and

8 See Philip Alston, 'The Populist Challenge to Human Rights' (2017) 9 *Journal of Human Rights Practice* 1.

the European Convention on Human Rights.[9] Although it may be theoretically disputable, essentially depending on definitional criteria, whether or not this is constituting *transnational* legal phenomena, it could for the sake of argument be assumed that such complexities and the ensuing scepticism represent some kind of model of the regulatory costs inherent in transnational or internationalised tendencies in the legal system.[10]

Democratic legitimacy versus international actors?

Another type of criticism, regularly combined with that challenging the scope and intensity of review as discussed earlier, is invoking the inherent democratic legitimacy of legislators and executive authorities at the national level and conversely questioning the legitimacy of international monitoring bodies as actors in the human rights system. Often reflecting concern for upholding democratic rule, this type of criticism is not one-dimensional as it includes different approaches and lines of reasoning. Some have primary focus on the institutional aspects of the human rights system while others primarily base themselves on notions of democracy.

The latter include those critics who are more fundamentally sceptical towards the entire system of human rights protection or the very concept of human rights, at least at the international level. Some proponents of this kind of human rights scepticism may even be prepared to discard the idea of fundamental rights at the national level insofar as such rights originating from national constitutions constrain the current policy choices that are open to governments and legislative majorities. Thus, domestic fundamental rights, properly enforced, could be subjected to similar challenges as the international human rights system by reference to notions of majoritarian rule as the sole basis of democratic legitimacy.

It is to be noted that such criticism rather frequently, at least implicitly, rejects or disregards the historical foundations of the human rights system as well as its broader connection to the principles of the rule of law. Without going into detail with the history of human rights, it should not be ignored that the international system for the protection of human rights that was established after World War II must reasonably be seen as the international community's response to the atrocities symbolised by the *Holocaust* with the clear aim of pre-empting similar developments in the future. Thus, the rationale of the human rights system warrants potential constraints on national decision-makers, indeed including legislative and executive authorities despite their ability to claim democratic mandate based on electoral support. Nonetheless, as an integral part of a qualitative understanding of democracy and its interconnectedness with the rule of law, human rights

9 For a general overview and discussion, see Louise Halleskov Storgaard, 'Composing Europe's Fundamental Rights Area: A Case for Discursive Pluralism' (2015) 17 *Cambridge Yearbook of European Legal Studies* 210.

10 See Roger Cotterrell, 'What is Transnational Law' (2012) 37 *Law & Social Inquiry* 500, 501–503.

norms and institutions basically serve the ultimate purpose of limiting the scope and exercise of majoritarian rule in democratic societies.

As regards the institutional aspects of the criticism against the international human rights system, it is recurrently being argued that its actors are not vested with democratic legitimacy as opposed to legislators and other decision-makers at the national level. Although apparently plausible, this tends to be a misconceived view inasmuch as members of most international monitoring bodies are actually appointed by political entities. Thus, members of the committees monitoring compliance with the various UN conventions pertaining to human rights are elected by the states that are party to these conventions on the basis of nominations by their respective governments.[11] Similarly, and indeed clearly reflecting political influence on the composition of monitoring bodies, the judges at the European Court of Human Rights are elected by the Parliamentary Assembly of the Council of Europe on the basis of a list of candidates nominated by the government of the Convention state in respect of which they are going to serve on the Court.[12]

Frustration, scepticism or rejection of human rights

The third prototype of critics mainly addresses issues of the lack of popular support for the human rights system. Their point of reference has frequently been sentiments that have developed in parts of the population influenced by specific experiences with the human rights system. Importantly, such sentiments may have become widespread as part of, or connected to, wider negative perceptions linked to internationalisation and globalisation. While in themselves often understandable in the light of real-life experiences of the socio-economic effects of these tendencies,[13] such sentiments would often appear to be based on a distorted perception of human rights and their operation and impact.

One of the most likely reasons is misrepresentation of that system in public debates. Certain politicians and the media often tend to simplify concrete cases, especially those concerning criminal suspects or offenders, blaming international human rights obligations for causing excessive procedural protection or resulting in insufficient sanctions with which they are dissatisfied. At least in Denmark, the prime example concerns offenders with an ethnic minority background, and

11 Cf. Arts 28–30 of the International Covenant on Civil and Political Rights; Art. 8 of the Convention on the Elimination of All Forms of Racial Discrimination; ECOSOC Resolution 1985/17 and Optional Protocol to the International Covenant on Economic, Social and Cultural Rights; Art. 17 of the Convention on the Elimination of All Forms of Discrimination against Women; Art. 17 of the Convention against Torture and Other Cruel, Inhuman or Degrading Treatment or Punishment; Art. 43 of the Convention on the Rights of the Child; Art. 34 of the Convention on the Rights of Persons with Disabilities.

12 Cf. Art. 22 of the European Convention on Human Rights.

13 On the issue of linkages between inequality and exclusion in the context of challenges to human rights, see Alston (n. 8) 6.

the dissatisfaction has specifically been triggered by the non-expulsion of non-nationals in rather prominent cases. In fact, this relates to only a rather small number of cases, yet mostly 'hard cases' with a high media profile partly due to distorted presentation of the facts and the context, ignoring more or less evident explanations of the outcome in the light of factual and legal circumstances of the individual cases.

Against that background, it was hardly surprising that an opinion poll initiated by a Danish political magazine was able to find 'remarkable scepticism' towards Denmark's commitment to the European Convention on Human Rights.[14] This finding was clearly not unrelated to the way in which the question had been presented to the respondents. It was first explained that the Danish government would attempt to renegotiate the European Convention on Human Rights in order to make it easier to expel non-national criminal offenders, followed by the question 'Should Denmark denounce the Convention in case it does not become easier to expel criminal offenders?'[15] The respondents gave the following answers to this question: 48% 'yes', 34% 'no' and 18% 'don't know'.[16]

This can be juxtaposed to another opinion poll carried out almost simultaneously, in which the question was formulated far more neutrally and openly: 'In your opinion, should Denmark remain party to the European Convention on Human Rights?'.[17] Here the answers came out quite differently: 73% 'yes', 12% 'no' and 15% 'don't know'.[18] The difference would seem to be explicable in the light of the assumptions underlying the question asked in the former opinion poll, most notably that the possibility of expulsion of non-national criminal offenders was too narrow and therefore ought to be widened; that this would necessitate renegotiation of the European Convention on Human Rights; that the consequence of failure in that endeavour could be Danish denunciation of the Convention in order to achieve the intended result in terms of enhanced scope for expulsion; and that denunciation would in such a situation have to be decided with no further consideration of the potential implications as regards in particular Danish membership of the Council of Europe and the European Union in case of unsuccessful renegotiation of the Convention.

The role of academia in these debates on the human rights system cannot be disregarded. As succinctly pointed out by Philip Alston on the role of scholars, it has 'become fashionable, especially at elite universities in the West, to disparage

14 Erik Holstein, Danish magazine *Altinget* 4 September 2017.

15 My translation. The Danish wording of the question was: 'Bør Danmark udtræde af konventionen, hvis det ikke bliver nemmere at udvise kriminelle?'; see *Altinget* 4 September 2017.

16 Internet panel poll carried out by Norstat on behalf of the magazine *Altinget* among 1,000 respondents between 16 and 22 August 2017.

17 My translation. The Danish wording of the question was: 'Synes du fortsat, at Danmark skal være medlem af Den Europæiske Menneskerettighedskonvention?'; see Jacques Hartmann, *Danmark og Den Europæiske Menneskerettighedskonvention* (Ex Tuto Publishing 2017) 132.

18 Internet panel poll carried out by YouGov on behalf of Jacques Hartmann between 25 and 27 August 2017; see Hartmann (n. 17) 130–133.

human rights by accentuating in dramatic and sometimes destructive ways the undoubted shortcomings of international human rights norms and institutions'.[19] Not least importantly from a European perspective, academics have contributed widely to discussions of the European Convention and Court of Human Rights over the past few years, as was amply illustrated in connection with the political initiatives taken by the Danish government in connection with its chairmanship of the Council of Europe in 2017–2018 that will be further discussed in the next section of this chapter.

Of particular relevance to the issue of popular scepticism, it should be mentioned that certain academic contributions to the domestic debate in Denmark appear to have aggravated the problem of misrepresentation of the impact of human rights in controversial cases. As a rather extreme example, it was argued by a legal expert that a specific criminal case had been 'enormously problematic' in terms of eroding the legitimacy of, and respect for, the European Convention on Human Rights because the case was a symbol of the inadequate balancing under the Convention.[20] Implying that the European Court of Human Rights was to blame for the fact that the convicted non-national in the case had not been expelled despite committing severe and recurring offences, the expert's comments[21] ignored the exact reasoning of the judgment that had actually been delivered not by the Strasbourg Court, but by the Danish Supreme Court and based on a rather exceptional concrete proportionality assessment under Article 8 of the Convention in which the Supreme Court specifically pointed to the prosecution's failure to claim expulsion of the offender at an earlier stage in his criminal career.[22]

Thus, rather than explaining the specific circumstances of the case and the legal reasoning behind the controversial outcome, such academic contributions seem to confirm distorted popular views on human rights in general and the European Convention and Court in particular, thereby actually creating or reinforcing the popular scepticism about which they claim to be concerned. The debate in Denmark before and during the preparation of the Copenhagen Declaration in 2016–2018 included a number of contributions that can hardly be seen as anything but aspirations to political influence disguised as dissemination of research findings. While academic contributions to policy processes can indeed be a legitimate endeavour, the appearance and timing of certain magazine articles and public statements may seem to suggest a somewhat concerted effort by some media and academic actors to deliver intellectual support for the initiatives that were underway from the Danish government which had at the relevant time

19 Alston (n. 8) 13.

20 Statement by Anders Henriksen, quoted by Erik Holstein in an article referring to him as expert of international law, *Altinget* 16 January 2017.

21 See also Anders Henriksen, 'EMRK, den nationale interesse og det danske formandskab for Europarådet' (working paper issued by think tank *Justitia*, Copenhagen 2017) 23.

22 Supreme Court judgment 12 May 2016, printed in (2016) *Ugeskrift for Retsvæsen* (weekly legal magazine) 2883, 2897.

already announced its intentions for the upcoming chairmanship of the Council of Europe.[23]

Reforming or curtailing the human rights system?

What is officially known as the Copenhagen Declaration, adopted by the 47 Member States of the Council of Europe at a high-level conference in April 2018, was the outcome of a protracted policy process at both national and European levels in which domestic attempts to push back human rights obtained a quite prominent and – in all likelihood intentionally – visible position. Whereas the draft Declaration became subject to rather unusual criticism in the extensive debate that followed its publication in early February 2018, the final Copenhagen Declaration can be considered as a quite logical extension of the previous declarations and reform initiatives concerning the Court and its mode of operation, i.e. the Interlaken, Izmir, Brighton and Brussels Declarations adopted from 2009 to 2015.

Already the 2016 governmental programme following the establishment of the Danish coalition government included expressions of scepticism towards the European Court of Human Rights, declaring the government's intention to critically examine the manner in which the Court's dynamic interpretation had 'extended the scope' of parts of the Convention as an initiative within Denmark's upcoming chairmanship of the Council of Europe.[24] While policy matters relating to the Council of Europe have traditionally been taken care of by the Ministry of Foreign Affairs, this particular strand of the Danish chairmanship priorities was referred to a special 'task force' that was established within the Ministry of Justice. With inputs and support from selected external advisers, the task force organised an expert conference in November 2017 and prepared the draft Declaration.

The draft was made public as soon as it was circulated among members of the Council of Europe Committee of Ministers, a fact that was generally recognised as an expression of transparency on the part of the Danish government. Apart from this procedural recognition, the draft was heavily criticised not only by non-governmental organisations (NGOs)[25] and academic commentators,[26] but also

23 See, in particular, the 'thematic issue' of *Juristen* (leading Danish legal magazine) in June 2017 with the introductory editorial article declaring the 'dynamic style of interpretation' of the Court of Human Rights up for debate, see Jens Kristiansen, 'Menneskerettighedsdomstolens dynamiske fortolkningsstil til debat' (2017) *Juristen* 71; see also articles by Jørgen Steen Sørensen, Mads Bryde Andersen and Anders Henriksen, whereas none of the Danish professors in human rights law had apparently been invited to contribute to this 'thematic issue'.

24 Danish government programme statement *Marienborgaftalen 2016 – For et friere, rigere og mere trygt Danmark* (Prime Minister's office November 2016) 55–56.

25 See, in particular, *Joint NGO Response to the Draft Copenhagen Declaration*, issued by Amnesty International, Open Society Justice Initiative, International Commission of Jurists and a number of other NGOs, 13 February 2018.

26 For a general critique, see Alice Donald and Philip Leach, 'A Wolf in Sheep's Clothing: Why the Draft Copenhagen Declaration Must be Rewritten', *EJIL: Talk!* (blog of *European Journal of International Law*) 21 February 2018.

caused critical observations by the European Court of Human Rights,[27] and not least by the Parliamentary Assembly of the Council of Europe.[28] In contrast, the Danish Institute for Human Rights officially expressed support of the draft Declaration, considering that it was well in line with the general reform process running over the period 2010–2019 and that it could result in strengthening the European human rights system.[29] Although a general account of this criticism, the ensuing debate and the actors involved would fall outside the scope of this chapter, a few elements pertaining to the topic of this contribution are relevant in order to illustrate the main line of legal reasoning and the policy agenda of the Danish government in attempting to reform the Court and, arguably, curtail its monitoring mandate when examining complaints and enforcing the human rights standards under the European Convention.

The Copenhagen Declaration focuses on *states' primary responsibility* for the effective national implementation of the European Convention on Human Rights and on 'ensuring a proper balance and enhanced protection' in this context; on the execution of the Court's judgments as a key obligation for Member States; on European supervision and the role of the Court; on interaction between the national and the European level and the need for dialogue; on the Court's case-load challenge and the need for further action in that regard; on the selection and election of judges; and on the accession of the EU to the Convention.[30] Insofar as the intensity of the European Court of Human Rights' review of complaints is concerned, the Declaration can be considered a rather neutral and diplomatic restatement of positions previously adopted in the abovementioned Council of Europe declarations, emphasising *shared responsibility* as an overarching term that has been used throughout the reform process to describe the link between the role of the Court and the States Parties.[31] Importantly, it is recalled from the outset in the Declaration that the concept of shared responsibility aims at achieving a balance between the national and European levels of the Convention system, and an improved protection of rights with better prevention and effective remedies available at the national level; it is made clear that 'strengthening the principle of subsidiarity is not intended to limit or weaken human rights protection, but to underline the responsibility of national authorities to guarantee the rights and freedoms set out in the Convention'.[32]

27 European Court of Human Rights, *Opinion on the draft Copenhagen Declaration*, 19 February 2018.
28 Council of Europe, Parliamentary Assembly, *Declaration on the Draft Copenhagen Declaration on the European Human Rights system in the future Europe*, 16 March 2018.
29 Danish Institute for Human Rights, 'Erklæring kan styrke Menneskerettighedsdomstol', press release 6 February 2018 quoting the Director of the Institute who was among the advisers to the government task force in preparing the draft Declaration.
30 Copenhagen Declaration, 13 April 2018, paras 6–18, 19–25, 26–32, 33–41, 42–54, 55–62 and 63–66, respectively.
31 Ibid., para. 6.
32 Ibid., paras 9 and 10.

The qualified application of the principle of *subsidiarity* becomes particularly clear when comparing the adopted and the draft text.[33] The Copenhagen Declaration states as follows:

> The principle of subsidiarity, which continues to develop and evolve in the Court's jurisprudence, guides the way in which the Court conducts its review.
>
> a The Court, acting as a safeguard for individuals whose rights and freedoms are not secured at the national level, may deal with a case only after all domestic remedies have been exhausted. It does not act as a court of fourth instance.
> b The jurisprudence of the Court makes clear that States Parties enjoy a margin of appreciation in how they apply and implement the Convention, depending on the circumstances of the case and the rights and freedoms engaged. This reflects that the Convention system is subsidiary to the safeguarding of human rights at the national level and that national authorities are in principle better placed than an international court to evaluate local needs and conditions.
> c The Court's jurisprudence on the margin of appreciation recognises that in applying certain Convention provisions, such as Articles 8–11, there may be a range of different but legitimate solutions which could each be compatible with the Convention depending on the context. This may be relevant when assessing the proportionality of measures restricting the exercise of rights or freedoms under the Convention. Where a balancing exercise has been undertaken at the national level in conformity with the criteria laid down in the Court's jurisprudence, the Court has generally indicated that it will not substitute its own assessment for that of the domestic courts, unless there are strong reasons for doing so.
> d The margin of appreciation goes hand in hand with supervision under the Convention system, and the decision as to whether there has been a violation of the Convention ultimately rests with the Court.[34]

This is in rather clear contrast to the draft Declaration by which States Parties were supposed to underline the need for a 'more effective, focused and balanced Convention system, where the Court can focus its efforts on identifying serious or widespread violations, systemic and structural problems, and important

33 See Janneke Gerards and Sarah Lambrecht, 'The final Copenhagen Declaration: fundamentally improved with a few remaining caveats', *Strasbourg Observers*, blog entry 18 April 2018.

34 Copenhagen Declaration, 13 April 2018, para. 28. As regards issues of general interpretation, it is explicitly recognised in para. 26 that the Court 'authoritatively interprets the Convention in accordance with relevant norms and principles of public international law, and, in particular, in the light of the Vienna Convention on the Law of Treaties, giving appropriate consideration to present-day conditions'; according to para. 30, the Conference '[a]ppreciates the Court's efforts to ensure that the interpretation of the Convention proceeds in a careful and balanced manner'.

questions of interpretation and application of the Convention', pointing out that 'Great emphasis has been placed on the principle of subsidiarity, by which the protection of human rights takes place primarily at the national level'.[35] Since the protection machinery established by the Convention is 'subsidiary and complementary to the national systems safeguarding human rights', the Court was here told that it 'should not take on the role of States Parties whose responsibility it is to ensure that Convention rights and freedoms are respected and protected at national level'.[36] It was further suggested that those rights should be '*secured and determined at national level*' and protected '*predominantly* at national level by State authorities in accordance with their *constitutional traditions* and in light of *national circumstances*'.[37]

Thus, the principle of primary state responsibility clearly appeared to be invoked by the Danish government's task force and its advisers preparing the draft Declaration as a basis for limiting the Court's review. Rather than operationalising states' primary protection responsibility, they would be encouraged to enforce their own 'constitutional traditions' – the draft Declaration essentially deferring to States Parties, including evolving authoritarian regimes for which this could be seen as an endorsement of their desire to take back control of human rights affairs. Whereas this endeavour did not succeed as apparently intended in the context of the Council of Europe, the politico-legal rhetoric inherent therein may well have reinforced more general tendencies in and beyond Europe towards restricting international human rights monitoring.

Concluding observations on the legal nature of controversies

As discussed earlier, it is theoretically debatable whether the attempts to push back international human rights law as examined in this chapter are really an issue of *transnational legal* phenomena and developments. Alternatively, it might be seen as just another feature of traditional struggles about the demarcation line between state sovereignty and *international* legal obligations. In either case, the current challenges to the human rights system are no coincidence in an era of rising nationalism, intolerance and resistance against binding international cooperative mechanisms.[38] In that sense, this is not exclusively an issue concerning human rights law as these phenomena affect the operation of international law and its interrelationship with national legal norms and institutions more generally.

In order to comprehend the nature of the dispute pertaining to international human rights, it would seem appropriate and possibly necessary to suggest certain conceptual distinctions between the various aspects or elements of the legal

35 Draft Copenhagen Declaration, 5 February 2018, para. 4.
36 Ibid., para. 22.
37 Ibid., paras 10 and 14 (italics added).
38 See Alston (n. 8) 2–4.

norms and their implementation to concrete situations, whether that is carried out by national authorities or international bodies. The debates criticising international monitoring bodies have, not least in Denmark, been fraught with generalising statements alluding to the phenomenon of 'dynamic interpretation' so as to imply that this is the core of the problem with judicial activism. In my view, however, this type of criticism reflects yet another misconception of the legal nature of human rights norms that is conveniently providing the basis for challenging the legitimacy of international actors. As an academic device that might help remedy this state of affairs, I would suggest distinguishing between some main elements in the process of transforming norms into real-life situations.

Thus, there is a fundamental difference between the *general interpretation* and the *concrete application* of human rights, and indeed other legal norms. This may seem banal or self-evident as these are well-known legal concepts. Nonetheless, the distinction could help clarify what is, and what is not, appropriate undertakings for judicial bodies at various levels. Insofar as general interpretation of norms is concerned, there can be no doubt about the need for uniform solutions – often referred to as *autonomous concepts* – which warrants the unlimited interpretive competence of the monitoring bodies, especially at the international level, yet with methodological constraints as described earlier. The concrete application of such norms, on the other hand, includes the balancing of interests, the assessment of evidence as well as procedural safeguards in connection with individual decisions applying human rights norms. This is where *subsidiarity* is called for, and where it is indeed well-established in the practice of international human rights bodies.

Such conceptual distinctions might facilitate the accommodation of the legal complexities flowing from transnational phenomena in law, thereby enhancing the capacity of both academic analysis and practical decision-making to tackle these complexities and challenges. In turn, that might offer just a little help to prevent the politicised pushing back of international norms being the consequence of relentless and unqualified criticism of the human rights system and, potentially, transnational tendencies challenging national legal systems in general.

10 Balancing legal obligations in Europe's cooperation with Libya in the fight against migrant smuggling

Fenella M.W. Billing and Nikolas Feith Tan

Introduction

Current European cooperation with Libya in the struggle to eliminate migrant smuggling presents legal dilemmas for the European Union (EU) and its Member States. These dilemmas arise from the tension between obligations in relation to crime control cooperation under international law, notably the Migrant Smuggling Protocol,[1] on the one hand, and human rights and refugee law,[2] on the other. This chapter addresses how Europe can resolve this tension through the balancing of obligations under these overlapping regimes of international law.

Europe–Libya cooperation focuses on stopping migrant departures from Libya to achieve migration control and combat migrant smuggling.[3] The means of cooperation is the provision of funding, equipment, training and technical assistance to the Libyan coastguard and land border authorities and has extended to the deployment of Italian vessels in Libyan territorial waters.[4] Another

1 The term 'migrant smuggling' is defined in the Protocol Against the Smuggling of Migrants by Land, Sea and Air, supplementing the United Nations Convention against Transnational Organized Crime (adopted 15 November 2000, entered into force 28 January 2004) 2241 UNTS 507 (hereinafter Migrant Smuggling Protocol) Art. 3(a).

2 Notably, European Convention for the Protection of Human Rights and Fundamental Freedoms, as amended by Protocols Nos. 11 and 14, 4 November 1950, ETS 5; European Union, Charter of Fundamental Rights of the European Union, 26 October 2012, 2012/C 326/02; International Covenant on Civil and Political Rights (adopted 16 December 1966, entered into force 23 March 1976) 999 UNTS 171 (ICCPR); The Convention against Torture and Other Cruel, Inhuman or Degrading Treatment or Punishment. Opened for signature 10 December 1984, 1486 UNTS 85 (entered into force 26 June 1987); Protocol Relating to the Status of Refugees (adopted 31 January 1967, entered into force 4 October 1967) 606 UNTS 267.

3 We use the term 'irregular migrant' to denote a person seeking entry without authorisation, including refugees and migrants.

4 European Council and Council of the EU, *Press Releases and Statements*, Malta Declaration by the members of the European Council on the external aspects of migration: addressing the Central Mediterranean route (3 February 2017) www.consilium.europa.eu/en/press/press-releases/2017/01/03-malta-declaration/ accessed 7 November 2017; European Commission, *EU Action in Libya on Migration: The Commission's Contribution to the Leaders' Agenda*, 7 December 2017 https://ec.europa.eu/home-affairs/sites/homeaffairs/

cooperation strategy is funding United Nations High Commission for Refugees (UNHCR) and International Organization for Migration (IOM) efforts to pursue adequate reception conditions in Libya and support evacuations, resettlement and repatriation.[5] The recorded loss of life in the Central Mediterranean stands at 4,581 deaths in 2016, 2,853 deaths in 2017 and 1,314 deaths in 2018.[6] A lack of cooperation with Libya may lead to a surge in smuggled migrant arrivals in the EU and, significantly, continuing high rates of migrant deaths at sea, as most deaths occur in or nearby Libyan territorial waters.

Previous cooperation with Libya on migrant smuggling included the much-criticised practice of interdiction and return of refugees and migrants by Italian authorities under the 2008 Treaty of Friendship, Partnership and Cooperation.[7] Falling short of similar 'pushback' operations, in the current cooperation with Libya, the EU and Italian actors are walking a fine line between mere assistance and active interdiction. Refugees and migrants in Libya suffer documented serious human rights abuses, including appalling conditions of detention, slavery, forced labour and physical and sexual violence.[8] In addition, there is a lack of proper asylum procedure, and irregular migrants are the target of criminal law sanctions. Against this background, the recent arrangements bring Italy and the EU closer to Libyan forces and raise complicated questions about legitimacy and the lawfulness of cooperation. Cooperation on migrant smuggling reflects not only on the legitimacy of Libya in relation to respect for human rights but also of the EU and its Member States in the decision to cooperate.

files/what-we-do/policies/european-agenda-migration/20171207_eu_action_in_libya_on_migration_en.pdf accessed 22 March 2018; Memorandum of Understanding (Libya-Italy) http://eumigrationlawblog.eu/wp-content/uploads/2017/10/MEMORANDUM_translation_finalversion.doc.pdf accessed 12 October 2017; Crispian Balmer, 'Italy begins naval mission to help Libya curb migrant flows' *Reuters* (2 August 2017) www.reuters.com/article/us-europe-migrants-italy-libya/italy-begins-naval-mission-to-help-libya-curb-migrant-flows-idUSKBN1AI1JC accessed 6 August 2017.

5 European Commission (n. 4); European Commission, *Press Release*: Delivering on Commitments: new programmes to protect migrants and support return and reintegration in Africa worth €150 million adopted, 26 February 2018, http://europa.eu/rapid/press-release_IP-18-1143_en.htm accessed 22 March 2018.

6 International Organization for Migration (IOM), 'Missing Migrants Project' https://missingmigrants.iom.int/region/mediterranean?migrant_route%5B%5D=1376, accessed 29 March 2019.

7 The European Court of Human Rights found that the Italian return operations violated the prohibitions against *refoulement* and collective expulsion: ECtHR (GC) *Hirsi Jamaa and Others v. Italy* Appl. No. 27765/09, 23 February 2012; see further Mariagiulia Giuffré, 'State Responsibility Beyond Borders: What Legal Basis for Italy's Push-backs to Libya?' (2012) 24 *International Journal of Refugee Law* 692.

8 See e.g. UN Security Council, *Report of the Secretary-General on the United Nations Support Mission in Libya* (4 April 2017) S/2017/283; UN Security Council, *Letter dated 1 June 2017 from the Panel of Experts on Libya*, S/2017/466.

Cooperation between states on the prevention of migrant smuggling is the cornerstone of the Migrant Smuggling Protocol,[9] which requires state parties to work together on combatting smuggling through criminalisation and strengthening borders. Cooperation on migrant smuggling raises particular concerns when obligations aimed at prevention conflict with other legal frameworks, such as international refugee law.[10] The balancing act may be problematic because transnational law enforcement requires international cooperation between states with varying protection commitments and standards.[11] The crucial question is *to what extent the duty to cooperate under the 2000 Migrant Smuggling Protocol is limited by human rights law, in light of the current circumstances in Libya.*

To answer this question, the chapter employs the concept of *trust*, which refers to expectations and predictions about the future behaviour of a cooperation partner, and is crucial to upholding human rights obligations in international cooperation.[12] In the context of migrant smuggling cooperation with Libya, we argue, the formation of trust requires an assessment by the EU and Member State authorities of the *legitimacy* of their partners. Legitimacy is defined here as a right to exercise authority deriving from a state's capacity to hold and exercise powers in compliance with accepted human rights law obligations.[13] Bodansky identifies respect for human rights as one normative standard giving a right to exercise authority consistent with the concept of legitimacy.[14] In the concrete case, Europe's trust in the legitimacy of Libyan authorities may be determined – at least in part – according to their respect for human rights standards, in law and in practice.

The chapter proceeds in five sections. First, we highlight the importance of upholding fundamental legal obligations in extraterritorial cooperation and, therefore, unfold the concept of trust in a decision to cooperate, based on legitimacy and respect for human rights obligations (section 2). The duty to cooperate

9 Anne T. Gallagher, 'Migrant Smuggling' in Neil Boister and Robert Currie (eds) *Routledge Handbook of Transnational Criminal Law* (Routledge 2015) 196.

10 Mariagiulia Giuffré, 'From Turkey to Libya: The EU Migration Partnership from Bad to Worse' (*Eurojus.it rivista*, 20 March 2017) http://rivista.eurojus.it/from-turkey-to-libya-the-eu-migration-partnership-from-bad-to-worse/ accessed 27 Mar 2017.

11 ECtHR *Soering v. United Kingdom*, Appl. No. 14038/88, Judgment 7 July 1989; see further Thomas Gammeltoft-Hansen and Jens Vedsted-Hansen, 'Human Rights in an Age of International Cooperation' in Thomas Gammeltoft-Hansen and Jens Vedsted-Hansen (eds), *Human Rights and the Dark Side of Globalisation* (Routledge 2017) 1–2.

12 Saskia Hufnagel and Carole McCartney, 'Introduction' in Saskia Hufnagel and Carole McCartney (eds), *Trust in International Police and Justice Cooperation* (Hart 2017) 1 and 15; James Coleman, *Foundations of Social Theory* (Harvard University Press 1990) 107–108.

13 See e.g. Daniel Bodansky, 'Legitimacy in International Law and International Relations' in Jeffrey Dunoff and Mark Pollack (eds), *Interdisciplinary Perspectives on International Law and International Relations: The State of the Art* (Cambridge University Press 2013) 324; Rüdiger Wolfrum, 'Legitimacy of International Law from a Legal Perspective: Some Introductory Considerations' in Rüdiger Wolfrum and Volkar Röben (eds), *Legitimacy in International Law* (Springer 2008) 6.

14 Bodansky (n. 13) 324 and 329ff.

is examined, detailing the range of specific forms of cooperation included in combating the transnational crime of migrant smuggling (section 3), followed by a brief overview of the most significant obligations owed to irregular migrants under human rights and refugee law in the Central Mediterranean (section 4). Finally, the chapter uses this approach to trust and legitimacy to analyse and conclude on the significance of the human rights situation in Libya to the lawfulness of EU/Italian cooperation to combat migrant smuggling (sections 5 and 6).

International cooperation based on respect for human rights

The need for internal and external consistency in compliance with legal obligations

Combating migrant smuggling does not provide the state with unfettered power. States are required to exercise balance between crime control obligations and the protection of human rights, in particular the rights of refugees and vulnerable migrants. Engaging in international cooperation and exercising powers extraterritorially does not extinguish this requirement of balancing obligations.

Moreover, EU law seeks to ensure that Member States apply the same fundamental legal obligations externally as are held and applied internally. This concept is established in relation to EU external action in Article 21(1) Treaty on European Union (TEU).[15] According to this provision, the Union's external action and relationships are guided by the fundamental principles upon which the EU was created, including the rule of law and fundamental rights. Standards of conduct that protect citizens and their fundamental rights do not stop at the border when state authorities exercise functions transnationally. Therefore, it may become a precondition of cooperation and cross-border exercise of authority that state agents anticipate partners will apply similar standards of protection, because cooperation entails a sharing or passing of control.

The issue of trust in decisions to cooperate with external partners

Trust in international cooperation allows state officers to take a 'leap of faith' about how public roles will be carried out by their potential or ongoing partners.[16] This trust may be based on any or all of three possible grounds: common values, common goals and personal contacts.[17] Common border securitisation and crime-fighting goals or common training initiatives that build personal

15 Treaty on European Union (Consolidated) OJ 2012/C326/01 (TEU).

16 Hufnagel and McCartney (n. 12) 1.

17 Saskia Hufnagel, 'Police Cooperation in Europe, China and Australia: Does Trust Depend on the Political System?' in Saskia Hufnagel and Carole McCartney (eds), *Trust in International Police and Justice Cooperation* (Hart 2017) 36ff.

contacts may be dominant factors in migrant smuggling cooperation.[18] However, Hufnagel uses the approach of linking trust and legitimacy with implementation of human rights obligations in the context of assessing how state authorities view each other in transnational policing cooperation.[19] Trust in a partner based on respect for common human rights norms ensures a balanced approach to complying with legal obligations and arguably provides greater strength to the legitimacy of the cooperation from the perspective of the international community.[20]

In order to move beyond 'blind faith' in a partner, expectations and predictions about future behaviour manifesting trust need to be well founded. Legitimacy deriving from a belief that a partner respects human rights, 'merely' because the state *holds* the same legal obligations, at most leads to a conclusion that the partner may be trusted in an abstract sense. Clearly, ratification of a human rights treaty does not in itself sufficiently demonstrate respect for fundamental values and human rights obligations.[21] Legitimacy is a quality that should be ascribed as a result of a concrete assessment that powers are both held and *exercised* appropriately in practice.[22] Therefore, trust in a concrete sense relies on the legitimacy of a partner because it holds similar obligations under an accepted human rights framework, and because it exercises and limits its powers accordingly.[23]

Trust is more readily achievable in partnership with states that share a comprehensive common value system, for example, within the EU. Such a system is highly indicative of legitimacy in relation to the actual human rights obligations being applied in law and practice.[24] Within the autonomous EU legal system, fundamental rights have not only developed under international law as a result of the consensus of states. In EU law, fundamental rights have developed as general principles of law inspired by the constitutional traditions of the Member States and the European Convention on Human Rights (ECHR),[25] and foremost as primary law in the EU's Charter of Fundamental Rights (CFR),[26] established under a supranational form of democracy, including the sharing of legislative powers

18 Douglas Guilfoyle, 'Jurisdiction at Sea: Migrant Interdiction and the Transnational Security State' in Thomas Gammeltoft-Hansen and Jens Vedsted-Hansen (eds), *Human Rights and the Dark Side of Globalisation: Transnational Law Enforcement and Migration Control* (Routledge 2017) 115–116 and 120ff, citing Stephen Humphrey's, *Theatre of the Rule of Law: Transnational Legal Intervention in Theory and Practice* (Cambridge University Press 2010) 10; ibid., 12, 43–49.

19 Hufnagel (n. 17) 33–35.

20 The question of legitimacy can also be addressed from other perspectives not specifically raised in this chapter, such as Libyan authorities or irregular migrants themselves.

21 *Hirsi Jamaa* para. 128.

22 Hufnagel and McCartney (n. 12) 1.

23 On 'mutual trust' '*in abstracto*' and '*in concreto*' in EU law, see Christine Janssens, *The Principle of Mutual Recognition in EU Law* (OUP 2013) 141ff.

24 On legitimacy of norms, see Bodansky (n. 13) 326–329; and Wolfrum (n. 13) 2 ff.

25 Convention for the Protection of Human Rights and Fundamental Freedoms (adopted 4 November 1950, entered into force 21 September 1970) as amended by Protocol No. 14 (entered into force 1 June 2010) CETS No. 194 (ECHR).

26 Charter of Fundamental Rights of the European Union OJ 2012/C 326/02 (CFR).

with the European Parliament.[27] Against this background, in EU law, the concept of trust has been elevated to a legal principle – the principle of mutual trust.[28] Thus, EU Member States must *presume* that other EU Member States comply with EU law and the same fundamental rights obligations. The presumption of compliance is only rebuttable, and obligations to cooperate limited, by significant evidence to the contrary and a balancing of interests.[29] However, this systematic level of confidence is not generally tenable beyond the level of European integration in cooperation between EU Member States. In EU external cooperation, the requisite legal basis to operate a presumption of compliance with human rights obligations is lacking. In addition, the record of compliance with obligations under relevant international human rights law frameworks should be taken into account already at the time cooperation agreements are made. Therefore, establishing trust may be problematic in transnational cooperation with states that have dissimilar political systems and varying attachments to the rule of law.[30]

In some situations, a lack of trust in another state's agency may be a reason not to cooperate because it does not hold similar values or implement human rights obligations in the same way.[31] However, risk is often inbuilt in international cooperation because of a time lag between agreeing to cooperate and the agreed activities taking place. Following Coleman's analysis of trust, cooperation requires an assessment of three elements: the probability that a partner is trustworthy; the potential loss of cooperation; and the potential gain.[32] This breakdown highlights the need to assess trust in light of legitimacy and by taking into account all the available information about the exigencies of the situation.[33]

27 TEU Art. 6.

28 See further Jens Vedsted-Hansen, 'Reception Conditions as Human Rights: Pan-European Standard or Systematic Deficiencies?' in Vincent Chetail, Philippe De Bruycker and Francesco Maiani (eds), *Reforming the Common European Asylum System* (Brill 2016) 295–296; Valsamis Mitsilegas, 'Mutual Recognition, Mutual Trust and Fundamental Rights after Lisbon' in Valsamis Mitsilegas, Maria Bergström and Theodore Konstadinides (eds), *Research Handbook on EU Criminal Law* (Edward Elgar 2016) 148–150.

29 See CJEU, *C.K. and others v. Republika Slovenija* C-578/16 PPU 16 February 2017 ECLI:EU:C:2017:127; CJEU (GC), *Pál Aranyosi and Robert Căldăraru*, joined cases C-404/15 and C-659/15 PPU, 5 April 2016, ECLI:EU:C:2016:198; CJEU (Full Court), Opinion 2/13, 18 December 2014, ECLI:EU:C:2014:2454; CJEU, *N.S. v. Secretary of State for the Home Department (England and Wales)* C-411/10, 21 December 2011, ECLI:EU:C:2011:865.

30 See Wolfrum (n. 13) 2 ff.

31 See e.g. Ludo Block, 'Establishing Trust Despite the Risk? An Analysis of the Need for Trust in Police Cooperation' in Saskia Hufnagel and Carole McCartney (eds), *Trust in International Police and Justice Cooperation* (Hart 2017) 21 and 25; Fenella Billing, *The Right to Silence in Transnational Criminal Proceedings: Comparative Law Perspectives* (Springer 2016) 341.

32 Coleman (n. 12) 91 and 99 ff.

33 Ibid. 103.

This may be based, for example, on reliable, independent reports by UN bodies and international organisations.[34]

Establishing trust where there is evidence that a state authority has been responsible for human rights violations will inherently involve a complex balancing between the needs for effective cooperation and protecting the individuals concerned. However, the *need* to place trust to satisfy border and crime control obligations may result in states 'grasping at straws' in the assessment of a partner state's human rights record.[35]

The duty to cooperate under the Migrant Smuggling Protocol

In principle, states have a legitimate interest and an obligation of protection under human rights law to cooperate in the fight against migrant smuggling, rather than ignore the 'very real harms that [it] … inflicts on individuals, States, and the international community as a whole'.[36] The crime is highly profitable and the perpetrators generally well connected to other criminal networks or corrupt state actors.[37] In addition to unseaworthiness of vessels, hard conditions at sea and scarcity of supplies, migrant smuggling by sea places migrants at a high risk of death.[38] Vulnerable refugees or poorer migrants may choose low-cost options that involve higher risks of abusive treatment by smugglers, including instances of smugglers selling migrants into slavery with impunity.[39] Due to the irregular status of refugees and migrants using migrant smuggling services and the lack of information and alternative options, they are almost powerless for the entire land and sea journey and are unlikely to seek assistance from law enforcement authorities.[40] Therefore, the Migrant Smuggling Protocol's triple purpose calls for an effective, comprehensive approach 'to prevent and combat the smuggling of migrants, as well as to promote cooperation among States Parties to that end, while protecting the rights of smuggled migrants'.[41]

Beyond this overarching call for international cooperation, the duty to cooperate is woven into various provisions of the Protocol. In relation to migrant smuggling by sea, for example, Article 7 requires cooperation 'to the fullest extent to

34 See e.g. *Hirsi Jamaa* paras 117–123, in particular at 121; *N.S. v. Secretary of State for the Home Department (England and Wales)*, paras 86–88, referring to ECtHR *M.S.S. v. Belgium and Greece* Appl. No. 30696/09 21 January 2011, paras 358, 360 and 367.

35 Coleman (n. 12) 107–108.

36 Anne T. Gallagher and Fiona David, *The International Law of Migrant Smuggling* (Cambridge University Press 2014) 13 and 493; and see Migrant Smuggling Protocol Art. 15.

37 UNODC, Issue Paper: Smuggling of Migrants by Sea, 2011, 18.

38 Ibid. 5.

39 Ibid. 20; and see e.g. Nima Elbagir, Raja Razek, Alex Platt and Bryony Jones, 'People for sale: where lives are auctioned for $400' (CNN 14 November 2017) http://edition.cnn.com/2017/11/14/africa/libya-migrant-auctions/index.html accessed 17 November 2017.

40 UNODC (n. 37) 22.

41 Migrant Smuggling Protocol preamble and Art. 2.

prevent and suppress the smuggling of migrants by sea', in accordance with the international law of the sea. The law of the sea sets out a framework for enforcement jurisdiction that is relevant to interdiction of migrant smuggling vessels, for example, to conduct a criminal investigation or enforce domestic immigration laws in territorial waters. In this context, Article 8 of the Protocol provides for *assistance in the suppression of vessels* used for migrant smuggling when requested by a party to the Protocol, requiring requested states to assist 'to the extent possible within their means'. In July 2017, the Government of National Accord requested Italian assistance in stopping the departure of smuggling boats from Libyan waters.[42]

In relation to the criminalisation of smuggling, Article 6 obliges state parties to create criminal offences relating to smuggling of migrants, participating as an accomplice, and the organisation of smuggling activities. Moreover, Article 6(3) requires state parties to provide for aggravating circumstances in national law, where offences risk the lives of migrants or amount to inhuman or degrading treatment. The danger inherent in the Central Mediterranean route means all smuggling offences would be aggravated.

Of relevance to cooperation between Europe and Libya, Article 14(2) of the Protocol further provides for cooperation between states to ensure *adequate training* to tackle smuggling. This may involve training on the investigation of migrant smuggling and the protection of smuggled migrants, including human rights education.[43] Cooperation between the EU and Italy and Libya currently comprises the operation of the Italian navy vessels in Libyan territorial waters providing 'logistical, technical and operational support' to their Libyan counterparts; EU training of 1,000 Libyan Coastguard officers and Italian funding of reception centres in Libya.[44]

In addition, Article 10 provides for an obligation to share information on migrant smuggling means and methods, in particular between states with common borders or located on smuggling routes. Article 18 requires cooperation on the *return* of smuggled migrants to their country of origin. States of origin are required to 'facilitate and accept, without undue or unreasonable delay', the return of their nationals, while receiving states are required to return smuggled migrants 'in an orderly manner and with due regard for the safety and dignity of the person'.[45]

42 Jason Horowitz, 'Italy Plans Naval Mission Off Libya to Stop Migrant Boats' *The New York Times* (27 July 2017) www.nytimes.com/2017/07/27/world/europe/italy-plans-naval-mission-off-libya-to-stop-migrant-boats.html?mcubz=1&_r=0 accessed 20 September 2017.

43 UN Security Council, 4 April 2017 (n. 8) 10–11, 13.

44 Memorandum of Understanding (Libya-Italy) (n. 4); European Council on Refugees and Exiles (ECRE), 'Italy further strengthens cooperation with Libya amid human rights concerns' (8 September 2017) www.ecre.org/italy-further-strengthens-cooperation-with-libya-amid-human-rights-concerns/ accessed 19 September 2017.

45 Migrant Smuggling Protocol Arts 18(1) and (5).

Perhaps most crucially, the duty to cooperate in relation to the above areas is subject to a savings clause in the Protocol. Article 19 provides:

> Nothing in this Protocol shall affect the other rights, obligations and responsibilities of States and individuals under international law, including international humanitarian law and international human rights law and, in particular, where applicable, the 1951 Convention and the 1967 Protocol relating to the Status of Refugees and the principle of *non-refoulement* as contained therein.

The savings clause limits the operation of the Protocol and its focus on cooperation in the combating of smuggling by special reference to other relevant branches of international law, including those protecting the rights of migrants and refugees. Article 16(1) thus requires state parties to take 'all appropriate measures' to protect the fundamental rights of those smuggled, 'in particular the right to life and the right not to be subjected to torture or other cruel, inhuman or degrading treatment or punishment'.[46]

Despite the Protocol's savings clause upholding the fundamental rights of smuggled migrants, including refugees, there remains a clear tension between the aims of the international law on smuggling and international refugee law.[47] Gallagher and David describe a potential 'collision of norms' between obligations to act against smuggling and obligations to ensure the rights of refugees,[48] while Hathaway warns of a 'slippery slope' into the criminalisation of transnational movement.[49] In the Central Mediterranean context, the EU faces the complex dilemma of preventing deaths of migrants and combating smuggling, on the one hand, or upholding the rights of refugees to access asylum in Europe and risking return of all migrants to inhuman and degrading conditions of detention in Libya, on the other.

Rights at risk in cooperation: obligation and reality

The right to asylum and non-refoulement

Unlike the Migrant Smuggling Protocol, international refugee law does not include a binding duty to cooperate. Rather, responsibility for refugees is generally territorial – the Refugee Convention prohibits the return to persecution of a refugee within a state's jurisdiction. While the preamble to the Refugee Convention recognises that refugee burden-sharing cannot be solved without

46 Anne Gallagher, 'Human Rights and Human Trafficking: Quagmire or Firm Ground? A Response to James Hathaway' (2009) 49 *Virginia Journal of International Law* 789, 839.

47 Gallagher (n. 9) 197.

48 Gallagher and David (n. 36) 65.

49 James C. Hathaway, 'The Human Rights Quagmire of Human Trafficking' (2008) 49 *Virginia Journal of International Law* 1, 5.

international cooperation, there are no substantive obligations to cooperate on refugees in the treaty.[50]

The Refugee Convention and relevant human rights treaties recognise the guarantee of *non-refoulement*, prohibiting the forced return to a real risk of persecution or serious harm.[51] As well as protecting refugees, *non-refoulement* protects all persons as an ancillary to the absolute prohibition against torture and inhuman or degrading treatment or punishment. EU Member States are bound by the principle of *non-refoulement* under a number of human rights instruments, including the ECHR, the CFR and the Refugee Convention.[52] Importantly, in the Libyan context, *non-refoulement* encompasses a prohibition against returning any person to torture or inhuman or degrading treatment or punishment, including in relation to detention.[53]

Significantly, the human rights law prohibition against *refoulement* is absolute and 'not subject to exception or limitation for any reason whatever'.[54] The absolute nature of the principle under international human rights law means that the EU, or one of its Member States, cannot derogate from its obligations in any circumstances.[55] The non-derogability of this obligation is an important element in the context of the current European migrant and refugee crisis as EU–Libya cooperation on migrant smuggling raises questions of compatibility with the principle of *non-refoulement*. While the nature of migrant flows crossing the Central Mediterranean is undoubtedly mixed, around 40% of irregular arrivals to Italy receive a form of international protection.[56] Therefore, any return of irregular migrants by the EU to Libya without an assessment of their international protection needs would violate the prohibition against *refoulement*. This is also the case because there is significant evidence of serious ill treatment of migrants detained in Libya. In addition, such returns may violate the prohibition against collective expulsion contained in ECHR Protocol 4 Article 4 and CFR Article 19(1). Further, Libya is not a party to the Refugee Convention and forced returns to

50 Convention Relating to the Status of Refugees (28 July 1951, entered into force 22 April 1954), 189 UNTS 137 (Refugee Convention), preambular para. 4.

51 On *non-refoulement*, see Elihu Lauterpacht and Daniel Bethlehem, 'The Scope and Content of the Principle of Non-refoulement: Opinion' in Erika Feller, Volker Türk and Frances Nicholson (eds), *Refugee Protection in International Law: UNHCR's Global Consultations on International Protection* (Cambridge University Press 2003).

52 ECHR Art. 3, CFR Arts 4, 18 and 19(2); Refugee Convention Art. 33(1); see also ICCPR Art. 7; and the Convention against Torture and Other Cruel, Inhuman or Degrading Treatment or Punishment (adopted 10 December 1984, entered into force 26 June 1987) 1486 UNTS 85 (CAT) Art. 3.

53 *Hirsi Jamaa* para. 114.

54 ECHR Art. 3; *Soering* para. 88; *Hirsi Jamaa* para. 120.

55 While the Refugee Convention includes narrow exceptions to *non-refoulement*, on the grounds of overriding reasons of national security and public safety, the ECHR and ICCPR allow no such exceptions, see Lauterpacht and Bethlehem (n. 51) 150 and 162.

56 Ministry of Interior (Italy), Asylum Statistics, 2015–2016, www.libertaciviliimmigrazione.dlci.interno.gov.it/sites/default/files/allegati/riepilogo_dati_2015_2016_0.pdf accessed 18 September 2017.

African countries of origin may also be an issue. Return of irregular migrants to Libya by Italy has previously been held to violate the principle of *non-refoulement* by the European Court of Human Rights (ECtHR).[57]

The right to leave

The right to leave any country, including one's own, is provided for in ICCPR Article 12(2) and ECHR Protocol No. 4 Article 2(2). Importantly, the scope of the right extends to both nationals and non-nationals and has been characterised as fundamental to international protection as a necessary condition of asylum in escaping one's own country.[58] However, the right to leave is not absolute;[59] and it does not amount to a right of entry into another country. States retain sovereignty over their borders, circumscribed only by the prohibition against *refoulement*, discussed earlier.

Human rights law jurisdiction

The application of human rights obligations in the context of transnational cooperation on migrant smuggling turns on the question of EU or member state jurisdiction. Human rights law jurisdiction relates to the applicability of a treaty to the conduct of a state party.[60] The finding of jurisdiction denotes factual and/or legal power over an individual or territory that reaches the threshold of engaging a state's international obligations. Human rights law jurisdiction is presumed to apply within the territory of a state but may be found extraterritorially in a range of circumstances. While the jurisdiction clauses of international human rights instruments vary, in general terms extraterritorial jurisdiction may be found where a state exercises effective control or authority over a territory or person.[61] This test would seem to require active interventions on the part of the state agent, such as to create a jurisdictional link between the individual and the state.[62]

57 *Hirsi Jamaa*.

58 Elspeth Guild and Jean Monnet, *The right to leave a country* (Strasbourg, Council of Europe Commissioner for Human Rights Issue Paper 2013) 6.

59 See ICCPR Art. 12(3), allowing necessary limitations to protect national security, public order, etc.; see e.g. Elspeth Guild, 'To protect or to forget? The Human Right to Leave a Country' (*EU Immigration and Asylum Law and Policy blog*, 27 December 2017) http://eumigrationlawblog.eu/to-protect-or-to-forget-the-human-right-to-leave-a-country/ accessed 3 May 2018.

60 ECtHR (GC) *Al-Jedda v. The United Kingdom* Appl. No. 27021/08, 7 July 2011, para. 74.

61 Karen Da Costa, *The extraterritorial application of selected human rights treaties* (Martinus Nijhoff Publishers 2012); Human Rights Committee, *General Comment 31: The nature of the general legal obligation imposed on States Parties to the Covenant* (CCPR/C/21/Rev.1/Add.13, 26 May 2004); Committee Against Torture, *General Comment 2: Implementation of article 2 by States Parties* (CAT/C/GC/2, 24 January 2008); ECtHR (GC) *Al-Skeini v. United Kingdom* Appl. No. 55721/07.

62 European Agency for Fundamental Rights, *Scope of the principle of non-refoulement in contemporary border management: Evolving areas of law* (Guidance Report 2016) 28.

Thus far, EU cooperation with Libya appears to have fallen short of reaching the standard triggering jurisdiction, as the activities of the EU or Italy do not appear to amount to the requisite authority or control over Libyan territory or irregular migrants seeking to depart the country. Accordingly:

> The training and assistance provided by the EU and Italy, in particular, aim to enable Libya to autonomously conduct rescue and 'pull-back' operations of all migrants and refugees sailing off from Libyan shores toward Europe as part of mixed operations to control borders and "rescue lives" at sea.[63]

To this point, neither EU nor Italian authorities have actively carried out return operations to Libya. This less interventionist form of cooperation on migrant smuggling appears to avoid EU jurisdiction over those irregular migrants prevented from departing Libya. Recently termed 'contactless control', neither the EU nor Italy exercise direct authority or control over irregular migrants in Libya.[64]

While the EU appears to be thus far avoiding human rights law jurisdiction over irregular migrants departing Libya, those migrants prevented from leaving the country face dire consequences. The Office of the High Commissioner for Human Rights, for example, reports a 'host' of human rights abuses, including arbitrary detention and inhuman treatment, in migrant detention centres in Libya.[65] The consequences, albeit indirect, of EU actions are extremely serious human rights violations to migrants prevented from departing or returning to Libya. At the same time, of course, preventing the departure of irregular migrants from Libya removes them from the risk of death at sea.

Europe's legitimacy dilemma

Resolving the tension between the duty to cooperate in preventing and suppressing migrant smuggling and concurrent human rights obligations is likely to result

63 Violeta Moreno-Lax and Mariegiulia Giuffré, 'The Rise of Consensual Containment: From "Contactless Control" to "Contactless Responsibility" for Forced Migration Flows' in S. Juss (ed.), *Research Handbook on International Refugee Law* (Edward Elgar forthcoming) 8; but see a recent application to the Strasbourg court contending that Italy's conduct does trigger jurisdiction under the ECHR: Global Legal Action Network. Legal Action Against Italy over its Coordination of Libyan Coast Guard Pull-backs Resulting in Migrant Deaths and Abuse (8 May 2018), www.glanlaw.org/single-post/2018/05/08/Legal-action-against-Italy-over-its-coordination-of-Libyan-Coast-Guard-pull-backs-resulting-in-migrant-deaths-and-abuse accessed 22 May 2018.

64 Global Action Legal Network (n. 63); see further ECtHR (GC) *Ilascu and Others v. Moldova and Russia* Appl. No. 48787/99, 8 July 2004; ECtHR *Ilascu and Others v. Moldova and Russia* Appl. No. 48787/99 (admissibility decision).

65 Office of the High Commissioner for Human Rights, *'Detained and Dehumanised': Report on Human Rights Abuses Against Migrants in Libya* (13 December 2016), 11.1; see also European External Action Service, *EUBAM Libya Initial Mapping Report* (Executive Summary, 25 January 2017) 37.

in a determination that Libya is not a legitimate or trustworthy partner. Although Libya holds certain common legal obligations through its ratification of the International Covenant on Civil and Political Rights (ICCPR) and the Migrant Smuggling Protocol, Libya is not a party to the Refugee Convention. Libyan law penalises irregular entry, exit and stays in the country without distinguishing between refugees, victims of smuggling and trafficking or other migrants.[66]

Moreover, reports about the exercise of power by Libyan authorities in practice are deeply problematic. Even with the formation of the UN-backed Government of National Accord, Libya remains a fragile state, with a number of factions vying for political authority since the fall of the Gaddafi regime in 2011, when Italy suspended the operation of its bilateral treaty with Libya on irregular migration.[67] The current situation of competing governments and militias continues to threaten citizens and migrants with armed clashes, chaos, a weak legal system and lack of accountability. Further, reports indicate the involvement of some armed groups and coastguards in smuggling enterprises in Libya, including people, weapons and fuel.[68] Moreover, despite EU funding, widespread reports document corruption and arbitrary detention of migrants in inhuman and degrading conditions in Libyan detention centres.[69] Highly relevant to the question of legitimacy, there is also a lack of proper asylum procedures in Libya and migrants risk forcible return to their countries of origin without proper consideration of their refugee status.[70]

In contrast, the EU is generally considered to possess high-level legitimacy by reference to the actual human rights obligations being upheld. However, even the provision of funding, training and equipment by the EU to combat migrant smuggling amounts to an extraterritorial security measure preventing access to asylum in the EU.[71] Thus far, however, European actors seem to have avoided directly carrying out violations of international human rights law in the course of cooperation. The absolute nature of some fundamental human rights protections, such as the prohibitions against *refoulement*, torture and ill treatment, places meaningful limits on cooperation between the EU, its Member States and Libya.

66 Office of the High Commissioner for Human Rights (n. 65) 11.

67 Giuffré (n. 7).

68 UN Security Council, 4 April 2017 (n. 8) paras 34–45; UN Security Council, 1 June 2017 (n. 8), summary and paras 57–59, 89–98, 240–245, 255–258 and Annex 17.

69 See e.g. UN Security Council, 4 April 2017 (n. 8) 8; UN Security Council, 1 June 2017 (n. 8) 20–21 and 133–136; Human Rights Watch, *World Report 2017* www.hrw.org/world-report/2017/country-chapters/libya accessed 7 September 2017.

70 See e.g. *Hirsi Jamaa* para. 153.

71 Guilfoyle (n. 18) 128ff. Moreover, such forms of 'aid and assistance' may raise questions of indirect legal responsibility, not addressed in this contribution. See Francesca Mussi and Nikolas Feith Tan, 'Comparing Cooperation on Migration Control: Italy–Libya and Australia–Indonesia' in Siobhán Mullally (ed.), *Irish Yearbook of International Law* (Hart-Bloomsbury 2017); Giuffré (n. 7) 692; Moreno-Lax and Giuffré (n. 63).

Simultaneously, the EU and Italy are attempting to raise the legitimacy of the Libyan authorities since the cooperation commenced, by allocating funding to the IOM and UNHCR to improve the conditions for irregular migrants detained in Libya, to facilitate assisted voluntary returns and, significantly, to remove and resettle vulnerable refugees.[72] The training and operational support provided by EU and Italian institutions to Libyan coastguards also aims to address human rights education and improved respect for the rights of migrants in operations at sea, particularly women and children.[73] In relation to the prosecution of migrant smugglers, lack of legitimacy on the part of the Libyan criminal justice system makes prosecutions under domestic law untenable. As a result, Italy appears to be taking on the prosecution of arrested smugglers.[74]

Conclusion

A decade ago, leading scholars debated the impact of the emerging international law framework on migrant smuggling on human rights and refugee law, foreseeing the potential for conflicts between the regimes.[75] Today, Europe is struggling to strike the balance between these tensions in its cooperation with Libya on 'breaking the business model of smugglers' while respecting the most fundamental rights of irregular migrants. This chapter argues that to strike such a balance, international cooperation between Europe and external states requires a certain level of *trust* that partners will act in accordance with common human rights obligations. Moving beyond a presumption of trust, cooperation relies on the *legitimacy* of the institutions of the partner state. Legitimacy in this context requires a record of holding similar norms, such as human rights obligations, in addition to the compliance with such norms.

Therefore, international cooperation between Europe and Libya requires trust based on the demonstrated ability of Libyan authorities to respect the fundamental rights of smuggled migrants. A straightforward analysis shows, however, that Libya lacks legitimacy in this regard. Rather than cooperate with Libya, Europe could conceivably confine itself to search and rescue operations on the high seas, transferring migrants to safety in the EU. Nevertheless, this approach arguably sustains the demand for migrant smuggling services, while withdrawing European support and presence in Libyan waters where most migrant deaths occur.[76]

72 European External Action Service (n. 65); European Commission (n. 4).

73 See e.g. UN Security Council, 4 April 2017 (n. 8) 10–11, 13.

74 European Council and Council of the EU, *Press Release*: EUNAVFOR MED Operation Sophia: mandate extended until 31 December 2018 www.consilium.europa.eu/en/press/press-releases/2017/07/25/eunavformed-sophia-mandate-extended/ accessed 6 August 2017.

75 Hathaway (n. 49); Gallagher (n. 46).

76 North Africa Mixed Migration Hub (MHub) 'Survey Snapshots', show for the majority of months that 100% of the migrants surveyed in Italy used the services of smugglers to make the journey by sea from Libya to Italy: www.mixedmigrationhub.org/survey-snapshots/ accessed 27 October 2017.

On this basis, despite Libya's low legitimacy in relation to respect for human rights, cooperation can lawfully continue with the principal aim of *preventing deaths at sea*, for example, through training and assistance on search and rescue. Such cooperation could also focus on improving the conditions of rescued migrants at sea. This type of cooperation is preferable to one that merely aims to stem irregular migration and combat smuggling. Moreover, people intercepted and returned to Libya face a situation of being forced 'out of the frying pan into the fire'[77] of immigration detention. *Improving conditions of immigration detention* in Libya and offering *legal pathways to asylum*, via evacuation and resettlement, must be given high priority alongside the primary goal of preventing deaths at sea.

77 English idiom.

Part III

Application, enforcement and the challenges of legitimacy

11 Enforcing transnational labour law in local contexts

Louise Munkholm

Introduction

The chapter investigates, from a sociology of law perspective, contemporary challenges and potential solutions to the local enforcement of safety and health standards formulated by the International Labour Organization (ILO).[1] Traditional ways of enforcing safety and health standards are under pressure from current trends in the global world of work characterised by unstable employment with short-term contracts and irregular hours due to the way production is organised.[2] Undeclared work and precarious working conditions are widespread.[3] To fill current gaps in the protection of workers, the ILO promotes the building of 'a culture of prevention in occupational safety and health'.[4] The ILO emphasises that 'safe and healthy work is a fundamental human right' and stresses the need for national and local implementation and enforcement of central ILO conventions on occupational safety and health (OSH), such as Convention 187 on 'Promotional Framework for Occupational Safety and Health' and Convention 155 on 'Occupational Safety and Health'.[5] The ILO has 187 Member States who have (most of them) ratified these conventions. In other words, almost all countries in the world subscribe to OSH, at least on paper. However, we cannot speak of OSH as purely international law. It is transnational in the sense that it is constituted through a complex overlap of different national, international, public and private norm-creation processes where a great variety of state and non-state actors

1 The chapter draws in part on empirical data gathered for my PhD project funded by Roskilde University. The full project is presented in Louise Munkholm, *Reinventing Labour Law Enforcement: A Socio-Legal Analysis* (Hart Publishing, forthcoming).
2 International Labour Organization, 'World Employment and Social Outlook: The Changing Nature of Jobs. Executive Summary' (2015) 3.
3 Guy Standing, 'Why the Precariat Is Not a "Bogus Concept"' (2014) www.opendemocracy.net/guy-standing/why-precariat-is-not-%E2%80%9Cbogus-concept%E2%80%9D accessed 10 September 2018.
4 International Labour Organization, 'ILO Flagship Programme OSH-GAP Occupational Safety and Health Global Action Plan for Prevention' (2017).
5 Ibid.

participate.[6] Against this background, OSH can be argued to be an example of a set of transnational legal norms that travels around the world. Importantly, OSH has to be implemented and promoted locally to have effect. Put differently, the legitimacy of transnational norms implies a local willingness to accept and follow the rules 'even if this goes against specific interests at specific times'.[7] One central dimension of legitimacy is then the extent to which 'persuasive reasons as to why a course of action, a rule, or a political order is right and appropriate' are provided.[8] As put by Andrew Hurrell, 'finding a stable language for the negotiation of legitimacy across [...] audiences remains perhaps the most serious challenge'.[9]

The chapter analyses how OSH norms are promoted by local labour inspectors in Prato, a small city in Northern Italy with a total population of 191,424 inhabitants.[10] Labour inspectors represent a governmental body established to enforce existing labour law with respect to working conditions, including OSH. Labour inspectors can thereby be seen as important communicators of OSH norms, in the sense that they play a central role in giving reasons and persuading employers and workers to accept and follow the standards established by the ILO. Since the 1980s, Prato has attracted thousands of Chinese migrants who own or work in small workshops active in different parts of the local clothing production chain. A recent report puts the actual Chinese population in Prato between 30,000 and 40,000.[11] The official number is a bit lower, however. The Municipality of Prato had, for instance, registered 16,182 Chinese-born residents in 2013.[12] On this basis, the picture is that approximately one in ten people in Prato is Chinese. The Prato Chamber of Commerce estimates that there are 5,842 Chinese-owned firms in Prato compared with a total of 33,453 firms.[13] The vast majority of the Chinese activities are concentrated in the clothing industry (3,641 firms) and much less in the traditional textiles-producing industry of Prato (389 firms).[14]

6 This definition builds on the work of Paulius Jurčys, Poul F. Kjær and Ren Yatsunami, *Regulatory Hybridization in the Transnational Sphere* (Martinus Nijhoff Publishers 2013). Jurčys et al. understand transnational law as a process of double hybridisation in which national and international domains as well as private and public spheres are mixed in a complex interplay between jurisdictions and between state and non-state actors.

7 Andrew Hurrell, 'Legitimacy and the Use of Force: Can the Circle Be Squared?' (2005) 31 *Review of International Studies* 15, 16.

8 Ibid., 24.

9 Ibid., 32.

10 Loretta Baldassar, Graeme Johanson, Narelle McAuliffe and Massimo Bressan, 'Chinese Migration to the New Europe: The Case of Prato' in Loretta Baldassar, Graeme Johanson, Narelle McAuliffe and Massimo Bressan (eds), *Chinese Migration to Europe, Prato, Italy, and Beyond* (Palgrave MacMillan 2015) 29.

11 Kevin Latham and Bin Wu, *Chinese Immigration into the EU: New Trends, Dynamics and Implications* (ECRAN 2013).

12 Baldassar et al. (n. 10).

13 The numbers have been found by searching in the statistical database of the Prato Chamber of Commerce www.po.camcom.it/servizi/datistud/stsint.php accessed 10 September 2018.

14 Ibid.

These figures indicate that the Chinese firms do not represent a direct competition for the Italian firms – a fact that has been stressed by various observers, including Baldassar et al., who emphasise that for Prato 'the Chinese in China are a greater economic threat than the Chinese in town'.[15] Perhaps, therefore, the Chinese firms in Prato were not given any special attention during the 1980s and 1990s. However, the financial crisis that hit hard in Italy in 2008 has fuelled debates about the Chinese in Prato, including the Chinese employers' use of undeclared work as well as the poor safety and working conditions of Chinese workers.[16] In 2014, the regional government gave the Chinese firms the choice of either entering into a process of legalisation or closing down.[17] The Provincial Labour Directorate (DPL) and the Local Health and Safety Authority (ASL) play key roles in this respect as they carry out control visits to Chinese firms and offer consultancy on how to turn OSH norms from paper into practice. Therefore, the chapter focuses on the work of labour inspectors in DPL and ASL in its analysis below. The selection of Prato as the case is a 'strategic choice', to use the typology of Bent Flyvbjerg. According to Flyvbjerg, '[a]typical and extreme cases often reveal more information because they activate more actors and more basic mechanisms in the situation studied'.[18] The case of Prato is extreme. The numbers alone (the proportion of Chinese in Prato's population and the proportion of Chinese firms in the local business environment that are not living up to basic requirements with regard to OSH) make it a strategic case for expecting processes of social change, including transformations in the way labour law is understood and enforced. Studying this extreme case provides insight into concrete actions taken by local labour inspectors to persuade firms about the legitimacy of OSH norms. The case study is then instrumental to learning about if, and how, legal actors seek to shape the legitimacy of existing transnational norms.

The chapter is divided into three parts. Part I presents the Italian labour inspection system with emphasis on defining the local labour inspector as a specific type of legal actor that promotes a culture of prevention when it comes to OSH. Part II analyses three specific tools developed by local labour inspectors to promote the benefits of labour law compliance to Chinese firms in Prato: video campaigning, distribution of guidelines and the offer of consultancy. Part III concludes the chapter by discussing the purposive strategies of local labour

15 Baldassar et al. (n. 10) 35. Baldassar et al. refer to the World Trade Organization (WTO) Multifibre Arrangement which was rescinded in 2005 in order to allow developing countries such as China the right to export textiles.

16 See Stefano C. Benvenuti, Fabrizio Cipollini, Gabi Dei Ottati, Camilla Ferretti, Piero Ganugi, Leonardo Ghezzi, Saverio Langianni and Stefano Rosignoli, 'Prato: Il ruolo economico della comunità cinese' (IRPET 2013) www.irpet.it/wp-content/uploads/2016/04/479_Prato_Cina-volume-Casini-con-cover.pdf accessed 10 September 2018.

17 The regional government distributed a flyer among citizens in Prato in 2014 titled 'Voglio Sicurezza. Non Rischio' http://allegati.usl4.toscana.it/dl/20140910114659749/volantinort.pdf accessed 10 September 2018.

18 Bent Flyvbjerg, 'Five Misunderstandings About Case-Study Research' (2006) 12 *Qualitative Inquiry* 395.

inspectors as examples of recent attempts to shape the legitimacy of transnational norms within the field of labour law.

Labour inspection in Italy

Since the turn of the millennium, an ambitious reform of labour inspection has been implemented in Italy.[19] Italy is a member of the ILO and the European Union (EU), and particularly when it comes to enforcement of OSH norms, Italy has been pushed by these international and supranational communities to develop a new approach to enforcement with emphasis on promoting a preventive culture at the workplace. The reform was initiated with the implementation of Legislative Decree no. 124 of 2004 on 'The measures of rationalisation of the functions of inspection and surveillance on social security and labour'. The Decree reflects an urgent need for advancing the level of labour law compliance through preventive measures and detection of labour legislation infractions. The ILO has had a significant impact on the reform process, particularly its 2006 call upon its Member States to adopt a series of policies to 'reinvigorate, modernize and strengthen labour inspectorates worldwide, in a move to boost the implementation of labour laws on the working conditions that protect the rights of millions of workers worldwide'.[20] Moreover, the EU has pushed the reform process of the Italian inspection system. An example can be found in the action taken by the European Commission in November 2011 where Italy was requested to fully apply the EU Directive (89/381/EEC) that establishes general principles concerning the prevention of occupational risks and the protection of the health and safety of workers.[21] Furthermore, the reform has been spurred by broader tendencies in the Italian labour market, including the general turn from permanent to flexible employment relationships, and a need for aligning protective measures to overcome the contrast between those workers who enjoy a high level of protection and those precarious workers with unstable and temporary employment conditions.[22] Mario Fasani (2011) summarises the ambition of the Italian labour inspection reform in this way:

19 The chapter focuses on the recent reforms initiated in the beginning of the 2000s and manifested with the implementation of Legislative Decree no. 124 of 2004. For a detailed historical account of the prior period of 120 years, see Mario Fasani (2011) 'Labour Inspection in Italy'. Working Document No. 11 (Geneva: LAB/ADMIN), Chs 1–2.

20 Ibid., 4.

21 European Commission, 'Health and Safety: Commission Requests Italy to Fully Apply EU Legislation' (Press release 21 November 2012) http://ec.europa.eu/social/main.jsp?catId=89&langId=en&newsId=1727&furtherNews=yes accessed 10 September 2018.

22 The dualism between insiders (with high protection) and outsiders (with low protection) has been a central ingredient in Italian labour law since World War II because Italian law establishes certain exemptions and conditions for small firms with less than 15 employees. For instance, such small firms are exempted from publishing financial results and excluded from the purview of bankruptcy and certain other aspects of insolvency. However, they must still live up to standards required within the area of safety and health at work. For more

> With this new reform, the labour inspection in Italy is contributing to a better compliance with labour legislation and the fight against undeclared work. It is also moving workers and employers in adapting a new approach vis-à-vis the introduction of a preventive culture specifically on occupational safety and health. All this in line with the European Union directives as well as international labour standards.[23]

The reform of the Italian labour inspection system has involved an important shift in the way law enforcement is understood by introducing a participatory and purposive orientation with a new definition of the labour inspector. Traditionally, the local labour inspector is the key person responsible for controlling and sanctioning breaches of labour law. Articles 7–8 of the Legislative Decree no. 124 of 2004 provide a new definition of the labour inspector as controller, promoter, consultant and trainer on all labour law issues. To be able to undertake this multitude of tasks, Article 18 of the Decree states that all labour inspection personnel must undergo continuing education that covers a variety of subjects, including labour and social security legislation, industrial relations, statistics, communication, use of information systems, methodology of social research and inspection investigation techniques.

Since 2004, several national legislative initiatives have added to the reform of the local labour inspector's role. Of particular importance is the 'Code of Conduct' of labour inspectors adopted by the Ministry of Labour and Social Policies in April 2006 to give 'harmonization to a matter that has been heterogeneous for a long time'.[24] The Code has four parts.[25] The first part describes the general principles of labour inspection as diligence, loyalty, fairness and impartiality.[26] The second part provides guidelines on conduct in the interaction between labour inspector and employer, summarised by the 'principle of cooperation' based on mutual respect as well as the least disturbance possible to the enterprise's activity subject to the inspection visit.[27] The third part establishes procedures to be followed during inspections, including preparation, investigative activities, the report of inspection findings and notification of sanctions and fines.[28] The fourth part provides a code of ethics to be followed by the inspectors when carrying out visits to firms. Here, the fundamental values are impartiality, objectivity, efficiency, professional adequacy, transparency, honesty and

information, see Michele Tiraboschi and Fashoyin Tayo, *Labour Law and Industrial Relations in Recessionary Times: The Italian Labour Relations in a Global Economy* (Cambridge Scholars Publishing 2014).

23 Fasani (n. 19) 39.

24 Ibid., 27.

25 'Codice di comportamento ad uso degli ispettori del lavoro' (Prot. n. 25/SEGR/0003540) http://sitiarcheologici.lavoro.gov.it/SicurezzaLavoro/Documents/CodiciEtici/codice_comportamento_ispettori_lavoro.pdf accessed 10 September 2018.

26 Ibid., Art. 3 (my translation).

27 Ibid., Art. 4 (my translation).

28 Ibid., Arts 11–19.

integrity.[29] Furthermore, inspectors are obliged to refrain from performing the inspection themselves if there are possibilities of personal or financial advantages, and all inspectors have the obligation to keeping secret the source of the complaint when the inspection visit is based on a request for intervention.[30]

It has been argued that the reform of the Italian labour inspection system has increased its effectiveness. According to the statistics from the Ministry of Labour and Social Policies published in 2009, there has been a significant increase in the number of maximum sanctions issued: for instance, the issuing of maximum sanctions for undeclared work increased by 61%, violations of working hours rules by 154%, fraud involving social security by 495% and penal offenses against safety and health by 155%.[31] In short, it seems that labour inspectors have become better at identifying and reporting labour law violations than they were prior to the reforms. At the same time, according to the Ministry of Labour and Social Policies, the reform has spurred a shift in employers' and workers' motivation for adopting a preventive culture with regard to labour law.[32] Still, huge challenges remain for this 'preventive culture' to become dominant. In 2013, national data on labour inspection report that 65% of all firms inspected breached central elements of labour law, including OSH.[33] The region of Tuscany was emphasised due to its high record of undeclared work, and the presence of Chinese workshops was specifically identified as the main reason.[34] This underlines the need for developing local actions to combat problems of non-compliance with labour law and to promote a culture of prevention in regards to OSH.

Reinventing tools for labour law enforcement in Prato

The violations of central elements of labour law found by labour inspectors in Chinese firms in Prato include the lack of working permits and contracts; non-compliance with maximum limits to working hours; safety and health problems related to the illegal presence of dormitories inside the factory as well as high risks of fire due to dangerous electric installations and the storage of gas cylinders close to machines.[35] According to labour inspectors, these irregularities are not found to the same degree at Italian firms or in cases of other types of migrants who run businesses or work in Prato.[36] As mentioned above, the regional government has

29 Ibid., Art. 20 (my translation).

30 Ibid., Art. 22 and Art. 23, respectively.

31 Fasani (n. 19) 39.

32 Ibid.

33 Dottrina Per il Lavoro (2014) 'Ministerio del Lavoro e delle Politiche Sociali: Vigilanza – Irregolari quasi il 65 % delle imprese inspezionate nel 2013' www.dottrinalavoro.it/notizie-c/min-lavoro-vigilanza-irregolari-quasi-il-65-delle-imprese-ispezionate-nel-2013 accessed 10 September 2018.

34 Ibid.

35 Interviews conducted by the author with Head of DPL Prato and Head of the ASL Unit of Prevention in June 2014.

36 Ibid.

recently given the Chinese firms the specific choice of entering into a process of gradually upgrading irregular activities to regular activities, or risking high fines and being closed down when labour inspectors pay their visits. Firms who choose to upgrade will receive consultancy and training in a 'preventive programme' where all relevant institutions participate, including inspection agencies, public health authorities and private consultants. The move from reactivism to proactivism is most clearly formulated in a flyer that was printed and distributed in Prato by the regional government in 2014.[37] The flyer is titled 'I want safety. Not risk'. In brief, the flyer promotes a preventive culture and encourages the Chinese firms to cooperate. At the same time, the flyer promises heavy sanctions (fines or closure of business) for those who do not accept to upgrade activities. This establishment of a 'preventive programme' reflects the new approach to labour law enforcement implemented in Italy as part of the labour inspection reform where consultancy and sanctions seem to go hand in hand. In Prato, the effort has been to have 74 labour inspectors control all Chinese firms in the region of Tuscany within a time span of two years (from September 2014 until the end of 2016).[38] Most of these inspections have been carried out in concerted action between the local labour inspectorate (DPL) and the local health and safety agency (ASL). At the same time, DPL and ASL have been involved in developing three new tools with the hope of shaping the legitimacy of existing law by giving reasons as to why the Chinese should choose to follow central requirements of labour law, including the transnational OSH standards.

The first tool is a video campaign developed by DPL in close cooperation with central local and regional institutions and associations.[39] It reflects the broadening of the tasks of the labour inspector from control activities towards encouraging the prevention of labour law violations. The 12-minute video is titled 'Protecting the Safety and Rights of Chinese Workers' (Tutela della sicurezza e dei diritti dei lavoratori cinesi). It is voiced in Italian and has Chinese subtitles.[40] The video begins by showing the impressive tower of the Cathedral S. Stefano rising against the blue sky and other central squares in the small town of Prato, before changing the scene to fabric halls where both Chinese and Italian employees are busy working. Meanwhile, the speaker describes Prato as 'a multi-ethnic city' and as full of 'job opportunities'. The scene shifts to a clothing lab where Chinese men and

37 Regione Toscana (n. 17).

38 Silvia Pieraccini, 'A Prato un "Patto fiduciario per la sicurezza" per incentivare l'emersione delle aziende cinesi' (*Il Sole 24 Ore* 17 July 2014) www.ilsole24ore.com/art/impresa-e-territori/2014-07-16/a-prato-patto-fiduciario-la-sicurezza-incentivare-emersione-aziende-cinesi-214604.shtml?uuid=AB8gEHbB&refresh_ce=1 accessed 10 September 2018.

39 The video campaign is the result of the cooperation of various entities, including DPL, the Municipal of Prato, the local Fireman Corps, INAIL, INPS and CNA. The campaign has been financed by the European Fund for the Integration of Third Country Nationals, the Prefecture in Prato and the Italian Ministry of Internal Affairs. The video is accessible here: www.utgprato.it/fei/Prato2015_ITALIANO.mp4 accessed 10 September 2018.

40 All excerpts from the video provided here are my translations of the original Italian version into English.

women produce clothes, surrounded by colourful threads. The speaker stresses that 'the Italian Constitution focuses on the worker and his rights, safety and health' and quotes Article 41 of the Constitution, which establishes that 'there is freedom of private economic initiative, but it cannot be conducted in conflict with the social utility or in a manner that could damage safety, liberty and human dignity'. The speaker underlines that 'in a city such as Prato where thousands of women and men are working it is important to comply with the rules'. Following these introductory remarks, the video tells the story of Jin, a young Chinese man who works in Prato:

> Jin is employed as worker in a textile firm. Workers like him contribute to the production of Italy. Regardless of ethnicity, age, gender, there are these fundamental standards for the protection of workers: safety at the workplace, a regular employment contract, health care and respect for working hours. [...] [These are] rights based on laws issued and administered by the Ministry of Labour and Social Policies.

The website of the Ministry is shown, followed by scenes from different public offices, including DPL, where personnel are busy consulting clients. Additional provisions from the Italian Constitution are quoted, including Article 37 regarding the equality between female and male workers in terms of rights and wages and the right for mother and child to have 'special adequate protection', as well as Article 36 which emphasises the right of a worker to receive a salary that reflects the quantity and quality of his/her work. It is emphasised that tax payment and social contributions allow workers to use health services, guarantee workers insurance in cases of work accidents or work-related disease and guarantee workers' pension upon retirement. It is further underlined that workers have the right to a minimum of two days off per week, and that each working day must entail a break so that workers can 'recreate and regain energy'. The video ends with pictures of Jin and his family, and the speaker summarises:

> Thanks to his employment, Jin has become integrated in Italy and he has had the opportunity to make a family. In the course of his working life, he will pay one quarter of this salary to INPS [the pension agency] and thereby is ensured a pension when his working life ends. Thanks to his employment and his contributions, he and his family are assured economically for the rest of his life.

Pictures from the multi-ethnic workplaces of Prato are shown again, and the speaker reframes the message:

> Workers represent an investment for entrepreneurs: investing in them as persons and in their health and safety permits an improvement of the quality of work and sends an important signal to the economic and cultural systems of other countries.

The video aims to communicate directly to the Chinese in Prato what labour law demands, with some reference to the intentions behind the legal requirements, including arguments for all the good reasons for establishing a safe and healthy workplace. The central message of the video is that all citizens, including the Chinese in Prato, need to re-orient behaviour toward the law and its principles on OSH. With the video, DPL promotes the safety and health of workers as transnational norms that should be respected by all citizens in Prato. The authority of labour law is emphasised. What is new is that the good reasons for law compliance become central in this form of communication. The logic seems to be that if citizens are better informed about the reasons for why certain norms should be seen as the legitimate ones, then they are likely to change behaviour. Using Jin, a Chinese migrant, as a key figure is symbolic of this effort of explaining to the target group that a Chinese worker in Prato, like themselves, has got a better life by playing by the rules. In this way, DPL seeks to generate the legitimacy of labour law, including OSH standards, by providing persuasive reasons as to why certain actions and rules are appropriate. At the same time, it can be argued that it is an attempt to justify and thereby legitimise the way in which DPL and other control bodies enforce law.

A second tool has been developed by ASL. It is a new set of guidelines titled: 'How to do risk assessment in the textile sector and in fast fashion'.[41] Each paragraph of the guidelines is provided first in Italian and then in Chinese. In his account of the development of this new tool, the Head of the ASL Unit of Prevention notes that before this instrument was implemented, it was tested by presenting it to a group of Chinese employers who were asked to comment on whether the guidelines were understandable.[42] ASL thereby seeks to take into account the ways in which Chinese might read and interpret the guidelines. Thus, the guidelines can be seen as an attempt to spell out in Chinese what existing labour law demands from employers and workers in the area of OSH. Its preamble stresses that the assessment of safety and health risks is mandatory for all firms in Italy[43] and defines the guidelines as 'a fundamental instrument for ensuring the correct management of safety and health in the firm, for detecting critical issues and for identifying individual solutions'. The guidelines are further described as a 'control list' aimed at supporting firms when assessing risks. Such assessment should, according to ASL, be an 'action of self-regulation' by companies. The preamble ends by warning about the various ways in which breaches of law will be sanctioned:

> WARNING: in case of the violation of law you risk serious consequences. These include the seizure of machinery or company, the obligation to put

41 The ASL guidelines are available online at http://allegati.usl4.toscana.it/dl/20140910120911468/ind_stand.pdf accessed 10 September 2018. All excerpts are my translations of the original Italian version into English.

42 Interview conducted by the author with Head of the ASL Unit of Prevention in June 2014.

43 Art. 15 of the Legislative Decree no. 81/2008 establishes the completion and updating of the Risk Assessment Document (DVR).

> machines, buildings and facilities (electricity, heating, gas) in accordance with law, very high fines and in case of default a process in court.[44]

The 'control list' is structured in three columns. The first column asks questions regarding the implementation of various legal demands. The second column provides room for employers and workers to note whether they comply or not. The third provides an explanation of the legal requirement by summarising the relevant law. The list contains 55 questions divided into 11 categories, including general requirements, information and training, organisation of the workplace, warehouse hygiene and toilets, electric installations, equipment and methane gas, work facilities, manual handling of loads, first-aid tools and personal protective equipment. The categories have several things in common. First of all, many of them focus on core documents that firms must complete to demonstrate law compliance. Documentation involves basing employment on written contracts, having receipts for the payment of social security contributions and being able to demonstrate authorisations. The case seems to be that law compliance is a matter of the degree to which the employer is able to document that practices are being performed according to the law. According to Italian law, it is the employer who has the primary responsibility for implementing and applying labour law.[45] Put differently, it takes documentation to implement a preventive culture. Secondly, whereas many of these categories would be relevant for Italian firms as well, the category regarding the organisation of the workplace is directed specifically toward the Chinese firms because it refers to the risks of living and working in the same place, which are among the most often found violations at Chinese firms.[46] The category deals with whether rooms are used for the purposes for which they have been authorised.[47] Regarding rooms used as kitchens, it is stressed that 'it is forbidden to eat in workplaces that are dusty or have harmful substances'; in general, rooms must be used as refectory and kitchen only if they are clean, well-aired, well-illuminated and have chairs and tables. 'You must wash hands before eating' also appears.[48] Rooms can be used for dormitory if they are 'separate from the workplace and with own bathroom and kitchen'.[49] With these admonitions, ASL underlines that certain social practices, which may be normal and widespread in the Chinese workplaces in Prato, are not tolerated in Italy. Instead, such practices are illegal and viewed as illegitimate. Thirdly, the ASL guidelines use an interesting set of response options. About half of the questions have the option of responding YES, PARTLY, NO, whereas the rest only have the option of YES or NO. There seems to be little logic as to which legal demands can be partly complied with and which must be fully complied with. It illustrates that it might

44 ASL guidelines (n. 41) (my translation).

45 G. Leroy Certoma, *The Italian Legal System* (Butterworths 1985) 383.

46 Interview conducted by the author with Head of the ASL Unit of Prevention in June 2014.

47 ASL guidelines (n. 41), questions 17–27.

48 Ibid., question 28.

49 Ibid., question 29.

be easier to explain the content of law in specific and clear terms than it is to assess the level of compliance. The assessment of compliance will in fact often be based on pragmatism.[50] According to the Head of the ASL Unit of Prevention, a company can be characterised as living up to an acceptable level of safety and health rules if the guidelines are followed.[51] The objective of ASL is then to support those firms who want to enter into the process of upgrading activities.[52]

Besides the video campaign and the distribution of guidelines for self-regulation, both DPL and ASL have been involved in the establishment of a new type of law consultant, publicly known as the 'ASCI technician'.[53] The need for a new type of actor in the existing law enforcement landscape is explained by the regional government in this way:

> In particular, this new profession is designed to meet the emerging demand for employees capable of working in a productive and multi-ethnic context, 'reading' the socio-economic context, planning, managing and evaluating business activities, encouraging cooperation processes between companies and institutions, formulating public policies for local development and affirming legality and the emergence of various forms of irregularities.[54]

In other words, there is a need for a new type of profession which can assist traditional ones, such as labour inspectors, in promoting the compliance with existing law and, thus, shaping the legitimacy of labour law. The context is multi-ethnic, and therefore tools for enforcement need to address multiple ways of understanding why and how workplaces ought to be organised. The ASCI technician carries out preventive visits to (primarily) foreign-owned firms in Prato, and by using a check-up tool in the form of a 30-page questionnaire they work with the firms to improve workers' protection. The questionnaire is comparable to the ASL guidelines presented above, however, it extends the perception of workers' protection from the focus on safety and health to other areas of law, such as labour contracts, taxation, environment and food hygiene that, according to the ASCI project coordinators, also influence the well-being of workers.[55] In the first

50 See Michael J. Piore and Andrew Schrank, 'Toward Managed Flexibility: The Revival of Labour Inspection in the Latin World' (2008) 147 *International Labour Review* 1.

51 Interview conducted by the author with Head of the ASL Unit of Prevention in June 2014.

52 Ibid.

53 ASCI stands for *Agente per lo Sviluppo di Cultura e Imprese* (in English: Agent for the Development of Cultures and Entrepreneurship). The idea was born with two regional legal initiatives taken by the regional government (Resolution n. 568/2013 and Resolution n. 274/2014) establishing the 'Integrated Project for the Development of the Area of Prato'.

54 Regione Toscana, 'Progetto Integrato per lo Sviluppo dell'area Pratese. Report breve delle attività al 30 Giugno 2014' (2014) 20 (my translation) www.poloprato.unifi.it/fileadmin/documenti/RICERCA/LABORATORI/RT-Progetto-Prato/Report/0.defintiiva_Report_breve10102014.pdf accessed 10 September 2018.

55 Mario Biggeri, Leonardo Borsacchi and Andrea Ferrannini, *Emersione, sviluppo ed integrazione nel territorio pratese. Professionalità e strumenti di facilitazione* (Pacini Editore SpA 2015) 40.

years after the implementation of the ASCI project, 15 ASCI technicians received training. They were selected for the training course based on certain criteria, one of them being their knowledge of Chinese language and culture.[56]

The experiences and practices of the new ASCI technician have been described elsewhere.[57] In comparison, this chapter looks at the role of local labour inspectors in contributing to the development of this new type of consultancy to support local enforcement of OSH. In general, the training of ASCI technicians consists of 240 hours of theoretical lectures combined with 360 hours of internship in trade associations, organisations and local companies.[58] Labour inspectors train ASCI technicians in conducting firm visits, observing and noting degrees of law compliance and making a final report on how firms can solve issues of non-compliance. The 30-page questionnaire is based on input from the various inspection agencies.[59] Furthermore, professors from Italian and Chinese universities are involved in the training sessions.[60] This mix of expertise used to train the ASCI technician and to invent the 30-page questionnaire emphasises the priority of traditional actors to establish a new type of legal professional that can contribute to the advancing of law compliance based on a multicultural, multilingual and multidisciplinary approach. According to the ASCI project coordinators, this cooperation between all relevant stakeholders is new in Prato; for the first time all stakeholders sat around the same table, deciding together what to do.[61]

The ASCI technicians visited 75 companies from May to August 2014: 69 Chinese-owned, two Pakistani-owned and four Italian-owned.[62] The main shortcomings of law compliance in the visited firms in relation to safety and health relate to the risk assessment document (DVR) that is only filled out in 'a generic form without reflecting the real situation of production in the firm'.[63] This indicates two interrelated problems: i) the ineffectiveness of some private firm consultants who are hired by Chinese firms to help with the paperwork (getting licenses, contracts, etc.) and ii) the lack of awareness and knowledge of the entrepreneur regarding the importance and usefulness of the DVR.[64] On this basis, the project coordinators conclude that it is necessary to improve information and support to entrepreneurs and workers to enhance their understanding of the importance of applying law:

56 Interview conducted by the author with ASCI project coordinators in June 2014.

57 Louise Munkholm, 'Creating a New Type of Law Enforcer: The Law Technician in Prato' (2018) 45 *Journal of Law and Society* 538. See also Biggeri et al. (2015) (n. 55).

58 Regione Toscana (n. 54).

59 Interview conducted by the author with ASCI project coordinators in June 2014.

60 Ibid.

61 Ibid.

62 Biggeri et al. (n. 55) 52–54.

63 Ibid., 59 (my translation).

64 Ibid.

> Overall, therefore, the needs and issues regarding safety in the workplace just outlined indicate a clear need for companies of foreign ownership to have a professional such as the ASCI technician able not only to analyse the compliance of the firm in a 360° integrated manner, but also to guide entrepreneurs through an informative, operational and managed process to [...] educate and inform entrepreneur and workers about the need for [...] management of the work environment to prevent risk to the safety of workers.[65]

The project coordinators thus stress guidance, information and education of employers and workers as central factors in the process towards establishing a culture of prevention at the workplace. Guidance seems to involve the communication of persuasive arguments from the Italian law enforcers to the Chinese regarding the reasons for why existing labour law should be followed. In this way, professionals such as ASCI technicians aim to shape the willingness of Chinese firms to comply with the rules.

Conclusion

The chapter has argued that OSH is one example of a set of transnational legal norms that travels around the world. It becomes clear, however, that OSH is applied and enforced with difficulties. It is particularly resource-demanding to shape the legitimacy of OSH locally when foreign-owned firms constitute new audiences as they can be hard to reach through traditional methods of reason-giving and persuasion. The extreme situation of having a foreign workforce which is far from being employed under legal conditions raises several questions: Which norms are legitimate in a multicultural, multi-ethnic world: The ones you bring from the country of your origin or the ones you meet in the country you enter? As mentioned, the legitimacy of transnational norms implies a local willingness to accept and follow the rules 'even if this goes against specific interests at specific times'.[66] In Prato, the willingness of the Chinese to organise their workplaces according to official OSH standards is unclear. According to the local labour inspectors, the Chinese might have had until now the excuse of not knowing and not understanding the rules. Therefore, resources have been devoted to intensifying communication campaigns using new types of media (e.g. video campaigning), new types of guidelines (e.g. in Chinese and with pictures and symbols) and new types of consultancy (e.g. the ASCI technician and the 30-page questionnaire). Thus, the local labour inspectors in Prato seek to shape the willingness of the Chinese employers and workers by referring to and explaining the substantive content of the OSH norms. Legitimacy is substantive, then. It stems from 'the congruence between the content of a rule or policy and the broader values that

65 Ibid., 61 (my translation).
66 Hurrell (n. 7).

are privileged in a community at a given moment'.[67] Labour inspectors in Prato seek to shape the legitimacy of OSH norms when promoting a preventive culture to the Chinese. Labour inspectors promote that we have to prevent danger; that is the main message from Italians to Chinese in Prato; and from the ILO to employers and workers worldwide. In Prato, prevention of safety and health risks is the transnational norm promoted. The establishment of a 'preventive programme' reflects the new approach to labour law enforcement implemented in Italy as part of the labour inspection reform. At the same time, the local labour inspectors have the mandate to sanction firms that are not willing to comply, even after they have received guidance. So the enforcement approach is flexible: 'legalistic and punitive when needed, but accommodative and helpful in others', to borrow the words of Robert A. Kagan.[68] Reading treaties and laws, one can detect various norms to be important, but what happens locally depends on the context and the audiences.[69] Now – based on the study presented in this chapter – we know more about how OSH can be promoted in situations where reactive responses, such as inspections, are no longer enough. New tools are needed. Tools that explain and visualise the intention of law with the aim of supporting employers and workers to create a safe and healthy workplace. Perhaps also new actors, such as the ASCI technician, are needed to shape the legitimacy of transnational norms. Persuasion and reason-giving are not enough for shaping the legitimacy of OSH, however. There is also a huge need for discussing input legitimacy[70] of OSH compliance, in this case, the extent to which the Chinese are heard at all in the recent initiatives taken in Prato. As shown, DPL used a Chinese worker as the central figure in its video campaign, ASL presented the new type of guidelines for Chinese to check for its usefulness and linguistics, and the ASCI technicians opened a channel for more knowledge about how the Chinese perceive the situation, including their difficulties with understanding and applying OSH standards and rules. Future research should closely follow these participatory and purposive initiatives taken by local law enforcers to learn in which ways such initiatives will in fact shape the willingness of individuals and groups to accept and follow the rules promoted by transnational law.

67 Magdalena Bexell, 'Global Governance, Legitimacy and (De)Legitimation' (2014) *Globalizations* 292.

68 Robert A. Kagan, 'Regulators and Regulatory Processes' in Austin Sarat (ed.), *The Blackwell Companion to Law and Society* (Blackwell Publishing, Blackwell Reference Online, 2004).

69 Hurrell (n. 7) 24.

70 Ibid. 18–19.

12 The principle of equality as a transnational principle

Natalie Videbæk Munkholm and Christian Højer Schjøler

Introduction

The chapter presents the shortcomings of the principle of equality as a source of European Union (EU) law[1] and discusses these shortcomings in light of the origin and development of the principle as a transnational phenomenon. The equality principle has been developed by the Court of Justice of the EU (the Court)[2] with reference to the common constitutional traditions of Member States and international law instruments. Elevating a principle found in some Member States to a general binding EU law principle can be viewed as the phenomenon of creating supranational law based on transnational principles. The chapter analyses the national transposition and implementation of a legal principle created through this process. The chapter examines resistance in transposition as a question of the procedural and substantive legitimacy of a supranational rule based on transnational principles. This is then interpreted in light of the theory of critical legal positivism. The theory gives insight into the possible interrelations between the application of a norm and the legal culture of the legal actors, which can act as a learning point for future developments in supranational EU law on the basis of transnational principles.

The use of a principle of equality can be portrayed in a number of contexts.[3] The chapter will use the principle as a freestanding principle challenging national acts. The chapter defines 'principle' as an unwritten rule or basic consideration recognised as a common interpretation vehicle. A principle, in this understanding, has a legal content of its own and can function as a source of law.

The principle of equality

The principle of equality can be traced back to the ancient Greek philosophers. Reference is often made to Aristotle: 'Things (and persons) that are alike should be treated alike, while things that are unalike should be treated unalike in proportion

1 EU law refers to Union Law as well as to Community Law.
2 The Court refers to the Court of Justice of the EU (earlier: the European Court of Justice).
3 Catherine Barnard, *EU Employment Law* (4th edn, Oxford University Press 2012) 270.

to their unalikeness.'[4] This form of equality is formal and does not specify the relevant normative aspects or criteria when assessing what is to be treated equally.[56] The perception of equality has accordingly shifted towards a concept of substantive equality.[7] Substantive equality can be seen as linked to the concept of social inclusion, whereby all persons, despite their preconditions, are awarded the same opportunity to participate in society.[8] The concept revolves around the individual's relationship with society, thereby encompassing several ideals, such as equality in outcome,[9] equality in opportunities and equality in respect.[10]

The principle of equality in an EU/EC context

At the Member State level, equality is a theme in the constitutions of many Member States. Equality is a complex concept.[11] Equality played a major part in the French revolution, in the motto *liberté, égalité, fraternité*. Equality emerged as a common constitutional principle in the post-World War II period, e.g. in Italy in 1947, where the public authorities were obligated to promote effective equality.[12] The principle of equality was recognised as a part of the legal heritage in Europe when forming the European Economic Community (EEC), without being mentioned in the original Treaty of Rome, 1957.[13]

From fair competition to non-discrimination

The principle entered EU law as Article 119, in the Treaty of Rome, on equal pay. The purpose of the provision was not to create equality between the sexes, but rather to create a level playing field between the textile industries of the Member States. As France had a provision on equal pay in its national legislation,[14] they feared unfair

4 Aristotle, *Nicomachean Ethics, V.3. 1131a10–B15; Politics, III.9.1280 A8–15, III. 12. 1282b18–23.*
5 E.g. slaves and women were not equal to free men.
6 H.L.A. Hart, *The Concept of Law*, with a postscript edited by Penelope A. Bulloch and Joseph Raz (Oxford University Press 1997) 159.
7 Joint publication of the European Union Agency for Fundamental Rights (FRA) and the European Court of Human Rights, 'PDF – Handbook on European Non-Discrimination Law' (*Council of Europe Publishing*) 13; Ann Numhauser-Henning, 'EU Equality Law – Comprehensive and Truly Transformative?' in Mia Rönnmar (ed.), *Labour Law, Fundamental Rights and Social Europe* (Hart 2011) vol. 4, 113.
8 Dagmar Schiek, Lisa Waddington and Mark Bell, *Cases, Materials and Text on National, Supranational and International Non-Discrimination Law* (Hart 2007) 28.
9 Sandra Fredman, *Discrimination Law* (2nd edn, Oxford University Press 2011) 14.
10 Schiek, Waddington and Bell (n. 8) 28.
11 See Bruno de Witte, 'From a "Common Principle of Equality" to "European Antidiscrimination Law"' (2010) 53 *American Behavioral Scientist* 1715.
12 Article 3 (2).
13 De Witte (n. 11) 2.
14 Numhauser-Henning (n. 7) 116.

competition from Member States allowing lower wages for female employees.[15] In 1976, the Council adopted Directive 76/207/EEC on equal treatment of men and women in employment (The Equal Treatment Directive).[16] The Commission drafted the Directive with reference to the resolution to take action for the purpose of achieving equality between men and women.[17] Reference was not made to any origin of the principle. The act aims at 'establishing the principle of equality between men and women'.[18] Likewise, in 1976, the Court in the *Defrenne II* case, concerning different mandatory retirement ages for female and male flight attendants, emphasised that

> the social objectives of the Community, which is not merely an economic union, but is at the same time intended, by common action, to ensure social progress and seek the constant improvement of the living and working conditions of their peoples, as is emphasized by the Preamble to the Treaty.[19]

In the ensuing *Defrenne III* case,[20] concerning compensation for damages suffered with regard to pension, the question was whether EU law contained a general principle at treaty level prohibiting gender discrimination in employment. The Court, however, refused to widen the scope of Article 119 to issues other than pay.[21] The Court found that although the elimination of discrimination based on gender is a fundamental right,[22] EU law had not at that time assumed any responsibility for supervising and guaranteeing the observance of the principle for individuals. The Court did not elaborate on how the principle of equality, introduced by the Equal Treatment Directive, should be implemented.

In 1994, the Court expressed that 'the directive is simply the expression, in the relevant field, of the principle of equality, which is one of the fundamental principles of EU law'.[23] But in 1996, with more caution, the Court stated that the equality principle could not extend the scope of the Treaty provisions beyond 'the competences of the Community'.[24]

Until 2000, the principle of equality was limited to the criteria of gender and nationality[25] and did not affect working conditions other than pay. In 2000,

15 Fredman (n. 9) 42.
16 Council Directive No. 76/207/EEC of 9 February 1976 on the implementation of the principle of equal treatment for men and women as regards access to employment, vocational training and promotion and working conditions.
17 COM (75) 36 final 1.
18 COM (75) 36 final 1, 31.
19 Case 43/75 *Defrenne II* [1976] ECR 455, paras 8–9.
20 Case 149/77 *Defrenne III* [1978] ECR 1365, para 25.
21 Ibid., paras 19–20.
22 Ibid., paras 26–29.
23 Case 13/94 *P. v. S. and Cornwall CC* [1996] ECR-I 2143, para 18, cf. Takis Tridimas, *The General Principles of EU Law* (2nd edn, Oxford University Press 2007) 107.
24 Case 249/96 *Grant v. South West Trains Ltd* [1998] ECR-I 621, para. 45.
25 Dagmar Schiek, 'The ECJ Decision in Mangold: A Further Twist on Effects of Directives and Constitutional Relevance of Community Equality Legislation' (2006) 35 *Industrial Law Journal* 333.

the right to non-discrimination became part of the EU Charter of Fundamental Rights (the Charter) adopted by the EU institutions. Also in 2000, the European Social Agenda was introduced; a programme of activities set up to provide sustainable growth in Europe, with more and better jobs and greater social cohesion.[26] In line with these developments, Directive 2000/78/EC was adopted, establishing a general framework for equal treatment in employment and occupation (the Employment Directive) across a range of criteria, including age, religion and disability.[27] By this, equal treatment was deemed an objective in its own right, applied to any direct or indirect discrimination, as a fundamental right entrusted to the individual.

The Mangold case

German legislation restricted the use of fixed-term contracts but only for employees under a certain age.[28] National law did not include a prohibition of age discrimination, and the age discrimination provisions of the Employment Directive had not yet been transposed. In the case of *Mangold* in 2005,[29] in order for a prohibition against discrimination on grounds of age to have any effect directly for the plaintiff, the EU principle of equality should be given direct horizontal effect. The Court stated:

> Directive 2000/78 does not itself lay down the principle of equal treatment in the field of employment and occupation. Indeed, in accordance with Article 1 thereof, the sole purpose of the directive is 'to lay down a general framework for combating discrimination on the grounds of religion or belief, disability, age or sexual orientation', the source of the actual principle underlying the prohibition of those forms of discrimination being found, as is clear from the third and fourth recitals in the preamble to the directive, in various international instruments and in the constitutional traditions common to the Member States. The principle of non-discrimination on grounds of age must thus be regarded as a general principle of EU law.[30]

Recital 1 of the preamble of the Employment Directive refers to Article 6 of the Treaty on European Union (TEU), according to which fundamental rights, as guaranteed by the European Convention on Human Rights (ECHR), and as they result from the constitutional traditions common to the Member States, shall constitute general principles of EU law. Recital 4 of the preamble of the Employment Directive refers to the universal right, recognised by the United Nation's Universal

26 COM (2000) 379 final.
27 Council Directive 2000/78/EC of 27 November 2000 establishing a general framework for equal treatment in employment and occupation.
28 Schiek (n. 25) 334.
29 Case 144/04 *Werner Mangold v. Rüdiger Helm* [2005] ECR-I 9981.
30 *Mangold* (n. 29) paras 74–75.

Declaration of Human Rights (UNHR), of all persons to equality before the law and protection against discrimination. Neither the ECHR nor the UNHR explicitly prohibits age discrimination.

In the constitutions of the Member States, only the Finnish and the Portuguese contained a prohibition on age discrimination.[31] The Greek and Spanish constitutions prohibited specific forms of age discrimination,[32] and a number of constitutions contained a general principle of equal treatment.[33] Seeking inspiration in the constitutions of the Member States was not new to the Court. When examining whether measures adopted by the EU are compatible with the fundamental rights in the constitutions of the Member States, reference was made to such constitutions.[34] In 1977[35] and 1979,[36] the Court stated that 'the Court is bound to draw inspiration from constitutional traditions common to the Member States, and it cannot therefore uphold measures which are incompatible with fundamental rights recognised and protected by the Constitutions of those States'.

In *Mangold*, the Court declared that the principle of non-discrimination on grounds of age must be regarded as an autonomous freestanding principle of EU law. The application of the general principle of equal treatment was not dependent on the national implementation of the principle of non-discrimination.[37] National courts were obliged to disapply national legislation incompatible with the principle of prohibition of age discrimination.[38] The obligation applies to the direct horizontal relationship between private parties as long as the matter comes within the scope of EU law.[39]

The transnational nature of the use of the constitutional traditions

The Court in *Mangold* used the constitutional traditions common to the Member States as the legal basis for recognising a general principle of EU law prohibiting discrimination on grounds of age. This use of the constitutional traditions of the Member States was novel.

A principle found in constitutional traditions common to Member States could be referred to as a *transnational* principle. The fact that the principle was common and at a constitutional level in the Member States was used as a legitimacy

31 Case 550/07 *Akzo Nobel Chemicals Ltd and Akcros Chemicals Ltd v. European Commission* [2010] ECR-I 8301, Opinion of AG Kokott, para. 96 footnote 78.
32 Felipe Temming, 'The Palacios Case: Turning Point in Age Discrimination Law?' 2007 *European Law Reporter* 382, 387.
33 Sandra Fredman and Sarah Spencer, *Age as an Equality Issue* (Hart 2003) 197.
34 Franz C. Mayer, 'Constitutional Comparativism in Action. The Example of General Principles of EU Law and How They Are Made – A German Perspective' (2013) 11 *International Journal of Constitutional Law* 1003, 1005.
35 Case 4/73 *Nold* [1977] ECR 1.
36 Case 44/79 *Hauer* [1979] ECR 3727.
37 *Mangold* (n. 29) paras 74–76.
38 Ibid., para. 77.
39 Case 555/07 *Seda Kücükdeveci v. Swedex GmbH & Co. KG.* [2010] ECR-I 365, para. 23.

argument for elevating a ***commonly recognised*** principle at the transnational level to a ***generally binding*** EU law principle at the supranational level.

The reference by the Court to the constitutional traditions was not further elaborated in the judgment nor in the subsequent cases.[40] Despite criticism, the Court upheld the doctrine.[41] In the 2007 ruling, *Kücükdeveci*, concerning shorter statutory notice periods for employees under the age of 25, the Court recognised the principle as expressed in the Employment Directive as well as in Article 21[42] of the Charter.[43] Further, the Court made clear that non-discrimination directives must be interpreted in light of the general principle of equal treatment derived from the individual right to equality and non-discrimination that is embedded in international human rights law and the constitutional traditions of the Member States.[44]

Legitimacy of the transnational principle as a supranational principle

The efforts of the Court in the *Mangold* case led to harsh criticism questioning its legitimacy and choice of reasoning. The response of AG Trstenjak is illustrative. In her Opinion in the *Dominguez* case, she raised concerns on the doctrine being an improper mixture of sources of law having different status within the EU legal system.[45] According to Trstenjak, the doctrine leaves completely open the scope of the protection of a general principle as well as the question of lack of congruence between the principle and its expression in the Directive. This again leads to concerns about legal certainty and the legitimacy of the Court:[46]

> as it will never be possible for a private individual to be certain when an unwritten general principle given specific expression by a directive will gain acceptance over written national law there would, from his point of view, be uncertainty as to the application of national law similar to that experienced where a directive is directly applied in a relationship between private individuals, which the Court, as so often affirmed in its case-law, has been at particular pains to avoid.

40 Elaine Dewhurst, 'The Development of EU Case-Law on Age Discrimination in Employment: "Will You Still Need Me? Will You Still Feed Me? When I'm Sixty-Four"' (2013) 19 *European Law Journal* 517.

41 Ibid., 524–525.

42 Jens Kristiansen, *The Growing Conflict between European Uniformity and National Flexibility: The Case of Danish Flexicurity and European Harmonisation of Working Condition* (Jurist- og Økonomforbundets Forlag 2015) 105.

43 *Kücükdeveci* (n. 39), paras 21 and 27.

44 Colm O'Cinneide, 'The Constitutionalization of Equality within the EU Legal Order: Sexual Orientation as a Testing Ground' (2015) 22 *Maastricht Journal of European and Comparative Law* 370, 379.

45 Case 282/10 *Dominguez* [2007] ECR-I 8531, Opinion of A.G. Trstenjak, para. 154.

46 Ibid., paras 155–166.

Trstenjak questioned the legitimacy of the Mangold doctrine inter alia as lack of procedural legitimacy, claiming that the Court acted outside its generally accepted conferred powers.[47]

Despite the criticism, the Court upheld the principle of non-discrimination on grounds of age as a fundamental EU principle.[48] In the aftermath of *Mangold*, the Court in ensuing case law added the Charter as a legal source likewise expressing the general principles of the constitutional traditions common to the Member States.[49]

The interplay between principles of national law, fundamental principles at the EU level and their application again in national law necessitates a suitability with regard to the legitimacy of the interpretational manoeuvres of the Court and the constitutional traditions of the Member States in order for it to function.[50] This was displayed most prominently in the German *Honeywell/Mangold* case[51] and the Danish *Ajos* case.[52]

The German case

In 2010, the German Federal Constitutional Court (GFCC), *Bundesverfassungsgericht*, assessed the constitutionality of a German Federal Labour Court ruling, applying the Mangold doctrine to a German employee. The Federal Labour Court disapplied a German national provision as it was found to be discriminatory on grounds of age.[53] The question before the GFCC was whether the Court had acted *ultra vires* and transgressed their competency of *interpretation* of EU law and instead *developed* EU law.[54] The GFCC elaborated on the long-lasting doctrine of collaboration between the Court and the Member States on the basis of the principle of conferral in Article 5 of the TEU.[55] In order to assess whether a transgression of the competency of the Court had taken place, a sufficiently qualified breach of Court competencies needed to present a significant shift to the detriment of Member State competences.[56] The GFCC, on the other

47 As defined in Magdalena Bexell, 'Global Governance, Legitimacy and (De)Legitimation' (2014) 11 *Globalizations* 289, 291.
48 Dewhurst (n. 40) 525.
49 The Charter became part of binding primary EU law on 1 December 2009 through Article 6(1) of the Treaty on European Union (TEU), as amended by the Treaty of Lisbon. The Charter was not yet legally binding at the time of the *Mangold* ruling in 2005.
50 O'Cinneide (n. 44) 382.
51 BVerfG, Order of the Second Senate of 6 July 2010 – 2 BvR 2661/06.
52 Case 441/14 *Dansk Industri (DI), acting on behalf of Ajos A/S v. Estate of Karsten Eigil Rasmussen* [2016] EU:C:2016:278 and Judgment of the Danish Supreme Court of 6 December 2016, *Dansk Industri (DI) acting for Ajos A/S vs. The estate left by A*, Ugeskrift for Retsvæsen 2017.824 H.
53 *BVerfG* (n. 51) para. 45.
54 Ibid., paras 47 and 56.
55 Ibid., para. 65.
56 Ibid., para. 71.

hand, focused on the procedural competencies and found it immaterial whether a general principle prohibiting discrimination based on age could in fact be derived from the constitutional traditions common to the Member States.[57]

The GFCC ruled that the Mangold doctrine did not create a new field of competences for the EU to the detriment of the Member States and did not expand the existing competences.[58] Ultimately, the GFCC found no transgression by the Court and rejected the claim of unconstitutionality of the Federal Labour Court ruling.

The Danish case

The question of Denmark's constitutional traditions took centre stage in the *Ajos* case. A Danish statutory provision on severance payment did not apply to employees eligible for old age pensions, regardless of whether the employee retired from the labour market or not. The provision in an earlier Court ruling[59] had been found to violate the prohibition of age discrimination in the Employment Directive. During the amendment work and while the provision was still in force, a second employee, eligible for pensions, did not receive severance payment, even though he planned to stay active in the labour market. The question before the Supreme Court was whether to rule against the employer in a situation where the employer had followed clear Danish provisions in force. The Supreme Court referred the case to the Court and inter alia presented the situation as a conflict between two principles: the principle of legal certainty versus the principle prohibiting discrimination on grounds of age.[60]

The Court clearly stated that if an EU consistent interpretation of the national provision is not possible, the national court must disapply the provision that is contrary to the general principle.[61] Legitimate expectations could not set aside a general principle prohibiting discrimination on grounds of age, even when a situation occurs before national legislation has been amended to align with Court case law.[62]

The Supreme Court then chose to investigate the question as one of procedural competencies, in particular whether the Danish State had conferred powers to the EU that allowed for the Court to develop a general EU law principle by the procedure in the *Mangold* case.[63] If the Danish Accession Act did not confer such rule-making power on the Court, the principle of prohibition of age discrimination would not have a direct horizontal effect in Denmark.

57 Ibid., para. 78.

58 Ibid., para. 77.

59 Case C-499/08, *Ole Andersen v. Region Syddanmark* [2010] ECLI:EU:C:2010:600.

60 *Ajos* (n. 52) para. 20. The incident took place in June 2009, i.e. before the Charter was elevated to primary EU Law. The question of EU conform interpretation and what constitutes *legem*, which was also assessed, is omitted here.

61 Ibid., para. 37.

62 Ibid., paras 40–41.

63 *Supreme Court* (n. 52) 40.

The Supreme Court ruled that such rule-making power had not been conferred on the Court, and that a principle at treaty level can only be given direct horizontal effect and allowed to take precedence over conflicting Danish provisions when such a principle has legal basis in a specific treaty provision.[64] The Supreme Court acknowledged that the Court can develop and establish general principles that are to be found in the European Convention on Human Rights and similar treaties and in the constitutional traditions common to the Member States. However, such general principles would not be directly applicable in Denmark by virtue of the Accession Act and cannot be relied on in disputes between individuals.[65]

The Supreme Court stated that disapplying the national provision in this situation would amount to acting outside the scope of its judicial powers.[66] The Supreme Court thus dismissed the guidelines of the Court and the principle of age discrimination as a general principle of EU law with binding direct horizontal effect in Denmark.[67] The ruling has been heavily debated.[68]

Remarks on legitimacy

The rulings of the national courts indicate that the development of EU law on the basis of a transnational principle was not considered legitimate by these legal actors. The application of the principle in national law with the effect of disapplying national provisions represented a fundamental conflict of authority between the EU and both Member States. The Mangold doctrine was viewed as lacking procedural legitimacy, as defined earlier, in both the German and the Danish case. According to Bexell, 'Procedural (input-based, democratic) legitimacy claims propose that a policy or institution is legitimate to the extent that it has come into being in accordance with generally accepted principles of right process'.[69]

As Denmark is one of the few Member States without a constitutional provision on equality and/or non-discrimination,[70] perhaps the doctrine also lacked substantive legitimacy. Substantive legitimacy can be defined as

> the need for policies or rules to be justifiable on the basis of shared broader norms and values. Substantive legitimacy thus stems from the congruence

64 Ibid., 45.
65 Ibid., 46.
66 Ibid., 48.
67 *Ajos* (n. 52).
68 Mikael Madsen, Henrik Palmer Olsen and Urska Sadl, 'Competing Supremacies and Clashing Institutional Rationalities: The Danish Supreme Court's Decision in the Ajos Case and the National Limits of Judicial Cooperation' (Social Science Research Network 2017) SSRN Scholarly Paper ID 2904012; Ruth Nielsen and Christina D. Tvarnø, 'Danish Supreme Court Infringes the EU Treaties by Its Ruling in the Ajos Case' (2017) *Europarättslig tidskrift* 303.
69 Bexell (n. 47).
70 Christopher McCrudden and Sacha Prechal, 'The Concepts of Equality and Non-Discrimination in Europe: A Practical Approach' (Social Science Research Network 2011) SSRN Scholarly Paper ID 1762815 3.

between the content of a rule or policy and the broader values that are privileged in a community at a given moment.[71]

First, in both courts, the crux of the matter was not the actual content of the principle of equal treatment. Instead, the rulings concerned the limits of competencies where the scepticism of both national courts was clear. The procedure was the centre of the investigations of both the *ultra vires* test by the GFCC and the Accession Act test by the Danish Supreme Court. This indicates a lack of procedural legitimacy.

Second, the GFCC chose to review the legitimacy of the Mangold doctrine within the framework of the institutional role awarded to the Court in the treaties. This approach is conducted on the terms of EU law itself and is open towards EU law.[72] The GFCC found that in order for the Court to transgress its institutional role, the act of the authority must be significantly in violation of competences.[73] The threshold set by the GFCC could indicate an inclination to go some of the way in accepting the procedure of norm-making based on transnational law. The GFCC used a pluralistic approach acknowledging the legitimacy of the constitutional powers of the Court. The Danish Supreme Court instead reviewed the Mangold doctrine with a formalistic and dualistic approach, taking the national constitutional law as the point of departure. The Supreme Court specifically stated that the Court can develop principles, but whether such principles would bind national legal actors depends on an interpretation of national constitutional law and statutory acts conferring rule-making powers on the EU.[74] The Danish court thus used a dualistic approach concentrating the test of validity on national legal sources. The approaches differ, but the questionable procedural legitimacy is evident.

Third, a lack of substantive legitimacy in the case of Denmark could also be indicated although not explicit in the ruling. In the Danish case, the general principle of equality in employment and the norm developed by the Court prohibiting discrimination on grounds of age are not expressed in the Danish constitution. The idea of a principle of equality overruling legal certainty was not congruent with the broader values of – at least – the Supreme Court judges at the given moment.

The lack of legitimacy could be indicated by this resistance in succumbing national judicial assessments to the overall guidance of the EU principle of equality. The rulings, more so the Danish ruling, illustrate a lack of judicial manoeuvring to accommodate the development of EU law by adhering to the Mangold doctrine.[75]

71 Bexell (n. 47).

72 *BVerfG* (n. 51) para. 58.

73 Ibid., para. 61.

74 Nielsen and Tvarnø (n. 68) 308.

75 Joxerramon Bengoetxea, 'Rethinking EU Law in the Light of Pluralism and Practical Reason' in Kaarlo Tuori, Miguel Maduro and Suvi Sankari (eds), *Transnational Law: Rethinking European Law and Legal Thinking* (Cambridge University Press 2014) 145, 167–168.

Procedural and substantive legitimacy – A legal theory perspective

The interplay between the transnational principle of equality common to the constitutions of the Member States and the freestanding EU principle of equality as well as the lack of legitimacy in its application by national actors can be interpreted in light of the theory of critical legal positivism.[76] The theory suggests that a legal order can be viewed as consisting of levels. Legislative initiatives and court decisions take place at *the surface level*. Underneath are the levels of *the legal culture* and *the deep structure of the law*.[77] Law at *the surface level* is constantly changing as regulations and developments continuously change and modify the contents of the legal order.[78] In our situation, this would refer to the expressions or manifestations of the equality principle in EU treaties, directives, the Charter and the surrounding case law of the Court.

The legal culture is the common legal understandings of the legal profession, as obtained through the legal education and work.[79] *The legal culture* is likewise dynamic and evolving, but at a lesser speed than *the surface level*. The common understandings are used as background knowledge when the legal profession interprets law at *the surface level*.[80] In our case, *the legal culture* would refer to the constitutional notions of formal and perhaps substantive equality in the Member States, as well as the reference in the preambles of EU instruments to non-EU instruments expressing similar principles.

The deep structure of the law consists of basic values underlying *the legal culture* in a given society, such issues that are common in a certain national or supranational culture.[81] It is the most stabile of the layers. When law develops, or fundamental concepts are fading away, it demonstrates that changes are taking place in *the deep structure* of the law. In our case, *the deep structure* could refer to a basic adherence to 'equality' between human beings.

The levels of law are in constant interaction. The interaction can be described as *recursive*. All activities of law-making, adjudication and legal science at *the surface level* are informed, interpreted and molded by legal notions found in *the legal culture*. At the same time, the legal notions are reproduced and perhaps even modified by the everyday use at the surface level. The content and application of the norms at the surface level draw on the legal culture of the legal actors when applying and interpreting a norm.[82] The *recursive* relation means that the legal practices at *the surface level* are dependent on *the legal culture* and *the deep structure of law* as a precondition. Likewise, the formation of law at *the surface level*

76 Kaarlo Tuori, *Critical Legal Positivism* (Ashgate 2002) 147–196.
77 Ibid., 147.
78 Ibid., 160.
79 Ibid., 161–162.
80 Ibid., 174.
81 Ibid., 184–185.
82 Ibid., 210–211.

over time contributes to amending and adjusting the principles and notions in *the legal culture* and *the deep structure* of law.[83] This interaction can be described as *sedimentary*, allowing the *surface level* to contribute to the continuous production and reproduction of the lower levels of law. This is what happens when common tendencies in judicial interpretation over time form a more general and firm principle of law.

First, the *recursive* relationship can be used to understand the national courts' foot-dragging approaches. When faced with applying a supranational principle of equality which has, as its basis, a transnational principle, the understanding and the interpretation of the supranational principle of equality will be influenced and informed by the legal culture of the legal actors in the Member State in which the application is carried out. In the Danish Supreme Court, the judges will align the interpretation and application of a rule with the legal culture and the deep structure of the legal community in Denmark. When the rule of law and the notion of legal certainty are very strong in the Danish legal culture, this renders a premonition against disapplying a legal provision in force. This is the case, even if the Danish legal culture and deep structure of law strongly agree with equality as a basic value in society. This means that more often a dualistic or formal legal culture will influence the application of a norm at the surface level, including supranational norms based on transnational principles. Second, when, as in this case, the principle at the surface level is vague, this would indeed require interpretation of the principle upon application; in particular, when in competition with the principle of legal certainty. This vagueness requires that the principle will be informed, adjusted and molded with reference to the legal culture in each specific case of interpretation and application. Third, in this case in particular, the lack of procedural and substantive legitimacy of the norm leaves the legal actors without pre-existing content and a common legal notion of the norm at the lower levels. As mentioned, the principle of non-discrimination on grounds of age is not found in the Danish constitution and is not part of the Danish legal tradition in employment.

From a national point of view, when the principle of equality is established on the basis of the constitutional traditions of *other* Member States, the theory could explain why such a development is likely to present problems in national application. The process of elevating a transnational principle to a supranational principle will, in itself, create resistance or lack of interpretational material at the level of the legal culture in the Member States not sharing the same legal understanding or basic value of such a principle. Examining the national cases, in light of the theory of critical legal positivism, thus gives a deeper understanding of possible interrelations and interplays between the lack of procedural and substantive legitimacy among national actors and the origin of norms as transnational law.

83 Ibid., 200–201.

Conclusion

An analysis of the development of the principle of equality in the EU and its resistance in certain Member States contributes with important aspects to the formation of legal theory.

First, the elevation of transnational principles, i.e. principles found in the common constitutional traditions of Member States, to general binding supranational principles, applicable to a larger group of Member States, has been presented with some resistance. The process of rule-making did not involve the democratic rule-making institutions of the EU and did also go beyond the existing substantial provisions on equality in the Treaty. This procedure created a lack of procedural legitimacy of the transnational norm and also – for the Member States which do not have the principle as their constitutional tradition – a lack of substantive legitimacy. The emerging tendency of the Court to create and expand EU law with reference to transnational principles as the legal basis was not welcomed by the national level legal actors.

Second, it could be viewed as the Court conferred a transnational principle as a new and independent legal principle of EU law by using the Member States as the legal source, not the Treaty nor the Framework Directive. The principle was then applied via the EU treaties directly in the horizontal relationship between private entities in Member States.[84] It could along the same lines be viewed as a norm diffusion from state to state, where the principle of equality originates from the domestic legal systems of Member States and through the Court becomes part of EU law and from then becomes a part of the domestic legal system through the Mangold doctrine.[85] This would be in line with Somek's notion of constitutionalism 3.0 by which the national constitution becomes strongly entangled with transnational regulatory processes.[86]

Third, future developments are unclear. In 2009, the Charter was elevated to treaty level by the Lisbon Treaty. With respect to the direct horizontal effect of provisions promoting non-discrimination, the legal consequences of this elevation naturally attract interest. The Danish Supreme Court in the *Ajos* case sweepingly stated that as a result of the Danish Accession Act the provisions in the Charter, including Article 21 on non-discrimination, cannot be given direct horizontal effect in Denmark.[87] The Court holds the opposite view. In the recent

84 Larry Catá Backer, 'On the Tension between Public and Private Governance in the Emerging Transnational Legal Order: State Ideology and Corporation in Polycentric Asymmetric Global Orders' (Social Science Research Network 2012) SSRN Scholarly Paper ID 2038103 24.

85 Gregory Shaffer, 'Transnational Legal Process and State Change' (Social Science Research Network 2011) SSRN Scholarly Paper ID 1901952 235.

86 Alexander Somek, 'The Cosmopolitan Constitution' in Kaarlo Tuori, Miguel Maduro and Suvi Sankari (eds), *Transnational Law: Rethinking European Law and Legal Thinking* (Cambridge University Press 2014) 97, 98.

87 *Ajos* (n. 52) 42

ruling of *Egenberger*,[88] the Court stated that the prohibition of discrimination on grounds of religion or belief is a general principle of EU law, and the prohibition, which is laid down in Article 21(1) of the Charter, is sufficient in itself to confer a right on individuals, even in disputes deriving from private contracts.[89] This could in effect be interpreted as the Court acknowledging an individual right to equal treatment and non-discrimination as laid down in Article 21(1) of the Charter. As the direct horizontal applicability of the Charter is not clear from the Charter provisions themselves or the implementing provision in the Lisbon Treaty elevating the Charter to Treaty level, the procedural legitimacy of the scope of equality in Article 21(1) could be questioned, e.g. 'based on any ground'. This new development allows for a new generation of rulings on the direct horizontal application of the principle of non-discrimination on a multitude of specific grounds.

Along the same lines is the enactment of the European Pillar of Social Rights in light of the differing national approaches to equality.[90] The pillar expresses principles and rights essential for fair and well-functioning labour markets and welfare systems in 21st-century-Europe.[91] The objective is obtained by reaffirming rights already existing as part of the EU *acquis* and by introducing new principles requiring measures or legislation to be adopted in order to be legally enforceable.[92] This development likewise allows for new rulings of the Court developing or confirming the existence of principles of equal treatment.

A transnational principle of equality elevated by the Court to supranational EU law has not had smooth sailing in the Member States. However, there is room for slight optimism with a view to the theory of Kaarlo Tuori. The legal culture of the Member States will potentially over time, by the process of *sedimentation* from the surface level to the lower levels, become influenced and developed by the rulings and regulations at the surface level. This would over time allow for increasing correspondence or recognition of the traditions of other Member States. This development would be supported by the case law of the Court, referencing their rulings to transnational principles of equal treatment, as expressed in the common constitutional traditions of the Member States, the Charter and the European Pillar of Social Rights.

88 Case C-414/16, *Vera Egenberger v. Evangelisches Werk für Diakonie und Entwicklung eV* [2018] ECLI:EU:C:2018:257.

89 Ibid., paras 76–78.

90 European Commission Communication of 26 April 2017 establishing a European Pillar of Social Rights, COM (2017) 250 final.

91 Sacha Garben, 'The European Pillar of Social Rights: Effectively Addressing Displacement?' (2018) 14 *European Constitutional Law Review* 210.

92 *European Pillar of Social Rights* (n. 90) preamble 14.

13 How domestic courts may shape international commercial law norms

Thomas Neumann

Introduction

The United Nations (UN) was established in the wake of World War II with the purpose of maintaining international peace and security, developing friendly relations among states, and solving international problems through international cooperation.[1] Resting on the old adage – if goods are not allowed to cross international borders, soldiers will – several legislative efforts have been made to create uniform legal norms for cross border commercial activities, and since 1966 this has predominantly been taking place under the auspices of the United Nations Commission on International Trade Law (UNCITRAL).[2]

Through conventions and model laws, the UN and UNCITRAL create international uniform law. When international uniform law is adopted by a state, it becomes applicable to private entities engaged in international economic activity within the scope of that uniform law, e.g. international sale of goods. More interesting, though, is that many of these commercially relevant international uniform laws require further interpretation and development by domestic courts in order to work in practice. However, without a supranational court or other supervising authority there is little official structure to ensure that this happens in a way that supports the instruments' uniform application. The fact that the power to develop international uniform commercial law through interpretation and application rests entirely with domestic courts questions both whether there are any limits to the Courts' exercise of discretion as well as their role as creators of transnational norms. The discretion to interpret, apply and thus also develop uniform commercial law is limited by statute in each uniform law instrument, in the sense that the domestic courts are required to exercise their discretion in a way that considers the international character of the instrument as well as the aim of reaching uniformity in practice. It is a crucial point that domestic courts thereby are expected by the drafters to rely on each other's experience – or in other words, to engage in a retrospective judicial dialogue – and thereby arrive at some degree

1 United Nations, Charter of the United Nations, 24 October 1945, 1 UNTS XVI, Art. 1.
2 UNCITRAL establishment, see General Assembly in 1966 (Resolution 2205(XXI) of 17 December 1966).

of uniform application of the uniform law text. However, this paper argues that the responsibility vested in the domestic courts to retrospectively rely on court practice inevitably also has a prospective aspect to it. A forward-looking court has the opportunity to shape the transnational norms that develop from uniform law if the Court is able to grasp the opportunity that lies in the non-hierarchical court structure in which uniform commercial law is interpreted and applied. In short – a court that understands how to exploit the opportunity of persuading future courts through its rationale may become the creator of transnational commercial law norms (rational persuasion).

This chapter analyses the responsibility that has been vested with domestic courts. The aim is to demonstrate how a court which aspires to shape transnational norms through its decisions is both allowed to do so and may do so through rational persuasion. The underpinning of the chapter is threefold. First, that the discretion to interpret and apply UNCITRAL instruments must be exercised under consideration of the instrument's international character and the aim of uniform application (see section "The authority for domestic courts to shape transnational norms"). Based on interpretation of one particular clause that is used repeatedly in UNCITRAL instruments, it is seen that it is a mandatory requirement that domestic courts engage in retrospective dialogue with each other in the sense that a court must exercise its discretion under informal influence by the already established court practice no matter if that court practice is established in the same or a foreign jurisdiction. Second, that domestic courts today rarely engage in judicial dialogue in a transparent way (see section, "The current state of the judicial dialogue"). Courts simply do not refer to the former court decisions that may or may not have played a role in the Courts' exercise of their discretion, and as such they generate less persuasive decisions since their use of retrospective judicial dialogue is not obvious to other courts. Third, that when courts do not transparently reveal how their discretion has been exercised, the decision holds less rational persuasive power when future courts engage in retrospective judicial dialogue themselves since the persuasive power of a decision that is not transparent is weaker than that of a transparent one (see section "Assessing the persuasive value of foreign court decisions"). Operating in a non-hierarchical court structure, such non-persuasive court decisions will wither away as other courts are neither formally required to follow them as precedent nor is the decision able to persuade a court to follow the decision's rationale voluntarily. However, the non-hierarchical structure of domestic courts also presents an opportunity for the prudent court to persuade future courts to voluntarily follow its decisions, and thus it may become the creator of transnational commercial norms. On this basis, it is concluded that domestic courts, as a minimum, are required to engage in retrospective judicial dialogue, but also that domestic courts both have the power and opportunity to shape international uniform law in practice (see section "Conclusion").

Before turning to the first part of the argument, it is fitting to summarise the terminology used in this chapter. The term judicial dialogue is used to describe the fact that the drafters of the international uniform laws subject of study have included an interpretation clause in almost every instrument which demands the consideration of former court practice including both practice from the same jurisdiction as the deciding court as well as court practice from other jurisdictions. Drawing on past court practice is addressed as a retrospective component of the judicial dialogue, whereas the opportunity to affect future courts' decisions through careful reasoning is a prospective component. Since domestic courts do not form part of a formal hierarchy, it all boils down to whether a court considers another court's decision to have persuasive character. Rational persuasion is the term used to describe the fact that a decision is considered legitimate in the sense that a court is more likely to voluntarily follow the decision's line of thought because the decision is rendered by an authority which ranks higher in power according to an official hierarchy.[3] In the words of Bodansky: 'an institution's lack of coercive power means that it must rely more on perceived legitimacy as a basis of influence'.[4] This chapter may thus be seen as a study of the legitimacy of court decisions in the shaping of transnational commercial law norms.

The authority for domestic courts to shape transnational norms

The UN General Assembly established the UNCITRAL as a tool to remove international legal barriers to trade through 'the codification and wider acceptance' of international trade terms, provisions and practices by way of uniform laws, conventions and model laws.[5] In other words, by creating international uniform law. The ultimate reason why the UN creates uniform law is to meet its goals of peace, international cooperation and common solutions to common problems.[6] These goals are reflected in the preambles of almost all commercially focused UN instruments, which are the subject of study in this chapter.[7]

Both the UNCITRAL and individual states have reiterated the UN's goals of peace and cooperation repeatedly either when drafting uniform law or when adopting it. However, one thing is to create a uniform instrument and have it adopted by as many states as possible, another is to achieve a uniform application of the instrument in practice. As we know, this task is to be performed by the domestic courts of each state though with due consideration of the interpretation and application experience that already exists with other domestic courts. When a state is a party to an international agreement in which it has promised to unify

3 Daniel Bodansky, 'Legitimacy in International Law and International Relations' in Jeffrey L. Dunoff and Mark A. Pollack (eds), *Interdisciplinary Perspectives on International Law and International Relations: The State of the Art* (Cambridge University Press 2013) 326.

4 Ibid., 325.

5 UNGA Res. 2205 (1966) GAOR 1497th plenary meeting.

6 United Nations, Charter of the United Nations, 24 October 1945, 1 UNTS XVI, Art. 1.

7 For one recent and elaborate example, see the preamble of United Nations Convention on Contracts for the International Carriage of Goods Wholly or Partly by Sea (adopted 11 December 2008; not yet entered into force) [the Rotterdam Rules].

certain commercial law rules, it means that the state, as such, must strive towards compliance. Notably, this includes also the behaviour of the Courts, and acting contrary to that promise could mean a breach of *pacta sunt servanda* – a breach of international obligations.[8] Therefore, it is salient to know the limits of the domestic courts' discretion when they interpret and apply international uniform law.

Looking across the commercial law instruments originating from the UNCITRAL, it becomes apparent that domestic courts must consider the '*international character*' and the '*need to promote uniformity*' in the application of the instrument they interpret and apply.[9] These two requirements are directly expressed in statutes in most of the UNCITRAL instruments, and the most recent example is seen in the Rotterdam Rules, Article 2, which reads: 'In the interpretation of this Convention, regard is to be had to its international character and to the need to promote uniformity in its application and the observance of good faith in international trade'.[10] The wording is identical, or nearly identical, to many other UN conventions in the field and can be traced to a total of nine conventions[11] drafted under the auspices of the UNCITRAL. In addition, six model laws,[12] which also originated from the UNCITRAL, rely on the same wording.

8 Jan Ramberg, 'Regionalism and Globalism from a Nordic Perspective' in Thomas Neumann (ed.), *Audiovisual Conference Book* (CISGNordic.net 14 November 2014) www.cisgnordic.net/conferencebook.shtml accessed 29 June 2018.

9 Citations from United Nations Convention on Contracts for the International Carriage of Goods Wholly or Partly by Sea (adopted 11 December 2008; not yet entered into force) [the Rotterdam Rules] Art. 2, but equally valid for all instruments listed later, n. 11 and n. 12.

10 United Nations Convention on Contracts for the International Carriage of Goods Wholly or Partly by Sea (adopted 11 December 2008; not yet entered into force) [the Rotterdam Rules].

11 United Nations Convention on Contracts for the International Sale of Goods (adopted 10 March to 11 April 1980, entered into force 1 January 1988) 1489 UNTS 3 (CISG) Art. 7; United Nations Convention on the Limitation Period in the International Sale of Goods (adopted 20 May to 14 June 1974, entered into force 1 August 1988) 1511 UNTS 3, Art. 7; United Nations Convention on the Use of Electronic Communications in International Contracts (adopted 23 November 2005, entered into force 1 March 2013) 2898 UNTS Doc. A/60/515, Art. 5; United Nations Convention on the Carriage of Goods by Sea (adopted 30 March 1978, entered into force 1 November 1992) 1695 UNTS 3 [the Hamburg Rules] Art. 3; United Nations Convention on the Liability of Operators of Transport Terminals in International Trade Article (adopted 19 April 1991, not entered into force) Doc. A/CONF/152/13, Art. 14; United Nations Convention on Contracts for the International Carriage of Goods Wholly or Partly by Sea (adopted 11 December 2008; not yet entered into force) [the Rotterdam Rules] Art. 2; United Nations Convention on International Bills of Exchange and International Promissory Notes (adopted 9 December 1988, not entered into force) Doc. A/RES/43/165, Art. 4; United Nations Convention on Independent Guarantees and Stand-by Letters of Credit (adopted 26 January 1996, entered into force 1 January 2000) 2169 UNTS 163, Art. 5; United Nations Convention on the Assignment of Receivables in International Trade (adopted 12 December 2001, not entered into force) Doc. A/RES/56/81, Art. 7.

12 UNCITRAL Model Law on International Commercial Arbitration with amendments as adopted in 2006 (1985) Art. 2A; UNCITRAL Model Law on International Commercial

For the sake of simplicity, the wording that is used repeatedly is dubbed the 'uniform interpretation clause'. The clause always instructs the interpreter – meaning the domestic courts – to consider the '*international*' character or origin, and the need to '*promote uniformity*' in the application of the uniform law. Thereby, it places restrictions on the discretion that domestic courts have.

The elements of '*international*' character/origin and the need to '*promote uniformity*' are closely related and presuppose each other.[13] Together, they call for an autonomous interpretation of the uniform law that is free from domestic traditions[14] and that acts as the framework within which a domestic court must exercise its discretion to interpret, apply and develop uniform law.

Having regard to an instrument's international character means to read the instrument in an international light, recognising, for example, that UN instruments exist in several equally authentic language versions. Should a court give preference to only one of the authentic language versions, it would violate the limits of the Court's discretion to interpret and apply the instrument[15] and potentially be contrary to the promise made by the state when it adopted the instrument. The international light in which to read the instrument appears from its legislative history, case law and scholarly writings.[16] Also, widely recognised non-governmental codifications may be used to provide the international light

Conciliation (2002) Art. 2; UNCITRAL Model Law on Electronic Commerce (1996) Art. 3; UNCITRAL Model Law on Electronic Signatures (2001) Art. 4; UNCITRAL Model Law on Cross-Border Insolvency (1997) Art. 8; UNCITRAL Model Law on Secured Transactions (2016) Art. 5.

13 Michael Joachim Bonell and Cesare Massimo Bianca, *Bianca-Bonell Commentary on the International Sales Law* (Giuffrè 1987) 72; John Honnold and Harry M. Flechtner, *Uniform Law for International Sales under the 1980 United Nations Convention* (4th edn, Wolters Kluwer 2009) 117–118; John Felemegas (ed.), *An International Approach to the Interpretation of the United Nations Convention on Contracts for the International Sale of Goods (1980) as Uniform Sales Law* (Cambridge University Press 2007) 12–13.

14 Hannu Honka in Alexander von Ziegler, Johan Schelin and Stefano Zunarelli (eds), *The Rotterdam Rules 2008* (Wolters Kluwer 2010) 32; 'Commentary on the Convention on the Limitation Period in the International Sale of Goods, Done at New York, 14 June 1974 (A/Conf.63/17)' in (1979) X UNCITRAL Yearbook, 145–173.

15 Honnold and Flechtner (n. 13) 118; Schwenzer and Hachem, in Ingeborg Schwenzer (ed.), *Schlechtriem & Schwenzer Commentary on the UN Convention on the International Sale of Goods (CISG)* (4th edn, Oxford University Press 2016) Art. 7, para. 8, 122 and para. 21, 129; Bonell and Bianca (n. 13); Fritz Enderlein and Dietrich Maskow, *International Sales Law* (Oceana Publications 1992) 55.

16 Ricardo Sandoval López in A.H. Boss and W. Kilian, *The United Nations Convention on the Use of Electronic Communications in International Contracts* (Wolters Kluwer 2008) 112.; Honka (n. 14) 32; Honnold and Flechtner (n. 13) 118–120; Bonell and Bianca (n. 13) 90–91. According to Konrad Zweigert and Hein Kötz, *Introduction to Comparative Law* (3rd edn, Clarendon Press 1998) 21; H.C. Gutteridge, *Comparative Law* (Cambridge University Press 1946) 81–82; and John Honnold, 'Uniform Words and Uniform Application – The 1980 Sales Convention and International Juridical Practice' in Peter Schlechtriem (ed.), *Einheitliches Kaufrecht und Nationales Obligationsrecht* (Nomos 1987). Scholarly works may act as a supplement for example when a country is not producing case law or the existing case law is difficult to discern due to reasons of access or language.

in which the instrument is to be read, though they may not be used to introduce new rules into the instrument being interpreted which have deliberately been excluded by the draftsmen.[17] To the extent that a uniform law instrument from the UN contains rules that are similar to that of codifications or restatements of international law and principles, the latter may act as interpretation aids, e.g. the rules of the 1980 UN Sales Convention may be read in light of the UNIDROIT Principles, Principles of European Contract Law and the TransLex Principles.[18]

The goal of uniformity is to be achieved by the domestic courts. In the absence of a formal hierarchy between the domestic courts of various jurisdictions, the Courts must operate as a community of courts joined by the fact that they all interpret and apply the same instrument and that they all must strive for uniformity in practice. Thus, domestic courts are supposed to engage in judicial dialogue in which they draw upon each other's experience, and in turn, voluntarily let themselves be persuaded by well-reasoned decisions from other jurisdictions as well as showing reluctance to deviate from a foreign line of precedents.[19] In short, domestic courts are required by the draftsmen through the uniform interpretation clause to consider, but not blindly follow, foreign court decisions when exercising their discretion. Due to the lack of a power structure between domestic courts and since no doctrine of *stare decisis* exists,[20] rational persuasion is the key[21] to achieving the aim of uniform application in the sense that only when a previous court decision itself openly has drawn upon the judicial dialogue, it may persuade other courts and thereby shape a transnational norm. It has been stated that sharing court experience in this way is a workable way to slowly reach uniform application of uniform law in practice.[22]

It may well be that a domestic court finds it unfamiliar to draw upon court experience from other jurisdictions. It is nonetheless what is being expected of it. Ignoring the limits to the discretion to interpret and apply uniform law would be

17 Enderlein and Maskow (n. 15) 55; and Ralf Michaels in Stefan Vogenauer and Jan Kleinheisterkamp (eds), *Commentary on the Unidroit Principles of International Commercial Contracts (PICC)* (Oxford University Press 2009) 57.

18 Felemegas (n. 13) 33–34; International Court of Arbitration, International Chamber of Commerce, *Food Products Case,* December 1996, no. 8817; 1999 The Principles of European Contract Law [PECL]; 2016 UNIDROIT Principles of International Contracts [PICC]; Trans-Lex Principles as presented on Trans-Lex.org. See further Klaus Peter Berger, *The Creeping Codification of the New Lex Mercatoria* (Wolters Kluwer 2010).

19 Marianne Roth and Richard Happ, 'Interpretation of the CISG According to Principles of International Law' (1999) 4 *International Trade and Business Law Annual 1,* 10.; Honnold and Flechtner (n. 13) 124; Schwenzer and Hachem (n. 15) Art. 7, para. 10, 123 and para. 13, 124–125; Enderlein and Maskow (n. 15) 56. Several decisions refer extensively to foreign case law, e.g. 26 November 2002 Tribunale di Rimini [District Court of Rimini, Italy].

20 Honka (n. 14) 32.

21 López (n. 16) 112.; Ulrich Magnus, 'Tracing Methodology in the CISG: Dogmatic Foundations' in Olaf Meyer and André Janssen (eds), *CISG Methodology* (Sellier 2009) 42; Roth and Happ (n. 19) 10–11.

22 Camilla Baasch Andersen, *Uniform Application of the International Sales Law – Understanding Uniformity, the Global Jurisconsultorium and Examination and Notification Provisions of the CISG* (Kluwer Law International 2007) 229.

inappropriate in the sense that it would counteract the aim of uniform application as well as the overarching goals of the UN. A domestic court may not reject this retrospective part of the judicial dialogue with the view that it is unfamiliar or 'foreign' to the domestic legal system. Uniform law originating from the UNCITRAL is not foreign to the domestic legal system in which it has been implemented in a way that the Courts should consider it less binding, less important or less legitimate than law of domestic origin. First, because the UNCITRAL consists of representatives from 60 nations, meaning that uniform law has some degree of a democratic anchor providing opportunity to affect the drafting.[23] Second, because adoption of an instrument is voluntary. If the content of an instrument is unacceptable to a particular state, then that state can choose not to ratify the document. Upon incorporation, the uniform law becomes part of the domestic legal body.

A domestic court may find it a burdensome practical challenge to draw on foreign court experience by having to locate relevant foreign court decisions, let alone understanding the language in which they are rendered. To overcome these practical barriers of the retrospective judicial dialogue, the UNCITRAL maintains a database[24] with domestic court decisions relevant to the application of UNCITRAL instruments, it publishes digests of case law in selected areas,[25] it maintains bibliographies giving an overview of current scholarly writings,[26] and various other autonomous initiatives collect and translate court decisions.[27] Hence, retrospective judicial dialogue may be a challenge for the domestic court, but not an impossible or unreasonable one to overcome. However, it does presume that courts are willing to engage in the judicial dialogue to begin with.

In summary, the draftsmen intended to establish an autonomous interpretation of uniform law through the uniform interpretation clause with the aim of reaching uniformity in practice. It is mandatory that courts engage in retrospective judicial dialogue in order to reach uniformity. However simple it may sound

23 Sixty members elected by the General Assembly for a six year period representing various geographic, economic, and legal regions, according to UNCITRAL, 'Origin, Mandate and Composition of UNCITRAL' (United Commission on International Trade Law) www.uncitral.org/uncitral/en/about/origin.html accessed 2 July 2018.

24 UNCITRAL, 'Case Law on UNCITRAL Texts' www.uncitral.org/clout/index.jspx#legislativeText accessed 2 July 2018.

25 Two digests are currently maintained. The UNCITRAL, *Digest of Case Law on the United Nations Convention on Contracts for the International Sale of Goods* (2016) and UNCITRAL, *2012 Digest of Case Law on the Model Law on International Commercial Arbitration*, both available at UNCITRAL 'Digests' www.uncitral.org/uncitral/en/case_law/digests.html accessed 2 July 2018.

26 See UNCITRAL, *Bibliography of recent writings related to the work of UNCITRAL*, www.uncitral.org/uncitral/publications/bibliography_consolidated.html accessed 2 July 2018.

27 Honnold and Flechtner (n. 13) 125–133; Schwenzer and Hachem (n. 15) Art. 7, para. 11, 123–124. The Institute of International Commercial Law at Pace Law School, New York provides a list of locally focused databases and has together with the University of London established the Queen Mary Case Translation Programme. See Pace Law, 'Autonomous Network of CISG Websites' http://iicl.law.pace.edu/cisg/page/autonomous-network-cisg-websites accessed 2 July 2018.

to make reference to a case law digest, it is not necessarily an obvious or straightforward task for a domestic court to then assess whether a previous court decision is one that is made under careful consideration of the uniform interpretation clause or not – meaning whether a foreign court decision should be persuasive or not. Before addressing this point, it is worth examining to which extent domestic courts in fact have embraced the judicial dialogue.

The current state of the judicial dialogue

One example of the UN and the UNCITRAL creating international uniform law is the 1980 UN Convention on Contracts for the International Sale of Goods (CISG).[28] While there are many more legislative initiatives than the CISG originating from the UNCITRAL, this particular convention is one of the more widespread ones with more than 80 states currently enforcing it.[29] This makes the CISG a suitable point of departure for observing how domestic courts handle the uniform interpretation clause, described earlier, in practice across several very different jurisdictions. Furthermore, the CISG is most often adopted by states in its authentic language version, meaning that courts from different jurisdictions are interpreting the same uniform law text as a starting point. Thus, the CISG is a useful lens through which one can observe how the retrospective judicial dialogue is handled by courts.

When looking systematically at domestic courts' practice, it can be observed that only a few domestic courts seem to engage openly in the retrospective judicial dialogue required by the UN. Others either do not rely on foreign court practice at all or they do it infrequently.[30] For example, in 42 court decisions by Chinese domestic courts applying international uniform law, it is not possible to observe a single reference to foreign court practice.[31] While this could be due to domestic traditions of how court decisions are reasoned, it is curious to see the same tendency in other quite different jurisdictions. In 258 decisions by German domestic courts applying the same international uniform law, it is only possible to observe reliance on foreign court practice in 5% (13 decisions) of the decisions.[32] In 29 decisions by Danish courts, no use of foreign court practice can be observed when the Courts apply international uniform law.[33]

28 Supra, n. 11.

29 *Status regarding the 1980 United Nations Convention on Contracts for the International Sale of Goods*, United Nations Commission on International Trade Law www.uncitral.org/uncitral/en/uncitral_texts/sale_goods/1980CISG_stat us.html accessed 29 June 2018.

30 Three percent of all reported case law applying the CISG refers to foreign case law according to Camilla Baasch Andersen, 'Nordic Legal Tradition – An Obstacle to Uniform Application?' in Thomas Neumann (ed.), *Audiovisual Conference Book* (CISGNordic.net 14 November 2014) www.cisgnordic.net/conferencebook.shtml accessed 29 June 2018.

31 Thomas Neumann, 'Is the Albert Kritzer Database Telling Us More than We Know?' (2015) 27 Pace International Law Review 119, 148–151.

32 Ibid.

33 Surveyed for the purpose of the present chapter: H-85-15 20 February 2017 Sø- og Handelsretten [Copenhagen Maritime and Commercial Court]; H-20-14 15 September 2015

It is important to emphasise that it is the *open* reliance on a judicial dialogue that is being surveyed at present. Courts may naturally consider foreign court practice behind closed doors, so to say. While this would comply with the mandatory aspect of the uniform interpretation clause as described earlier, it inhibits the persuasive value of the decision, as will be described later. It has been established earlier that courts are obliged to consider and voluntarily rely upon foreign court decisions when applying uniform law instruments containing the uniform interpretation clause. Due to the lack of an official hierarchy between the Courts, it is critical that a court is able to assess the persuasive value of foreign court practice, especially since foreign practice may vary in its approach to similar issues instead of establishing a uniform line of precedent. The assessment of persuasive value is key to the success of uniformity in practice, and the current reticence of domestic courts to make their considerations of persuasive value transparent has created a welcome opportunity for individual domestic courts to become creators of transnational norms.

Assessing the persuasive value of foreign court decisions

A persuasive court decision is one where the domestic court has utilised the discretion vested with it by the UN and the UNCITRAL within the limits of the uniform interpretation clause. It has already been mentioned that uniformity in practice is to be achieved by domestic courts,[34] and so the interpretation

Sø- og Handelsretten [Copenhagen Maritime and Commercial Court]; H-67-14 23 October 2015 Sø- og Handelsretten [Copenhagen Maritime and Commercial Court]; H-0102-09 21 December 2012 Sø- og Handelsretten [Copenhagen Maritime and Commercial Court]; H-0037-10 30 June 2011 Sø- og Handelsretten [Copenhagen Maritime and Commercial Court]; S-0020-06 30 August 2011 Sø- og Handelsretten [Copenhagen Maritime and Commercial Court]; H-95-06 26 February 2010 Sø- og Handelsretten [Copenhagen Maritime and Commercial Court]; UfR2008.181H [Supreme Court of Denmark]; H-23-05 1 December 2008 Sø- og Handelsretten [Copenhagen Maritime and Commercial Court]; 19 October 2007 Københavns Byret [District Court of Copenhagen]; UfR2004.1869H [Supreme Court of Denmark]; 8 July 2004 Retten i Randers [District Court of Randers]; 3 December 2004 Vestre Landsret [Western High Court of Denmark]; 21 December 2004 Vestre Landsret [Western High Court of Denmark]; 6 February 2003 Retten i Grenaa [District Court of Grenaa]; 12 September 2003 Retten i Randers [District Court of Randers]; 4 December 2003 Retten i Aarhus [District Court of Aarhus]; UfR2002.1370Ø [Eastern High Court of Denmark]; 31 January 2002 Sø- og Handelsretten [Copenhagen Maritime and Commercial Court]; 30 October 2002 Vestre Landsret [Western High Court of Denmark]; UfR2001.713Ø [Eastern High Court of Denmark]; 15 February 2001 Højesteret [Supreme Court of Denmark]; 10 December 2001 Retten i Esbjerg [District Court of Esbjerg]; UfR2000.706Ø [Eastern High Court of Denmark]; 10 November 1999 Vestre Landsret [Western High Court of Denmark]; UfR1998.1092Ø [Eastern High Court of Denmark]; 4 November 1998 Retten i Randers [District Court of Randers]; UfR1996.616Ø [Eastern High Court of Denmark]; UfR1992.920SH Sø- og Handelsretten [Copenhagen Maritime and Commercial Court].

34 Felemegas (n. 13) 5–6.

of uniform law has to support that goal of unification.[35] In securing uniform interpretation, the uniform interpretation clause is crucial, since, in the words of another scholar, it is 'taking on metaphorically the mantle of a supranational tribunal or court'.[36]

It is easy to find examples of stray domestic court decisions that do not consider the international character or the aim of uniformity of the international uniform law applied. The interpretation clause does not demand that a domestic court follows such stray decisions as they have no rational persuasive value. A terrible, but very illustrative example of a court not engaging in the mandatory retrospective judicial dialogue, was seen in *Raw Materials Inc. v. Manfred Forberich GmbH.*[37] Here the domestic US court interpreted an international uniform law (CISG) and stated expressly that domestic law could serve as guidance on how to understand a particular uniform concept. The Court then ignored all foreign court decisions as well as all scholarly materials on the uniform concept and relied purely on domestic sources. Obviously, this is contrary to the intentions behind the uniform interpretation clause given by the UNCITRAL. The US court decision has aptly been described as a 'flagrant and depressing example of a court ignoring its obligations'.[38]

What the Court should have done instead was to consider the sources which could provide the necessary international lens through which the uniform law should be observed. In line with general treaty interpretation,[39] these sources do not form a hierarchy of sources. Instead they should all be considered.[40] However, it is possible to speak of primary sources and supplementary sources that may be used to confirm an interpretation, but not as the primary outset.[41]

Primary sources include the uniform law text expressing the rule being interpreted, the purpose of the rule and the application of the rule by other courts – including also foreign domestic courts.[42] Secondary sources are the preparatory

35 Magnus (n. 21) 34.

36 Bruno Zeller, *The United Nations Convention on Contracts for the International Sale of Goods – A Methodology for its Interpretation and Application* (The University of Melbourne 2001) 235. Another scholar aptly states: 'Uniformity achieved during the legislative process (in the ratification and implementation of the Convention) could be jeopardised by non-uniform interpretation'. López (n. 16) 112.

37 6 July 2004 Northern District of Illinois, Eastern Division, United States, *Raw Materials Inc. v. Manfred Forberich GmbH.*

38 Joseph Lookofsky and Harry Flechtner 'Nominating Manfred Forberich: The Worst CISG Decision in 25 Years?' (2005) 1 *Vindobona Journal of International Commercial Law and Arbitration* 199, 204.

39 Vienna Convention on the Law of Treaties (adopted 23 May 1969, entered into force 27 January 1980) 1155 UNTS 331, Arts 31 and 32.

40 Anthony Aust, *Modern Treaty Law and Practice* (2nd edn, Cambridge University Press 2007) 231 and 234; Mark E. Villiger, *Commentary on the 1969 Vienna Convention on the Law of Treaties* (Martinus Nijhoff 2009) Art. 31, para. 29, 435–436.

41 Villiger (n. 40) 447.

42 *1969 Vienna Convention* (n. 39) Art. 31.

works of the uniform law in question[43] and soft law which may be used to confirm the interpretation arrived at when using the primary sources to the extent the former express the same underlying principle.

Scholarly works are not easily placed in either group. On one hand, scholarly works may be considered a primary source since they may provide a clearer picture of the purpose and context of the uniform law in question, especially when there is a lack of application experience. On the other hand, scholarly works are secondary as they should not be consulted first in establishing the rights and obligations of the commercial parties subject to the uniform law.

An illustrative example of a court observing its authority is the Italian court decision in *Rheinland Versicherungen v. Atlarex*.[44] The decision has received high acclaim for its approach.[45] The domestic Italian court applied international uniform law (the CISG) and did so, well aware that no official court hierarchy could be relied upon. Still, it engaged in retrospective judicial dialogue when it took foreign court decisions into consideration. In fact, it did so more than 50 times in its reasoning. This style of reasoning is not only in line with the mandatory requirement of the uniform interpretation clause, it also enables future courts to assess the persuasive value of the Italian decision itself as the reasoning is transparent in its use of retrospective judicial dialogue.

Court decisions that consider foreign case law, but without making this clear in the reasoning of the decision itself, fall in between the two polar opposites exemplified by *Raw Materials Inc. v. Manfred Forberich GmbH* and *Rheinland Versicherungen v. Atlarex* earlier. On one hand, these decisions observe the mandatory retrospective aspect by considering also foreign court practice as part of the judicial dialogue. On the other hand, they do not enable further judicial dialogue since the lack of reasoning makes it impossible to assess whether the decision is one of domestic nature like *Raw Materials Inc. v. Manfred Forberich GmbH* or one of international nature like *Rheinland Versicherungen v. Atlarex*. The problem being that the rational persuasive value of such decisions is not easily established. For obvious reasons, it is extremely difficult to provide an example of such a middle ground decision. If one accepts the premise that courts are diligent and aware that participation in judicial dialogue is mandatory, it may be that most court decisions actually fall in this middle category.

The most apparent example of a court decision falling between the two polar opposites is the decision of 31 January 2002 by the Maritime and Commercial Court in Denmark.[46] In this decision, the Court decided on a number of points

43 *1969 Vienna Convention* (n. 39) Art. 32.

44 12 July 2000 Tribunale di Vigevano [District Court of Vigevano, Italy].

45 See, for example, Franco Ferrari, 'Applying the CISG in a Truly Uniform Manner: Tribunale Di Vigevano (Italy), 12 July 2000' (2001) *Uniform Law Review – Revue De Droit Uniforme* 203. See also 17 March 2009 בית המשפט העליון, Beit haMishpat ha'Elyon [Supreme Court of Israel], *Pamesa Ceramica v. Yisrael Mendelson Ltd.* in which two approaches were accounted for before the adjudicator picked what was believed to be the appropriate one.

46 31 January 2002 Sø- og Handelsretten [Copenhagen Maritime and Commercial Court].

with reference to international uniform law (CISG). Like so many other decisions, this one too is stripped of any reference or mention of foreign court decisions or any other indication of the Court actually engaging in retrospective judicial dialogue. However, the wording of the Court's reasoning is obviously inspired by the wording of a relevant decision from the Netherlands, thus demonstrating that the Court, in fact, engaged in retrospective judicial dialogue and was persuaded by foreign court practice.[47] The Court faced the question of whether a transnational norm requiring frozen goods to be thawed as part of the buyer's examination of the goods when the uniform law in question merely stated that the goods had to be examined. In the Courts' reasoning, it 'paraphrased the exact reasoning'[48] of foreign court decisions, but without referring to them. Though the lack of reference to those foreign court decisions is not a violation of the uniform interpretation clause, it makes it difficult, if not impossible, for future judges or legal counsel to decipher whether the decision should be persuasive on a court or not. In this particular situation, scholarly works have assisted interpreters in understanding that the decision of the Maritime and Commercial Court is, in fact, a decision of persuasive value.[49] However, for the vast amount of decisions that still do not refer to the foreign case law that may have persuaded the Court, and for which no supplementary scholarly works exist, the careful interpreter has good reason to consider such court decisions to be of no or little persuasive value. Consequently, neither a uniform approach nor a judicial dialogue shaping the transnational norms developing from uniform law is formed.

Conclusion

It has been established in this chapter that rational persuasive power originates from the Court's transparent use of retrospective judicial dialogue in its reasoning as prescribed by the uniform interpretation clause. Studies of court practice demonstrate polar opposite examples of the persuasive value of court decisions, but also that most decisions fall in-between, in the sense that they may be the result of a retrospective judicial dialogue, but without the Court making this apparent in its reasoning. Such decisions are problematic as it is difficult for future courts to assess their persuasive character.

In summary, it has been demonstrated that there is room for the prescient and ardent court to shape the transnational norms that may develop from uniform law more than happens today. The opportunity to influence future court decisions by prudent and transparent reasoning is allowed, but not required, by the uniform interpretation clause. Should a court choose this prescient and visionary path, it

47 Netherlands 19 December 1991 District Court Roermond (Fallini Stefano v. Foodik); Baasch Andersen (n. 30); and Thomas Neumann, 'International Commercial Law from a Nordic and Baltic Perspective: Status and Current Challenges' (2014) 2 *Nordic Journal of Commercial Law* 1, 7–8.

48 Baasch Andersen (n. 30).

49 Baasch Andersen (n. 30).

would seize the opportunity to speed up the otherwise slow process of developing international uniform law in practice. In turn, legal barriers to international commercial trade would deteriorate faster, commercial activity across borders would flow more freely and peaceful international relations would be cemented. Domestic courts often, perhaps inadvertently, let this opportunity slip at the cost of the removal of legal barriers and business opportunity. For every time a court does not indicate, in its reasoning, its willingness to draw upon the judicial dialogue, and for every time it does not consider the legitimacy of its own decisions for future judicial dialogue, it fails to seize this opportunity. The Courts 'must accept the fact that pure isolationism is no longer possible, and that the responsible way to exercise sovereignty is by recognizing the impact of that sovereignty on the global marketplace'.[50]

From the present chapter, it is possible to make some general observations relevant to the focal point of this book regarding transnational tendencies, legal actors and legitimacy of law. First, in the field of international commercial law there is a distinct tendency that attempts are being made for the goals of the United Nations to be fulfilled by creating international uniform commercial law instruments. It is a common trait that the UN leaves it to the domestic courts to achieve uniformity in practice, and it has been so the last many decades in the field of international commercial law. The power to reach uniformity in practice has been vested in the domestic courts, which in turn are supposed to exercise their discretion using the retrospective judicial dialogue. It is a common trend that courts seldom rely on foreign court practice in a transparent manner, which has the consequence that the pursuit of uniform application, in practice, is developing slowly.

Second, it can be observed that while the creators of international commercial law may be the UN and its Commission on International Trade Law, the uniform interpretation clause embedded in most uniform commercial law instruments allows courts to develop transnational norms from the uniform law. A persuasive application by a court in one jurisdiction may *qua* the retrospective judicial dialogue be applied by a court in another jurisdiction, and hence a transnational norm is born. Such court-developed norms are applicable to private commercial parties without being expressed in the uniform law adopted by the state. Therefore, an important legal actor in the field of international commercial law is the domestic courts as they, in fact, may act as creators of transnational commercial law norms.

Finally, with regard to legitimacy, it is seen that the UN and the UNCITRAL, as legal actors, still rely on uniformity being developed by the domestic courts in a non-hierarchical community. Thus, the assertion that it is often assumed that 'normative standards of legitimacy, such as transparency, participation, and representativeness, are, in fact, widely shared'[51] is confirmed in the present context.

50 López (n. 16) 113.
51 Bodansky (n. 3) 323.

Since there is no remedy to pressure courts who do not utilise the method of the uniform interpretation clause, the UN assumes that courts are willingly persuaded by well-reasoned foreign court decisions. Why the Courts are reticent in advancing the goals of UN uniform instruments in a transparent way is not possible to say. Whether the Courts assess the legitimacy of foreign decisions based on an analysis of the rational persuasive character or rely on other criteria is unknown as no study exists in this regard. Thus, it is confirmed that there is a need for empirical study.[52]

52 Bodansky (n. 3) 323.

14 Transnational religious law – Exemplified by the United Methodist Church

Lisbet Christoffersen

Introduction

Religion law,[1] including religious law, is one of the favourite examples in the literature analysing the development of transnational law as a perspective or a methodology.[2] It is a central argument in this contribution that religious law as an example of transnational law is neither new nor related solely to the impact of Islam while of course the new immanence of Islam in Northern Europe has made the societal challenge more obvious.

In this chapter, transnational law is understood as a methodological framework,[3] allowing for analysis of local and transnational actors and norms, connected through 'networks' and 'migrating standards', however, not as entirely detached from national political and legal orders, but as emerging out of and reaching beyond them. Transnational law in this chapter is further understood as an approach to analyse the frustration with possible lack of accountability,

1 I thank Reverend Jørgen Thaarup and Bishop Christian Alsted, the Danish Methodist Church, for good and informative comments to the factual content of earlier versions of this chapter. The chapter, including all evaluations, is of course my responsibility. The collection of material for this chapter ended mid-November 2018. Further update on the events discussed in the article are mentioned in footnote '37'.

2 Larry Catá Backer, 'On the Tension between Public and Private Governance in the Emerging Transnational Legal Order: State Ideology and Corporation in Polycentric Asymmetric Global Orders' (2012) Consortium for Peace and Ethics http://ssrn.com/abstract=2038103 accessed 12 November 2018; Roger Cotterrell, 'What is Transnational Law?' (2012) Queen Mary University of London, School of Law. Legal Studies Research Paper No. 103/2012, p. 9. See also King's LLM: Transnational Law modules descriptions for prospective students, Full Year Module on Contesting Globalisation: New Theories on Transnational Law and Global Governance, where 'religious relations' is highlighted as 'one of the perspectives, placing enormous pressure on established theories of democracy, the rule of law and social order'. The transnational perspective on religious law is analysed in Anne Hellum, Shaheen Sardar Ali and Anne Griffiths, *From Transnational Relations to Transnational Laws. Northern European Laws at the Crossroads* (Routledge 2016, reprint from Ashgate 2011). They do, however, only analyse the case of Muslims in the European Diaspora.

3 Peer Zumbansen, 'Defining the Space of Transnational Law: Legal Theory, Global Governance & Legal Pluralism', Osgoode Hall Law School Comparative Research in Law & Political Economy, research paper no. 21/2011, p. 30 ff.

access to justice and democratic legitimacy of such regulatory frameworks. The chapter will also draw on contributions from H. Patrick Glenn[4] on the 'margin-of-appreciation-doctrine' and from Kaarlo Tuori[5] on perspectivism with a focus on interlegality instead of a radical pluralism.

The governance system in transnational religious communities, that keeps the internal coherence and order in such communities, is and has always been a central example of a 'parallel' legal structure, challenging the nation state's sole capacity to regulate the legal conflicts among their citizens. Religious law, such as the Canon law of the Catholic or the Orthodox churches,[6] is the main examples of what in German theory is named 'Internes Recht der Religionen'.[7] These systems are transnational in nature as far as the churches or religious communities they are governing are transnational.

Transnational elements also influence the legal analysis of purely national churches or religions, such as the German or Scandinavian Lutheran churches. The Scandinavian state churches are just about to develop internal legal governance structures, independent from state laws, since church autonomy did not exist for these churches from the Reformation in 1529/1536 and until the changed relations with the states around 2000,[8] e.g. in Norway where the Church of Norway gained legal personality (2017), but also opened up for a transnational legal analysis of the extent to which the Church of Norway on the basis of international and European human rights norms and the Norwegian Constitution and Norwegian legislation has acquired or is about to acquire church autonomy. An additional question is to which extent this 'autonomy' also includes the existence of parallel religious legal orders in the country, or whether the autonomy is based on delegation from and within state law, or, as a third possibility, is based

4 H. Patrick Glenn, 'Transnational Legal Thought: Plato, Europe and Beyond' in Miguel Maduro, Kaarlo Tuori and Suvi Sankari (eds), *Transnational Law. Rethinking European Law and Legal Thinking* (Cambridge University Press 2014) 61.

5 Kaarlo Tuori, 'Transnational Law: On Legal Hybrids and Legal Perspectivism', in Miguel Maduro, Kaarlo Tuori and Suvi Sankari (eds), *Transnational Law. Rethinking European Law and Legal Thinking* (Cambridge University Press 2014) 11.

6 See e.g. Richard Potz and Eva Synek (unter Mitarbeit von Spyros Troianos), *Orthodoxes Kirchenrecht. Eine Einführung* (Verlag Plöchl 2007).

7 Josef Berkmann Buckhard, *Internes Recht der Religionen. Einführung in eine vergleichende Disziplin* (Verlag Kohlhammer 2018). For other examples, see e.g. Francis Lyall, *Of Presbyers & Kings. Church & State in the Law of Scotland* (Aberdeen University Press 1980); Mark Hill, *Ecclesiastical Law* (4th edn, Oxford University Press 2018).

8 See, for this concept, Gerhard Robbers, *Church Autonomy. A Comparative Survey* (Peeters 2001). For a discussion of the developing autonomy in the Scandinavian, previously established churches, see Lisbet Christoffersen, Kjell Å. Modéer and Svend Andersen (eds), *Law & Religion in the 21st Century. Nordic Perspectives* (Jurist- og Økonomforbundets Forlag 2010) and Lisbet Christoffersen, 'The Argument for a Narrow Conception of "Religious Autonomy"' (2015) 4 *Oxford Journal of Law and Religion* 278.

on an understanding of collective freedom of religion and belief with autonomy as legitimised through constitutional law/human rights law.[9]

The question of the existence of 'parallel religious legal orders' is currently discussed all over Europe. For some the answer is easy: Religious law is a social system of its own with its own legitimacy and its own legality.[10] Religious pluralism is a legal principle leading to the acknowledgement of parallel religious legal orders;[11] and the acknowledgement of these parallel legal orders is based on an understanding of freedom of religion and belief as not only covering individual rights, but also group rights.[12] The Reformation, in these perspectives, did not change the understanding of churches having a right to internal governance systems of a legal nature.[13]

In the Nordic context, the question of parallel religious legal orders is a burning issue.[14] The entire legal order is established as a monolithic system on the basis of the Reformation and the 19th century constitutions, establishing legislative powers through parliament. Freedom of religion and belief in the constitutions, from 1814 and onwards, does not in these countries seem to change the picture.[15] Freedom of religion and belief gives individual rights and freedoms. It also gives rights and freedoms to religious groups. However, the question to which groups such rights and freedoms can exist as a parallel legal order or in contrast to existing legislation is in these countries at best not settled; for most scholars the answer would be a simple and clear 'no' since it is the parliament which interprets the content of the basic rights to freedom of religion

9 Lisbet Christoffersen, 'Towards Re-Sacralisation of Nordic Law' in Marius Mjaaland (ed.), *Formatting Religion* (Routledge, forthcoming).

10 See Russel Sandberg, 'Religious Law as a Social System' in Russel Sandberg (ed.), *Religion and Legal Pluralism* (Ashgate 2015), Ch. 15.

11 See Dorota A. Gozdecka, 'Religious Pluralism as a Legal Principle' in Russel Sandberg (ed.), *Religion and Legal Pluralism* (Ashgate 2015), Ch. 11.

12 See e.g. Ch. 11: 'Religious Group Autonomy' in Rex Adhar and Ian Leigh, *Religious Freedom in the Liberal State* (Oxford University Press 2005).

13 John Witte, Jr, *Law and Protestantism. The Legal Teachings of the Lutheran Reformation* (Cambridge University Press 2020); Wim Decock et al. (ed.), *Law and Religion. The Legal Teachings of the Protestant and Catholic Reformations* (Vandenhoeck & Ruprecht 2014). See, however, also Virpi Mäkinen (ed.), *Lutheran Reformation and the Law* (Brill 2005).

14 See, as an example, the qualitative analysis of the existence of private religious law in Denmark in Anika Liversage and Tina Gudrun Jensen, *Parallelle retsopfattelser i Danmark. Et kvalitativt studie af privatretlige praksisser* (SFI – Det Nationale Forskningscenter for Velfærd 11:37). The analysis leads to legislative initiatives aimed at stopping the development of such practices. See also Rubya Mehdi et al., *Law and Religion in Multicultural Societies* (Jurist- og Økonomforbundets Forlag 2008) and Lisbet Christoffersen, 'Is Shari'a Law, Religion or a Combination?' in Jørgen S. Nielsen and Lisbet Christoffersen (eds), *Shari'a as Discourse. Legal Traditions and the Encounter with Europe* (Ashgate 2010) 57.

15 Christoffersen et al., *Law & Religion in the 21st Century. Nordic Perspectives* (n. 8). See also the HERA-funded research project (2016–2019) *Protestant Legacies in Nordic Law: Uses of the Past in the Construction of the Secularity of Law* https://teol.ku.dk/pronola/ accessed 12 November 2018.

and belief.[16] Therefore, an acknowledgement of religious law on the basis of a transnational law analysis could be regarded as a challenge to the entire legal system.

This question of the existence of a legal right to organise transnational religious law and the obligation for national legal orders to accept such legal norms is in this chapter seen as the question of the existence of a transnational religion law. The analysis in this chapter takes its point of departure in the empirical fact that religious governance systems of a legal nature actually exist, also in the Nordic countries, and that many of these religious laws are transnational.

The example analysed in this chapter is the internal legal system of the United Methodist Church. The material for the analysis is the regulatory levels, actors and norms within the 'hard' law of the United Methodist Church. The United Methodist Church was created on 23 April 1968 by a unification of different Methodist and Brethren churches worldwide, including the Danish Methodist Church. The churches trace their historical roots back to the Wesleyan awakening, starting in America in March 1736.[17] After World War II, the Methodist churches were active in developing worldwide organisations of Methodists as well as supporting the development of the World Council of Churches as a parallel to the United Nations. Three elements were central for the uniting of the Methodist churches: the concern for further church ecumenicity; a growing uneasiness with the problem of racism in both the nation and the church; and the full clergy rights for women established in 1956 in the Methodist Church. Since the establishment in 1968, the United Methodist Church has included more member churches all over the world, and since 1980 it has included female bishops. The Methodist Church sees itself as 'a community in which all persons, regardless of racial or ethnic background, can participate in every level of its connectional life and ministry'.[18]

Methodism includes a central statement[19] on the relation to the laws of the land:

> It is the duty of all Christians, and especially of all Christian ministers, to observe and obey the laws and commands of the governing or supreme authority of the country of which they are citizens or subjects or in which they reside, and to use all laudable means to encourage and enjoin obedience to the powers that be.[20]

16 Jens Peter Christensen, Jørgen Albæk Jensen og Michael Hansen Jensen, *Dansk Statsret* (Jurist- og Økonomforbundets Forlag 2012) 371.

17 *The Book of Discipline of the United Methodist Church*, 2012 and 2016, Historical Statement.

18 *The Book of Discipline of the United Methodist Church*, 2012, 22. *The United Northern Europe and Eurasia Central Conference 2012 supplement to the Book of Discipline*, 2012, explains how the European, Nordic and Baltic churches as well as the Russian Methodist churches became affiliated with the United Methodist Church; see 'Addition to the Historical Statement', pp. 7–14.

19 In one of the 25 foundational norms in the Book of Discipline.

20 *The Book of Discipline of the United Methodist Church*, 2012, p. 70, quoted in full length.

At the same time, Methodism expects from governments and legislators that they ensure civil rights and take responsibility for developing just societies.[21]

It is, among other things, against this background that the current (Danish born) bishop of the Nordic and Baltic area of the United Methodist Church Northern Europe and Eurasia Central Conference claims: 'Methodism is moderate and not fundamentalist'.[22] It could, seen in that light, at least for a scholar from the Nordic countries, appear surprising that the United Methodist Church is legally organised with its own internal constitution, with by-laws and with a Judicial Court (Judicial Council) on both a global and regional level, delivering rulings on the constitutionality of legislative changes to the Book of Discipline and declaratory decisions on interpretation or constitutionality of existing paragraphs.[23] This transnational, legally based organisation with a division of powers between legislative, executive and judiciary, including a right to judiciary review, is a key to the understanding of the Methodist Church, e.g. the Danish Methodist Church has thus also been bound by the internal transnational regulation of the church since its establishment in 1859.

The choice of the legal structure of the United Methodist Church as the empirical example of this analysis of religious law as transnational law is taken exactly on the background of such a (possible) surprise; thus, it is not only 'bad religions'[24] that set up their own transnational legal structure, parallel to the legal structures of the home countries. As mentioned earlier, even 'good religions', such as the Methodist Church, do so, and even in our countries.

The first level analysis in this article then explains how the hard law of the United Methodist Church identifies the different legal actors, norms and procedures in the internal, religious law.[25] The second level analysis discusses this legal system seen in relation to the 2017 Danish *law on religious communities*[26] and the presumptions in that law regarding collective freedom of religion and belief. This analysis has been performed in order to identify possible areas of conflict between the religious law and the religion law of Denmark. The third part of the analysis

21 This position also opens up for the possibility of non-violent civil disobedience, and the individual must be prepared to accept the costs of disobedience; see Social Principles, *Book of Discipline* 164 F.

22 Christian Alsted, 'Overvejelser om styreform i en mindretalskirke i lyset af de nordiske flertals kirkemodeller'. Paper given at a conference at Roskilde University, 25 August 2015 (can be required by the author of this chapter).

23 About the Judicial Council and the Central Conference, see: www.umc.org/who-we-are/about-the-judicial-council accessed 12 November 2018; www.umc-ne.org/central-conference/boards-and-committees accessed 12 November 2018.

24 As it is formulated in a research project at the Faculty of Theology, University of Oslo: bad religions – good religions.

25 The material for the analysis of the Methodist Church law is *The Book of Discipline of the United Methodist Church*, 2012, *The Book of Discipline 2012 Supplement*, adapted by the Northern Europe and Eurasia Central Conference, 17–21 October 2012; and *The Book of Resolutions of the United Methodist Church*, 2012.

26 Lov nr. 1533 af 19.12.2017 om trossamfund udenfor folkekirken www.retsinformation.dk/Forms/R0710.aspx?id=196402 accessed 12 November 2018.

discusses questions of legitimacy and legality concerning transnational religious law in a system of religion law, the main question being how citizens, who are both religious and secular in their life style, can give legitimacy to a religious law such as the Book of Discipline of the United Methodist Church.

The Book of Discipline and the Book of Resolutions of the United Methodist Church: a transnational legal order of religious law

It is central in Methodism that faith and order are congruent.[27] It is equally central that the churches are independent from any state regulation. That the members are expected to abide by the law of the land, as mentioned earlier, is not the same as to accept state regulation of church affairs. The United Methodist Church has grown in American law and religion structures with a constitutional wall of separation between church and state; that is also what is expected around the world.[28]

The churches are organised in a synodal structure. The first level is the local congregation where all eligible members have a voice and vote in the church conference and elect delegates to the annual conference in the area (i.e. in Denmark). Eligibility is obtained by being baptised and additionally having publicly declared to be prepared to support the church through active membership, payment, etc. Of course, it is also a condition that no declaration of lack of eligibility is formulated by a decision of the Court due to, e.g. lack of moral. The annual conferences elect delegates to the General Conference for all churches within the United Methodist Church (the denomination's highest legislative body) and to the Central Conference (which has the authority to make adaptions to the Book of Discipline for the area). The Central Conference has the authority to elect and appoint bishops. The Central Conference, to which the Danish Methodist Church belongs, is the Central Conference for Northern Europe, and Eurasia Decisions by bishops on law are mandatory referred for judicial review to the Judicial Council, which assembles on a regular basis four times a year with a fixed calendar, also for bringing in petitions.[29] Members of the Judicial Council cannot be elected as members of the legislative body, the conferences. Likewise, as further dimension of distinction of powers, the bishops do not have the power to propose legislation in the conferences, and they do not have voting rights in the councils.

27 Alsted (n. 22) 1. This paper serves in the following as an easy access to the explanation of legal actors, norms and procedures.

28 See e.g. Cole W. Durham, Jr, 'Facilitating Freedom of Religion and Belief through Religious Association Laws' in Tore Lindholm et al. (eds), *Facilitating Freedom of Religion and Belief: A Deskbook* (Martinus Nijhoff 2004) Ch. 15.

29 See the Calendar for the Judicial Council www.umc.org/who-we-are/calendar-for-judicial-council accessed 12 November 2018.

In the following, I will explain the actors, the norms and the procedures in regard to one single case which might enforce the United Methodist Church to split up – or to change its faith and order.

On 16 July 2016, an openly lesbian female priest, Karen Phyllis Olieveto, living in registered partnership, was elected, consecrated and assigned to an episcopal area as a bishop in the Western Jurisdiction of the Methodist Church in the United States.[30] The immediate response from the neighbouring district, the South Central Jurisdictional Conference, was to petition a motion to the Judicial Council of the United Methodist Church. They asked the council to explain whether the nomination, election, consecration and/or assignment as bishop of a person who claims to be a 'self-avowed practicing homosexual' or is a spouse in a same-sex marriage or civil union could really be in accordance with the Book of Discipline.

In order to petition a case before the Judicial Council, the council must have jurisdiction. That became clear in another decision from the council, related to the same conflict. The UMC Denmark Annual Conference had petitioned the Judicial Council for a declaratory decision on the legality of the sentence added to the Book of Discipline (161.G),[31] '[...]and considers this practice incompatible with Christian teaching'. The General Conference in 2016 had thus strengthened its disciplinary ordering regarding homosexual marriage by saying not only that the church does not condone the practice of homosexuality, but also that the church considers this practice incompatible with Christian teaching. As a reaction to this strengthened wording in the doctrine came, first, the consecration of an openly lesbian female bishop – and next, a petition from Denmark that the strengthened wording was against the doctrine of the Methodist Church.

However, the Danish petition was deemed outside the jurisdiction of the Judicial Council.[32] The Judicial Council can answer questions from the General Conference and from parallel jurisdictions, but only from the local, annual conferences (the local national churches) if the wording is directly relevant for the work in that church. So, if the Danish church should have received an answer, then they should have shown directly that the changed wording would order them to dismiss a loyal worker or the like. Or the Danish church should have persuaded the entire Northern Europe Central Conference to petition with them.

That was what the South Central Jurisdictional Conference did. At the moment the female lesbian bishop was consecrated, they declared the entire process illegal and against the order and faith of the Methodist Church. This petition

30 See Kathy L. Gilbert, 'Married lesbian consecrated United Methodist bishop' (16 July 2016) www.umnews.org/en/news/married-lesbian-consecrated-united-methodist-bishop accessed 12 November 2018.

31 The Book of Discipline uses a reference system, equally to paragraphs, which is also used in this sentence.

32 Memorandum no. 1347 from the Judicial Council of the United Methodist Church http://s3.amazonaws.com/Website_Properties/who-we-are/judicial-council/decisions-pdf/Memorandum_1347_-_final.pdf accessed 12 November 2018.

was – partly – deemed within the jurisdiction of the Judicial Council.[33] The majority of the council voted that the consecration of the bishop was against the Book of Discipline; a minority found that not only the consecration, but also the nomination, the election and the placement of the bishop and thus the entire process was to be evaluated within the jurisdiction of the Court and seen as illegal, whereas another minority found that the Court had no jurisdiction at all in the case. The consecration of a bishop is, according to the majority in this case, a question for the entire United Methodist Church. Therefore, the Judicial Council ordered the Western Jurisdiction to raise a case against Karen Olieveto in order to analyse whether she can remain in office.

The norms in play concerning the procedure, the jurisdictional questions and the norm on whether a bishop can live in a same-sex relationship are all to be found in the Book of Discipline, which is a full law book.

Facing a threatening schism based on different positions to homosexual practice, the 2016 General Conference asked the Council of Bishops to organise a commission to analyse a possible 'Way Forward'[34] for the church and eventually call an extraordinary General Conference, focusing on this thematic. Such a Special Session of the General Conference is called to be held in St Louis 23–26 February 2019. The three different solutions are 1) the One Church Plan, allowing for individual churches and conferences to decide on these questions locally, while the United Church remains as one church – this is a plan which includes a series of changes to the Book of Discipline, leaving questions of same-sex marriage and ordination to a local and annual conference decision; 2) the Connectional Conference Plan, which basically divides the United Methodist Church into two or three different sub-churches and includes several amendments to the constitution of the Church; and 3) the Traditionalist Plan, which leaves the Book of Discipline as it is while it strengthens accountability of pastors, annual conferences and bishops with strict judicial enforcement and leaves it to local churches if they do not want to continue their membership. But plans 2 and 3 involve questions of payment for the pension of bishops and priests as well as questions of ownership of churches. Making it easier for local churches to leave the denomination with all their property and assets is a separate set of petitions. Currently, local churches are able to leave the denomination only with the approval of the annual conference as all property and all assets by law belong to the annual conference. The Judicial Council has now been asked by the Council of Bishops to make a declaratory decision regarding the constitutionality of all three plans. The decision was taken at the Judicial Council meeting of

33 Decision no. 1341 from the Judicial Council of the United Methodist Church http://s3.amazonaws.com/Website_Properties/who-we-are/judicial-council/decisions-pdf/decision-1341.pdf accessed 12 November 2018. Decisions and memoranda can be found at www.umc.org/decisions/search, accessed 28 March 2019.

34 Commission on a Way Forward's Report to the General Conference, July 2018; for an explanation in the Danish Methodist church about the conflict, see www.metodistkirken.dk/2017/06/08/kirke-med-alle-mennesker/ accessed 12 November 2018.

23–26 October 2018 in Zürich.[35] The decision was unanimous. The Judicial Council found that the One Church Plan (no. 1) with few exceptions is constitutional while the Traditionalist Plan (no. 3) contains several problems with the constitution, mainly in separating out one chargeable offence and moral issue over others. Since the Connectional Conference Plan (no. 2) contains constitutional changes required for implementation, the Judicial Council ruled that it had no authority to scrutinise the plan at this time.[36]

Seen through the lenses of *transnational law as a methodological approach*, it is thus possible to identify all the common elements of a legal order in the internal religious law of the United Methodist Church. We can identify legal norms in the Book of Discipline, consisting of Part I, the constitution, which sets up the different institutions, here explained, including a distinction between legislative, executive and judiciary powers. Parts II–III explain the doctrinal standards; Part IV, the ministry and the requirements for a person who wishes to join the ministry; and Part V, the Social Principles. It is in Part V that the rulings regarding the understanding of 'the Social Principles', including norms regarding the family, marriage, divorce, single persons, women and men and human sexuality, are described, and it is these norms, which of course also apply to the ministers, that are currently under discussion. Part VI then regulates organisation and administration, including the organisation of the local church, the ministry of the ordained, the bishops, the conferences, the administrative order, the church property and the judicial administration, as explained earlier. All of these regulations are in play in the proposed three different solutions to be discussed in February 2019.[37]

Chapter seven of Part VI regulates in further detail the judicial administration. It sets up the Judicial Council and regulates investigations, trials and appeals. Procedures are set up for referral and investigation of a judicial complaint, for trials and for appeals. Even a list of chargeable offences for bishops, clergy members of an annual conference, local pastors, clergy on honourable or administrative

35 Linda Bloom, Kathy L. Gilbert and Vicki Brown, 'Court docket details proposed plans for UMC' (18 July 2018) www.umnews.org/en/news/court-docket-details-proposed-plans-for-umc accessed 12 November 2018. See also Docket no. 1018-12 www.umc.org/who-we-are/judicial-council-october-2018-docket accessed 12 November 2018.

36 The decision will be published at the home page of the Court.

37 The 2019 special session General Conference in the United Methodist Church took place in St Louis 23–26 February 2019, see http://www.umc.org/topics/general-conference-2019-special-session, accessed 1 April 2019. Apart from the three plans, previously mentioned, there was also a fourth plan, called The Simple Plan proposed, http://www.umc.org/who-we-are/general-conference-2019-legislation, accessed 1 April 2019. The conference ended by passing the Traditionalist Plan (438 for, 384 against). Added to this was a Disaffiliation plan (or exit plan). The result is thus a strengthening of the overview and check on the anti-homosexual dimensions of the book of discipline, especially against practicing pastors. Before the 2019 Special Session of General Conference closed, a motion was passed (405-395) to request a decision from the Judicial Council on the constitutionality of the Traditional Plan's legislative petitions. The bishops have requested a ruling on the constitutionality of the disaffiliation plan also. These issues will be addressed by the Judicial Council when they gather in Evanston, Illinois, 23–25 April 2019.

location or diaconal ministers (Art. 2702) is made. The list includes immorality, including but not limited to not being celibate in singleness or not faithful in a heterosexual marriage, practices declared by the United Methodist Church to be incompatible with Christian teachings, including but not limited to being a self-avowed practicing homosexual, etc. The formulations concerning homosexuality (including but not limited to [...]) were added in the 2004 Book of Discipline, which entered into force from 1 January 2005. The list further includes, among other things, crime and disobedience to the order and discipline of the United Methodist Church. The list proceeds and includes also child abuse (listed from 1996). The list ends with racial or gender discrimination.

Thus, it is possible to conclude that the Book of Discipline of the United Methodist Church establishes a legal order with actors, norms and procedures. The legal order is transnational. It is not bound to any national legal order. Neither is it international, being constituted by relations between national states. It is a legal order which establishes norms that are binding for private individuals, living in diverse countries, following the institutional and judicial commands on the basis of them being part of the church. The Book of Discipline includes all the elements that we on a methodological basis[38] (cf. the Introduction to this chapter) normally require of a transnational legal order.

The Danish law on religious communities versus the religious law of the Methodist Church

Full freedom of religion and belief is ensured in the Danish Constitution and has been so since 1849, also without any formal recognition from the side of the state.[39] However, a system of royal acknowledgements was established during Absolutism. The Catholic Church, the Reformed Churches and the Jewish Community were acknowledged already in the constitution. The religious communities understood this system of acknowledgement as a formal approval of their existence from the side of the public authorities. It was a condition for performing marriages with civil authority, and later on it became a condition for indirect economic support.[40] Thus, as the first example after the constitution, the Methodist Church was also granted acknowledgement by a royal decree in 1865.

38 Cf. Zumbansen (n. 3).

39 ‘Citizens shall be at liberty to form congregations for the worship of God in a manner which is in accordance with their convictions, provided that nothing contrary to good morals or public order shall be taught or done’, My Constitutional Act with Explanations, section 67, published by the Parliament, see www.ft.dk/~/media/pdf/publikationer/english/my_constitutional_act_with_explanations.ashx accessed 12 November 2018. The translation of the wording is at the same time an interpretation of the text. See also Lisbet Christoffersen, ‘State, Church and Religion in Denmark at the Beginning of the 21st Century’ in Lisbet Christoffersen, Kjell Å. Modéer and Svend Andersen (eds), *Law & Religion in the 21st Century: Nordic Perspectives* (Jurist- og Økonomforbundets Forlag 2010) 145–161.

40 See Lisbet Christoffersen, ‘A Long Historical Path Towards Transparency, Accountability and Good Governance: On Financing Religions in Denmark’ in Francis Messner (eds), *Public Funding of Religions in Europe* (Ashgate 2015) 125–149.

The system behind the public acknowledgement and not least the system of royal decrees have been changed a number of times during the second half of the 20th century. The conditions laid down by a committee analysing the applications from different religious communities were, however, evaluated as increasingly illegitimate without firm basis in public legislation. Especially conditions concerning equal treatment of men and women in the organisational structure (*not* in the ministry) were seen as requiring a legislative basis. Therefore, a committee suggested a new Danish law regulating the formal conditions for being a religious community in Denmark.[41] The committee suggested that it should still be possible to exist as a religious community without any public consent, approval or acknowledgement. However, if a religious community wanted to obtain indirect economic support or to perform marriages with civil authority, an acknowledgement would be a condition. The majority of the committee further proposed that a condition for such an approval should be that religious communities live up to principles of equality (between men and women, non-discrimination on grounds of race or sexuality, etc.). A minority recommended, on the basis of a tradition for free organisational rights in Denmark, that such a condition should not be set up and thus suggested that previous practice be changed. It should be added that Denmark, in 2012, by law introduced marriage for same-sex partners and at the same time introduced such marriages both at the civil authorities and in the national church. The possibility for other religious communities to perform marriages with civil authorisation was upheld, and this possibility is open also for other religious communities. In order to receive authorisation to perform marriages, the religious communities must live up to the regulations in the new law on religious communities. However, it is worth underlining that no religious community is forced to perform marriages of partners of the same sex. In this regard, the Danish Methodist Church follows the regulations of the United Methodist Church – even though there are voices arguing for other solutions.[42]

Thus, Danish law does not jeopardise the current practice and interpretation of the Book of Discipline within the Danish Methodist Church. Depending, however, on the developments in the United Methodist Church, as explained earlier, the question could become of relevance. The Council of Danish Churches, of which the Danish Methodist Church is a member, in their comments to the committee report, therefore, also stressed the necessity that no Danish legislative initiatives would interfere with the internal affairs of religious communities.[43]

41 Kirkeministeriet, En samlet lovregulering om andre trossamfund end folkekirken. Betænkning 1564/2017.

42 Claus Vincent, 'Det siger trossamfundene om homoseksuelle vielser', *Kristeligt Dagblad* (14 December 2011) www.kristeligt-dagblad.dk/kirke-tro/det-siger-trossamfundene-om-homoseksuelle-vielser accessed 12 November 2018.

43 See https://frikirkenet.dk/sites/default/files/pdf-upload/170425_dkr_hoeringssvar_til_betaenkning_fra_trossamfundsudvalget.pdf accessed 12 November 2018.

The subsequent law on religious communities outside the national church,[44] approved by Parliament in December 2017, did not include requirements concerning equal treatment in the religious organisations. Neither did the law include equal treatment regarding members and their rights nor equal treatment regarding eligibility in internal elections to organisational posts or access to religious rituals. Already, when the commission report was published, the government informed the public that the minority would be supported, and no majority in Parliament wished to follow previous practice. The responsible minister stated in Parliament that she would not propose a law requiring equal treatment of men and women in the organisational framework of religious communities (however, *outside* ministry). Her argument was that such a proposal would affect the Catholic Church. The effect on the Catholic Church is, however, not legal, and no legal conflict between such a requirement in Danish law and Canon law would have been established.

One could, of course, have expected that the argument behind this position would be an argument formulating respect for transnational religion law, including the 'no-interference-into-internal-affairs' argument or the 'church-autonomy' argument. The argument could have run as follows: The European Convention on Human Rights includes a right to freedom of religion and belief. That right is understood, in a series of Strasbourg cases, as also securing collective and organisational freedom of religion and belief, including to some extent a 'ministerial exemption' from the general law, however, balanced against other human rights.[45] Thus, *church autonomy* seems to be an acknowledged right, at least in American jurisprudence and at least to a certain extent in European jurisprudence.[46]

However, the Danish legislators did not argue their case on the basis of respect for transnational religious law. It is still debated among Danish legal scholars on religion to which extent church autonomy is a legal requirement binding the Danish legislative authorities, and it is especially debated when it comes to legislation giving the religious communities rights on the basis of public authorisation.

The law states that a religious community can freely organise itself within the limits of the law as well as freely organise and perform rituals on the condition that these are within the limits of the law. The formulation could be understood as a possibility for the legislative authorities to limit freedom of religion and belief further than stated in international conventions. That is, however, not the purpose – the bye-law (para. 2.2.2) underlines that any legislative proposal must live

44 Lov nr. 1533 af 19/12 2017 om trossamfund uden for folkekirken (n 26).

45 See, for a discussion of some of the latest cases, Emma Svensson, 'Religious Ethos, Bond of Loyalty, and Proportionality – Translating the "Ministerial Exception" into "European"' (2015) 4 *Oxford Journal of Law and Religion. Special Issue on Ministerial Exemption* 224–243.

46 See the Special Issue 2015 of *Oxford Journal of Law and Religion on Ministerial Exemption*, discussing exactly to which extent ministerial exemption from the law of the land is part of an international law understanding of freedom of religion and belief.

up to the general (transnational religion law) standards, requiring proportionality, among other things, for a law to be seen as constitutional.

The government's decision not to go further into the legal requirements to the religious communities must instead be evaluated as an attempt to escape a *legal* transnational conflict within religion law concerning the proportionality of a central point in religious laws among the oldest 'minority' religions in Denmark. The transnational legal order of religion law is not directly approved of – but it is also not directly confronted.

Legitimacy behind a transnational religion law allowing discrimination on the basis of sexuality

> The transnational dimension of hybrid regulatory actors and newly emerging forms of norms radicalizes the semi-autonomous nature (of hybrid legal spaces, my insertion) and we begin to conceive of regulatory spaces as being marked by a dynamic tension between formal and informal norm-making processes.

This is a quotation from Peer Zumbansen,[47] who proceeds by illustrating 'the frustration with the lack of accountability, access to justice and democratic legitimacy of the evolving regulatory frameworks'.

In his recent contribution on transnational legal thought, H. Patrick Glenn underlines the 'multivalent logic' in existing European legal practice.[48] In order to unpack that concept, he especially refers to the *margin of appreciation* of the European courts. The idea is that European courts, especially when it comes to the interpretation of fundamental freedoms and rights such as protection of family life, freedom of religion and speech, freedom of association, etc., have to some extent a tendency to interpret these rights in accordance with the national cultural understanding. The margin of appreciation is especially in use if the national authorities at the highest possible, legislative level have themselves balanced these rights against each other and have included the basic conditions concerning necessity and proportionality regarding regulation in a democratic society.[49] The idea is that the national parliaments are the first interpreters of international conventions, and they must (also) abide by international law. Such compliance can take many shapes – among them not making a legal conflict and just refer to cultural norms, keeping freedoms and rights for religious minorities, as in the mentioned Danish example. In this regard it is a central point that legitimacy and accountability are upheld in the understanding of both sides: the Danish parliamentary understanding of representative democracy as the sole law-maker is kept,

47 Zumbansen (n. 3) 31 ff.

48 Glenn (n. 4) 69.

49 See also the Copenhagen Declaration of April 2018 on the reform process of the European Court of Human Rights, www.justitsministeriet.dk/sites/default/files/media/Forsidebilleder_2018/copenhagen_declaration.pdf accessed 12 November 2018.

and at the same time the religious communities are free to keep their internal understanding of (lack of) equal treatment. Left behind is a general concept of equal treatment in 21st century society.

Kaarlo Tuori discusses transnational law as an example of legal perspectivism. He identifies transnational law as a deficiency of the black box model not least in regard to legal orders that have emerged from autonomous operation of denationalised social subsystems.[50] Religious law, as I have analysed it earlier, is such an example. He then analyses the fundamental conflict of authority established by the existence of such systems where 'rival legal orders, with diversely defined jurisdictions and enforced and ensured by at least partly different institutions, are competing for authority in the same territorial and social space'.[51] Conflicts of authority, according to Tuori, are almost bound to arise in areas where 'the substantively limited claims of transnational law confront the universal and exclusive pretensions of national law'.[52]

Tuori, against this background, identifies three versions of radical pluralism: (1) the Kelsenian position, which is behind Nordic legal positivism, as represented also behind the legislation presented above, (2) a critical legal version of legal pluralism and (3) as well as a Luhmannian version of legal pluralism. Both versions of legal pluralism (2 and 3, mentioned here) are represented by different versions of the American argument in favour of a *wall of separation* between secular law and religious law. Recent representatives of these critical or Luhmannian versions of legal pluralism within the field of religion law are, e.g. Levey and Modood arguing for a multiculturalist version of religious law's right to exist parallel to secular law in society.[53] Another example is a Swedish legal scholar who argues that Muslims want to follow Islamic law, also when living in Sweden, and that they have a cultural, legitimate right to do so.[54] More Luhmannian in his approach (without directly quoting him) is perhaps Rivers claiming the legal freedom of the Anglican Church in England, based on the concepts of legal secularism.[55] Also, the publications from the RELIGARE project build on the idea that societal law is secular and as such does not have any legitimacy in regulating (internal) religious affairs.[56]

50 Tuori (n. 5) 23.

51 Tuori (n. 5) 27.

52 Tuori (n. 5) 31.

53 Tariq Modood, 'Muslims, Religious Equality and Secularism' in Geoffrey B. Levey and Tariq Modood (eds), *Secularism, Religion and Multicultural Citizenship* (Cambridge University Press 2009) Ch. 7.

54 Mosa Sayed, *Islam och arvsrätt i det mångkulturella Sverige. En internationellt privaträttslig och jämförande studie* [Islam and Law on Inheritance in the Multicultural Sweden. A Private International Law and Comparative Law Analysis] (Iustus Förlag 2009) Ch. 1.

55 Julian Rivers, *The Law of Organized Religions. Between Establishment and Secularism* (Oxford University Press 2010) Ch. 11. See also Sandberg (n. 10).

56 Marie-Claire Foblets et al. (eds), *Belief, Law and Politics. What Future for a Secular Europe?* (Ashgate 2014).

Tuori puts his hopes in *legal dialogists*.[57] They realise that perspectivism does not necessarily condemn legal orders, but may imply resources for dialogue and cooperation. Tuori refers to the development of a new *ius commune* with *ius gentium* norms prevailing over the different *iura propria* conflicts and norms. The idea is the existence of an emerging *non-state constitutionalism* to which such transnational legal orders relate.

Thus, transnational law on religion points to two different strands of legitimacy: either the clear-cut idea of parallel legal orders – a secular order for the state and religious legal orders for the religious communities. This type of legitimacy builds on the idea that citizens are either religious (thus supporting religious legal orders with legitimacy) or secular (thus providing states with legitimacy). Tuori's own suggestion is legitimacy gained for the entire legal order, including transnational legal religious norms in the churches, based on a dialogue format, including all citizens in the state. According to that idea, legitimacy builds on citizens, no matter how religious or non-religious they are. That is, of course, a type of legitimacy which has a much better empirical foundation since there is no doubt that people are both religious and secular at the same time. It is, on the other hand, a type of legitimacy which does not establish a clear power foundation for the internal forces in religious communities.

Conclusion

I want to listen optimistically to Tuori's ideas of a developing legal dialogism, keeping legal order with developing transnational legal orders, attached to a common *ius commune* based on *non-state constitutionalism*. My empirical example for this chapter, the United Methodist Church, is relevant in that context. The church was leading, in the United States, in Europe and elsewhere, in fighting against discrimination of women and of black people. Should we therefore ever expect to find an organisation within the increasing transnational religion law, which in its religious law would also include homosexuals on an equal human basis; it would be expected from the United Methodist Church.

However, the United Methodist Church is becoming global. The increasing identification of homosexuality as against the church order during the last 20 years has led to a confrontation which comes before the board at the extraordinary global meeting in February 2019 as well as in the Judicial Council late October 2018. The church builds on transnational law. The understanding until now has been that the religious law of the church is never in conflict with societal law. However, the religious law of the church now faces a conflict where an increasing radical pluralist transnational legal understanding in the church confronts a tradition of transnational law, based on legal dialogue. A conflict between internal legitimacy solely versus internal legitimacy, confronting and leading society on the basis of its identity as a liberal, Christian church.

57 Tuori (n. 5), 34, 37–41.

15 Is formality legitimacy? Defining the obligations of non-state armed groups

Lauren Neumann

Introduction

Non-state armed groups (NSAGs) – such as the Revolutionary Armed Forces of Colombia (FARC), the Liberation Tigers of Tamil Eelam (LTTE) or Boko Haram – can have a considerable effect on the displacement of civilians, the commission of international crimes and the protection or abuse of human rights; yet international law addresses them directly in only limited ways. Despite the role and influence of non-state actors in situations covered by international conventions, most treaty-law is directed exclusively to states.[1] The applicability of human rights norms to NSAGs is often argued for, given these actors' significant influence on the enjoyment of human rights in both armed conflict and peacetime,[2] but the legal or theoretical basis for extending international law to NSAGs is uncertain. This is despite its relevance for both the legitimacy of its application and the possible future regulation of the conduct of NSAGs. In addition, armed groups often have internal codes of conduct, commit to international norms in formally non-binding ways and make unilateral declarations regarding their perceived obligations. The precise effect[3] of these measures or instruments under international law remains contested at best: are they legitimate (and legitimate according to whom), and what then is their effect?

This chapter examines the legitimacy and binding nature of the obligations of NSAGs under established international law, as well as ad hoc agreements and more recent initiatives that challenge the definitions of 'legal' and 'non-legal' regulation. The legitimacy of instruments from the point of view of international law and the armed groups themselves will be considered, concluding that obligations may arise from sources other than traditional law, but that the international legal system is yet to fully recognise them. The analysis also highlights the role

1 An exception is found in the law of armed conflict, discussed later in Part two.

2 See, for example, Daragh Murray, *Human Rights Obligations of Non-State Armed Groups* (Hart Publishing 2016); Katharine Fortin, *The Accountability of Armed Groups under Human Rights Law* (OUP 2017); Andrew Clapham, *Human Rights Obligations of Non-State Actors* (OUP 2006) 271–312.

3 For example, whether they are binding and in which forum.

of various actors, including non-government organisations, in generating and shaping norms.

The chapter proceeds in five parts. Part one begins by explaining the transnational nature of the topic and offers working definitions of NSAGs and legitimacy. Part two considers the extent to which international law applies to NSAGs. The rationale for the application of the law of armed conflict is examined, before turning to the question of whether international human rights law could also apply. Parts three and four address informal[4] means of engaging with NSAGs that could potentially result in binding such groups to international human rights or humanitarian norms. The legitimacy of these means and initiatives is considered within the framework of the actors, norms and processes involved.[5] A key example here is Geneva Call's Deeds of Commitment, in addition to special agreements,[6] voluntary codes of conduct and unilateral declarations on the part of NSAGs. Part five concludes by offering an examination of the relationship between legitimacy and formality in determining the sources and application of the law. Finding the balance in this relationship raises questions of who can create binding obligations, when these become binding, and what this means for the efficacy and stability of the international legal system. While the chapter purports to only modestly answer these significant questions, it is hoped that it contributes to discussions reconsidering the nature and application of international law in transnational situations.

Transnationalisation, non-state armed groups and legitimacy

Armed groups do not necessarily operate entirely within one sovereign state,[7] and may therefore not fall wholly under the jurisdiction and responsibility of that state.[8] Moreover, a number of the initiatives and mechanisms taken both by and towards NSAGs fall outside traditional international law doctrine, particularly when international law is described in its most statist form. As such, defining

4 'Informal' here describes agreements established outside the processes of the international legal system rather than the degree of ceremony or procedure involved in their conclusion. Informal processes can therefore follow strict ceremony or prescribed procedures.

5 Peer Zumbansen, 'Lochner Disembedded: The Anxieties of Law in a Global Context Symposium: Part I: Globalization: Critical Engagements with Territoriality' (2013) 20 *Indiana Journal of Global Legal Studies* 29, 57–59.

6 Under Common Article 3 of the Geneva Conventions, e.g. Geneva Convention Relative to the Protection of Civilian Persons in Time of War (adopted 12 August 1949, entered into force 21 October 1950) 75 UNTS 287 (Fourth Geneva Convention).

7 Al-Qaeda and the Islamic State of Iraq and the Levant (ISIL) are examples of groups operating across international borders. See also Jan Klabbers, '(I Can't Get No) Recognition: Subjects Doctrine and the Emergence of Non-State Actors' in Jarna Petman and Jan Klabbers (eds), *Nordic Cosmopolitanism: Essays in International Law for Martti Koskenniemi* (Martinus Nijhoff Publishers 2003) 359.

8 For a more detailed analysis of transnational armed groups, see Marco Sassòli, 'Transnational Armed Groups and International Humanitarian Law' [2006] Program on Humanitarian Policy and Conflict Research, Harvard University, Occasional Paper Series.

the law as it applies to NSAGs necessarily challenges the state focus of international law[9] and can be seen as contributing to the growing body of transnational regulation.[10]

In legal literature, NSAGs are commonly referred to as operating in situations of armed conflict. Armed groups exist, however, in situations that do not meet the threshold of armed conflict,[11] and may even exert significant control there.[12] NSAGs come in many forms and structures, with varied ideologies and motivations. The present chapter does not delve into the effect of the heterogeneity of armed groups on their legal obligations and likelihood of compliance with international norms.[13]

A point to note with regard to legitimacy and NSAGs (as compared with other non-state actors) is that a great number of them are actively seeking to challenge the control and sovereignty of a state. NSAGs consciously and publicly undermine the state and due to this, any action by them is often subject to vehement state opposition. Any moves by an armed group, however well meant, to engage with the international community or formally become party to international norms can be expected to be met with hostility and obstruction and perceived as illegitimate by a state or states.

Weber described legitimacy (of rule) in three categories: charismatic, traditional or rational.[14] Charismatic legitimacy is based on the characteristics of an individual (for example, a heroic leader), and traditional legitimacy comes from

9 The treatment of NSAGs by states in international law has been described as 'ostrich-like', that is, attempting to ignore the uncomfortable truth of their existence and influence, Marco Sassòli, 'Taking Armed Groups Seriously: Ways to Improve Their Compliance with International Humanitarian Law' (2010) 1 *Journal of International Humanitarian Legal Studies* 5, 50 and generally. See also Sophie Rondeau, 'Participation of Armed Groups in the Development of the Law Applicable to Armed Conflicts' (2011) 93 *International Review of the Red Cross* 649, 649–650.

10 On transnational regulation, see Gregory Shaffer, 'Theorizing Transnational Legal Ordering' (2016) 12 *Annual Review of Law and Social Science* 231, 237–242.

11 The law of armed conflict applies to all parties to a conflict (including internal armed conflicts). Human rights law applies predominantly to states (rather than NSAGs) and has more recently been accepted as applying, subject to modifications, in armed conflict, see e.g. Gerd Oberleitner, *Human Rights in Armed Conflict: Law, Practice, Policy* (CUP 2015) 81–127, 210–219. As such, the existence – or otherwise – of an armed conflict has significant effects on the applicable legal regime.

12 The operation of Boko Haram in Nigeria is an example.

13 For example, the motivation and ideology of a group will likely inform its political willingness to comply with international norms: Olivier Bangerter, 'Reasons Why Armed Groups Choose to Respect International Humanitarian Law or Not' (2011) 93 *International Review of the Red Cross* 353; Hyeran Jo, *Compliant Rebels: Rebel Groups and International Law in World Politics* (CUP 2015), and their level of organisation or control may affect their legal obligations: Murray (n. 2) 120–154, 172–202; Konstantinos Mastorodimos, *Armed Non-State Actors in International Humanitarian and Human Rights Law: Foundation and Framework of Obligations and Rules on Accountability* (Ashgate Publishing 2016) 183–197.

14 Max Weber, 'The three types of legitimate rule' (1958) 4 *Berkeley Publications in Society and Institutions* 1, 1.

historical precedent or inheritance, as in monarchies. The third type of legitimacy – the most common in society, according to Weber – can also be described as legality, whereby it is adherence to the legal system and processes that makes a norm legitimate, rather than its content or effect.[15] As such, rational legitimacy and legality both refer to the pedigree of law as stemming from the formal processes and authorised actors involved in its creation and enforcement, with that pedigree then giving the law legitimacy. Within rational rule, legitimacy can either be procedural (wherein a norm, actor or process is legitimate if it has 'come into being in accordance with generally accepted principles of right process'), substantive (for example, they are considered just) or efficiency-based (providing solutions to collective problems).[16] This chapter considers the legitimacy of various measures from the perspective of procedure and effect, noting also that the perspective of an individual actor is relevant to the determination of legitimacy. As Hurd asserts, legitimacy can '[refer] to the normative belief by an actor that a rule or institution ought to be obeyed', that is, the subjective perception of legitimacy is an important element.[17]

Applying the state-based international legal system to non-state armed groups

NSAGs have a complex position in international law. The law is generally focused on states as the dominant actors within a system both established by and addressed to them, however, a notable exception exists within the law of armed conflict. Common Article 3 of the Geneva Conventions and Additional Protocol II (on the protection of civilians in non-international armed conflicts) apply to all parties to a conflict,[18] thereby including at least some NSAGs as bearers of direct duties under international law.[19] This legal anomaly had a difficult birth, with the drafting history of the provisions reflecting attempts to balance the efficacy of the law with a desire to prevent inadvertent political legitimisation of armed groups

15 Alexander P. d'Entrèves, 'Legality and Legitimacy' (1963) 16 *The Review of Metaphysics* 687, 689–690.

16 Magdalena Bexell, 'Global Governance, Legitimacy and (De)Legitimation' (2014) 11(3) Globalizations 289, 291–292.

17 Ian Hurd, 'Legitimacy and Authority in International Politics' (1999) 53 *International Organization* 379; see also Michaels, who proposes that legal systems must recognise themselves as law in order to be law, but to (potentially) be binding on another system, the latter system must accept the first as legal, Ralf Michaels, 'What Is Law Beyond the State? An Introduction' in Michael A. Helfand (ed.), *Negotiating State and Non-State Law: The Challenge of Global and Local Legal Pluralism* (CUP 2015) 56.

18 Rather than 'states' or 'High Contracting Parties'.

19 E.g. *Fourth Geneva Convention* (n. 6) Art. 3; Protocol Additional to the Geneva Conventions of 12 August 1949, and relating to the Protection of Victims of Non-International Armed Conflicts (Protocol II) (adopted 8 June 1977, entered into force 7 December 1978) 1125 UNTS 609. Additional Protocol II requires a higher level of organisation in order to apply to non-state parties to a conflict, compared with Common Article 3.

by virtue of their status as international duty-bearers.[20] This resulted in the somewhat awkward phrasing of common Article 3, wherein the provision's final sentence states that '[t]he application of the preceding provisions shall not affect the legal status of the Parties to the conflict'.[21] After establishing that NSAGs have legal obligations under international law, the provision in one fell swoop denies any acknowledgement or legal recognition of the group(s) and attempts to deny their elevation to subjects of international law on this basis alone.[22]

Endowing obligations on NSAGs but maintaining their legal status as inferior to that of states begs the question of how international law can be directly binding on such groups. The answer affects not only the current obligations of NSAGs during armed conflict, but also future attempts to bind these groups to international rules or norms. Despite recent scholarly efforts, the legal basis for binding obligations remains at best contested.[23]

Given that NSAGs have no opportunity to formally submit to (or reject) international law, consent is clearly not the source of its purportedly binding nature.[24] While it is argued that NSAGs are bound by norms that have become customary international law, this can create unequal obligations between warring parties.[25] The doctrine of prescriptive jurisdiction states that NSAGs are bound by the law of armed conflict as a result of the consent of the state in which they operate, though as Klabbers points out, this logic would not create direct international obligations on armed groups, and it is 'implausible' that an armed group would consider itself bound by the commitments of those it seeks to fight.[26] More recently, scholars have argued that it is the level of organisation and control of the armed group that makes it subject to international law.[27]

These arguments have been extended to the possible human rights obligations of NSAGs. Human rights treaties are explicitly directed towards states as obligation-bearers,[28] and despite persuasive arguments that NSAGs can and ought

20 For a summary, see Murray (n. 2) 34–41.

21 *Common Article 3 of the Geneva Conventions* (n. 6).

22 See also Klabbers (n. 7) 359.

23 See for example Murray (n. 2); Fortin (n. 2); Jann K. Kleffner, 'The Applicability of International Humanitarian Law to Organized Armed Groups' (2011) 93 *International Review of the Red Cross* 443; Nadarajah Pushparajah, *Human Rights Obligations of Armed Non-State Actors in Non-International Armed Conflicts* (Wolf Legal Publishers 2016); Mastorodimos (n. 13).

24 For a discussion of theories of consent, see Kleffner (n. 23) 456–460; Daragh Murray 'International Humanitarian Law Treaties Bind Non-State Armed Groups' (2015) 20(1) *Journal of Conflict and Security Law* 101, 120–121, 130–131.

25 Kleffner (n. 23) 454–456; Murray (n. 2) 83–89; Murray (n. 24), 105–109.

26 Klabbers (n. 7) 358–359.

27 See e.g. Murray (n. 2) 120–154, 172–202; Tilman Rodenhäuser, *Organizing Rebellion: Non-State Armed Groups under International Humanitarian Law, Human Rights Law, and International Criminal Law* (OUP 2018).

28 See e.g. International Covenant on Civil and Political Rights (adopted 16 December 1966, entered into force 23 March 1976) 999 UNTS 171 (ICCPR) Art. 2(1) ('Each State Party'); International Covenant on Economic, Social and Cultural Rights (adopted 16 December

to incur obligations under these instruments,[29] this position lacks unanimous acceptance.[30] The uncertainty surrounding the basis for international legal obligations offers a problem of legitimacy; NSAGs are bound by at least part of the law of armed conflict, but there is no clear explanation of how, or whether, this basis provides for broader legal obligations.

The very existence of NSAGs is highly problematic for international law, as these groups can control territory, establish governance, policing and municipal services, act in place of the state, and yet the content of their direct legal obligations is uncertain.[31] The state-based mechanisms of protecting human rights vis-à-vis the conduct of non-state actors offer (often) inadequate protection to individuals under the control of such groups and do little by way of inducing direct compliance with international human rights norms by NSAGs. The groups themselves may not accept the legitimacy of norms or instruments over which they have had no influence, and states have demonstrated a reluctance to implicitly recognise the legitimacy of armed groups, despite including them as (albeit limited) duty-bearers under international law.

This stalemate has led, unsurprisingly, to the development of other means of transnational regulation that potentially enhance, complement and challenge international law. The following sections outline some examples of these, beginning with the work of the non-government organisation, Geneva Call.

1966, entered into force 3 January 1976) 993 UNTS 3 (ICESCR) Art. 2 ('Each State Party'); International Convention on the Elimination of All Forms of Racial Discrimination (adopted 21 December 1965, entered into force 4 January 1969), UNGA Res. 2106 (xx) (CERD) Art. 2 ('States Parties' and 'Each State Party'); Convention on the Elimination of All Forms of Discrimination against Women (adopted 18 December 1979, entered into force 3 September 1981), UNGA Res. 34/180 (CEDAW) Art. 2 ('States Parties').

29 It is controversial to claim that NSAGs are subject to legal obligations beyond those found in Common Article 3 of the Geneva Conventions and Additional Protocol II, however, a number of authors are increasingly championing this position, see e.g. Clapham (n. 2); Murray (n. 2); Rodenhäuser (n. 27); Mastorodimos (n. 13); Even Rodley, commonly cited as an opponent to the human rights obligations of non-state actors, has acknowledged that armed groups exercising state-like functions may be bound by international human rights law: Nigel Rodley, 'Can Armed Opposition Groups Violate Human Rights?' in Kathleen E. Mahoney and Paul Mahoney (eds), *Human Rights in the Twenty-First Century: A Global Challenge* (Martinus Nijhoff Publishers 1993) 299–300; Nigel S. Rodley, 'Non-State Actors and Human Rights' in Scott Sheeran and Nigel S Rodley (eds), *Routledge Handbook of International Human Rights Law* (Routledge 2013) 523.

30 For example, the negotiations on the Optional Protocol to the Convention on the Rights of the Child on the involvement of children in armed conflict. For a brief summary, see Michael J. Dennis, 'Newly Adopted Protocols to the Convention on the Rights of the Child' (2000) 94 *American Journal of International Law* 789, 792–793.

31 See e.g. Ana Arjona, 'Wartime Institutions: A Research Agenda' (2014) 58 *The Journal of Conflict Resolution* 1360; Marika Sosnowski, 'Violence and Order: The February 2016 Cease-Fire and the Development of Rebel Governance Institutions in Southern Syria' [2018] Civil Wars 1.

Beyond states: direct contact with non-state armed groups

Although a number of organisations, for example, the International Committee of the Red Cross (ICRC), engage directly with NSAGs on matters of compliance with the law and protection of civilians, Geneva Call is an example of an organisation whose primary focus is on armed groups. They have developed novel 'Deeds of Commitment' as a means of engaging armed groups and seeking to garner compliance with international norms.

Deeds of Commitment are instruments through which NSAGs undertake to respect humanitarian norms. While originally focusing on prohibiting anti-personnel landmines,[32] there are now Deeds of Commitment aimed at protecting children[33] and preventing sexual and gender-based violence and discrimination in situations of armed conflict.[34] The Commitments are entered into voluntarily and deposited with the Canton of Geneva,[35] and Geneva Call monitors compliance.[36]

There are clear advantages in terms of human rights protection to initiatives that engage directly with the potential perpetrators of criminal activity or breaches of human rights. A good deal of research suggests that compliance with norms is more likely if actors have contributed to the creation of the norms applying to them, or their submission to the norms has been voluntary[37] – that is, the substantive legitimacy of the norms is high. Other factors are of course relevant,

32 Deed of Commitment for Adherence to a Total Ban on Anti-Personnel Mines and for Cooperation in Mine Action, 2000.

33 Deed of Commitment for the Protection of Children from the Effects of Armed Conflict, 2010.

34 Deed of Commitment for the Prohibition of Sexual Violence in Situations of Armed Conflict and towards the Elimination of Gender Discrimination, 2012.

35 *Deed of Commitment, Mines* (n. 32) Art. 10; *Deed of Commitment, Children in Armed Conflict* (n. 33) Art. 16; *Deed of Commitment, Sexual Violence* (n. 34) Art. 14.

36 For a discussion of the monitoring and review mechanisms employed by Geneva Call, see Pascal Bongard and Jonathan Somer, 'Monitoring Armed Non-State Actor Compliance with Humanitarian Norms: A Look at International Mechanisms and the Geneva Call Deed of Commitment' (2011) 93 *International Review of the Red Cross* 673.

37 Rondeau (n. 9) 654; Sassòli (n. 9) 28–30; Ezequiel Heffes and Marcos D. Kotlik, 'Special Agreements as a Means of Enhancing Compliance with IHL in Non-International Armed Conflicts: An Inquiry into the Governing Legal Regime' (2014) 96 *International Review of the Red Cross* 1195, 1203–1204; Sandesh Sivakumaran, 'Courts of Armed Opposition Groups: Fair Trials or Summary Justice?' (2009) 7 *Journal of International Criminal Justice* 489, 512–513. With regard to law more generally, Duquet and others find that '[t]o the extent [informal law] is not legally binding, for it to be effective, addressees will need to be convinced to follow its normative guidelines, more so than with legally binding norms whose effectiveness is backed-up by formal sanctions', Sanderijn Duquet and others, 'Upholding the Rule of Law in Informal International Lawmaking Processes' (2014) 6 *Hague Journal on the Rule of Law* 75, 83; Cedric Ryngaert, 'Non-State Actors in International Humanitarian Law' in Jean d'Aspremont (ed.), *Participants in the International Legal System: Multiple Perspectives on Non-State Actors in International Law* (Routledge 2011) 288.

including the structure of groups, local norms and levels of training in the content of the law.[38]

But the legitimacy of any such 'informal' commitment is open to discussion. NSAGs invested in a written commitment to Geneva Call demonstrate a belief in the binding nature of the instruments they sign, whether such instruments can rightly be called 'law' (and therefore legally binding) or not.[39] This speaks in favour of the Deeds being legitimate sources of international regulation according to Hurd's definition.[40] Further, the creation of the Deeds of Commitment follows a procedure not unlike that undertaken in international law-making. NSAGs contribute to the content of the instrument by negotiation (though not drafting).[41] In one Deed of Commitment, NSAGs have the opportunity to make reservations, provided that the reservation is within the 'object and purpose' of the Deed.[42] Furthermore, they consent to being bound by it through signature, and the Deed of Commitment is deposited with a third party. Monitoring is conducted by Geneva Call (an organisation external to the group subject to the Deed of Commitment, akin to an international organisation vis-à-vis states) and through self-reporting. There is no overarching mechanism for ensuring compliance or imposing sanctions in case of non-compliance, but neither is there in international law. A significant difference, of course, between the state-based system and the Deeds of Commitment is the actors involved. Rather than sovereign states and an international organisation (the United Nations and its bodies), it is a NSAG and a non-government organisation working together.

The role of both armed groups and Geneva Call as legal actors capable of drafting and entering into binding commitments clearly challenges what international law and the state-based system would tend to define as formally (or procedurally) legitimate.[43] As a non-government organisation, Geneva Call cannot claim democratic legitimacy as a representative of the people (or another group of constituents), and they have not been granted a mandate by states.[44] However, that the agreements it facilitates are entered into voluntarily speaks in favour of its position as facilitating norm-creation. Similarly, NSAGs are not recognised as

38 See International Committee of the Red Cross, 'The Roots of Restraint in War' (ICRC 2018); Bangerter (n. 13); Jo (n. 13).

39 Though as with states and international conventions, Deeds of Commitment are not immune as forms of propaganda, entered into without genuine commitment to adherence.

40 Hurd (n. 17).

41 This can be likened to situations of succession or secession in international law, in which new states may determine their willingness to be bound by existing conventions – possibly subject to reservations – but cannot redraft their content.

42 Deed of Commitment for the Protection of Children from the Effects of Armed Conflict, 2010, Art. 15.

43 For a brief definition of types of legitimacy, see Bexell (n. 16) 291–292.

44 In contrast to, for example, the ICRC. Note though that determining the legitimacy of international organisations is difficult, Daniel Bodansky, 'The Legitimacy of International Governance: A Coming Challenge for International Environmental Law' (1999) 93 *American Journal of International Law* 596.

fully legitimate under international law, but determining the criteria for legitimacy (beyond 'sovereignty' or membership of the United Nations) in a manner that incorporates all sovereign states, yet excludes all NSAGs, would appear impossible. Democratic principles, respect for fundamental rights or compliance with the law are all followed and breached by states and non-state groups alike.

The legitimacy of the instruments themselves, and the substantive norms that they contain, is also a source of contention. The content of the Deeds of Commitment mirrors the norms found in international conventions, so an armed group 'bound' by a Deed of Commitment and a state party to the corresponding conventions would often have the same obligations. This is a case of regulatory hybridisation,[45] wherein the norms of the international legal system merge (at least to some degree) with a form of agreement accepted by NSAGs.

A lack of coherence may though arise in situations where a NSAG may have (for example, human rights) obligations under international law[46] and have signed a Deed of Commitment. If the norms or their interpretation conflict, international legal doctrine would dictate that the convention(s) contain the applicable obligations, whereas the armed group may well argue that it considers itself solely or primarily bound by the obligations to which it actively consented (i.e. the Deeds of Commitment).

Special agreements, unilateral declarations and codes of conduct

A third source of potential obligations for NSAGs comes from the groups themselves, in the form of special agreements, internal codes of conduct or unilateral declarations. Special agreements are concluded under the auspices of recognised international bodies such as the ICRC or the United Nations,[47] and their legal basis is justified by Common Article 3 (i.e. international law). Unilateral declarations or internal codes of conduct are not provided for, but nevertheless exist as indicators of the norms groups feel bound by.

Special agreements

Common Article 3 provides in part that '[t]he Parties to the conflict should further endeavour to bring into force, by means of special agreements, all or part of the other provisions of the present Convention'.[48] In short, all parties (including NSAGs)

45 Paulius Jurčys, Poul F. Kjaer and Ren Yatsunami (eds) *Regulatory Hybridization in the Transnational Sphere* (Martinus Nijhoff Publishers 2013). On regulatory hybridisation and international law, see particularly Jan Klabbers, 'Of Round Pegs and Square Holes: International Law' 29–48 in that volume.

46 See earlier n. 29.

47 Sassòli (n. 9).

48 See Common Article 3 (n. 6). For a more detailed discussion of the importance of Special Agreements in ensuring compliance with international humanitarian norms, and the law that governs them, see Heffes and Kotlik (n. 37).

may simultaneously agree to the expansion of the obligations they otherwise have under Common Article 3[49] and make this publicly known. Special agreements can include norms from the law of armed conflict, as well as human rights norms, though the latter are somewhat more controversial.[50] The negotiation and conclusion of a special agreement requires contact between parties to the conflict,[51] and for each party to consider both their obligations and their capacity to implement international norms. They are a 'unique opportunity for [armed groups] to actually have some input on what their concrete rights and obligations will be', and therefore also an instrument that may lead to greater compliance with international norms.[52]

The legal effect of these agreements, as well as the law governing them, is not clear. International law recognises, primarily, only agreements between states as treaties.[53] Common Article 3 provides formal international legal justification for the conclusion of special agreements, and the consent of the parties (generally the state and a NSAG) may be assumed by their participation in the agreement. It is unclear, however, how such agreements should be interpreted in relation to the international legal obligations of the groups (particularly in cases of variance), or how these instruments can or ought to be enforced.[54] Heffes and Kotlik argue that 'the process of creation of special agreements as understood under the framework of international law serves to enhance the perceived legitimacy of the rules agreed upon, hence increasing the chances of voluntary compliance in the first place'.[55] This may well be true in the eyes of contributors to the agreement, though doubts may be raised in regard to the perspective taken by third states, or international law more generally (hereunder, importantly, accountability and enforcement mechanisms).[56]

There is mixed international practice regarding the normative status of special agreements, with the Security Council having referred to them[57] and the

49 Heffes and Kotlik (n. 37) 1205–1207. A special agreement cannot reduce the obligations of a party to the conflict below the minimum standard provided for in Common Article 3: Heffes and Kotlik (n. 37) 1203, 1208–1209.

50 Ibid., 1207, cf. Liesbeth Zegveld, *Accountability of Armed Opposition Groups in International Law* (CUP 2002) 50.

51 Special agreements may be concluded under the auspices of, for example, the ICRC or the United Nations: International Committee of the Red Cross, 'Increasing Respect for International Humanitarian Law in Non-International Armed Conflicts' (ICRC 2008) 16–18; Sassòli (n. 9) 29–32.

52 Heffes and Kotlik (n. 37) 1200.

53 Vienna Convention on the Law of Treaties (adopted 23 May 1969, entered into force 27 January 1980) 1155 UNTS 331, Arts 1, 3.

54 Heffes and Kotlik (n. 37) suggest that the VCLT could give interpretative guidance by analogy, but leave enforcement largely unexplained, 1221–1222.

55 Ibid., 1222.

56 It should be noted though, that this problem may be equally true with regard to ensuring the accountability and enforcement of legally binding international obligations such as Common Article 3.

57 UNSC Res. 1127 (1997) The situation in Angola, UN Doc S/RES/1127.

International Criminal Tribunal for the former Yugoslavia (ICTY) using them as evidence of other treaty norms.[58] However, other bodies have maintained that states alone can create internationally binding instruments.[59]

Unilateral declarations and codes of conduct

Special agreements differ from unilateral declarations and codes of conduct in that they are an expression of the will of (at least) two parties to a conflict.[60] Unilateral declarations, in contrast, are expressions of only one party's will and willingness to be bound by a given norm, and codes of conduct are guidelines for the behaviour of members of the relevant group.

Unilateral declarations can be made by any party to a conflict.[61] They can be oral or written and may be general commitments to abide by international law (or a body of international law, such as the law of armed conflict) or undertakings to respect specific rules.[62] Internal codes of conduct establish the rules by which members of the group must abide/conduct themselves.[63] These are often written documents and their influence on the behaviour of groups and their members can be significant.[64] The Kosovo Liberation Army has stated that

> [f]rom the start, we had our own internal rules for operations. These clearly lay down that the UCK recognises the Geneva Convention [sic] and the conventions governing the conduct of war, even though it has not been offered the chance of signing them, as it would have done.[65]

Can these mechanisms be seen as legitimate and potentially having legal force? They operate in fact to control behaviour and are intended to be binding on a

58 *Prosecutor v. Hadžihasanović and Kubura* (Decision on Joint Defence Interlocutory Appeal of Trial Chamber Decision on Rule *98BIS* Motions for Acquittal, Appeals Chamber) IT-01-47-AR73.3 (11 March 2005) fn. 51; *Prosecutor v. Duško Tadić* (Decision on the Defence Motion for Interlocutory Appeal on Jurisdiction) ICTY-95 (2 October 1995), para. 73.

59 See e.g. *Prosecutor v. Kallon and Kamara* (Decision on Challenge to Jurisdiction: Lomé Accord Amnesty) SCSL-2004-15-AR72(E) and SCSCL-2004-16-AR72(E) (13 March 2004), paras 45–50. For further examples, see Sandesh Sivakumaran, *The Law of Non-International Armed Conflict* (OUP 2014) 109–110 and the references therein.

60 Heffes and Kotlik (n. 37) 1198, 1200.

61 For examples of unilateral declarations, see Sivakumaran (n. 59) 113–118.

62 For examples, see Sivakumaran (n. 59) 118–124.

63 For detailed analysis and examples of NSAG codes of conduct, see Olivier Bangerter, *Internal Control: Codes of Conduct within Insurgent Armed Groups* (Small Arms Survey, Graduate Institute of International and Development Studies 2012); 'A Collection of Codes of Conduct Issued by Armed Groups' (2011) 93 *International Review of the Red Cross* 483; ibid., 124–152.

64 Bangerter, (n. 63).

65 *Prosecutor v. Limaj, Bala and Musliu* (Transcript) IT-03-66 (14 February 2005) p. 3385. See also Krasniqi Explains UCK's Origins, Structure, Pristina *Koha Ditore*, 12 July 1998, Exhibit P48 in ICTY *Limaj* trial (ICTY translation) cited in Sivakumaran (n. 59) 135.

group's members.[66] They lack the formal pedigree of international law instruments, but in the eyes of at least some actors, they have legitimacy as binding norms. This is an important factor with regard to ensuring compliance and seeking accountability for, or enforcement of, these particular norms.

It seems clear that a code of conduct does not render the law of armed conflict inapplicable.[67] There is some international practice to suggest that unilateral and internal instruments may nonetheless have some normative status,[68] and scholarly support exists for such a position,[69] but there is far from universal acceptance. These are politically sensitive legal questions, but the political nature of the subject ought not automatically result in a finding that the unilateral or internal instruments of NSAGs are necessarily illegitimate.

For example, should a NSAG establish a court, would the international legal system recognise the norms applied by the groups (assuming they recognised the court at all), if those norms were established in a code of conduct, unilateral declaration or Deed of Commitment? This is of significant importance as international criminal law assigns individual criminal responsibility in the case of grave breaches of some international legal obligations, and prior appropriate prosecution can either be a defence[70] or render the International Criminal Court (ICC) without jurisdiction.[71]

Pedigree or effect? The future for international law and transnational regulation

In many ways, international law has fashioned itself as an ultimate arbiter of legitimacy. Had international law taken a more reflexive approach[72] to NSAGs and a more inclusive understanding of legitimacy, some of the challenges posed by such groups (and raised in this chapter), including the emergence of new 'legal' instruments, would have at least been reduced.

66 Sivakumaran (n. 59) 108 notes that the distinction between a statement being propaganda or an actual expression of the intention of the party is determined only by the level of compliance with the measure.

67 '*A Collection of Codes of Conduct Issued by Armed Groups*' (n. 63) 484–485; Jean-Marie Henckaerts and Louise Doswald-Beck, *Customary International Humanitarian Law* (CUP 2005) xxxvi.

68 *Prosecutor v. Akayesu* (Judgment) ICTR-96-4-T, T Ch. I, (2 September 1998), para. 627.

69 Sivakumaran (n. 59) 110–113.

70 See UN General Assembly, *Rome Statute of the International Criminal Court (last amended 2010)*, (17 July 1998, entered into force 1 July 2002) Art. 28.

71 See ibid., Arts 17(1)(c) and 20(3), wherein no one may be tried by the International Criminal Court if they have previously been appropriately tried for those crimes. The Statute does not explicitly refer to state courts in these sections.

72 Menno T. Kamminga, 'Final Report on the Impact of International Human Rights Law on General International Law' in Menno T. Kamminga and Martin Scheinin (eds), *The Impact of Human Rights Law on General International Law* (OUP 2009) 3.

The instruments and mechanisms utilised in attempting to bind NSAGs by international norms challenge definitions of law and raise questions as to what is required for their legitimacy. Particularly, questions of who can make or be subject to binding regulations, and from whose perspective their legitimacy should be measured,[73] reflect a conflict between maintaining the formalistic pedigree of norms and instruments (i.e. a specific type of procedural legitimacy) and efforts to ensure the effectiveness of the law in practice (efficiency-based legitimacy).

It is argued here that procedural legitimacy,[74] or legality, is an important but insufficient element in determining the law. Procedural requirements act as safeguards against abuses of power and arbitrary demands.[75] They also increase certainty in the law as it can be far more easily 'known' if it only becomes binding subject to specific prerequisites being met. But rigidity in those requirements, such as international law only recognising certain subjects as capable of law-making and to some degree law-taking, can lead to situations in which a blind eye is turned to the reality of how actors behave and therefore can be regulated. Those realities do not cease to exist, but other measures arise that run parallel, and potentially contrary, to the established system. This can undermine the practical functioning of the established system as well as the respect it commands and even its legitimacy in the eyes of those subject to the system.[76]

Bianchi argues that

> [t]he contemporary international community, which provides the terrain in which the game of international law is played, is no longer perceived as consisting solely of states and, inevitably, the inclusion/exclusion mode with which the traditional theory of subjects has been set and used in a restrictive fashion to preserve the integrity of the system needs to be reconsidered.[77]

Bianchi opens here for the possibility of international law becoming more expansive in its approach to actors such as NSAGs and Geneva Call. In so doing, one must consider the processes and norms that may result, and the status they can or should have on the international plane. In this case, the lens of transnational regulation can help to find legal solutions to factual problems that extend beyond national borders and challenge existing law.

73 For example, those bound by it, those creating it, those benefiting from it, or a third, impartial party?

74 Part of Weber's rational legitimacy (n. 14).

75 Jan Klabbers, 'The Undesirability of Soft Law' (1998) 67 *Nordic Journal of International Law* 381.

76 For example, the victims of human rights abuses by NSAGs for whom no effective remedy is available through the state-based system, as the state who would otherwise be responsible for the NSAG cannot be identified or is unwilling or unable to adequately control the group.

77 Andrea Bianchi, 'Relativizing the Subjects or Subjectivizing the Actors: Is That the Question?' in Andrea Bianchi (ed.), *Non-state Actors and International Law* (Ashgate 2009) xxvi.

It is submitted that, in the transnational sphere, the Geneva Call Deeds of Commitment as well as codes of conduct and special agreements can be legitimate, though it is acknowledged that they currently lack the acceptance of the international system.[78] As such, the actors, norms and processes involved in these instruments are still in conflict, or at best in uneasy competition with the established system of public international law.[79] From the transnational perspective, these relationships can also be described as regulatory hybridisation, a concept that alludes to the mixing of private/public regulation and accepts that different actors and sources of regulation can combine to create new – and legitimate – forms of obligation.[80]

From the perspective of international law, and in simplified terms, the international system can respond to informal transnational regulation in three ways. It can ignore the emergence of informal regulation and maintain that the law is in conflict or competition with it. At the other extreme, all informal actors, norms and processes could be considered as legitimate and binding, with potential discrepancies and conflicts between the formal and informal to be determined as need arises. This approach negates, however, the importance of determining what can be considered legitimate, and within the rule of law, such that the subjects of a given norm are adequately protected from arbitrary uses of power. It would seem that the better approach to the relationship between formal and informal law and processes – at least with regard to regulating NSAGs – is to accept that the process of negotiation (hopefully leading to cooperation in Halliday and Shaffer's paradigm[81] or genuine hybridisation) is ongoing. The precise parameters of what makes a measure or an actor legitimate must be redrawn, with less emphasis on the formal mechanisms employed and greater emphasis on the content and effect of the norms and instruments that result.

Resolving the issues raised in this chapter is important for ensuring the stability and functioning of the international legal system as a whole, as trust in, and respect for, an overall system is made up of the legitimacy of its constitutive parts.[82] However, internally developing and adjusting the technicalities of various bodies of international law is inadequate to ensure that the law can respond to the increasingly influential international actors who are not (or cannot be) defined as sovereign states.[83] It is therefore argued that accepting and understanding the possible concurrent application of formal and informal law-making mechanisms is essential. As a result, the means of defining legitimacy in international law ought to be revisited, as the current, formal requirements do not reflect the actual influence of the informal norms, actors and processes at work.

78 See Michaels (n. 17).

79 Halliday and Shaffer suggest that transnational legal orders can be in conflict, competition, negotiation or cooperation with each other: Terence C. Halliday and Gregory Shaffer, 'Transnational legal orders' in Terence C. Halliday and Gregory Shaffer (eds) *Transnational Legal Orders* (CUP 2015), 41 figure 1.2.

80 See Jurčys, Kjaer and Yatsunami (n. 45).

81 Shaffer (n. 10) 238.

82 Kamminga (n. 72).

83 Ibid.

Conclusion

Transnationalisation and legal actors: Legitimacy in question

Louise Munkholm, Cécile Pelaudeix and Bettina Lemann Kristiansen

The book has set out to investigate how legal actors interact in transnational settings with special attention paid to the understudied question of the effect these interactions have on legitimacy. In this context, the following research questions have guided the inquiry: Who are the legal actors on the transnational scene today and how do they generate or shape existing norms? What are the emerging transnational tendencies in law? What does this mean for how the legitimacy of norms is understood, defined, constructed and contested? To answer these questions, the book has considered the issue of legitimacy from a broad range of legal areas, including environmental law, human rights law, commercial law, labour law and religion law, and covered developments in Europe and its neighbouring states in the Arctic region, and in China. The contours of legitimacy have been mapped with an emphasis on the legitimacy seeking practices or delegitimation attempts of actors like supranational, intergovernmental and international organisations, states and courts, and non-state actors who operate in transnational settings. Accordingly, the book has been divided into three analytical parts emphasising i) critical perspectives on transnational tendencies in law; ii) the development of law in the transnational context and iii) the challenges of transnationalisation of law to the application and enforcement of law.

The concluding chapter discusses crosscutting issues based on the different cases in the book on the relationship between transnationalisation, legal actors and legitimacy. The first part of the chapter takes stock of the different analyses of legal actors on the transnational scene and the role they play in generating, shaping and/or contesting norms. The second part of the chapter discusses transnational tendencies that emerge from these actor-centered analyses. The third, and final, part of the chapter points to future challenges and problem-solving mechanisms while designing pathways for further reflection on legal actors and legitimacy in the transnational context.

Legal actors on the transnational scene

Many different actors are involved in norm creation and norm shaping on the transnational scene. The authors of the volume have considered supranational and international organisations (the European Union and the United Nations), states (China, Denmark, the UK, Italy, Libya and other African countries), courts (the Court of Justice of the European Union, the European Court of Human Rights, the International Court of Justice, the International Criminal Court, the Permanent Court of Arbitration and national courts), enforcement agents (labour inspectors) as well as non-state actors, including private companies, indigenous peoples organisations (the Inuit Circumpolar Council), religious communities (the United Methodist Church) and armed groups, such as the Revolutionary Armed Forces of Colombia (FARC), the Liberation Tigers of Tamil Eelam (LTTE) and Boko Haram. The question of who a legal actor is constitutes the central concern in L. Neumann's chapter, which argues that international law faces a dilemma when denying any acknowledgement or legal recognition of specific types of non-state actors such as armed groups. The author demonstrates that regardless of the status of armed groups under international law, these types of actors are creating and shaping legal norms on the ground, as these groups can control territory, establish governance, policing and municipal services and act in place of the state. According to Neumann, the concept of 'a legal actor' can be interpreted in three ways as covering 1) only those actors who participate in law development processes based on official membership of the local, national or international community, 2) the actors that are officially recognised by these communities and 3) those actors who establish rules for conduct on the ground. Various authors of the book also stress that in order to achieve a deeper understanding of norm creation and norm-shaping processes in the transnational context, the analysis of legal actors needs to be broadened to include also those actors who might not have clear legal obligations and rights under official law but who nonetheless influence the legitimacy seeking practices of, for instance, the United Nations (UN) and the European Union (EU).[1] Thus, interactions and negotiations of norms take place among many different types of actors, which thereby engage in what can be called legitimacy seeking practices as well as delegitimation attempts. Legitimacy seeking practices involve inter alia the pursuit of procedural (democratic), substantive (justifiable norms based on shared norms and values) and output (efficiency-based) legitimacy.[2] The following subsections look into the decisions, actions and positions taken by the different types of actors as part of their legitimacy seeking practices or delegitimation attempts in transnational contexts.

1 See Chapter 2 by Thomas Gammeltoft-Hansen and Tanja Aalberts (the role of NGOs, academics, technical experts and private corporations), Chapter 5 by Reza Banakar (the role of the public sphere, including the media, political interest groups, grassroot movements and ordinary citizens), Chapter 9 by Jens Vedsted-Hansen (the role of the media and academia) and Chapter 14 by Lisbet Christoffersen (the role of the Methodist Church).

2 Magdalena Bexell, 'Global Governance, Legitimacy and (De)Legitimation' (2014) 11 *Globalization* 289, 291–292.

Supranational and international organisations

The UN and the EU have been the focus of several authors of this volume to analyse the current attempts of large, intergovernmental organisations to shape the legitimacy of transnational law, particularly human rights law, environmental law, commercial law and labour law. Although the UN and the EU have different legal status (impacting their definition of constituency and their enforcement capacity), they both share the procedural legitimacy challenge related to being representative, transparent and participatory. They both seek to establish procedural legitimacy by inviting all stakeholders concerned to participate in the drafting of new frameworks for ordering social spaces. They also share a challenge related to substantive legitimacy as the universal character of the norms promoted by the UN and the EU are increasingly met with scepticism and counter reactions from states and non-state actors.

In their analysis of the UN-based business and human rights regimes, Buhmann and Azizi underscore the new practices of the UN aimed at ensuring, through the use of information and communication technologies (ICTs), the legitimacy of its norms and activities related to sustainable development. The UN focuses on establishing procedural legitimacy by providing the global public access to participation in defining sustainability norms and steps for implementation. The use of mobile phones in remote areas of African countries shows that the bottom-up approach of the UN and the use of ICTs in combination offer a potential for transnational governance that is inclusive of non-state actors, including non-governmental organisations (NGOs) and individuals, i.e. this is seen as a positive step taken by the UN in terms of enhancing the procedural and substantive legitimacy of UN-based business and human rights norms.

In comparison, Petersen draws attention to the difficulties of the EU in maintaining procedural legitimacy in the 21st century, which has resulted in threats to the internal cohesion of the Union. According to the author, the EU has substituted its prior legitimacy-seeking practices based on economic growth and market rationality with the principle of solidarity in its strategy for strengthening its legitimacy. Petersen emphasises that it remains to be seen whether this use of top-down normative arguments of solidarity will transform into bottom-up expressions and practices at local, national and transnational levels. The legitimacy seeking practices of the EU are also central in the analysis of Banakar, who argues that Brexit is evidence of the EU's failed integration policy and its inability to generate a collective European identity. The author shows how EU law has been used for building a European identity based on a set of core values aimed at integrating the Member States into a political union. According to the author, the problem of using EU law as a device for European identity building and integration is that EU law enforces a hierarchy of political power and legal authority that threatens the sovereignty and identity perception of the Member States, including its citizens. Thus, for Banakar, Brexit is a clear result of the fragmented experiences, attitudes and expectations of UK citizens, politicians and the media towards EU law. According to the author, to overcome EU scepticism in the public sphere, the EU will have to strengthen its efforts in bottom-up identity building processes. Within these processes, EU institutions concentrate on facilitating cross-border collaboration among EU citizens to enhance intercultural intersubjectivity and solidarity rather than imposing supranational norms from above. In this respect, both Petersen and Banakar point to the lack of bottom-up procedural legitimacy in the EU.

When it comes to EU legitimacy seeking practices in relation to the governance of the Arctic Ocean, Pelaudeix shows that the EU is relying on procedural legitimacy deriving from the fact that three Member States (Denmark/Greenland, Sweden and Finland) are Arctic states. However, regardless of the questioning of its procedural legitimacy by some Arctic states, the EU is mainly active in developing substantive legitimacy by incorporating and designing a wide range of norms of environmental protection and sustainable development, some with relevance for the European Economic Area, as well as engaging in output legitimacy activities. Likewise, Basse shows that the EU, in cooperation with the OSPAR Commission for the Protection of the North-East Atlantic, seeks to impact national legislation in Denmark when it comes to the management of the marine environment in the Arctic. In essence, the EU seeks to shape the legitimacy of OSPAR norms (characterised by an ecosystem-based approach) by monitoring and reporting on the environmental status of the Arctic marine area, thereby putting pressure on the national legislation in its Member States. This indirect impact of the EU on national legislation is a clear example of transnational norm diffusion in which different layers of legal obligations meet and compete. The EU is party to the OSPAR Convention, the Biodiversity Convention and the Law of the Sea Convention, and its institutions are – based on the Lisbon Treaty – in their relations with the wider world obligated to do all that lies in their power to enhance the international legal order. At the same time, the internal relations between Greenland and Denmark establish an obstacle to the EU legitimacy seeking practices as Denmark does not accept that the obligations of OSPAR are relevant in the Danish/Greenlandic marine area.

By their activities of norm creation and norm diffusion, the UN and the EU are both transcending national borders, and thereby bridging national legal cultures, or establishing 'interlegality', to use Tuori's notion.[3] While the EU in many situations incorporates UN norms into EU law, the norms of the UN and the EU are not always compatible. In their chapter, Billing and Tan warn that the current EU-Libya agreement, related to the combatting of migrant smuggling, results in violations against the UN-based principle of non-refoulement, which is one of the central pillars of international refugee law. Libya, as the authors argue, should not be seen as a partner since international partnership needs to be based on a shared set of moral and ethical values. The analysis is driven by the argument that the UN is supposed to deliver substantive justice, i.e. norms and rules that

3 See Chapter 1 by Kaarlo Tuori in this volume.

can be used to evaluate the legitimacy of actions and practices of other actors. In other words, the transnational human rights regime established by the UN can be used to formulate delegitimation claims regarding activities of other actors, such as the EU, Italy and Libya.

Legitimation and delegitimation attempts of nation states

The analyses presented in this book leave no doubt that nation states engage in both shaping and contesting the legitimacy of norms created in transnational settings. Delegitimation attempts occur, for instance, in relation to sustainable development and human rights, i.e. norms that have been developed in transnational settings. A case in point is the regulation of the Arctic marine areas analysed by Basse. As mentioned above, Basse shows that Denmark, with its environmental marine strategy and practices in the Arctic, is undermining the legitimacy of the EU Marine Strategic Framework Directive. The tension stems from a mismatch between the ecosystem-based approach of the UN and the traditional pollution reducing approach applied by Denmark. According to Basse, Denmark insists on being only responsible for reducing the pollution from ships and not for damage caused by hydrocarbon extraction activities, as these have been taken over by Greenland. In contrast, Greenland is of the opinion that the protection of the marine environment is the responsibility of the Danish authorities. The consequence is that there are no rules in the Danish nor in the Greenlandic legislation of relevance for the protection of the marine environment inside the exclusive economic zone against the pollution of the marine ecosystem. Conflicting interests on sovereignty issues stand in the way.

Vedsted-Hansen analyses the increasing critical engagement with international human rights law among nation states. The author shows that at the level of political discourse, the main argument is that international human rights obligations reduce the scope of manoeuvre for sovereign states and their democratically elected bodies at the national level. According to the author, this factor is frequently exacerbated by domestic policymakers' frustration over judicial control of the legislative and executive branches of government. Based on the analysis of three major strands of criticism: one concerned with the interaction between international and national authorities; one invoking the inherent democratic nature of national authorities; and one discarding human rights outright, the author argues that more radical positions have been developing in recent years. In all likelihood, this is closely connected to tendencies of resistance towards any increase in binding international cooperation mechanisms in general, sometimes articulated with reference to ideas of 'taking back control' in policy areas characterised by dissatisfaction with the modalities or outcomes of international cooperation.

In a similar vein, Gammeltoft-Hansen and Aalberts point to processes whereby nation states participate in delegitimisation activities in regard to international law by means of 'creative legal thinking' where, for instance, national foreign policy responses operate at the fringes of the UN-based legal framework. According to

Gammeltoft-Hansen and Aalberts, at the same time, and perhaps therefore, we are witnessing networks of NGOs, academics and activists that create so-called global advocacy alliances that contribute to ensuring the procedural legitimacy of international law. Furthermore, they argue, networks of government officials create new modes of cooperation to fill gaps in politically sensitive areas where binding international agreements are difficult to obtain.

Pelaudeix highlights China's legitimacy seeking strategy and shows that in the Arctic Ocean it is based on a different set of arguments and approaches than other stakeholders, such as the Inuit Circumpolar Council (ICC) and the EU. Although it enjoys some legitimacy in the governance of the Arctic Ocean, China, in order to support further its economic interests, resorts to conceptual ambiguity whereby it creates a 'flou artistique' that slightly distorts the procedural argument (related to the idea that China should be involved in the development of norms because it claims that it is a "near-Arctic state") and also the substantive aspects of sustainable development or environmental protection. In this context, Pelaudeix stresses the need to also look into economic leverage to have a full understanding of China's legitimation seeking activities. This effort is undertaken by Petersen in her chapter. Petersen underlines that China 'may lead or influence normative processes globally by way of size and power',[4] however, at the same time, according to the author, size is not decisive in its own right when it comes to discussions of who has authority to create and shape norms. In addition, economic power is essential. The author underlines this argument by pointing to the fact that many Nordic countries have small populations but are still wealthy and play central roles in international and transnational law- and policymaking.

Law enforcers

Several chapters in the book highlight the important role that law enforcers, such as domestic courts, play in either contributing to, or invalidating, the legitimacy-seeking practices of international or supranational organisations. T. Neumann stresses the divergence of domestic court practices and how it hinders the development of transnational commercial law. The author emphasises that the United Nations Commission on International Trade Law (UNCITRAL) establishes the potential for domestic courts to develop uniform interpretation mechanisms and, from there, shape transnational norms based on rational persuasion. However, until now, only a few national courts have engaged in the required judicial dialogue where domestic courts consider the international character of the case at hand and rely on experiences from other courts – or at least only a few courts document transparently if they do that. The consequence, according to the author, is that other courts are not able to assess the persuasive values of prior decisions: the learning potential is lost, and so is the potential for uniformity in the transnationalisation of commercial law.

4 See Chapter 6 by Hanne Petersen in this volume.

In contrast to the UN example, Vedsted-Hansen stresses the well-established practice of the European Court of Human Rights (ECtHR) related to the principle of 'dynamic interpretation' as a means to ensure that the European Convention of Human Rights will be 'practical and effective, not theoretical and illusory'.[5] According to the author, the principle implies some potential for judicial activism, which has been subjected to a rather imbalanced criticism from nation states. In response, the author argues that the ECtHR has made persistent and gradually enhanced efforts to pre-empt or accommodate accusations of 'judicial activism' by developing the principle of subsidiarity and the ensuing margin of appreciation as a general feature of its examination of the cases brought before it. In addition to this method of reviewing the decisions adopted by domestic authorities, the Court has also based significant rulings on the so-called comparative method. In doing so, the question of a European 'consensus' is normally considered decisive to the Court in settling issues of either dynamic interpretation, modification of the balancing of interests or other kinds of development of standards that might extend the protective scope of the Convention and could therefore be seen as an expression of judicial law-making.

In another area of EU law, Videbæk Munkholm and Schjøler discuss the unsolved tension between national courts and the Court of Justice of the European Union (CJEU), which arguably result in the dilution of the EU principle of equality at work as a common prism of interpretation when introducing fundamental rights into labour law. According to the authors, the CJEU ascribes constitutional status to the principle of equality both in EU law and in Member States' law, and, on that basis, domestic courts are obliged to disregard national legislation which is incompatible with the principle. This has led to harsh criticism from advocates general and national courts who question the legitimacy of the CJEU and its reasoning. The analysis reminds us that the interplay between legal actors is pivotal in any discussion of legitimacy – the willingness of one group to accept a set of norms created by another group or legal actor 'even if this goes against specific interests at specific times'.[6]

It can take other actors than courts to help enforce norms developed in the transnational sphere. L. Munkholm investigates the facilitating role of local labour law enforcers in legitimising transnational legal norms regarding the protection of workers. The author analyses the reason-giving and persuasion activities of local labour inspectors who interact on a daily basis with multiple audiences (e.g. small firms as well as big industrial companies that can be domestic or foreign-owned). The analysis shows that labour inspectors have had to customise communication strategies in an attempt to persuade new types of audiences (Chinese companies in Italy) to comply with central areas of labour law. Put differently, traditional ways of seeking legitimacy have had to be rethought, resulting in new tools for

5 See Chapter 9 by Jens Vedsted-Hansen in this volume.

6 Andrew Hurrell, 'Legitimacy and the Use of Force: Can the Circle Be Squared?' (2005) 31 *Review of International Studies* 15, 16.

law enforcement, involving video campaigning, guidelines for self-regulation and consultancy.

Non-state actors

Non-state actors are very active when it comes to legitimation and delegitimation practices in a transnational context. In her analysis of the legal obligations of non-state armed groups (NSAGs), L. Neumann argues that NSAGs engage in a norm creation process that currently falls under the radar of much political debate as the NSAGs are rarely recognised as subjects of international law. According to the author, informal instruments of the NSAGs can no longer be ignored as they are used to establish some sort of order in situations where conditions are far from normal, i.e. where UN norms and principles face a hard time in solving conflicts. On that basis, the author argues that international law needs to develop an expansive approach characterised by the involvement of non-state actors in the attempt to find legal solutions to factual problems that extend beyond national borders and challenge existing law. The author names such an approach a 'lens of transnational regulation'.

Moving to the private law sphere, in her analysis of the use of a US-originated boilerplate provision in contracts governed by Danish law, Mitkidis establishes how norm-setting in the private sphere might be one solution to the lack of a predictable legal framework in international commerce. According to the author, we are witnessing convergence in contracting practices of companies, a so-called 'new lex mercatoria', but not convergence among national contract laws. Thus, as companies' practice still rests on national dispute resolution bodies, diversity in application and enforcement of contract law and principles remains a great obstacle for transnational commercial law. The norm-creation process that takes place in the private sphere provides important lessons for discussion of legitimacy-seeking practice and delegitimation attempts. It questions the role of international organisations such as the UN and the EU. As private companies generate new norms to fill gaps in the international legal frameworks, they call for recognition as norm creators and for attention of states and international and supranational organisations.

Looking yet at another non-state actor, Pelaudeix analyses the ICC and its legitimacy strategy related to governance of the Arctic Ocean. The author shows that this non-state actor strives for legitimacy by applying several simultaneous approaches: the referring to international law (human rights and indigenous peoples' rights) to put pressure on state actors to include the interests of the Inuit People in politics related to the governance of the Arctic; and at the same time, a bottom-up approach based on the innovative concept of 'indigenous protected areas' (a free-travel zone for Inuit managed by an authority led by Inuit representatives regulating activities such as transportation, shipping and off-shore industrial development). This first illustrates that international law, although relying on state sovereignty, which is contested by the ICC, remains useful for transnational actors striving to be granted legitimacy. It also shows that local stewardship gains in momentum.

Finally, Christoffersen argues that the governance system in transnational religious communities is, and has always, been a central example of a parallel legal structure, challenging the nation state's sole capacity to regulate legal conflicts among its citizens. The election of a lesbian priest for the position as bishop in the Western Jurisdiction of the Methodist Church in the United States and the position taken by the Methodist Church in relation to same-sex marriage are used as illustrative examples of the ongoing struggles under transnational religious law. Regarding the case of the election of a lesbian bishop, the neighbouring Methodist church in the United States (the South Central Jurisdictional Conference) petitioned against the decision with reference to the Book of Discipline, i.e. the religious norms of the community. At the same time, the Methodist Church in Denmark claimed that condemnation of homosexuality would be against the doctrine of the Methodist Church. The internal disagreement among the Methodist Churches in respect of homosexuality (whether it is to be condemned or tolerated) has led to a rethinking of the governance system in this transnational religious community with more local decision-making capacity as one of the potential outcomes. This means that legitimacy seeking practices that rest solely on the Book of Discipline are challenged by requests to follow also the development of local interpretations and applications of religious rules when it comes to same-sex marriages and the hiring practices of the Methodist Church.

Emerging tendencies

Transnational tendencies in law have been analysed by Zumbansen as the co-existence, competition and interaction between regulatory levels, between hard and soft law, between official and unofficial law and between public and private law.[7] According to Zumbansen, actors, norms and processes are the central elements in the analysis of transnational law.[8] Based on the contributions to this book, we see a number of emerging transnational tendencies in law. First of all, regarding procedural aspects of law, we argue that democracy and legitimacy are inextricably linked. Secondly, we find a movement towards basing legitimacy seeking strategies on substantive arguments. Thirdly, there is a need to rethink the traditional hierarchy of norms. This section looks into each of these themes.

Legitimacy and democracy in a transnational context

Does legitimacy presuppose democracy? A traditional approach is to answer affirmatively. As pointed out by Habermas, the people affected by the regulation

7 Peer Zumbansen, 'Defining the Space of Transnational Law: Legal Theory, Global Governance, and Legal Pluralism' (2012) 21 *Transnational Law and Contemporary Problems* 305, 307.

8 Ibid.

should have a say in the drafting of the regulation.[9] Habermas also made the point that democracy does not only relate to borders of the state. He pointed out the legitimacy-deficit of the EU. In this approach, procedural legitimacy is pivotal. But at the same time, it is an important aspect of democracy to secure the rights of minorities to be involved in decision-making on issues that affect their lives.

Democracy as the basis for law's legitimacy is still strong. But it does not stand alone: other ideas of legitimating sources are found.[10] Human rights are mentioned by many of the authors in the book as the basis for various arguments for changing regulations and also for challenging the substantive legitimacy of norms. In some cases, human rights are seen as a modern form of natural law standing above any other legal orders (see Chapter 10 by Billing and Tan). In other cases, arguments regarding sustainability (see Chapter 8 by Buhmann and Azizi), a better environment (see Chapters 3 and 4 by Pelaudeix and Basse, repectively) and the protection of workers are focal (see Chapters 11 and 12 by L. Munkholm, and N. Videbæk Munkholm and Schjøler, respectively), and also religious legitimacy (see Chapter 14 by Christoffersen) is a basis for challenging normative structures. It has been suggested in the academic literature that the legitimacy discourse in the transnational context has moved away from democracy towards less-demanding standards of legitimacy, such as accountability, deliberation and administrative procedure.[11] The reason for this is that it is difficult, maybe illusory, to rely on a democratic process when adopting law or legal decisions at the transnational level. Democracy on a global, or even a broad transnational level, remains highly challenging. Thus, the efforts must be focused on creating decision-making procedures best suited to ensuring a legitimate outcome.

There is a trend towards the development of bottom-up practices or procedures to supplement the more traditional top-down (yet democracy based) procedures (see Chapter 8 by Buhmann and Azizi, Chapter 2 by Gammeltoft-Hansen and Aalberts, Chapter 9 by Vedsted-Hansen, Chapter 3 by Pelaudeix, Chapter 15 by L. Neumann and Chapter 7 by Mitkidis). In contexts where there is no such bottom-up practice, this is recommended as a way forward (see Chapter 5 by Banakar). Also, Petersen stresses that 'we need to understand other normative expressions beyond the written – be they visual, oral, factual or customary – both in local and personal relations and beyond' (see Chapter 6).

'Bottom-up' sometimes refers to smaller groups or communities being the senders where states are addressees of information or requests. And sometimes 'bottom-up' means from nation states to international or supranational legislative

9 Jürgen Habermas, *Faktizität und Geltung* (Suhrkamp 1992).

10 Jørgen Dalberg-Larsen, 'From Jean Bodin to Michael Böss – on Legitimacy Crisis in a Historical Perspective' in Per Andersen, Cecilie Eriksen and Bjarke Viskum (eds), *Law and Legitimacy* (Jurist- og Økonomforbundets Forlag 2015) 37.

11 Daniel Bodansky, 'Legitimacy in International Law and International Relations' in Mark A. Pollack and Jeffrey L. Dunoff (eds), *Interdisciplinary Perspectives on International Law and International Relations: The State of the Art* (Cambridge University Press 2013) 321.

bodies, e.g. in transnational law development. In these 'bottom-up' approaches, 'democracy' is not only perceived as a value in itself but also as a device: a way of informing the legislator or norm creators in question. And the traditional ways of getting this pertinent information, including through democratic representation, are either not possible yet or not sufficient in a transnational context. New mechanisms to ensure input from those affected by the regulation are being created and further developed.

A risk is that the input received is not only relevant input from actors in the field or from individuals or entities affected by a potential regulation. There is a risk that those shouting the loudest get heard, and that the norms will lack protection of minorities – that strong actors (e.g. private international corporations or religious communities) will have a clear advantage, thus resulting in a privatisation of legislation. The role of economic power is addressed by several authors (e.g. Petersen, Gammeltoft-Hansen and Aalberts, Pelaudeix). And there is a risk of dilettantisation of legislation – of actors who are dilettantes developing norms or rules that are arbitrary. On the other hand, there is also a risk of transnational law development being formed primarily by a technocratic elite defending the system that they are part of and the norms therein.

Towards substantive legitimacy?

A traditional distinction is made between descriptive legitimacy and normative legitimacy. The former builds on people's beliefs about political authority.[12] Weber derives his concept of legitimacy from his perception of power as being rational, i.e. based on the belief of others that the actor in question has the right to exercise power ('Legitimitätsglaube'). The origin of the regulation is pivotal whilst the content of the legal regulation is not questioned. Normative legitimacy on the other hand entails some sort of benchmarks of acceptability or justification of the regulation.[13] Only regulation meeting the benchmark criteria is perceived as legitimate.

Actors have different perceptions of legitimacy and strive for different forms of legitimacy – or perhaps they strive for the form of legitimacy which is available for them. Different strategies are used in the pursuit of legitimising the norms that the actor in question wants to promote. One strategy is to make the strongest possible argument for getting a place at the table. Being a legal actor provides a place at the table where decisions are made, thus the actor tends to stress the procedural legitimacy (e.g. the EU or the UN), whereas actors who are not invited to the table concentrate on arguing the norms they find most important or most suitable to their particular interests (e.g. non-state armed groups). As demonstrated above, delegitimation practices show that the actor in question puts forward the argument that without this particular actor at the table, the

12 Max Weber, *The Theory of Social and Economic Organization* (The Free Press 1964).
13 John Rawls, *Political Liberalism* (Columbia University Press 1993).

decisions made lack procedural legitimacy. Another strategy is also delegitimation but through substantive arguments. The point is that a set of norms lack legitimacy because their contents conflict with what is perceived as more important substantive norms, e.g. human rights or the fundamental principles of the EU. The foundations for substantive legitimacy arguments vary depending on the actor in question and the context.

Since some of the very important actors in various fields are non-state actors and they tend to focus more on substantive legitimacy and output/effectiveness legitimacy, there seems to be a trend towards a more substantively based form of legitimacy in transnational law. Legitimacy is based on the transnational regulation being perceived as legitimate by actors in the field. This potentially influences both the perceived procedural and the perceived substantive legitimacy of transnational normative structures. On the contrary, this also has the potential to open up for increased interlegality. If legitimacy cannot be primarily based on procedural elements (who has the power to create legally binding norms), but also needs to live up to substantive requirements (what is the content of the regulation), the transnational normative structures might be more prone to openness towards other normative structures and contexts.

A commonality between the actors' different approaches to legitimacy practices is that transnational law is not perceived as either legitimate or not – but rather as legitimate for some, in some contexts and to some degree.

Weber operates with two different forms of material rationality on which a general regulation can build. In one understanding, material rationality means realisation of certain, concrete values, e.g. human rights. The other understanding of material rationality means setting up procedural frameworks for decision-making without predetermining the values that should lead to the decisions – this is what Teubner means by reflexive law.[14] The idea here is not only to develop a framework for solving concrete conflicts but, more importantly, to further develop democracy through training people's autonomy and self-determination. The legitimacy perceptions among the various actors might be a form of material rationality in the transnational law development – as understood in the latter form.

A preliminary finding of the book is that local approaches to development and enforcement of transnational law are found to be more effectful (see Chapter 14 by Christoffersen, Chapter 7 by Mitkidis, Chapter 15 by L. Neumann and Chapter 11 by L. Munkholm). The legitimacy of transnational law is better served – when it comes to law development and enforcement – by local actors. This might be so because this setting leaves more room for material rationality. But effectiveness arguments lie implicitly in substantive ways of arguing for legitimacy: even if it takes the form of a substantive argument, there is a purpose-orientation behind it. The risk is that it is not the values, or 'the better argument', that prevails in the end.

14 Gunther Teubner, 'Reflexives Recht, Entwiklungsmodelle des Rechts in vergleichender Perspektive' (1982) 68 *Archiv für Rechts- und Sozialphilosophie* 13.

Hierarchy of norms

Are transnational norms then challenging the traditional formal hierarchy of norms? Can reactions from nation states stressing authority and procedural legitimacy be understood as counter reactions? How is the interplay between the various legal orders and norms (international, national, local)? Which norms should prevail and on which ground? Some authors claim that legitimacy of international law should prevail (see Chapter 4 by Basse, Chapter 10 by Billing and Tan and Chapter 9 by Vedsted-Hansen), but this is met with arguments regarding issues of authority and subsidiarity (see Chapter 12 by N. Videbæk Munkholm and Schjøler and Chapter 5 by Banakar).

In Chapter 1 in this book, Tuori emphasises

> the pluralist relations between EU law and Member State law: EU law defines its jurisdiction mainly in substantive (functional) terms, while Member State law adheres to the territorial principle of authority, specified, in state sovereigntist terms, by a claim to universal and exclusive jurisdiction within its territory.

Tuori emphasises interlegality as a means of handling or solving pluralist conflicts, but what does it mean – in practice?

In some of the chapters in this book, the aim is to look for new ways to ensure a hierarchy or a harmonisation or uniformity in the regulation (see Chapter 13 by T. Neumann), e.g. through the development of new lex mercatoria (see Chapter 7 by Mitkidis). Others look to a form of rational persuasion or substantive legitimacy, e.g. stressing human rights, sustainability, the principle of equality or the concepts of solidarity and harmony as potentially ranking above nation state law (see Chapter 4 by Basse, Chapter 3 by Pelaudeix, Chapter 6 by Petersen and Chapter 12 by N. Videbæk Munkholm and Schjøler).

The constitutional approach and its hierarchy between norms are challenged by a sociological approach, e.g. legal pluralism where there is no clear hierarchy between the various normative orders. Some rules that have been developed might not be seen as legitimate by all actors, but they are still part of life. Empirical studies have shown different legal orders at the same time. But theories on legal pluralism have not answered how to solve disputes and conflicts between the different legal orders. There is a deficiency in normativity to decide on which norms should prevail in a particular context. But is this lack necessarily a shortcoming or a failure?

Schiff Berman[15] argues that in a global legal pluralistic view it is good to preserve different normative spaces when dealing with the coexistence of multiple normative communities. He clearly argues against harmonisation. Schiff Berman develops six principles and nine mechanisms to help solve conflicts between the

15 Paul Schiff Berman, 'Global Legal Pluralism' (2007) 80 *Southern California Law Review* 1155.

different normative orders. Among the principles are: do not deny the reality of pluralism, not all norms are embraced, you might end up with hybrid forms, the need for development of procedural mechanisms along the lines of Habermas' communicative rationality[16] but with a more international approach. Among the mechanisms are: dialectical legal interactions, margins of appreciation, limitations in autonomous regimes (e.g. religious groups), subsidiary schemes, hybrid participation arrangements and a pluralist approach to conflicts of law. But still it is not always easy or even possible to solve these conflicts through this type of approach. There is a risk of overlooking or disregarding power and power structures. In the end, somebody must be able to solve conflicts. Habermas' appeal to the moral arguments and dialogue is very alluring, but they only work if there is an alternative to the dialogue such as, e.g. the possibility to bring the case or question to court. Another problem here is that we are left without a clear definition of 'law' – can we live with this?

In this book, we get a clearer picture of how 'law' is perceived by actors in the field, thereby adding a more internal view on law to the predominately external perspective most common in legal pluralism theories. This book shows that there are, in fact, some normative elements here. Norms can be perceived as legitimate among actors, i.e. a sort of 'living law', even though they are not legitimate in a traditional sense. There is an interaction between different legal orders. In practice they tend to merge or melt together, which might result in hybrid forms of regulations. Principles develop from practice and can form actual solutions to conflicts. International law has different effects and interpretations because it is seen in the light of national law when interpreted in courts of law and when applied by actors. This might result in a post-modern concept of law where the concrete contents, intentions and effects of law depend on the actual balance of powers involved. The creation of norms through the practice of solving disputes and conflicts can result in the 'best argument' wins – or in fundamental norms, such as human rights, being used to legitimate or delegitimate regulation.

Perspectives

Even with a greater attention to transnational tendencies in law, the existing academic research suffers from gaps in the understanding of the effects of these tendencies on legitimacy.[17] Indeed, there has been far more focus on theoretical aspects than on empirical work.[18] This book has presented a wide range of case studies interlinking empirical work and theory: e.g. research on the kind of authority, and how much authority an institution is exercising, including the

16 Jürgen Habermas, *Theorie des kommunikativen Handelns* (Suhrkamp 1981) vols 1 and 2.

17 T. Alexander Aleinikoff, 'Transnational Spaces: Norms and Legitimacy' (2008) 33 *Yale Journal of International Law* 479.

18 Daniel Bodansky, 'Legitimacy in International Law and International Relations' in Jeffrey L. Dunoff and Mark A. Pollack (eds), *International Perspectives on International Law and International Relations* (Cambridge University Press 2013) 321.

ways in which legitimacy may depend on the issue area or domain.[19] Three scenarios have been suggested by other scholars engaged in the debate about the relationship between transnationalism and international governance: (1) a tighter form of governance and oversight at the national level (return of the state), (2) increased transnationalisation (that would require more delegation of resources and authority) and (3) a building upon the existing architecture of transnational governance and overcoming its shortcomings.[20]

The research conducted for this book contributes with insight into different problem-solving mechanisms in this respect. It is clear that many states aim to take back control, calling for a tighter form of governance with regard to transnational affairs. Thus, the legitimacy of central transnational regimes such as the human rights system, the ecosystem-based approach and commercial law is increasingly questioned by states and non-state actors. Still, transnationalisation is a process that can hardly be rolled back. The most constructive way forward is therefore to overcome the shortcomings of the existing architecture of transnational governance. As argued by several authors of the book, the key is to support interaction across borders: judicial dialogue, interlegality, common prisms for interpretation and intercultural intersubjectivity are all concepts invoked by the different contributors to this book in their attempt to suggest paths forward. What these concepts have in common is their quest for solidarity and bottom-up approaches to law. Legitimacy in relation to transnationalisation is closely related to the issue of whether there is such a thing as a transnational public sphere. Not only supranational and international bodies, but also academia, in general, and the media, in particular, have important roles to play when it comes to creating a public sphere that transcends national borders as well as traditional divisions of public/private law and soft/hard law. As mentioned in several of the chapters, academics and journalists more often than not fuel nationalism, political rhetoric and popular discontent through their nation-centric studies and often superficial and critical coverage of international law and its institutions. The lack of a global or transnational public sphere is central; the public sphere so far remains nation-bound.

Also practitioners – all those who engage in the development, the application and the enforcement of law – need to direct attention towards the above-mentioned ideas of judicial dialogue, interlegality, common prisms for interpretation and intercultural intersubjectivity. If these professional legal actors do not see themselves as part of a transnational community, a lens of transnational regulation will never be established. In this context, there is a need to rethink the idea of a legal actor. By its empirical focus, the book has demonstrated that non-state actors are de facto heavily engaged in the development of transnational norms. However, the activities of these actors are likely to fall under

19 Ibid., 332.

20 Marie-Laure Djelic and Kerstin Sahlin, 'Reordering the World: Transnational Regulatory Governance and its Challenges' in David Lévi-Faure (ed.), *The Oxford Handbook of Governance* (Oxford University Press 2012) 745.

the radar as the concept of 'a legal actor' is often interpreted in a narrow sense comprising those actors who participate in law development processes based on official membership of national and international communities. It is crucial that not only academics, but also practitioners, support the development of a transnational public sphere, not only for the sake of democracy, but also for achieving more justice and equity in the world.

Index

Page numbers in **bold** denote tables.

accountability 29, 71–72, 208, 213, 225, 227, 239; lack of 153, 201, 213; personal 72; political 72

act: Danish 51; Danish Accession 180–182, 185; on Greenlandic Self-Government 56–57; Human Rights 76–77; Inatsisartut Mineral Resources 51, 57–59; Inatsisartut on Marine Environmental Protection 59; legal 9; national 51; on the Protection of the Marine Area in the exclusive Economic Zone (EEZ) 58–59; subnational 51

activism: dilemma of 129; judicial 24–25, 129, 131, 140, 236; perceived 131

actors: academic 135; central 83–84, 230; commercial 98, 107; domestic 128; European 153; governmental 18; international 140, 229; judicial 18; legal 161, 173, 181–185, 199, 205, 223, 230–231, 236, 240, 244–245; media 135; national 65, 183–184; non-state 18, 20, 22, 82, 101, 113, 117, 120, 159, 216, 218, 221, 230–232, 237, 241, 244; normative 94; private 61, 98; regional 50; regulatory 50, 213; religious 87; social 72; state 85, 147, 159, 237; transnational 201, 237

administrative: competences 56; decisions 77; location 209–210; obstacles 79; order 209; procedure 239; rights 36; systems 73

agreement 28, 36, 38, 55, 57, 99–100, 112–113, 119, 146, 216–217, 223–225; bilateral 23; contemporaneous 100; Entire (EA) 98–99; integrated 103; intergovernmental 27; internal 238; international 18, 39, 54–55, 57, 189, 235; legal 25–26; multi-lateral 27, 30; non-binding 22; political 119; regional 55; self-government 37; special 224–226, 229

Agreement on Trade-Related Aspects of Intellectual Property Rights (TRIPS) 30

Ajos 179–180, 185

Anwendungsvorrang 12–13

Arab Spring 122, 126

Arctic 35–36, 40–41, 45, 49; coastal states 37, 43–44, 49; indigenous peoples 37, 56; marine area 47, 49–50, 52–54, 59–61, 233–234; Marine Strategic Plan (AMSP) 54, 61; Ocean (AO) 33–34, 37, 39–42, 44–48, 233, 235; policy 39, 45; region 33, 38, 52, 230; states 33–34, 40, 42, 44, 54, 57, 233, 235; *see also* Council

asylum 26, 28, 90, 140, 149; seekers 28, 90

authority: centres of 27; civil 210–211; claims of 5; conflicts of 9–11, 181, 214; direct 152; hierarchy of 62, 81; International Sea-Bed 43; legal 53, 80, 232; legitimate 37; political 153, 240; principles of 8–9, 242; state 147; supreme 204; top-down 80

autonomy 5, 9–10, 13, 71, 73, 145, 152, 177, 202–203, 241; concepts 140; initiatives 193; interpretation 191, 193; legal system 106; operation 214; regime 243; semi- 213; *see also* church

black box model 3–4, 8, 10, 214
Boko Haram 216, 231
Book of Discipline 205–211, 238
borders 44, 66, 83, 94, 116, 143, 151–152, 199, 239, 244; common 148; corporate 76; crossing 82; hard 67; internal 69; international 187; linguistic 94; national 34, 69, 72, 80, 97, 228, 233, 237, 244; soft 67; state 37; territorial 116; without 68
Brexit 25, 27, 62–63, 66–67, 73, 79–80, 232

charter 77, 176, 178–179, 183, 185–186; of citizens' rights 78; of criminals and terrorists 80; European 87; of Fundamental Rights of the European Union 71, 73, 86, 145
Chinese Arctic Policy (CAP) 42, 46
church 202–204, 206–212, 214, 215; autonomy 202, 212; Catholic 88, 90–91, 202, 210, 212; Christian 90, 215; Danish Methodist 204–207, 211; One 208–209; Orthodox 86, 202; United Methodist 204–211, 215, 231, 238
comparative method 129, 236
conservation 38, 40, 43–44, 58
conservative 77–78, 86
constitution: changes 209; Chinese 84; deadlocks 10; democracy 71; duelling 9; framework 71–72; impact 77; internal 205; Italian 166; law 9, 182, 203; multinational 75; national 132, 185; Norwegian 202; notions 183, 185; powers 182; principle 174; provision 181; Spanish 177; state 108; traditions 139, 145, 173, 176–181, 184–186; *see also* court; Danish
contracts 64, 98–102, 104, 106–108, 110–111, 164, 170, 237; commercial 99, 102–103; common law 99; fixed-term 176; international 109; labour 169; lengthy 101; private 186; short-term 159; transnational 107; written 104, 168
Convention: Aarhus 61; Biodiversity 49, 51–56, 59–60, 223; on Biodiversity Beyond National Jurisdiction 33; on Biological Diversity 30; Geneva 226; on Human Rights 76; International Labour Organisation's 56, 61; Law of the Sea 233; on Occupational Safety and Health 159; on Promotional Framework for Occupational Safety and Health 159; on the Protection of the Marine Environment of the North-East Atlantic (OSPAR) 49, 56, 59–60; Refugee 149–150, 153; Reservations to the Genocide 20; Vienna 55, 60
Copenhagen Declaration 128, 135–138
Council: Arctic 33, 37, 45–46, 51, 54, 60–61; Barents Euro-Arctic 38; of Bishops 208; Human Rights 27; of Danish Churches 211; of Europe 23, 26, 76, 127–128, 133–137, 139; Inuit Circumpolar (ICC) 33, 231, 235; Judicial 205–209, 215; Security 225
court: American 103; British 76; constitutional 9; Copenhagen Maritime and Commercial 103, 197–198; Danish Supreme 24, 135, 180–182, 184–185; decisions 105, 183, 188–189, 192–200; domestic 138, 187–196, 199, 235–236; European 213; foreign 188, 192–200; German constitutional 9–10; German Federal Constitutional (GFCC) 179–180, 182; German Federal Labour 179–180; international 20, 25, 105, 138; Italian 197; Judicial 205; local 105; of Justice of the European Union (CJEU) 9, 24, 40, 51, 55, 60, 69, 71, 80, 173, 231, 236; Member State 10; national 10, 13, 78, 105, 110, 177, 180–182, 184, 231, 235–236; regional 21, 24, 105; ruling 180; Strasbourg 135; supranational 187
crisis: economic 86; financial 74, 161; identity 62, 78–80; legitimacy 127; of national identity 63, 76, 80; refugee 87, 150; regulatory 114
culture 56, 92, 94, 97, 103, 170; British 73, 75; deep 6, 15; indigenous 11; individualistic 79; legal 6, 15–16, 82, 92–93, 109, 173, 183–184, 186, 233; local 65; national 70–71, 183; political 70; of prevention 159, 161–165, 168, 171–172; of respect 76–77; supranational 183; of victimhood 90

Danish: Accession Act 180, 185; Act on the Protection of the Marine Area in the Exclusive Economic Zone 51, 58–59; Constitution 56–57,

182, 184, 210; contract law 98, 107; government 25, 134–137, 139; -Greenlandic Arctic marine area 49–50, 52, 56, 58–59, 233; jurisdiction 56, 105; law 98, 104, 107–108, 110, 211–212, 237; legal system 98, 100–101; Realm 49, 56; *see also* church; Court, Danish Supreme
declaration 23, 30, 37, 136–139, 206; of the *Arctic 5* 40; Brighton 136; Brussels 136; Circumpolar Inuit 37; Copenhagen 128, 135–138; Council of Europe 137; Ilulissat 34; Interlaken 136; Izmir 136; on resources 37; Rio 61; of Sovereignty 37, 44; unilateral 216–217, 224, 226–227; Vienna 114
Deeds of Commitment 217, 222–224, 229
Defrenne III 175
democracy 47, 71, 91, 113, 213, 238, 239, 240, 241
democratic 6, 34, 47, 70, 89–90, 113, 126, 132, 145, 193, 231, 238–241, 245; constitutional 71; control 108; decision-making 24; elections 68, 78, 127, 234; factual 91; identity 71; institutions 70; legitimacy 68, 108–109, 118, 132–133, 181, 202, 213, 238; mandate 132; nature 130, 234; notions of 132; outcomes 122; participation 125; political culture 70; principles 224; processes 70, 111, 118, 239; representative 213, 240; rule 132, 185; semi- 84; society 133, 213; structures 70; values 71; weaker 108
Directive: EIA 40, **46**; environmental 61; Equal Treatment 175; Framework 176, 178, 180, 185; Habitats 40, **46**; for Marine Spatial Planning (FMSP) 40, **46**, 53; Marine Strategic Framework (MSFD) 53, 57, 234; non-discrimination 178; Offshore Safety 40, **46**, 53, 61; SEA 40, **46**; Wild Birds 40, **46**
discourse: cross-boundary 15; deliberative 119; human rights 11; intercontinental 86; inter-regime 15; legal 15; legitimacy 239; official 46; political 25, 79, 127, 234; public 24, 91, 118
diversity 5, 237; cultural 33; legal 8, 10; simple 3–5, 8
Durkheim, E. 86, 88
dynamic: developments 26, 130; interpretation 24, 128–129, 136, 140, 236; multi-level 50; of regime complexity 30; tension 213

economic: activities 33, 68, 114, 187; aspects 47; benefits 36, 74; calculation 66; challenges 114; character 121; considerations 106, 110; crisis 86; development 20, 42, 87; disparities 86; downturns 122; egoism 74; equality 89; gains 66; growth 83–84, 86, 121, 232; incentives 91; inequalities 82, 85–86; initiative 166; integration 63; issues 53; leverage 48, 235; losses 66; needs 88; obligations 87; participation 115, 125; partners 121; perspective 44; policies 90; power 107, 235, 240; practice 85; relations 69; socio- 121, 133, 169; structures 85; sustainability 112; systems 166; threat 161; transactions 108; union 175; use of resources 44; zones 28, 51, 58–59, 234
Egenberger 186
Entire Agreement (EA) clause 98–111
environment 39, 42, 63, 169, 239; aspects 40, 54; challenges 114; competence 51; consequences 51, 58; governance 50, 54; issues 53; law 20, 54, 59, 116, 230, 232; legislation 39, 58; liability 45; marine 50, 52, 54, 56–59, 233–234; movements 72; natural 42; obligations 58; political 19; protection 30, 36, 39, 41, 44, 46, 52, 58, 233, 235; provisions 58; quality 57–58; restrictions 28; rules 58; safeguarding 45; status 50, 53, 57, 61, 233; sustainability 112, 118; targets 57; work 171; *see also* directive; values
equality 70, 85, 166, 174–176, 181, 184, 186; effective 174; perception of 174; principle of 173–176, 182–186, 236, 242; right to 178; social 89; substantive 174, 183
ethnic 166; background 204; belonging 71; differences 72; markers 73; minorities 67, 127, 133; multi- 165–166, 169, 171; signifiers 75; unity 74–75
European: Atomic Energy Community 87; Charter 87; Commission 61, 162;

Community 69; Convention on Human Rights (ECHR) 23, 77, 80, 128–130, 132, 134–135, 137, 145, 176, 181, 212, 236; Court of Human Rights (ECtHR) 21, 23–24, 26, 76, 78, 128–131, 133, 135–137, 151, 231, 236; Court of Justice (ECJ) 9, 23, 51; Economic Area (EEA) 39, 233; Economic Community (EEC) 82, 87, 174; Free Trade Association (EFTA) 39; governance 72; human rights 9, 11, 137, 202; identity 62–63, 67–72, 76, 232; integration 10, 15, 72, 146; jurisprudence 212; law 70; legal practice 213; migration challenge 92, 150; Parliament 77, 146; Pillar of Social Rights 186; political elite 67; populations 73; Social Agenda 176; trawlers 28; Union (EU) 25, 49–50, 62, 70–71, 73, 75–76, 82, 84, 86, 90, 134, 141, 162–163, 173, 185, 231–232
Exclusive Economic Zone (EEZ) 28, 34, 39, 44, 51–52, 57–59, 234

Free Prior and Informed Consent principle (FPIC) 38, 44

Geltungsvorrang 12–13
Geneva: Call 217, 221–223, 228–229; Canton of 222; Conventions and Additional Protocol II 219
German: Constitutional Court 9–10; Federal Constitutional Court (GFCC) 179–180, 182
global: advocacy 18, 235; arena 36; business community 104; challenges 90; citizenry 115, 117, 125; civil society 18; collaboration 118; commercial practice 106; commons 20; community 109; concern 115–116, 126; consensus 109–110; economy 99; geopolitical 84; governance 24, 33, 41, 115, 118, 125; government 107; growth 121; impacts 38; interactions 114; interest 47, 50; law 3, 14, 106, 115; legal landscape 83–84; legal world 105; level 15, 47, 98, 205; marketplace 199; membership 39; order 114; power 51; practice 106; public 112–113, 125, 232; regulation 124; rule-making 126; social justice 31; society 118–119; stage 41, 114; sustainability 112–114, 118, 125; value chains 28; world 83, 159
globalisation 5, 15, 33, 66, 74, 76, 86, 88–90, 107, 118, 133; anti- 82, 89; of law 111; normative 83
governance 18, 27, 33–34, 37, 39–41, 45, 50, 62, 65, 67–68, 70, 113, 117–118, 124, 221, 231, 233, 235, 237, 244; bottom-up 123–126; effective 112; environmental 50; good 20; inclusive 122; institutionalist 19; international 244; internet 109; maritime 39, 49, 52, 54, 61; prospective 125; public 114; regulatory 47; self- 121; structures 202; systems 119, 202–204, 238; traditional 44; transnational 31, 48, 51, 53, 60–61, 73, 232, 244; *see also* global
growth 19, 86–87, 118, 120; economic 83–84, 86, 121, 232; sustainability 176; unprecedented 86
Grundnorm 4, 10, 12–13

Holocaust 127, 132
human rights: abuse 124, 142, 152, 216; commitments 25–26; committees 21; discourses 11; education 148, 154; fundamental 71; infringements 120; instruments 21, 150; international 71, 127–133, 135, 139–140, 146, 217, 221; jurisdiction 29; law 9, 11, 26, 28–29, 117, 120, 127, 139, 141, 143, 147, 149–152, 178, 203, 217, 230, 232, 234; obligations 131, 143, 145–146, 151–154, 220, 224, 234; protection 71, 76, 80, 129, 132, 137, 139, 144, 153, 216, 221–222; regime 123, 126, 232, 234; scepticism 132; standards 130, 137, 143; treaties 21–22, 128, 145, 150, 220; violations 147, 152; *see also* values
Human Rights Act (1998) 76–77

identity: British 73–75; building 71, 73, 76, 233; collective 63, 68, 70, 72–73; common 70; communal 11; constitutional 9; crisis 78, 80; cultural 11; European 62–63, 67–68–72, 76, 232; formation 72; institutional 76; liberal democratic 71; national 63, 68, 74–76; perception 232; politics 62, 67, 75, 79, 90; project 76; solidarity-based 76

Ilulissat Declaration 34, 37
immigration 24–26, 90, 148, 155
indigenous: Australians 38; cultures 11; law 4, 7, 9, 11; legal concepts 11; legal regimes 5; organisations 33; peoples 33, 37, 44–45, 54, 56, 61, 231, 237; Protected Area (IPA) 38, **46**, 237; *see also* values
inequality 86; economic 85–86; income 85; social 86
interlegality 3–5, 8, 10–12, 14, 62–63, 65–66, 68–69, 71, 73, 78–81, 202, 233, 241–242, 244
International: Committee of the Red Cross (ICRC) 222, 224; Court of Justice 21, 43, 231; Covenant on Civil and Political rights (ICCPR) 37, 151, 153; Criminal Court 21, 227, 231; Criminal Tribunal for the former Yugoslavia (ICTY) 226; Labour Organization (ILO) 56, 61, 159–160, 162, 172; Maritime Organisation (IMO) 33, 39; Organization for Migration (IOM) 142, 154; Union on the Conservation of Nature (IUCN) 38
internet 91, 115, 120, 123; access 115, 121, 125; governance 109; platform 120; sites 125
Inuit 34, 36–38, 56–57, 237; circumpolar 36; homeland 37; Nunaat 37–38, 44; regions 36; rights 36, 45, 57; sovereignty 36–37; values 45; *see also* Council
Inupiat 35; Assembly 34
Islam 86, 201, 214

judicial: activism 24–25, 129, 131, 140, 236; administration 209; assessments 182; bodies 4, 140; commands 210; competences 56; complaint 209; control 127, 234; dialogue 187–189, 192–199, 235, 244; enforcement 208; forum shopping 30; institutions 20, 106; interpretation 184; law-making 130, 236; manoeuvring 182; powers 181; practices 8; review 129, 206; sovereignty 4; whim 130
Judicial Council 205–209, 215
jurisprudence 86, 110, 138, 212
justice 80, 93, 245; access to 202, 213; criminal 154; social 31, 78; substantive 233; transnational 105

Kompetenz – Kompetenz question 9–10

legislative: authorities 132, 212; basis 211; bodies 4, 206, 239; branches of government 127, 234; changes 205; competence 102; efforts 187; history 191; initiatives 163, 183, 194, 211; level 213; majorities 132; powers 108, 146, 203, 205, 209; practice 4; proposal 212; sovereignty 4
legitimacy: definition of xii; democratic 34, 68, 108, 109, 118, 132, 133, 181, 202, 213, 223; descriptive 45, 71, 109, 240; expert-based 109; input 50, 59, 60, 61; - of legal actors 161, 173, 181, 184, 199, 236; normative 71, 73, 240; - of norms 221, 230, 234, 239; outcome 113, 239; output 34, 41, 45, 50, 60, 61, 233; procedural 38, 40, 44, 47, 179, 181, 182, 185, 186, 228, 232, 233, 235, 239, 240, 241, 242; - strategies 36–38, 40–41, 42–44, 45; substantive 34, 38, 41, 45, 47, 181, 182, 184, 185, 232, 233, 239, 240–241
Liberation Tigers of Tamil Eelam (LTTE) 216, 231
Local Health and Safety Authority (ASL) 161, 165, 167–169, 172

Mangold 176–182, 185
margin of appreciation 129, 131, 138, 213, 236, 238
Master Rule 5, 8, 12–14
migrant: Asian 74; black 74; Chinese 160, 167; deaths 142, 149, 154; departures 141; detention 152–153; EU 67; European 150; illegal 77; ill treatment of 150; irregular 142, 144, 150–152, 154; poorer 147; return of 149; rights of 149, 154; smuggling 141–145, 148–154, 233; vulnerable 144, 147
Migrant Smuggling Protocol 141, 143, 147, 149, 153
migration: anti- 67, 74; Asian 75; black 75; control 28–29, 141; curbing 67; European 92; irregular 153, 155; laws 148; from poorer regions 90
minority 127, 208, 211–212; ethnic 67, 133; protection of 240; religious 213; rights 24, 239; sexual 25

new lex mercatoria 106, 108, 110, 237, 242
non-governmental organizations (NOGs) 18, 22, 120, 123–124, 136, 232, 235
non-state armed groups (NSAGs) 216–225, 227–229, 237, 240
normativity 5–8, 14, 64, 81, 242

Offshore Safety Directive 40, 53, 61

Paris Accord 84, 125; Paris Agreement on climate change 25, 33; Paris Climate Change Accord 112
Parliament 65, 203, 212; Assembly 133, 137; Danish 56, 213; devolution of power 75; EU 68, 80; European 77, 146; Greenland 56, 58; involvement of 108; national 68, 213; sovereignty 74, 77, 108; statute 12; UK 76–78; will of 77
Permanent Court of Arbitration (PCA) 21, 231
pluralism 5, 10; anti- 89; legal 5, 8, 10, 214, 242–243; post-national 9; radical 3, 8, 202, 214; reality of 243; religious 203
Pope Francis 87–88, 90
populism 83, 88–91
positivism 4, 8; legal 4–5, 7, 12, 173, 183–184, 214
postnational: age 3, 8; condition 14; constellation 116; developments 15; era 5, 14; law 3, 5–8, 14; legality 6; plurality 3–5, 12–14; systematisation 14
Powell, E. 74–75
principle: of authority 9, 242; of consent 20, 36; constitutional 174; of cooperation 163; core 31; of dynamic interpretation 128, 236; of effectiveness 128; of equality 42, 173–178, 182–186, 211, 236, 242; of European Contract Law 192; of free admissibility of evidence 100; of free movement 67; fundamental 144; interpretive 129; of law 145, 173, 178, 184; legal 106, 146, 173, 180, 184–185, 203; loyalty 55, 60; of mutual recognition 10; of mutual trust 146; of non-discrimination 176–177, 179–181, 184, 186; of *non-refoulement* 149–151, 233; normative 10, 127; of organising 5; personal 8–9; primary state responsibility 139; reconciling 9; of right process 34; of self-determination 38; of sincere cooperation 60; soft law 109; of solidarity 232; of subsidiarity 26, 64, 129, 137–139, 236; substantive 4, 9, 13; of supremacy 12; territorial 8–9; transnational 173, 177, 181, 183–186; unifying 14
propaganda 83, 90–92; commercial 91; political 82
Provincial Labour Directorate (DPL) 161, 165–167, 169, 172

Raw Materials Inc. v. Manfred Forberich GmbH 196–197
reform 41, 80, 90, 137, 162–165, 172; initiatives 136; institutional 26; market 85; process 26, 137, 162
Reformation 90, 202–203
regulatory 82; activities 60; actors 50, 213; approach 47, 50; competence 56; costs 132; crisis 114; frameworks 202, 213; gaps 102; hybridisation 224, 229; institutions 50; levels 204, 238; mechanisms 81; micro- 64; policies 36; power 50, 57; processes 185; regime 64, 107; responses 115; spaces 213; strategies 114
Revolutionary Armed Forces of Colombia (FARC) 216, 231
Rheinland Versicherungen v. Atlarex 197

solidarity 62–63, 67, 70, 72–73, 76, 78–79, 82–83, 86–90, 92, 232–233, 242, 244
sovereignty 20, 25, 37, 42, 66, 75, 77, 83, 151, 199, 224, 232; claim 38; commercialisation of 28; concept of 37, 62; declaration of 37, 44; Inuit 36–37; issues 59, 234; legal 82; manoeuvrability 19; national 24, 89; notion of 37; parliamentary 68, 74, 77, 108; political 68; power 26; rights 42; state 4–5, 20, 127, 139, 217–218, 223–224, 229, 234, 237, 242; traditional 25; will 76; *see also* judicial
Stufenbau 12, 14
Sustainable Development Goals (SDG) 112, 115, 124–125

technology 91, 123, 125–126; information and communication (ICT) 113, 125, 232; mobile 121; mobile phone 120, 124–125; progress 91; SMS messaging 122

terrorist 77–78, 80; 7 July 2005 (London) 75, 77; 9/11 (Twin Towers) 77; incidents 75; suspects 28
Thatcher, M. 74, 78
transnationalisation 98, 101, 106, 108, 116, 244
transnational law 7, 8, 9, 11, 17, 33, 82, 90, 109, 115, 116, 143, 201, 204, 205, 214, 215, 241
Trans-Pacific Partnership Agreement (TPPA) 25, 27
Treaty: Arctic 41; on European Union (TEU) 60, 64, 144, 176, 179; of Friendship, Partnership and Cooperation 142; Lisbon 39, 46, 51–52, 54, 56, 86–87, 185–186, 233; of Rome (1957) 65, 77, 87, 174; Svalbard 42
Trump, D. 25, 84, 89, 91

UNIDROIT principles 106, 109, 192
unification 97–98, 104, 196, 204
United Nations (UN) 22, 33, 82–83, 90, 112–113, 118–119, 124, 126, 133, 147, 153, 187, 189–195, 199–200, 204, 223–224, 231–232–234, 235–237, 240; Business and Human Rights Regime (BHR) 113, 116, 123, 232; Charter 37, 44; Commission on International Trade Law (UNCITRAL) 187–190, 193–196, 199, 235; Convention on Biodiversity 49; Convention on Contracts for the International Sale of Goods 1980 (CISG) 97, 194; Convention on the Law of the Sea (UNCLOS) 23, 34, 36–37, 39–40, 43–45, 49, 52, 55–57, 59; Declaration on Refugees 77; Declaration on the Rights of Indigenous Peoples (UNDRIP) 37–38, 44; Economic and Social Council 37; Fish Stocks Agreement 40; General Assembly 189; Guiding Principles on Business and Human Rights (UNGP) 113, 119–120, 123, 126; High Commission for Refugees (UNHCR) 142, 154; Human Rights Council 113; Office of Legal Affairs 43; Protect, Respect and Remedy Framework 113, 119–120; Sales Convention 192; Universal Declaration of Human Rights (UDHR) 176–177
unity 3–5, 13–16, 70; comprehensive 13; discursive 3; ethnic 74; formal 3–5, 12–14; inter-instance 14; internal 3, 5, 12, 14; of law 5, 14; lost 13

values 39, 46–47, 51, 67, 72, 76, 79, 103, 118, 146, 171, 181–183, 231, 241; common 144; community 78; conflict of 66; core 63, 70, 232; democratic 71; environmental 35; ethical 233; ethno-cultural 70; fundamental 145, 163; human rights 72, 79, 127; Indigenous 38; international 41; Inuit 45; persuasive 235; shared 67, 70; spiritual 88; transformations of 93; understandings of 94; vacuum of 88
victim: of abuse 124; -hood 90; of smuggling 153
Vienna: Convention on the Law of Treaties 55, 60; Declaration and Programme of Action on human rights and sustainable development 114
Vorverständnis 6, 16

Westphalian: model 34, 37; order 82; state 4
World Trade Organization (WTO) 9, 30, 47, 67, 119
World War II 82, 127; post- 13, 18, 75–76, 132, 174, 187, 204

For Product Safety Concerns and Information please contact our EU representative GPSR@taylorandfrancis.com
Taylor & Francis Verlag GmbH, Kaufingerstraße 24, 80331 München, Germany

www.ingramcontent.com/pod-product-compliance
Ingram Content Group UK Ltd.
Pitfield, Milton Keynes, MK11 3LW, UK
UKHW010958180926
475701UK00004B/430
* 9 7 8 0 3 6 7 7 2 7 9 6 3 *